REAL LATIN

Praise for *Wiley's Real Latin: Learning Latin from the Source*

"The use of all ancient texts for illustrations of grammar, translation exercises, and longer passages is a real asset – this is the best way for students to learn the Latin language in its own terms and gives good opportunity for exploration of literature, history, and culture along with grammar."
Erika J. Nesholm, Kenyon College

"Many Latin students have experienced that dreadful letdown, in which they have difficulty with 'real' Latin after months of textbook instruction. This book, with its guidance through unchanged Latin passages, offers a practical approach to a demanding language; it will be especially gratifying to students eager to read ancient texts."
Dustin Heinen, University of Texas at Arlington

"*Wiley's Real Latin* prepares students to read Latin by using real Latin from the start. It features a clear exposition of grammar, cultural background, attractive illustrations, frequent reviews, and helpful 'Hints' throughout."
Barbara Gold, Hamilton College

"Traditional, rigorous, but also fun: experienced Latinists set out Latin as it really is, with clarity and through real Latin written by Romans. *The* textbook for *ab initio* teaching."
Calum Maciver, University of Edinburgh

"A most valuable and absorbing guide for students of Latin at all levels: clear exposition, all examples from real Latin authors, biographies and illustrations to provide contexts. Use and enjoy it."
J. B. Hall, Hildred Carlile Professor of Latin Emeritus, University of London

"Clarity, depth, opportunity to practice, helpful tables, images from Roman material culture, and information on the context of genuine Latin sentences set as translation exercises make *Wiley's Real Latin* an attractively produced rival to *Wheelock's Latin*."
Costas Panayotakis, University of Glasgow

"This engaging guide provides students with the skills they need to read and enjoy real Latin texts. Features include clear and concise grammatical explanations, practice exercises all based on Latin authors, user-friendly layout with images, helpful hints, and vocabulary."
Sophie Weeks, University of York

"An elegant and succinct introduction to Latin. Using only passages from 'real Latin' throughout, it brings Classical writers like Cicero, Caesar, Catullus, and Ovid into the classroom from the beginning."
Anne Rogerson, University of Sydney

"Very interesting approach! Material presented simply, clearly, meaningfully. Well paced. Interesting 'asides,' linguistic and historical, with helpful hints and chapter reviews. Sentence-based exercises from authentic Latin and into English challenge both recognition and production skills. Well done!"
Margaret Palczynski, McGill University

WILEY'S REAL LATIN

Learning Latin from the Source

Robert Maltby
and Kenneth Belcher

WILEY-BLACKWELL
A John Wiley & Sons, Ltd., Publication

This edition first published 2014
© 2014 John Wiley & Sons, Inc.

Wiley-Blackwell is an imprint of John Wiley & Sons, formed by the merger of Wiley's global Scientific, Technical
and Medical business with Blackwell Publishing.

Registered Office
John Wiley & Sons Ltd, The Atrium, Southern Gate, Chichester, West Sussex, PO19 8SQ, UK

Editorial Offices
350 Main Street, Malden, MA 02148-5020, USA
9600 Garsington Road, Oxford, OX4 2DQ, UK
The Atrium, Southern Gate, Chichester, West Sussex, PO19 8SQ, UK

For details of our global editorial offices, for customer services, and for information about how to apply for per-
mission to reuse the copyright material in this book please see our website at www.wiley.com/wiley-blackwell.

Library of Congress Cataloging-in-Publication Data

Maltby, Robert.
  Wiley's real Latin : learning Latin from the source / Robert Maltby and Kenneth Belcher.
      pages. cm.
  Includes bibliographical references and index.
  ISBN 978-0-470-65506-1 (hbk) – 978-0-470-65507-8 (pbk)
  ISBN 978-1-118-56180-5 (cs) – ISBN 978-1-118-56185-0 (epdf) – ISBN 978-1-118-56175-1 (epub) –
ISBN 978-1-118-56168-3 (mb) – ISBN 978-1-118-56161-4   1. Latin language–Grammar.
I. Belcher, Kenneth.   II. Title.
  PA2080.2.M35 2013
  478.2'421–dc23
                                                          2012050377

Cover image: © Nekiy - Fotolia.com
Cover design by Simon Levy

A catalogue record for this book is available from the British Library.

Set in 10/13 pt Minion by Toppan Best-set Premedia Limited
Printed and bound in Singapore by Markono Print Media Pte Ltd

1   2014

Chapter 2 18

Chapter 3 31

Chapter 4 42

Chapter 5 54

Chapter 6 66

Chapter 7 77

Chapter 8 91

Chapter 9 103

Chapter 10 111

Chapter 13 144

Chapter 14 161

Chapter 15 179

Chapter 18 216

Chapter 19 227

Chapter 20 240

Chapter 21 251

Conclusion 263

Appendices 265

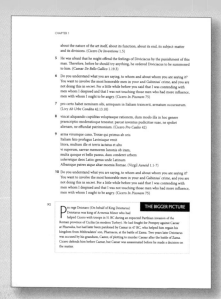

Feature: **The Bigger Picture** The Bigger Picture sidebars present valuable historical and literary background information that gives the reader context for the sentences they are translating.

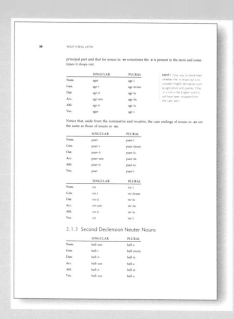

Feature: **Hint!** Marginal Hints! provide the reader with helpful mnemonics and other tools to help them learn and retain material more easily.

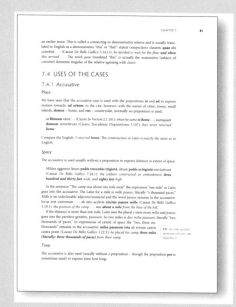

Feature: **FYI** Marginal FYI notes highlight exceptions and anomalies to the main grammatical rules, include helpful and clarifying information, and refer the reader to supporting materials in the Appendices.

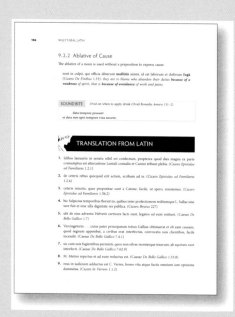

Feature: **Sound Bites** Sound Bites are short pithy sayings from famous Romans and offer the reader a quick, fun translation exercise.

Feature: **Try This** Try This exercises appear after the introduction of each key part of speech and major grammatical concept and give the reader the opportunity to test and solidify their understanding of the material.

Feature: **English Derivations** English Derivations assist the reader in learning key vocabulary by helping him/her make connections between familiar English words and less familiar Latin ones.

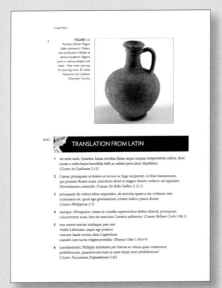

Feature: **Sentences for Translation** The Sentences for Translation are all derived from key Latin authors, including Cicero, Caesar, Virgil, Catullus, Ovid, and Plautus. Translations from both Latin to English and English to Latin afford the reader the opportunity to apply and reinforce their knowledge by immediately engaging with actual ancient texts.

Feature: **Extra Passage** Extra Passages give the reader the opportunity to continue to strengthen their skills and facility by translating longer excerpts. Like the *Sentences for Translation* these passages are all taken from ancient texts.

www.wiley.com/go/reallatin

The *Wiley's Real Latin* companion website features a wealth of resources created by the authors to help instructors teach and students learn for no additional cost.

FOR INSTRUCTORS

A comprehensive Instructor Manual, including:

- Sample syllabi
- Answers to all sentences for translation and other exercises in the text
- Additional translation sentences for homework or test hand-outs
- Translation tips
- Dictionary practice exercises
- Tense synopsis charts
- A selection of practice tests
- Helpful student hand-outs
- Extra passages for translation with commentary and questions
- Quizzes and word games
- Full declension and conjugation tables

FOR STUDENTS

- Flashcards and word games
- Vocabulary lists
- Grammar tables
- Author biographies
- Timeline

I suppose the first question one may ask is, "Why another Latin textbook?"

The impetus behind our text has been twofold. Firstly, in teaching Latin at different levels over a number of years we have found that students have constantly requested a Latin text that sets out the material in a clear, concise, and accessible way. Secondly, we have found that students who complete a beginners' course in Latin are often at a loss when they come to read Latin authors at an advanced level. In order to meet the first problem, we have considered carefully feedback from students on the content, delivery, and accessibility of the approach offered in the text. Students have been intimately involved in selecting many of the sentences, especially from Cicero and Caesar, that appear in the Latin to English translation sections of each chapter and their input is one of the strengths of the text. In the printed version we have adopted a number of suggestions that students have made over the years and many other student-led exercises appear in the online resources that accompany the text. The enthusiasm of our students for the study of Latin has been a driving force in the development of this text.

In response to the second issue, we have used passages from Latin authors throughout. This has caused some problems, not the least of which is finding "simple" examples that actually reflect the grammar introduced in each chapter; however, the benefits of using examples from Latin authors are clear even early on: students appreciate and are enthusiastic about dealing with ancient texts instead of "made-up" Latin sentences, which research has shown reflect English and not Latin idiom; by introducing readings from ancient texts the flexibility of Latin word order becomes apparent; it is possible to engage in meaningful discussions of various stylistic features of the passages; and when students have completed the course, they approach longer texts with less trepidation and greater confidence. Of course, it is not possible (nor would it be useful) to introduce all of the difficult constructions and irregularities that occur; however, we feel that the text covers just the right amount to allow students to begin to come to grips with the Latin of Caesar, Cicero, Ovid, and other authors (students may be directed to Appendix 6 for biographies of the authors as they appear in the text).

We also believe strongly in the importance of translation practice from English into Latin as a means of promoting an active knowledge of grammatical constructions and vocabulary. Even here, the sentences to be translated are chosen from Latin authors so that the students can compare their own translations with the Latin original and thus improve their understanding of the style and idiom of different authors. This is a unique approach and feedback from students on this exercise has been uniformly positive.

In each chapter we aim for variety – a mixture of forms, grammatical explanations, and vocabulary – and here again student feedback and suggestions have been invaluable. Some difficult choices have been made in the order of presentation of grammatical constructions and accidence. For example, we have chosen to introduce formally the comparative and superlative relatively late, supplying early instances as items of vocabulary. Once the subjunctive has been introduced in Chapter 13, more complicated passages are introduced and in each chapter a reading is provided without any vocabulary help in order to increase students' confidence and skill in using a Latin dictionary. These are best used selectively.

We have found that it is neither possible nor advisable to attempt to translate every sentence in class; rather the most successful approach, especially early on, is to limit the number to four each per chapter (of Latin to English and English to Latin). This method allows for detailed discussion of the constructions involved. In the online material one sentence has been selected from each of the first 12 chapters and a detailed list of questions and points for discussion is provided for each. This material reflects an in-class method that has proven very successful and that allows student to engage fully with the Latin texts. Sentences not prepared in advance for class may be assigned to be handed in. In this regard it has also been useful to offer further advice and tips on translating, for example, pointing out apparent oddities in word order and forms. Translations of all of the sentences will be available online and so instructors may choose when or if to give these to the students.

We have included some suggestions for shorter drills in the review chapters that appear throughout the text; however, there is not sufficient space to offer as many as we would like. When using the text we have found it helpful to ask students, for example, to decline noun adjective combinations or conjugate verbs; short vocabulary tests every other week are also a helpful tool. Various additional exercises are available online: suggested format for semester tests; tense synopses; questions about English derivatives from Latin words; extra short connected passages from other Latin authors (here, for example, mythological stories from Hyginus have proved very popular with students); further examples to illustrate complicated constructions such as the ablative absolute; and for those who are more ambitious we have created commentaries for Cicero *In Catilinam* 1.1–1.13, *In Verrem* 2.5.1–7 and Ovid *Metamorphoses* 4.55–166 (Pyramus and Thisbe).

A word on presentation: in the vocabularies for the separate chapters the same Latin word may appear more than once. This is because the word may have different meanings in each of the chapters concerned or it may be considered an important one to learn. In the consolidated vocabulary at the end all these different meanings are brought together under each lemma. In the individual chapter vocabularies the principal parts of regular first conjugation verbs, e.g., *portō, portāre, portāvī, portātum*, and of third declension nouns, e.g., *opinio, opiniōnis*, are given in different formats, whereas in the final consolidated vocabulary these are abbreviated, e.g., *portō, -are, opinio, -ōnis*; the principal parts of all other verbs (including deponents) are written out in full in the consolidated vocabulary. The use of different styles allows students to become familiar with various traditions.

Learning vocabulary is a perennial issue with students. We have found that assigning frequently occurring items to be learned for short vocabulary tests is useful, but only to a certain extent. Reading as much Latin as time allows and focusing on translation skills is the best way for students to begin to acquire a solid basic vocabulary.

We teach the text over two 11-week semesters and this works well; however, there is a clear break at Chapter 12 before the subjunctive is introduced and so a flexible approach is possible; depending on the class and requirements, more time may be spent on the basic constructions (for example 1–12 over two semesters).

Last, but perhaps most important: we have tried to strike a balance in our approach. On the one hand, our students have responded most favorably to what may be called our academic approach. Latin is a difficult language to learn and we make no excuses or apologies for this. Students respond well to this approach rather than to something they feel is "watered-down." On the other hand, we have tried to make the learning of the language fun by introducing some of the technical rhetorical terms and pointing out, for example, how politicians today are as fond of a tricolon as were Cicero, Virgil, and Ovid; also by setting the historical context, rather than simply focusing on grammar and forms. It is also inspiring to remind students that they are among the few who are setting out on a journey that will allow them to begin to appreciate the great literature of Rome, its influence on later authors and its importance for 2000 years of scholarship.

The authors would like to thank those who reviewed an earlier manuscript of the text and offered valuable criticisms; also Haze Humbert, Deirdre Ilkson, Galen Young, and Louise Spencely for all of their help and advice; finally, and above all, our students whose enthusiasm and eagerness to learn have made the effort of putting this text together worthwhile. In this regard we would particularly like to thank James Brookes, Sam Penberthy, Tara Strange, Chris Lill, Ian Greenfield, and above all Anna Reeve and Sally Baume.

INTRODUCTION

FIGURE 0.1 The Colosseum, Rome. Begun by the emperor Vespasian, the Colosseum was completed in AD 80 by his son, the emperor Titus. As many as 50,000 people came to watch games (*ludi*) presented there. *Source: courtesy Sam Penberthy*

CHAPTER CONTENTS

Wiley's Real Latin: Learning Latin from the Source, First Edition.
Robert Maltby and Kenneth Belcher.
© 2014 John Wiley & Sons, Inc. Published 2014 by John Wiley & Sons, Inc.

0.1 PARTS OF SPEECH

Latin has eight main parts of speech: nouns (also called substantives), adjectives, pronouns, verbs, adverbs, prepositions, conjunctions, interjections.

0.1.1 Nouns

A noun is the name of a person (*Caesar*), place (*Rome*), thing (*tree*), or abstract idea (*love*). Nouns which refer to the names of persons or places are called proper nouns; all other nouns are called common nouns (for reference: concrete nouns refer to objects we can perceive with our five senses, for example, *tree*; collective nouns refer to a group of individuals or things which can be regarded as forming a single unity such as *army*; and an abstract noun denotes a quality or implies an action, for example *beauty, peace, love*, etc.).

In Latin a noun has gender (i.e. is masculine, feminine, or neuter), number (i.e. is either singular or plural), and case (for the definition of the term case, see Chapter 1).

0.1.2 Adjectives

An adjective is a word that is applied to a noun to indicate a quality of the noun that the adjective is said to modify. Examples: *good, bad, many, three, his*, and so forth. An adjective may be used **attributively**: *she reads **good** books*; or **predicatively**: *these books are **good***. The first example defines the noun more closely (not simply books, but good books); the second denotes a quality which is said to belong to the noun (a predicative adjective occurs after its noun and frequently in the predicate of a sentence containing forms of the verb "to be" or other copulative or linking verbs such as "to become" and "to seem"). Note also the following: *we are painting the **white** house* (attributive adjective); *we are painting the house **white*** (predicative adjective).

Like nouns, adjectives in Latin also have three genders as well as number and case. A fundamental principle in Latin: adjectives take the same case, gender, and number as the nouns they modify.

0.1.3 Pronouns

Pronouns are words used in place of a noun to indicate a person or thing without actually naming the person or thing. There are various types of pronoun: personal – *I, you, he, she*, etc.; impersonal – *it*; demonstrative – *this, that*, etc.; relative – *who, which*, etc.; and others which will be discussed as they arise.

0.1.4 Verbs

A verb is a word which denotes an action or state: *I **run**, people **live***. Verb forms may be finite or non-finite.

Finite verbs are defined by five qualities: **person** 1st (I/we), 2nd (you), 3rd (he, she, it, they, and all nouns generally: e.g., *Virgil **writes** poetry*), **number** (singular or plural), **tense** (present, future, perfect, imperfect, future perfect, pluperfect), **mood** (indicative, subjunctive, imperative), **voice** (active where the subject of the verb performs the action or passive where the subject of the verb is the recipient of the action).

> Examples: *Virgil* **wrote** *the Aeneid*. The verb *wrote* is 3rd person, singular, perfect, indicative, active.
>
> *The Aeneid* **was written** *by Virgil*. The verb form *was written* is 3rd person, singular, perfect, indicative, passive.

There are also non-finite verb forms. An example of a non-finite verb is the infinitive: in English *to see*, for example. Notice that an infinitive does not have **person**. You cannot say, for example, *I to see you*.

In addition verbs may be transitive, i.e., those which take a direct object: *I am reading* **a book**, or intransitive, i.e., those which do not take a direct object: *I am going* **to Athens**.

Finally, there is a further class of verbs called copulative or linking verbs which simply link the subject of the sentence with another noun, pronoun, or adjective in the predicate of the sentence: *he* **is** *tall*. The most important of these is the verb *to be*.

0.1.5 Adverbs

Adverbs, generally speaking, modify verbs, adjectives, or other adverbs. They are words that express manner: *she ran* **quickly**; time: *he went out* **then**; place: *I fell* **there**. An example of an adverb modifying an adjective: *he is* **incredibly** *wise*.

0.1.6 Prepositions

Prepositions are words that are usually placed before nouns and pronouns to define more closely their relation to other words in the sentence: *to, for, from, by, with, on*, etc. Example: *we are coming* **to** *the city* **with** *our friends*.

0.1.7 Conjunctions

Conjunctions are words that join together words, phrases, and sentences. They are divided into two classes: co-ordinating and subordinating. Co-ordinating conjunctions simply join together words or clauses of equal grammatical rank: *you are leaving* **but** *I shall see you soon* **and** *then we shall be together again*. Notice that each of the three clauses forms a complete grammatical sentence and that each could stand on its own as an independent sentence. There are various co-ordinating conjunctions: *and, but, or*, etc.

Subordinating conjunctions join together clauses which are not of equal grammatical rank, i.e., the one is subordinate to, or dependent upon, the other: **when you come**, *I will see you*. The clause *when you come* cannot stand on its own as a grammatical sentence; it depends upon the main clause to complete its sense and for that reason is called a subordinate clause. There are many subordinating conjunctions: *when, after, while, since, if, unless, although*, etc.

0.1.8 Interjections

Interjections are words which are "thrown in among" the other words of a sentence. They are grammatically independent and usually express some feeling or emotion as, for example: *O! What a mess.*

0.2 THE PRONUNCIATION OF LATIN

Although Latin is no longer a living, spoken language, it is possible to establish with a fair degree of certainty how it was pronounced by using such evidence as inscriptions, transcriptions into Greek letters, and by working back from the history of its descendants, the Romance languages (French, Spanish, Italian etc.).

The alphabet is the same as our own, except that **i** was used by the Romans for both the vowel i and the consonant j (pronounced **y**), and **u** (with its upper case equivalent **V**) was used for both the vowel u and the consonant v (pronounced **w**). In this book, following the conventions of most modern printed Latin texts, **v** will be used for consonantal u throughout, e.g., *vacca* (not *uacca*), but **i** will be used both for the vowel and for consonantal i, e.g., *iacio* (not *jacio*). Students must, however, be prepared to see consonantal u written as u (e.g., *uacca*) in other texts, e.g., the Oxford Classical Texts series, and also, occasionally for consonantal i to be written as j (e.g., *jacio*) in some older texts, e.g., C.T. Lewis and C. Short's *A Latin Dictionary*.

0.2.1 Consonants

The consonants **d, f, h, l, m, n, p, q, r,** and **z** are pronounced as in English. The remainder have the following modifications:

b as in English, except it is pronounced as *p* before **s** and **t**: e.g., **urbs** (*urps*), **obtestor** (*optestor*)

c always a hard *k* sound, as in *cat*, never a soft *s* sound, as in *civil*, even before **i** and **e**: e.g., **cibus** (*kibus*), **cēna** (*kena*)

g always a hard *g* sound, as in *good*, never a soft sound as in *general*, even before **i** and **e**: e.g., **gerō**

i before vowels is pronounced like the consonant *y* in *yes* and *yacht*: e.g., **iaceō** (*yakeo*), **iam** (*yam*)

s always "unvoiced" as in *set*, never a "voiced" *z* sound as in *his*: e.g., **semper, bis**

t as in English, except it never changes to a *sh-* sound before *i* as in *exception*: e.g., **tam, contiō**

v before vowels is pronounced like the consonant *w* in *watch*: e.g., **vacca** (*wacca*), **volō** (*wolo*).

x always a *cs* sound as in *excellent*, never a *gs* sound as in *examine*: e.g., **ex, maximus**

Double consonants should be pronounced twice as in English compounds such as *bus-service, unnamed, book-keeper*: e.g., **agger, annus** (as contrasted with **ager, anus**).

0.2.2 Vowels

Latin has the same five vowels as English, **a, e, i, o, u**. Each vowel has a long and short pronunciation. Sometimes long forms are marked in dictionaries by a macron (a bar over a vowel is used to indicate that the vowel is long), e.g., **frāter**; you will find other texts often indicate the length of vowels. Vowel lengths need to be learnt for pronunciation and scansion of poetry. Long vowels will be marked when they appear in declensions and conjugations and in the vocabulary lists. Following the convention of scholarly texts we have not marked vowel lengths in the sentences for translation. The pronunciation of vowels is as follows:

a long as in *father*, e.g., **fānum**

a short as in *at*, e.g., **annus**

e long as in *they*, e.g., **rēmus**

e short as in *let*, e.g., **celsus**

i long as in *speak*, e.g., **mīles**

i short as in *bit*, e.g., **cibus**

o long as in *boat*, e.g., **ōtium**

o short as in *cot*, e.g., **quot**

u long as in *coot*, e.g., **sūmo**

u short as in *put*, e.g., **sub**.

Occasionally **y** is found in words borrowed from Greek, mainly proper names. Its correct pronunciation is as a French *u* (as in *tu*) or German *ü* (as in *über*), although it is often assimilated to *i*. The vowel may be either long, as in **Lȳdia**, or short, as in **Lycoris**.

0.2.3 Diphthongs

A diphthong is a combination of two vowels. Diphthongs regularly count as one long syllable. The most common examples in Latin are:

ae pronounced like the *i* in *blind*, e.g., **terrae**

au pronounced like the *ou* in *couch*, e.g., **aurum**

oe pronounced like the *oi* in *foil*, e.g., **proelium**.

Latin, like English, has a stress accent. In words of more than two syllables (polysyllables) the stress falls on the second last syllable (penultimate) if that is long, e.g., *conféctus*, or on the third last syllable (antepenultimate) if the penultimate is short, e.g., *confício*. In words of two syllables the accent falls on the first syllable, e.g., *régo*. A syllable may be long if it contains a naturally long vowel, e.g., *dōnum*, or a diphthong, e.g., *causa*, or if it contains a short vowel followed by two or more consonants (except *r*, where the syllable can be either long or short), e.g., in the penultimate syllable in *confectus*, but not always, as in the first syllable of *apri*.

CHAPTER 1

FIGURE 1.1 Romano-British mosaic of the wolf and twins. Shortly after the birth of the twins, Romulus and Remus, their uncle, who had usurped power, had them exposed so that they would not be able to challenge his rule. However, the boys were found by a shepherd and given to a she-wolf who raised them. When they grew to manhood, they established the city of Rome. © *Leeds Museums and Galleries (Discovery Centre)*

Wiley's Real Latin: Learning Latin from the Source, First Edition.
Robert Maltby and Kenneth Belcher.
© 2014 John Wiley & Sons, Inc. Published 2014 by John Wiley & Sons, Inc.

1.1 INFLECTED LANGUAGE

Latin is an inflected language. In effect this means that the sense of a sentence is determined to a large extent not by word order (as is usually the case in English) but by word endings (inflections).

The ending of a Latin noun changes depending, for example, on whether it is the subject of a verb or its object, and the ending of a Latin verb also changes to reflect, for example, person (1ˢᵗ, 2ⁿᵈ, or 3ʳᵈ) and number (singular or plural).

Consider the following:

> *Our men* (subject) *swiftly* (adverb) *took up* (verb) *the weapons* (object).

and

> *The weapons* (subject) *swiftly* (adverb) *took up* (verb) *our men* (object).

When the word order is changed in English, the sense also changes and, as shown in this example, may become nonsense. However, in Latin, Caesar (Caesar *De Bello Gallico* 3.28.4) writes the following: **nostrī** (*subject*: "our men") **celeriter** (*adverb*: "swiftly") **arma** (*object*: "the weapons") **cēpērunt** (*verb*: "took up"); he could also have written **arma** (*object*) **nostrī** (*subject*) **celeriter** (*adverb*) **cēpērunt** (*verb*) and the meaning would have been virtually the same. Notice that the endings of the words are the same in both sentences: word endings, not word order, determine the sense. Note also that Latin has neither a definite article (the) nor an indefinite article (a, an).

> **HINT!** Note that English also has examples of inflection such as: I (subject); me (object); who (subject); whom (object); friend (singular); friends (plural); friend's (singular, possessive); friends' (plural, possessive).

1.2 NOUNS

The function of a Latin noun in a sentence is determined by its case and each case has a specific ending (in the example above the object of the verb has the ending **-a**). In Latin there are six cases and each case has certain uses. The names and basic uses of cases are as follows:

Nominative – used for the subject of the sentence
Genitive – used to show possession
Dative – used for the indirect object of the sentence
Accusative – used for the direct object of the sentence
Ablative – used with the meanings "by," "with," "from," "in," or "on"
Vocative – used to address someone or something directly.

Latin nouns are said to decline: that is they change their forms for each of the cases in the order that they are listed above. Latin nouns belong to different declensions (there are five declensions in all, but in this chapter only one of these will be introduced). Latin nouns also have number (singular or plural) and gender (masculine, feminine, or neuter).

1.2.1 Vocabulary Lists

In vocabulary lists and dictionaries Latin nouns are presented as follows:

    vīta, -ae (f.) – life. The first two items are called the principal parts and these are (1) the nominative singular and (2) the genitive singular; next comes the gender – in this case **vīta** is feminine (f. = feminine, m. = masculine, and n. = neuter); finally, the meaning of the word (here it should be noted that some Latin words have more than one English equivalent). The second principal part is regularly abbreviated, as in the example above. In full the principal parts for this noun are: **vīta, vītae**.

1.2.2 First Declension Nouns

As noted above, Latin has five different declensions: nouns that decline in the same way (that is, have the same case endings) belong to the same declension. The declension to which a noun belongs (and, hence, its case endings) is identified by the genitive singular (the second principal part of the noun in the vocabulary lists). For **vīta**, the genitive singular ends in -**ae**. This indicates that the noun belongs to the so-called first declension: all nouns with a genitive singular ending in -**ae** belong to the first declension. In order to decline a noun in full, it is necessary to establish the stem and this is done by removing the ending from the second principal part. A noun is declined by adding the case endings to the stem. The stem of **vīta, vītae** is **vīt-** and the noun is declined as follows:

	SINGULAR	PLURAL
Nom.	vīt-a	vīt-ae
Gen.	vīt-ae	vīt-ārum
Dat.	vīt-ae	vīt-īs
Acc.	vīt-am	vīt-ās
Abl.	vīt-ā	vīt-īs
Voc.	vīt-a	vīt-ae

The difference between the nominative singular and ablative singular is in the pronunciation. The ablative singular ends in long **ā**, whereas the nominative and vocative singular end in a short **a**.

    Almost all nouns of the first declension are feminine; there are a few masculine nouns of the first declension, but they decline in precisely the same way as the feminine nouns of this declension; there are no neuter nouns in the first declension. An example of a masculine first declension noun is **poēta, -ae** (m.) – poet (here **oe** is not a diphthong). It is worth pointing out here that although nouns may belong to different declensions and have different case endings, the uses of the cases remain the same. It is also important to note that the rule for forming the cases (stem + endings) is the same as for all declensions and that the stem is found by removing the ending from the second principal part.

Declension of Poēta, -ae

	SINGULAR	PLURAL
Nom.	poēt-a	poēt-ae
Gen.	poēt-ae	poēt-ārum
Dat.	poēt-ae	poēt-īs
Acc.	poēt-am	poēt-ās
Abl.	poēt-ā	poēt-īs
Voc.	poēt-a	poēt-ae

Notice that **poēta**, although masculine in gender, has the same endings as **vīta**. Both have genitive singular ending -**ae** and so both belong to the first declension.

All first declension masculine nouns decline in this way. As will be obvious, some cases have exactly the same form but usually this does not present a problem as the context makes the sense (and accordingly the case) clear. Notice that the nominative and vocative, both singular and plural, are exactly the same in form. This is true for all first declension nouns.

TRY THIS

Identify the following noun forms, giving all the possible answers:

e.g., *puellae* – genitive singular, dative singular, or nominative plural of *puella* – girl

Remember that vowel lengths are not normally printed in Latin texts; so the form **agricola** could be either nominative, ablative, or vocative singular of **agricola, -ae** – farmer.

(i) *fortuna*
(ii) *poetarum*
(iii) *Galliae*
(iv) *gloriam*
(v) *fama*
(vi) *vitae*
(vii) *puellis*
(viii) *poetas*
(ix) *poenarum*
(x) *pecunia*

1.3 VERBS

Like nouns, verbs also change their endings to reflect their use in a Latin sentence. The main verb in a Latin sentence or clause is usually a finite verb. Finite verbs are defined as having five qualities: **person** (1st, 2nd, 3rd), **number** (singular, plural), **tense** (present, future, perfect, future perfect, imperfect, pluperfect), **mood** (indicative, subjunctive, imperative), and **voice** (active, passive). We begin with the present indicative active: simply stated the indicative is the mood used to express a fact; active voice is used when the subject is performing the action of the verb.

Whereas nouns are said to decline, verbs are said to conjugate. To conjugate simply means to list the forms of a verb in all persons, singular and plural. Latin verbs belong to different conjugations (there are five conjugations in all, but in this chapter only one will be introduced).

HINT! Note that English verbs also have principal parts: sing, sang, sung.

Like nouns, verbs also have principal parts. For regular verbs, these are four in number; just as is true for nouns, so the principal parts of Latin verbs offer much in the way of information. First though, it is important to define the principal parts of a Latin verb. For the verb **amō**: its principal parts are **amō, amāre, amāvī, amātum**. The first principal part is the first person singular present indicative active (*I love, I am loving, I do love*); the second is the present infinitive active (*to love*); the third is the 1ˢᵗ person singular perfect indicative active (*I loved, I did love, I have loved*); the fourth is called the supine (English does not have a supine; its use in Latin is explained in Chapter 15). For the moment we will be using only the first two principal parts; however, it is worthwhile to memorize the principal parts of all verbs in the learning vocabularies now in order to save time later. Generally (for example, in dictionaries) principal parts are given in abbreviated form: **amō, -āre, -āvī, -ātum**. In the first 12 chapters of this text principal parts of verbs are written out in full; however, most first conjugation verbs follow the pattern **-ō, -āre, -āvī, -ātum**; from Chapter 13 on and in the consolidated vocabulary at the end of the text only the first two principal parts of regular first conjugation verbs are given.

Why do we need to know principal parts? They are important because it is possible to create all Latin verb forms from the principal parts of each verb. The first principal part gives the present stem on which the forms of the present, imperfect, and future tenses are built. The second principal part defines the conjugation to which a verb belongs: all verbs whose second principal part ends -**āre** belong to the first conjugation (as noted above there are five conjugations in all), and all first conjugation verbs conjugate in the same way. The third principal part provides the stem for all active forms of the perfect tenses. More detail about the use of the perfect stem and uses of the fourth principal part will be explained in later chapters.

1.3.1 First Conjugation: Present Indicative Active

In order to conjugate a verb of the first conjugation in the present indicative active, the simplest method is to remove the -**ō** from the first principal part (the 1ˢᵗ person singular) then add the following endings: -**ō, -ās, -at, -āmus, -ātis, -ant**.

So for the verb **amō**:

HINT! In effect the personal endings -ō,-s, -t, -mus, -tis, -nt are added to the characteristic a-stem of the first conjugation. Notice that the letter *a*, called the connecting vowel, is sometimes long (marked with a macron), sometimes short. Look for this in other conjugations.

	SINGULAR	PLURAL
1ˢᵗ **person**	am-ō – I love, am loving, do love	am-āmus – we love, etc.
2ⁿᵈ **person**	am-ās – you love, etc.	am-ātis – you love, etc.
3ʳᵈ **person**	am-at – he, she, it loves, etc.	am-ant – they love, etc.

Notice the following points: there is no need for the pronoun subject as in English (I, you, he, etc.); rather the subject of the verb in Latin is denoted by the ending. The subject of the 3rd person singular may be "he," "she," or "it" – the context usually will make clear which is appropriate; all regular verbs of the first conjugation form the present indicative active in this way.

1.3.2 Irregular Verbs

Latin has very few irregular verbs; most follow a set pattern depending on the conjugation to which they belong and their tense, mood, and voice. The most important and common of the irregular verbs is the linking or copulative verb "to be": **sum** – I am; **esse** – to be. The present indicative is conjugated as follows:

	SINGULAR	PLURAL
1st person	sum – I am	sumus – we are
2nd person	es – you are	estis – you are
3rd person	est – he, she, it, there is	sunt – they, there are

Related to the verb **sum** is the verb **possum** – *I am able; I can*; **posse** – *to be able*. The present indicative conjugates as follows:

	SINGULAR	PLURAL
1st person	possum – I am able	possumus – we are able
2nd person	potes – you are able	potestis – you are able
3rd person	potest – he, she, it is able	possunt – they are able

Notice that the endings are -**sum**, -**es**, -**est**, -**sumus**, -**estis**, -**sunt** (that is the present of the verb **sum**); **po-t** + endings for the endings beginning with a vowel and **po-s** for endings beginning with the letter "s."

Possum is frequently followed by an infinitive in Latin:

THE BIGGER PICTURE

*I*n Catilinam (*Against Catiline*), delivered in four parts by Cicero in 63 BC against the senatorial candidate for the following year, Lucius Sergius Catilina, accusing him of a plot aimed at the seizure of government and the cancellation of debts. Parts I and IV of the speech were delivered before the senate and parts II and III before the assembly of the people. As a result of his speeches before the senate the city was in effect placed under martial law and Cicero, as consul, had the conspirators, including Catiline, executed in summary fashion.

sed ea . . . **dissimulāre nōn possum** (Cicero *In Catilinam* 4.14): *but **I cannot/am unable to conceal** these things.*

FYI For a list of some verbs followed by a complementary infinitive see Appendix 1.

Dissimulāre is called a complementary infinitive because it complements or completes the meaning of the verb **possum**. There are a number of verbs in Latin that are followed by a complementary infinitive.

TRY THIS

Identify (i.e., give person, number, tense, mood, and (where appropriate) voice) and translate the following verb forms, giving all the possible answers:

e.g., *potes* – present indicative 2nd person singular (active – see FYI) – you can; you are able

Remember that the present indicative of most verbs can be translated into English in three ways, so the form **sperant** could mean they hope, they are hoping, or they do hope.

HINT! Technically the verbs *sum* and *possum* are neither active nor passive. Try putting the verb "to be" into the passive in English (= I am been). Is this correct English?

(i) *es*	(vi) *exspectant*
(ii) *possumus*	(vii) *superatis*
(iii) *paras*	(viii) *pugnamus*
(iv) *spero*	(ix) *portat*
(v) *dat*	(x) *amas*

1.4 PRONOUNS: *HIC, HAEC, HOC*

Of the pronouns in Latin three of the most common are the demonstrative pronouns **hic, haec, hoc** – this, **ille, illa, illud** – that (introduced in Chapter 3), and the rather weaker demonstrative **is, ea, id** – this; that; he; she; it, which is introduced in the next chapter. Each has a slightly irregular declension (and none has a vocative case). **Hic** is declined as follows:

	SINGULAR			PLURAL		
	m.	f.	n.	m.	f.	n.
Nom.	hic	haec	hoc	hī	hae	haec
Gen.	huius	huius	huius	hōrum	hārum	hōrum
Dat.	huic	huic	huic	hīs	hīs	hīs
Acc.	hunc	hanc	hoc	hōs	hās	haec
Abl.	hōc	hāc	hōc	hīs	hīs	hīs
Voc.	NO VOCATIVE			NO VOCATIVE		

HINT! Note the use of the accusative neuter singular and plural of pronouns such as *haec* = these things (as in *haec dant* – they are giving these things). You do not need a word for "things." The singular is also used in this way: *hoc dant* – they give this (thing).

1.5 PREPOSITIONS

Latin has a number of prepositions, which, you will be pleased to learn, neither decline nor conjugate – their forms do not change! In general, prepositions are followed by the accusative or ablative case. Some prepositions that take the accusative case only are: **ad** – to; **ante** – before; **post** – after; the following take the ablative case only: **ab** – from; by; **cum** – with. The prepositions **in** and **sub** take the accusative when they are used to express motion and the ablative when there is no motion involved: **in** (+ acc.) – into: **in Ītaliam** contendit (Caesar *De Bello Gallico* 1.10.3): *he is marching **into Italy***; *sub* (+ acc.) – under: exercitum **sub iugum** [mittit] (Caesar *De Bello Gallico* 1.12.6): *he [Caesar] sends the army **under the yoke***; **in** (+ abl.) – in (on): castra **in Ītaliā** sunt (Cicero *In Catilinam* 1.5): *there is a camp **in Italy***; **sub** (+ abl.) – under; beneath: **sub monte** consēdit (Caesar *De Bello Gallico* 1.48.2): *he halted **beneath/at the foot of a mountain***.

FIGURE 1.2 Casa dei Cervi (House of the Stags – named for a statue found in the garden of the house), Herculaneum. An ancient Roman looking out from this vantage point would have been able to see the sea. Herculaneum, along with Pompeii, was destroyed by the volcanic eruption of Mt Vesuvius in AD 79. *Source: courtesy Sally Baume*

1.6 ADVERBS

Adverbs in Latin as in English are used to modify verbs, adjectives, and other adverbs. Like prepositions they do not decline. Adverbs may express time, **tum** – then; at that time; place, **ibi** – there; in that place, **hīc** – here; in this place; manner, **sīc** – so; thus. More adverbs will be introduced as we proceed through the course.

1.7 CONJUNCTIONS

Conjunctions are used to join nouns, adjectives, or clauses together: *I went to Rome <u>and</u> I saw my friends there*. Like adverbs and prepositions, conjunctions do not decline. Some examples: **et** – and; **et . . . et** – both . . . and; **sed** – but.

FIGURE 1.3 Romano-British flagon (date unknown). Pottery was produced in Britain at various locations; flagons came in various shapes and sizes – their main use was for pouring wine. © *Leeds Museums and Galleries (Discovery Centre)*

VOCABULARY TO LEARN

Nouns; Pronouns

agricola, -ae (m.) – farmer
audācia, -ae (f.) – boldness
cōpia, -ae (f.) – supply; plenty (in the plural (military) forces)
dea, -ae (f.) – goddess
fāma, -ae (f.) – report; rumor; fame
fēmina, -ae (f.) – woman
fortūna, -ae (f.) – fortune
Gallia, -ae (f.) – Gaul
glōria, -ae (f.) – glory; honor
hic, haec, hoc – this; this man; this woman; this thing
insula, -ae (f.) – island
patria, -ae (f.) – homeland
pecūnia, -ae (f.) – money
poena, -ae (f.) – penalty; punishment
poēta, -ae (m.) – poet
puella, -ae (f.) – girl
Rōma, -ae (f.) – Rome
vīta, -ae (f.) – life

Verbs

amō, amāre, amāvī, amātum – love
dō, dare, dedī, datum – give
exspectō, exspectāre, exspectāvī, exspectātum (+ acc.) – wait for; await

parō, parāre, parāvī, parātum (+ inf.) – prepare (to)
portō, portāre, portāvī, portātum – carry
possum, posse, potuī (+ inf.) – be able (to); can
pugnō, pugnāre, pugnāvī, pugnātum – fight
spērō, spērāre, spērāvī, spērātum (+ acc.) – hope; hope for
sum, esse, fuī – be; exist (note: *est* can mean "there is" and *sunt* can mean "there are")
superō, superāre, superāvī, superātum – overcome; surpass

Adverbs; Prepositions; Conjunctions

ab (+ ablative) – from; by (sometimes written **a** before a consonant)
ad (+ acc.) – to; towards; against
cum (+ abl.) – with
et – and
ex (+ abl.) – from; out of; in accordance with (sometimes written **e** before a consonant)
hīc – here; in this place
in (+ abl.) – in; on
in (+ acc.) – into; onto
post (+ acc.) – after
sed – but
ubi – when; where; where?

English Derivations

From which Latin roots do the following English words derive?

e.g., patriotic from *patria*
(i) possible
(ii) porter
(iii) pecuniary
(iv) copious

1. What are the eight parts of speech in Latin?

2. In your own words describe what is meant by the term "inflected language."

3. Decline the following: *hic, haec, hoc* in the masculine and feminine singular and neuter plural; *dea* in the singular; *copia* in the plural.

4. Conjugate the verb *possum* in the present indicative and *do, dare* in the present indicative active; give translations for all forms.

5. Give all possible meanings for the following:
    (i) huic
    (ii) poetae
    (iii) Italia
    (iv) puellis
    (v) estis
    (vi) exspectant

6. For the following English sentences parse each word and, without translating, state how you would express each in Latin:

    Example: (Poets) (are not able) (to fight) (but) (they are able) (to love) (girls).

    poets: noun; subject of the verb; in Latin, nominative case, masculine, plural

    are able: finite verb; 3rd person plural present indicative (active); in Latin as in English

    not: adverb; in Latin as in English

    to fight: present infinitive active; in Latin as in English (complementary infinitive)

    but: conjunction

    they: pronoun; subject of the verb; in Latin it is not necessary to translate; remember the ending is sufficient to indicate the person and number (review the definition of inflected language)

    are able: 3rd person plural present indicative (active) – 3rd person plural because the subject is "they"

    to fight: present infinitive active; in Latin as in English (complementary infinitive)

    girls: direct object of the infinitive "to love"; in Latin accusative case, feminine plural

    (i) This man is giving money to the girls.
    (ii) When a poet praises boldness, he hopes for fame.
    (iii) They are preparing to carry these things to the island.
    (iv) I can overcome the forces of Gaul.

FYI Parsing is a time-honored tradition; simply put to parse means to identify each part (from Latin *pars* = part) of speech in a sentence and to define its grammatical function.

CHAPTER 2

FIGURE 2.1 Roman glass vessel (date unknown). Early on glass was a luxury item; however, technological advances (glass-blowing was invented in the 1st century BC) meant that glass was able to be mass-produced. Glass works were found in many Roman provinces. © *Leeds Museums and Galleries (Discovery Centre)*

Wiley's Real Latin: Learning Latin from the Source, First Edition.
Robert Maltby and Kenneth Belcher.
© 2014 John Wiley & Sons, Inc. Published 2014 by John Wiley & Sons, Inc.

2.1 SECOND DECLENSION NOUNS

Almost all nouns of the second declension are either masculine (nominative ending **-us**, **-er**, or **-r**) or neuter (nominative ending **-um**). The characteristic identifying feature of second declension nouns is that the second principal part (genitive singular) ends in -ī: **animus**, **-ī** (m.) – soul; spirit; **Marcus**, **-ī** (m.) – Marcus; **bellum**, **-ī** (n.) – war. Although the group of nouns classed as second declension has different endings from the first declension, the uses of the cases remain the same. The rule for forming the cases (stem + endings) is the same as for the first declension and the stem is found by removing the -ī from the second principal part.

2.1.1 Second Declension Nouns in *-us*

	SINGULAR	PLURAL
Nom.	anim-us	anim-ī
Gen.	anim-ī	anim-ōrum
Dat.	anim-ō	anim-īs
Acc.	anim-um	anim-ōs
Abl.	anim-ō	anim-īs
Voc.	anim-e	anim-ī

FYI Normally the vocative ends in -e; however, if the stem ends in -i (e.g., *fīlius, fīliī*), the vocative is merely the stem, i.e., *fīlī*. Another exception: the vocative of *deus* is *deus*.

In most declensions the vocative has the same form as the nominative. Second declension nouns ending **-us** in the nominative are the only exception to this rule.

2.1.2 Second Declension Nouns in *-er; -r*

There are a few second declension nouns where the nominative does not end in **-us**, for example: **ager**, **agrī** (m.) – field; **puer**, **puerī** – boy; **vir**, **virī** (m.) – man. For nouns of this type the nominative must be learnt (and here the vocative is the same as the nominative). All other cases are formed regularly: stem + endings. Note that the stem is still obtained from the second principal part and that for nouns in -**er** sometimes the -**e** is present in the stem and sometimes it drops out.

	SINGULAR	PLURAL
Nom.	ager	agr-ī
Gen.	agr-ī	agr-ōrum
Dat.	agr-ō	agr-īs
Acc.	agr-um	agr-ōs
Abl.	agr-ō	agr-īs
Voc.	ager	agr-ī

HINT! One way to remember whether the -e drops out is to consider English derivatives such as agriculture and puerile. If the -e is not in the English word it will have been dropped from the Latin stem.

Notice that, aside from the nominative and vocative, the case endings of nouns in -**er** are the same as those of nouns in -**us**.

	SINGULAR	PLURAL
Nom.	puer	puer-ī
Gen.	puer-ī	puer-ōrum
Dat.	puer-ō	puer-īs
Acc.	puer-um	puer-ōs
Abl.	puer-ō	puer-īs
Voc.	puer	puer-ī

	SINGULAR	PLURAL
Nom.	vir	vir-ī
Gen.	vir-ī	vir-ōrum
Dat.	vir-ō	vir-īs
Acc.	vir-um	vir-ōs
Abl.	vir-ō	vir-īs
Voc.	vir	vir-ī

2.1.3 Second Declension Neuter Nouns

	SINGULAR	PLURAL
Nom.	bell-um	bell-a
Gen.	bell-ī	bell-ōrum
Dat.	bell-ō	bell-īs
Acc.	bell-um	bell-a
Abl.	bell-ō	bell-īs
Voc.	bell-um	bell-a

All neuter nouns have the same form in the nominative, vocative, and accusative; however, the context usually removes any ambiguity. In the nominative, vocative, and accusative plural all neuter nouns end in -**a**.

There are a few feminine nouns of the second declension; however, none is particularly common. Again, the distinctive feature is genitive singular ending in -ī (**humus**, -ī (f.) – ground).

2.2 ADJECTIVES

Adjectives modify nouns: *a **good** book*; *the **bad** men*, etc. In English the position of the adjective or the context makes clear which noun the adjective modifies. While the position of an adjective in Latin is significant (it usually follows but may precede the noun it modifies), it is the ending, and therefore the case, of the adjective that is most important. Like nouns, adjectives decline and like nouns adjectives belong to different declensions.

2.2.1 Adjectives of the First/Second Declension

One type of adjective of the first/second declension appears in vocabulary lists as follows: **bonus**, -**a**, -**um** – good. These are the principal parts and meaning of the adjective. The first principal part is the nominative masculine singular, the second is the nominative feminine singular, and the third is the nominative neuter singular. In order to decline adjectives of this type, it is necessary first to find the stem: this can be done by removing the -**us** ending from the first principal part. Then the endings of the first declension are added to the stem to create the feminine forms of the adjective and the endings of the second declension are added to the stem to create the masculine and neuter forms of the adjective. So the adjective **bonus**, -**a**, -**um** declines as follows:

	SINGULAR			PLURAL		
	m.	**f.**	**n.**	**m.**	**f.**	**n.**
Nom.	bon-us	bon-a	bon-um	bon-ī	bon-ae	bon-a
Gen.	bon-ī	bon-ae	bon-ī	bon-ōrum	bon-ārum	bon-ōrum
Dat.	bon-ō	bon-ae	bon-ō	bon-īs	bon-īs	bon-īs
Acc.	bon-um	bon-am	bon-um	bon-ōs	bon-ās	bon-a
Abl.	bon-ō	bon-ā	bon-ō	bon-īs	bon-īs	bon-īs
Voc.	bon-e	bon-a	bon-um	bon-ī	bon-ae	bon-a

Adjectives ending in -**us**, -**a**, -**um** thus make use of the endings for nouns of the first declension (for feminine forms) and of the second declension (for masculine and neuter forms).

There is another type of first/second declension adjective with a nominative, masculine, singular ending in **-er**: e.g., **miser, -era, -erum** – wretched, miserable, and **pulcher, -chra, -chrum** – beautiful. Compare these with the second declension nouns **puer** and **ager** and notice the following: only the endings of the nominative and vocative, masculine, singular differ from first/second declension adjectives in **-us, -a, -um** and it is necessary to go to the second principal part to see if the letter "e" has dropped out of the stem.

	SINGULAR			PLURAL		
	m.	f.	n.	m.	f.	n.
Nom.	pulcher	pulchr-a	pulchr-um	pulchr-ī	pulchr-ae	pulchr-a
Gen.	pulchr-ī	pulchr-ae	pulchr-ī	pulchr-ōrum	pulchr-ārum	pulchr-ōrum
Dat.	pulchr-ō	pulchr-ae	pulchr-ō	pulchr-īs	pulchr -īs	pulchr-īs
Acc.	pulchr-um	pulchr-am	pulchr-um	pulchr-ōs	pulchr-ās	pulchr-a
Abl.	pulchr-ō	pulchr-ā	pulchr-ō	pulchr-īs	pulchr-īs	pulchr-īs
Voc.	pulcher	pulchr-a	pulchr-um	pulchr-ī	pulchr-ae	pulchr-a

	SINGULAR			PLURAL		
	m.	f.	n.	m.	f.	n.
Nom.	miser	miser-a	miser-um	miser-ī	miser-ae	miser-a
Gen.	miser-ī	miser-ae	miser-ī	miser-ōrum	miser-ārum	miser-ōrum
Dat.	miser-ō	miser-ae	miser-ō	miser-īs	miser-īs	miser-īs
Acc.	miser-um	miser-am	miser-um	miser-ōs	miser-ās	miser-a
Abl.	miser-ō	miser-ā	miser-ō	miser-īs	miser-īs	miser-īs
Voc.	miser	miser-a	miser-um	miser-ī	miser-ae	miser-a

2.2.2 Agreement of Adjectives with Nouns

It is a cardinal rule of Latin that an adjective agrees with the noun that it modifies in case, number, and gender. If a noun is nominative, singular, masculine, then an adjective modifying the noun will also be nominative, singular, masculine and so on: **socius bonus** – a/the good ally; **sociī bonī** – good allies, the good allies. Consider the following: **vir bonus** – a/the good man. Notice that although the endings are not the same, both are nominative masculine singular and so the adjective does, in fact, agree with the noun. An adjective may have a different ending from that of the noun that it modifies; however, the case, gender, and number must be the same.

Supply the correct form of the adjective [in brackets] to agree with the following nouns; identify the case(s), giving all the possible answers:

　e.g., *agricolam* [*bonus*] – *bonum* (accusative masculine singular)

Remember that the same noun form can have a number of different meanings so *agricolae* [*bonus*] would have the answers *boni* and *bono*, as *agricolae* could be either genitive singular or nominative plural (hence *boni*) or dative singular (hence *bono*).

(i) *auxilio* [*bonus*]	(vi) *viro* [*Romanus*]
(ii) *bellum* [*novus*]	(vii) *fama* [*verus*]
(iii) *foro* [*magnus*]	(viii) *locis* [*pulcher*]
(iv) *filii* [*miser*]	(ix) *equorum* [*miser*]
(v) *naturae* [*bonus*]	(x) *deo* [*magnus*]

2.2.3 Adjectives and Pronouns Used as Nouns

Adjectives in English may be used as nouns often by the addition of the definite article: ***The Good, The Bad, and The Ugly***; but notice also examples such as ***goods***. In English this use of adjectives is somewhat restricted, but in Latin any number of adjectives can be used as nouns: **bonus** – a/the good man; **bonae** – good women, the good women; **bona** (neuter, plural) – good things; goods; **Rōmānus** as an adjective means *of Rome* or *Roman*, as a noun it means *a/the Roman* and in the plural **Rōmānī** it means *Romans* or *the Romans*.

　As we have seen, the pronoun **hic** may be used by itself – this man; however, it may also be used as an adjective **hic vir** (Cicero *In Pisonem* 6): ***this man**.*

HINT! As noted earlier the accusative neuter singular and plural of pronouns may stand alone: e.g., *haec* = these things (as in *haec dant*). Adjectives may be used in the same way: *multa* = many things (*multa dant*). There is no need for the word "things."

THE BIGGER PICTURE

In Pisonem (*Against Piso*) a speech delivered against L. Calpurnius Piso before the senate in 55 bc. Piso was an ally of Caesar, who, together with the tribune Clodius, had plotted against Cicero during Caesar's absence in Gaul from 58 bc. As a reward, Piso had been given the province of Macedonia. In 57 bc Cicero had spoken against Piso's government of Macedonia and had him recalled from his province. Piso spoke against Cicero in the senate on his return home and this is Cicero's reply.

2.3 SECOND CONJUGATION: PRESENT INDICATIVE ACTIVE

The defining feature of verbs of the second conjugation is that the second principal part (the present infinitive active) ends in -**ēre** (where the first **ē** is long), for example **videō**, -**ēre** – see. It is also true that the letter e precedes the final in all second conjugation verbs. In order to conjugate a verb of the second conjugation in the present indicative active, begin by removing the -**ō** from the first principal part then add the following endings: -**ō**, -**s**, -**t**, -**mus**, -**tis**, -**nt**:

	SINGULAR	PLURAL
1ˢᵗ **person**	vide-ō – I see, am seeing, do see	vidē-mus – we see, etc.
2ⁿᵈ **person**	vidē-s – you see, etc.	vidē-tis – you see, etc.
3ʳᵈ **person**	vide-t – he, she, it sees, etc.	vide-nt – they see, etc.

2.4 IMPERFECT INDICATIVE ACTIVE

The imperfect tense in Latin is used to denote a continuous or habitual action in the past and may be translated, for example, *I was loving* or *I used to love* (and occasionally simply as *I loved*). In order to conjugate verbs of the first and second conjugations in the imperfect indicative active, simply remove the -**re** from the second principal part (the present infinitive) and add the following endings: -**bam**, -**bās**, -**bat**, -**bāmus**, -**bātis**, -**bant** (notice the familiar endings -**s**, -**t**, -**mus**, -**tis**, -**nt** in the second person singular, etc.).

2.4.1 First Conjugation

	SINGULAR	PLURAL
1ˢᵗ **person**	amā-bam – I was loving, etc.	amā-bāmus – we were loving
2ⁿᵈ **person**	amā-bās – you were loving	amā-bātis – you were loving
3ʳᵈ **person**	amā-bat – he, she, it was loving	amā-bant – they were loving

HINT! Write out conjugations and declensions: repetition is the best way to learn the forms. Keep repeating the active endings of verbs: -o, -s, -t, -mus, -tis, -nt. For the imperfect: -bam, -bas, -bat, -bamus, -batis, -bant (notice that except for the first person singular, the personal endings are the same).

2.4.2 Second Conjugation

	SINGULAR	PLURAL
1ˢᵗ **person**	vidē-bam – I was seeing, etc.	vidē-bāmus – we were seeing
2ⁿᵈ **person**	vidē-bās – you were seeing	vidē-bātis – you were seeing
3ʳᵈ **person**	vidē-bat – he, she, it was seeing	vidē-bant – they were seeing

2.4.3 Irregular Verbs: *Sum, Esse; Possum, Posse*

	SINGULAR	PLURAL
1ˢᵗ person	eram – I was	erāmus – we were
2ⁿᵈ person	erās – you were	erātis – you were
3ʳᵈ person	erat – he, she, it was	erant – they were

	SINGULAR	PLURAL
1ˢᵗ person	poteram – I was able	poterāmus – we were able
2ⁿᵈ person	poterās – you were able	poterātis – you were able
3ʳᵈ person	poterat – he, she, it was able	poterant – they were able

Here the endings are the same as the imperfect indicative of **sum**. Since all endings begin with a vowel the imperfect stem is **pot**- (compare the conjugation of the present).

2.5 DEMONSTRATIVE PRONOUN: *IS, EA, ID*

The pronoun **is**, **ea**, **id** – he; she; it; this; that, is a weaker demonstrative than the pronoun **hic**. It is frequently used where English uses the 3ʳᵈ person personal pronoun: nuntios **ad eum** mittit (Caesar *De Bello Gallico* 2.6.4): *he sends messengers to him*. Like **hic** it may be used as an adjective: **ob eam** causam (Caesar *De Bello Gallico* 1.17.6): *for that reason*.

	SINGULAR			PLURAL		
	m.	**f.**	**n.**	**m.**	**f.**	**n.**
Nom.	is	ea	id	eī (iī)	eae	ea
Gen.	eius	eius	eius	eōrum	eārum	eōrum
Dat.	eī	eī	eī	eīs	eīs	eīs
Acc.	eum	eam	id	eōs	eās	ea
Abl.	eō	eā	eō	eīs	eīs	eīs
Voc.	NO VOCATIVE			NO VOCATIVE		

Related to the pronoun **is**, **ea**, **id** is **īdem**, **eadem**, **idem** – the same. Notice that the declension closely follows the declension of **is**; however, the suffix -**dem** is added. Only the first part declines.

> **FYI** For the full declension of **īdem** see Appendix 2.

idem Caesar facit (Caesar *De Bello Gallico* 1.15.1): *Caesar does the same thing*.

Like **hic** and **is**, **īdem** may be used as an adjective: **eandem** bellī **fortūnam** (Caesar *De Bello Gallico* 2.16.3): *the same fortune* of war.

FIGURE 2.2 Mosaic of Neptune's wife, Amphitrite, Ostia. Amphitrite is shown on a hippocampus (a sea-horse), accompanied by Hymenaeus (a winged Eros with a torch, referring to marriage). Ostia was the sea-port at the mouth of the river Tiber (still called Ostia today). *Source: courtesy Sally Baume*

TRANSLATION FROM LATIN

1. id ubi vident, mutant consilium. (Caesar *Bellum Civile* 2.11.2)

   FYI For biographies of authors, see Appendix 6.

2. consul castra Aequorum oppugnabat. (Livy *Ab Urbe Condita* 3.23.4)

3. Polemarchus est Murgentinus, vir bonus atque honestus. (Cicero *In Verrem* 2.3.56)

4. hic, ubi nunc Roma est, . . . silva virebat. (Ovid *Fasti* 1.243)

5. bellum parat administrare. (Caesar *De Bello Gallico* 7.71.9)

6. Romanus sum . . . C. Mucium vocant. (Livy *Ab Urbe Condita* 2.12.9)

   HINT! Latin will often omit a word if it is easily understood from the context. In sentence 6 the word for "me" is easily understood.

7. hi . . . agros, aedificia, vicosque habebant. (Caesar *De Bello Gallico* 4.4.3)

8. Ennius "sanctos" appellat poetas. (Cicero *Pro Archia* 18)

9. hunc ego amicum habere non curo. (Cicero *Epistulae ad Familiares* 3.8.7)

> *In Verrem (Against Verres)* a prosecution speech on behalf of the Sicilian people, dating from late summer 70 BC, against Gaius Verres, former governor of Sicily, on a charge of extortion and misgovernment. The speech consists of two separate parts for two separate hearings. Verres was defended by the leading orator of the day, Hortensius, and Cicero's success in this prosecution was a career breakthrough.

THE BIGGER PICTURE

> *Pro Archia (On behalf of Archias)* written in 62 BC, in defense of the Greek poet Archias, who was threatened with expulsion from Rome on the grounds that he did not have Roman citizenship. Cicero deals only briefly with the facts of the case supporting the poet's citizenship and dedicates most of the speech to a famous panegyric on the value of literature in society.

THE BIGGER PICTURE

> *Epistulae ad Familiares (Letters to his Friends)* a collection of letters between Cicero and his friends, including several letters from his friends to Cicero. These were collected and edited by Cicero's secretary, Tiro, and published in 16 books, in no particular order, chronological or otherwise. The earliest letter is to Pompey (from 62 BC) and the latest to Cassius (43 BC), a few months before Cicero's assassination.

THE BIGGER PICTURE

TRANSLATION INTO LATIN

1. I ought not to fear. (Cicero *In Verrem* 2.5.171)

2. Country life is hard. (Plautus *Vidularia* 31)

3. They are moving camp from that place. (Caesar *De Bello Gallico* 1.15.1)

4. A few fearless horses were standing by. (Livy *Ab Urbe Condita* 37.20.12)

5. However, there are also learned girls. (Ovid *Ars Amatoria* 2.281)

6. This was the nature of the place. (Caesar *De Bello Gallico* 2.18.1)

7. For I cannot deny this. (Cicero *In Verrem* 2.3.110)

8. And he gives his daughter in marriage to that man. (Caesar *De Bello Gallico* 1.3.5)

9. The crops in the fields were not ripe. (Caesar *De Bello Gallico* 1.16.2)

FIGURE 2.3 Silver denarius, 19–18 BC, with image of a comet and inscription: DIVUS IULIUS. After the assassination of Julius Caesar in 44 BC a comet appeared in the sky and it was said that the comet was a sign of Caesar's deification. See Ovid *Metamorphoses* 15.843–50. © *Leeds Museums and Galleries (Discovery Centre)*

VOCABULARY TO LEARN

Nouns; Pronouns

ager, agrī (m.) – field

amīcus, -ī (m.) – friend

animus, -ī (m.) – mind; spirit

auxilium, auxiliī (n.) – help; aid; (in the plural – reinforcements)

bellum, -ī (n.) – war

castra, -ōrum (n. pl.) – camp

consilium, consiliī (n.) – plan

deus, deī (m.) – god

equus, -ī (m.) – horse

filius, filiī (m.) – son

forum, -ī (n.) – forum; market place

hic, haec, hoc – this; this man, etc.

is, ea, id – he; she; it; this; that, etc.

liber, librī (m.) – book

locus, -ī (m.) – place

nātūra, -ae (f.) – nature

oppidum, -ī (n.) – town

puer, puerī (m.) – boy

servitium, servitiī (n.) – slavery

socius, sociī (m.) – friend; ally

verbum, -ī (n.) – word

vir, -ī (m.) – man

FYI Note: nouns with genitive singular in -*iī* are often written with only one -*ī*; e.g., *auxilī* for *auxiliī*.

FYI The declension of the noun *deus* is irregular. The vocative singular is regularly *deus* and in the plural the nominative is *deī, diī* or *dī*; dative and ablative plural: *deīs, diīs* or *dīs*.

Verbs

dēbeō, dēbēre, dēbuī, dēbitum – owe; (+ inf.)
  ought (to)
doceō, docēre, docuī, doctum – teach
habeō, habēre, habuī, habitum – have
oppugnō, oppugnāre, oppugnāvī, oppugnātum
  – attack
teneō, tenēre, tenuī, tentum – hold; have
timeō, timēre, timuī – fear
videō, vidēre, vīdī, vīsum – see
vocō, vocāre, vocāvī, vocātum – call

Adjectives

bonus, -a, -um – good
magnus, -a, -um – great; big
miser, -era, -erum – wretched; unhappy;
  unfortunate

novus, -a, -um – new
pulcher, -chra, -chrum – beautiful; handsome
Rōmānus, -a, -um – Roman
vērus, -a, -um – true

Adverbs; Prepositions; Conjunctions

enim – for
et . . . et – both . . . and
nōn – not
nunc – now
ob (+ acc.) – on account of; because of
-que – and (added to the end of a word: **arma
  virumque canō** – I sing of arms **and** the
  man)

VOCABULARY SPECIFICALLY FOR CHAPTER 2 PASSAGES

Nouns; Pronouns

aedificium, aedificiī (n.) – building
Aequī, -ōrum (m. pl.) – a people of Italy
Ennius, Enniī (m.) – Ennius (a Roman poet
  239–169 BC)
C. Mūcius, -iī (m.) – Gaius (abbreviated C.)
  Mucius; a sixth-century BC Roman hero
gladius, gladiī (m.) – sword
īdem, eadem, idem – same; the same (see
  Appendix 2)
magister, magistrī (m.) – teacher
mundus, -ī (m.) – world
pīlum, -ī (n.) – javelin
Polemarchus, -ī (m.) – Polemarchus (a man's
  name)
silva, -ae (f.) – forest; wood
vīcus, -ī (m.) – village

Verbs

administrō, administrāre, administrāvī,
  administrātum – assist; take charge of
appellō, appellāre, appellāvī, appellātum –
  address; call (by name)
cūrō, cūrāre, cūrāvī, cūrātum – care to (+ inf.);
  care for
mūtō, mūtāre, mūtāvī, mūtātum – change
vireō, virēre, viruī – be green; flourish

Adjectives; Adverbs

ferē – approximately; almost
honestus, -a, -um – honorable; honest
Murgentīnus, -a, -um – Murgentian (Murgentia
  – a city in Sicily)
quidem – indeed; certainly
sanctus, -a, -um – holy; sacred

English Derivations

From which Latin roots do the following English words derive?

(i) social
(ii) debt
(iii) forensic
(iv) vocation

CHAPTER 3

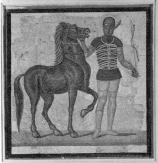

FIGURE 3.1 Mosaic: four horse riders. Chariot racing was very popular at Rome. There were four "teams": white, red, blue, green. Each team was followed with the same enthusiasm as sports teams are today. *Source: Terme Museum, Rome, Italy/The Bridgeman Art Library*

Wiley's Real Latin: Learning Latin from the Source, First Edition.
Robert Maltby and Kenneth Belcher.
© 2014 John Wiley & Sons, Inc. Published 2014 by John Wiley & Sons, Inc.

3.1 DIRECT QUESTIONS

In English the subject and verb are regularly inverted in questions: Why **are you** ordering me? This is not possible in Latin but there are various ways of introducing questions including adverbs such as **cur?** – why? and **ubi?** – where?:

> **cur** Albānum venīre iubet? (Cicero *Pro Flacco* 92): **why** is he ordering the Alban to come?

THE BIGGER PICTURE

Pro Flacco (*On behalf of Flaccus*), a defense speech for Lucius Valerius Flaccus, who had been praetor during Cicero's consulship in 63 BC and had helped in putting down the Catilinarian conspiracy. He was charged with extortion during his governorship of Asia in 62 BC and was defended at his trial in 59 BC by Cicero and Hortensius, the prosecutor being Decimus Laelius. Flaccus was acquitted despite his probable guilt.

Latin may also indicate a question by adding -**ne** to the first word in a sentence: **vidēsne** hoc? (Cicero *In Verrem* 2.3.157): **do you see** this?

3.1.1 Interrogative Pronoun: *Quis?*, *Quid?*

Latin also has an interrogative pronoun, **quis?, quid?** – who?, what? (genitive – whose?), which declines as follows:

	SINGULAR			PLURAL		
	m.	**f.**	**n.**	**m.**	**f.**	**n.**
Nom.	quis	quis	quid	quī	quae	quae
Gen.	cuius	cuius	cuius	quōrum	quārum	quōrum
Dat.	cui	cui	cui	quibus	quibus	quibus
Acc.	quem	quam	quid	quōs	quās	quae
Abl.	quō	quā	quō	quibus	quibus	quibus
Voc.	NO VOCATIVE			NO VOCATIVE		

> **quid** dīcis? (Cicero *In Verrem* 2.5.5): **what** are you saying?

3.1.2 Interrogative Adjective

Latin also has an interrogative adjective. In the plural its declension is exactly the same as that of the interrogative pronoun; in the singular, the forms are slightly different (note the nominative singular of all genders and the accusative neuter singular).

	SINGULAR			PLURAL		
	m.	**f.**	**n.**	**m.**	**f.**	**n.**
Nom.	quī	quae	quod	quī	quae	quae
Gen.	cuius	cuius	cuius	quōrum	quārum	quōrum
Dat.	cui	cui	cui	quibus	quibus	quibus
Acc.	quem	quam	quod	quōs	quās	quae
Abl.	quō	quā	quō	quibus	quibus	quibus
Voc.	NO VOCATIVE			NO VOCATIVE		

Like all adjectives the interrogative adjective agrees with the noun that it modifies in case, gender, and number.

> **quam rem pūblicam** habēmus? **in quā urbe** vīvimus? (Cicero *In Catilinam* 1.9): **what state** do we have? **in what city** are we living?

> **quī reliquī**? **quō** ex **bellō**, **quā** ex **vastitāte**? (Cicero *In Verrem* 2.3.124): **what survivors?** From **what war**, from **what devastation?**

TRY THIS

Supply the correct form of the interrogative adjective to agree with the following nouns; identify the case(s) giving all the possible answers:

e.g., *poetae* (gen. m. sing., dat. m. sing., nom. m. pl.) – *cuius, cui,* or *qui*

(i) *populi*

(ii) *servorum*

(iii) *agros*

(iv) *deis*

(v) *bello*

(vi) *filium*

(vii) *fori*

(viii) *libris*

(ix) *castra*

(x) *consilio*

3.2 PERSONAL PRONOUNS

As we have seen, it is not necessary to express the pronominal subject of a verb since the ending tells whether the form is first person singular and so on. However, Latin does have forms for the first person and second person pronouns, singular and plural. The nominative is used when the speaker or writer wants to emphasize the subject; the other cases are used in the standard way: for example, accusative for direct object, etc.

3.2.1 First Person

	SINGULAR	PLURAL
Nom.	ego	nōs
Gen.	meī	nostrum (*also* nostrī)
Dat.	mihi	nōbīs
Acc.	mē	nōs
Abl.	mē	nōbīs
Voc.	NO VOCATIVE	NO VOCATIVE

3.2.2 Second Person

	SINGULAR	PLURAL
Nom.	tū	vōs
Gen.	tuī	vestrum (*also* vestrī)
Dat.	tibi	vōbīs
Acc.	tē	vōs
Abl.	tē	vōbīs
Voc.	tū	vōs

3.3 DEMONSTRATIVE PRONOUN: *ILLE, ILLA, ILLUD*

Latin has three common demonstrative pronouns, two of which we have already met: **hic, haec, hoc** – this, etc. and the weaker demonstrative, **is, ea, id** – this; that; he, she, it. The third is the pronoun **ille, illa, illud** – that; that man; that woman; that thing. It is declined as follows:

	SINGULAR			PLURAL		
	m.	f.	n.	m.	f.	n.
Nom.	ille	illa	illud	illī	illae	illa
Gen.	illīus	illīus	illīus	illōrum	illārum	illōrum
Dat.	illī	illī	illī	illīs	illīs	illīs
Acc.	illum	illam	illud	illōs	illās	illa
Abl.	illō	illā	illō	illīs	illīs	illīs
Voc.	NO VOCATIVE			NO VOCATIVE		

Like **hic** and **is**, **illa** may be used as an adjective: e.g., **hic vir**; **illae fēminae**, etc.

3.4 THIRD CONJUGATION

3.4.1 Present and Imperfect Indicative Active

The defining features of verbs of the third conjugation are that the first principal part ends in **-o** and the second principal part (the present infinitive active) ends in **-ere**, for example **pōnō, -ere** – place; put (however, here the **e** is short; compare the second conjugation where the second principal part has a long **e**). By looking at the first two principal parts of any Latin verb one can tell the conjugation to which the verb belongs:

first conjugation: -ō, -āre

second conjugation: -eō, -ēre

third conjugation: -ō, -ere

In order to conjugate a verb of the third conjugation in the present indicative active, begin by removing the **-ō** from the first principal part then add the following endings: **-ō, -is, -it, -imus, -itis, -unt**:

	SINGULAR	PLURAL
1st **person**	pōn-ō – I place, am placing, do place	pōn-imus – we place, etc.
2nd **person**	pōn-is – you place, etc.	pōn-itis – you place, etc.
3rd **person**	pōn-it – he, she, it places, etc.	pōn-unt – they place, etc.

In order to conjugate a verb of the third conjugation in the imperfect indicative active, simply remove the **-re** from the second principal part and add the following endings: **-bam, -bās, -bat, -bāmus, -bātis, -bant**:

	SINGULAR	PLURAL
1st **person**	pōnē-bam – I was placing, etc.	pōnē-bāmus – we were placing
2nd **person**	pōnē-bās – you were placing, etc.	pōnē-bātis – you were placing
3rd **person**	pōnē-bat – he, she, it was placing, etc.	pōnē-bant – they were placing

HINT! The imperfect endings *-bam, -bas, -bat*, etc. are the same for all conjugations.

Compare this with the conjugation of **amābam** and of **vidēbam**.

3.5 NEGATIVES

The negative in Latin is the adverb **nōn**; it regularly precedes the word it negates: quis enim hoc **nōn** videt? (Cicero *Pro Caelio* 57): *for who does **not** see this?*

THE BIGGER PICTURE

*P*ro Caelio (*On behalf of Caelius*), a defense speech for M. Caelius on a charge of disturbing the public peace with armed bands. The charge was probably instigated by Claudia, known as Lesbia in the poems of Catullus. The Claudii were political enemies of both Caelius and Cicero. The prosecutor was Atratinus, whose father Caelius had prosecuted in the previous year. It is probable that Caelius was acquitted.

TRY THIS

Verb form practice.

Conjugate the following verbs in the present indicative active: *ago, dico, laudo, pono, possum.*

Conjugate the following verbs in the imperfect indicative active: *credo, iubeo, timeo, sum, voco.*

3.6 USES OF THE CASES

3.6.1 Partitive Genitive

As noted above the personal pronouns **nōs** and **vōs** have two different forms of the genitive: **nostrum** and **nostrī** and **vestrum** and **vestrī**. The forms ending in **-um** are used only when part of a greater group or number is meant (called the partitive genitive). E.g., in English: *some of us; ten of you; no one of us; who of us?* In Latin: quis enim **nostrum**, iūdices, ignōrat? (Cicero *Pro Sestio* 91): *for who **of us**, judges, is unaware?*

THE BIGGER PICTURE

*P*ro Sestio (*On behalf of Sestius*), a defense speech for Sestius, who was charged with using an armed bodyguard during his tribunate in 57 BC. The trial dates from February and March of 56 BC. Sestius was defended by the best lawyers of the day, Hortensius, Crassus, the poet Calvus, and Cicero who delivered the concluding speech for the defense. Sestius was acquitted unanimously.

Neither form is used to show possession. For this Latin uses the adjectives **noster**, **nostra**, **nostrum** – our, and **vester**, **vestra**, **vestrum** – your (plural): exercitus **noster** (Caesar *De Bello Gallico* 2.1.2): *our army*. Note also the following use (frequent, e.g., in Caesar): **nostrī** – *our men* (soldiers). Similarly, the adjectives **meus**, **-a**, **-um** – my, and **tuus**, **-a**, **-um** – your (singular) are used to show possession: monet **amīcus meus** tē (Cicero *Pro Caecina* 35): *my friend advises you.*

THE BIGGER PICTURE

*P*ro Caecina (*On behalf of Caecina*), a speech made in 69 BC on behalf of Aulius Caecina's claim to an estate, left to him in her will by a certain Caesennia. Caesennia's agent, Aebutius, challenged Caecina's qualification to be heir and claimed the estate for himself. It is probable that Caecina won his case.

3.6.2 Subjective and Objective Genitive

Where nouns have a verbal equivalent (e.g., love, hate, etc.) the genitive may express the subject or object of the action inherent in the noun. If the genitive represents the person or thing doing the action, it is called a subjective genitive; however, if the genitive represents the person or thing that "receives" the action, it is called an objective genitive. The forms **nostrī** and **vestrī** are used only as objective genitives. Certain adjectives, for example **cupidus**, **-a**, **-um** – desirous (of), are also followed by an objective genitive.

The simplest way to tell whether a genitive is subjective or objective is to convert the noun to a verb and decide whether the genitive is the subject or object of the verb: *love of Caesar* may mean *Caesar loves* (subjective genitive) or *someone loves Caesar* (objective genitive): **bellī** . . . metus (Cicero *Pro Plancio* 87): *fear **of war*** (objective genitive); **bonōrum** odium (Cicero *In Pisonem* 43): *hatred **of good men*** (note that this example appears to be ambiguous: it could mean *good men hate* or *someone hates good men*; however, the context makes it clear that the genitive is subjective); quis erit tam cupidus **vestrī**? (Cicero *In Verrem* 2.3.224): *who will be desirous of/devoted to **you**?* (objective genitive).

THE BIGGER PICTURE

*P*ro Plancio (*On behalf of Plancius*), a speech delivered in 54 BC in defense of Gnaeus Plancius who had been accused of electoral bribery in his candidature for the aedileship in 55 BC. The charge had been brought by an unsuccessful candidate in the same elections, a certain Laterensis. It is not known whether Plancius was acquitted.

TRANSLATION FROM LATIN

1. ubi estis, servi? (Plautus *Cistellaria* 660)

2. quis hic est? (Plautus *Miles Gloriosus* 276)

3. quid agis, Sceledre? (Plautus *Miles Gloriosus* 276)

4. multa miser timeo. (Ovid *Amores* 1.4.45)

HINT! In sentence 6, notice that *te* is the direct object of the infinitive *laudare*. Infinitives can take the same constructions as finite verbs (e.g., direct object; preposional phrase).

5. Troia et huic loco nomen [= name] est. (Livy *Ab Urbe Condita* 1.1.5)

6. te quidem . . . satis laudare non possum. (Cicero *Pro Milone* 99)

7. si enim sunt viri boni, me adiuvant. (Cicero *Pro Caecina* 3.8)

8. ligna hic apud nos nulla sunt. (Plautus *Aulularia* 352)

9. deditisne vos populumque . . . agros, aquam? (Livy *Ab Urbe Condita* 1.38.2)

THE BIGGER PICTURE

*P*ro Milone (*On behalf of Milo*), a speech in defense of T. Annius Milo, who had been tribune of the plebs in 57 BC. Just as Clodius had raised the city rabble in support of Caesar, so Milo led similar urban gangs in favor of Cicero and the senate. During the elections of January 52 BC the two men and their gangs met on the Appian Way. In the ensuing scuffle Clodius was killed and Milo was tried for murder. Cicero's original defense speech was unsuccessful and Milo was exiled to Marseilles.

FIGURE 3.2 Roman wall mosaic, comic and tragic masks, 1st century BC–1st century AD. Actors wore masks on stage. Different masks were used to depict different characters and it seems that there was a standard repertoire of masks, each of which was representative of a particular character. *Source: Musei Capitolini, Rome, Italy/Ancient Art and Architecture Collection Ltd/The Bridgeman Art Library*

TRANSLATION INTO LATIN

1. He had a large number of captives. (Caesar *De Bello Gallico* 5.23.2)

2. Who of you is unaware of this? (Cicero *De Lege Agraria* 2.41)

3. What is it, Catiline? (Cicero *In Catilinam* 1.13)

4. I have silver (money). (Plautus *Curculio* 530)

5. I love this woman and she loves me. (Plautus *Asinaria* 631)

6. For your Catullus' purse is full of spiders' webs. (Catullus 13.7–8)

7. They say so many things. (Cicero *De Finibus* 4.2)

8. The Fates rule me also. (Ovid *Metamorphoses* 9.434)

9. Who does not see this, judges, or who does not know this? (Cicero *Pro Caelio* 57)

THE BIGGER PICTURE

*D*e Lege Agraria (*On the Agrarian Law*), delivered by Cicero at the beginning of his consulship in January 63 BC against a bill by the tribune P. Servilius Rullus proposing the purchase of public land for distribution amongst the people. Part I was made before the senate and parts II and III before the people's assembly.

VOCABULARY TO LEARN

Nouns; Pronouns

ego, meī – I; me
nōs, nostrī (nostrum) – we
populus, -ī (m.) – people
quis?, quid? – who?; what?
servus, -ī (m.) – slave; servant
tū, tuī – you (sing.)
vōs, vestrī (vestrum) – you (pl.); yourselves

Verbs

agō, agere, ēgī, actum – lead; act; do (quid agis?
    "How are you?")
crēdō, crēdere, crēdidī, crēditum (+
    dat.) – believe
dīcō, dīcere, dīxī, dictum – say
iubeō, iubēre, iussī, iussum – order; bid
laudō, laudāre, laudāvī, laudātum – praise
timeō, timēre, timuī – fear; be afraid of

Adjectives

doctus, -a, -um – learned
līber, -era, -erum – free (m. pl. līberī, -ōrum
    – children)
longus, -a, -um – long
multus, -a, -um – much (pl. many)
novus, -a, -um – new
parvus, -a, -um – small
stultus, -a, -um – stupid

Adverbs; Prepositions; Conjunctions

hīc – here; in this place
sī – if
ubi? – where?

VOCABULARY SPECIFICALLY FOR CHAPTER 3 PASSAGES

Nouns

aqua, -ae (f.) – water
lignum, -ī (n.) – wood (pl. logs; firewood)
populus, -ī (m.) – people
Sceledrus, -ī (m.) – Sceledrus (slave name)
Troia, -ae (f.) – Troy

Verbs

adiūvō, adiuvāre, adiuvī, adiutum – help; assist
arcessō, arcessere, arcessīvī, arcessītum – send for
dēdō, dēdere, dēdidī, dēditum – surrender; hand over
dēsīderō, desīderāre, desīderāvī, desīderātum – desire; long for

Adjectives

antīquus, -a, -um – ancient
dignus, -a, -um – worthy

laetus, -a, -um – happy
nullus, -a, -um – no
pūblicus, -a, -um – public
tantus, -a, -um – so much

Adverbs; Prepositions

apud (+ acc.) – at the house of
iam – now
enim – for
etiam – even
quidem – indeed
satis – enough

> **FYI** *Enim* is regularly the second word in a clause or sentence, never first. The technical term for this is postpositive (i.e., "placed after").

English Derivations

From which Latin roots do the following English words derive?

(i) doctor
(ii) novel
(iii) stultify
(iv) servile

CHAPTER 4

FIGURE 4.1 Roman two-handled glass cup (date unknown). © *Leeds Museums and Galleries (Discovery Centre)*

Wiley's Real Latin: Learning Latin from the Source, First Edition.
Robert Maltby and Kenneth Belcher.
© 2014 John Wiley & Sons, Inc. Published 2014 by John Wiley & Sons, Inc.

4.1 THIRD DECLENSION NOUNS

Although the group of nouns classed as third declension has different endings from the first and second declensions, the uses of the cases remain the same. An example of a third declension noun is **mīles**, **mīlitis** (m.) – soldier. Notice that for third declension nouns, the genitive singular ends in **-is** and notice too that for many third declension nouns the stem cannot be predicted from the nominative case.

4.1.1 Masculine Nouns of the Third Declension

The rule for forming the cases (stem + endings) is the same as for the first and second declensions; for the third declension the stem is found by removing the **-is** from the second principal part: e.g., **mīles**, **-itis** (m.) – soldier (stem = **milit-**):

	SINGULAR	PLURAL
Nom.	mīles	mīlit-ēs
Gen.	mīlit-is	mīlit-um
Dat.	mīlit-ī	mīlit-ibus
Acc.	mīlit-em	mīlit-ēs
Abl.	mīlit-e	mīlit-ibus
Voc.	mīles	mīlit-ēs

All regular third declension masculine nouns decline in this way. As will be obvious, some cases have exactly the same form but usually this does not present a problem as the context makes the sense (and accordingly the case) clear. Notice that the nominative and vocative both singular and plural are exactly the same in form. This is true for all third declension nouns.

HINT! You need to know principal parts of nouns, especially of third declension nouns, as you need the nominative to find a word in a dictionary: there is no point in looking up *militis*, you must look up *miles*.

4.1.2 Feminine Nouns of the Third Declension

The endings for feminine nouns of the third declension are the same as those for masculine nouns: **cīvitās**, **-tātis** (f.) – state (stem = **cīvitāt-**):

	SINGULAR	PLURAL
Nom.	cīvitās	cīvitāt-ēs
Gen.	cīvitāt-is	cīvitāt-um
Dat.	cīvitāt-ī	cīvitāt-ibus
Acc.	cīvitāt-em	cīvitāt-ēs
Abl.	cīvitāt-e	cīvitāt-ibus
Voc.	cīvitās	cīvitāt-ēs

All regular third declension feminine nouns decline in this way (stem + endings).

4.1.3 Neuter Nouns of the Third Declension

The endings for neuter nouns of the third declension have some endings different from masculine and feminine nouns: **corpus**, **-oris** (n.) – body:

	SINGULAR	PLURAL
Nom.	corpus	corpor-a
Gen.	corpor-is	corpor-um
Dat.	corpor-ī	corpor-ibus
Acc.	corpus	corpor-a
Abl.	corpor-e	corpor-ibus
Voc.	corpus	corpor-a

Note that for neuter nouns the nominative, vocative, and accusative cases have exactly the same forms (both in the singular and in the plural). Note also that the nominative, vocative, and accusative plural end in **-a**, not in **-ēs**. All regular neuter nouns of the third declension decline in the same way as **corpus**.

4.1.4 Basic Rules of Declension

The nominative must be learnt; the cases are formed by adding the appropriate endings to the stem (from the second principal part). Although the group of nouns classed as third declension has different endings from the first and second, the uses of the cases remain the same. The rule for forming the cases (stem + endings) is the same as for the first and second declensions and the stem for third declension nouns is found by removing the **-is** from the second principal part.

4.1.5 Adjectives with Third Declension Nouns

As noted in Chapter 2, adjectives modify nouns and the adjective agrees with the noun that it modifies in case, gender, and number. However, the ending of an adjective need not be the same as that of the noun with which it agrees; for example, a third declension noun may be modified by a second declension adjective, as follows:

	SINGULAR	PLURAL
Nom.	mīles bonus	mīlites bonī
Gen.	mīlitis bonī	mīlitum bonōrum
Dat.	mīlitī bonō	mīlitibus bonīs
Acc.	mīlitem bonum	mīlites bonōs
Abl.	mīlite bonō	mīlitibus bonīs
Voc.	mīles bone	mīlites bonī

It is necessary, therefore, to look at the case, gender, and number in order to establish whether an adjective modifies a noun.

4.1.6 Third Declension i-Stem Nouns

There is a class of third declension nouns, traditionally referred to as i-stems, that displays minor differences in its declension. General guidelines for determining whether a noun is an i-stem are:

(a) the nominative ends in -**is** or -**es** and the genitive has the same number of syllables as the nominative: **cīvis**, **cīvis** (m.) – citizen; **nūbes**, **nūbis** (f.) – cloud;

(b) the nominative singular is only one syllable and the stem ends in two consonants: **urbs**, **urbis** (f.) – city;

(c) neuter nouns whose nominative ends in -**e**, -**al**, or -**ar**: **mare**, **maris** (n.) – sea; **animal**, **animālis** (n.) – animal.

These nouns decline as follows:

	SINGULAR	PLURAL
Nom.	cīvis	cīv-ēs
Gen.	cīv-is	cīv-ium
Dat.	cīv-ī	cīv-ibus
Acc.	cīv-em	cīv-ēs or cīv-īs
Abl.	cīv-e	cīv-ibus
Voc.	cīvis	cīv-ēs

Note that the only differences between i-stems of this type and non-i-stems regularly occur in the genitive plural and the accusative plural (here the **-ī** in the alternative form is long).

	SINGULAR	PLURAL
Nom.	urbs	urb-ēs
Gen.	urb-is	urb-ium
Dat.	urb-ī	urb-ibus
Acc.	urb-em	urb-ēs or urb-īs
Abl.	urb-e	urb-ibus
Voc.	urbs	urb-ēs

Again, note that the only differences between i-stems of this type and non-i-stems occur in the genitive plural and the accusative plural.

	SINGULAR	PLURAL
Nom.	animal	animāl-ia
Gen.	animāl-is	animāl-ium
Dat.	animāl-ī	animāl-ibus
Acc.	animal	animāl-ia
Abl.	animāl-ī	animāl-ibus
Voc.	animal	animāl-ia

For neuter i-stem nouns, note the ablative singular, nominative, genitive, accusative, and vocative, plural.

4.1.7 Third Declension Adjectives

Like adjectives of the first/second declension, adjectives of the third declension have a full case system and for most third declension adjectives the case endings are the same as the endings of third declension neuter i-stem nouns.

There are three basic types: so-called adjectives of one termination; so-called adjectives of two terminations; and so-called adjectives of three terminations. These designations refer to the differences in the nominative singular of the three genders. The principal parts of the adjective **fēlīx**

FYI There are various anomalies especially with neuter i-stems. For example, the genitive plural of *mare* is very rare and only occurs in the form *marum*.

FYI Some adjectives of the third declension are so-called consonant stems and these have the same endings as *mīles*; the most important of these are *vetus*, **-eris** – old, *pauper*, **-eris** – poor, and *memor*, **-oris** – mindful.

are **fēlīx, fēlīcis** – fortunate; happy. The first principal part represents the nominative masculine, feminine, and neuter singular, the second principal part is the genitive singular (note the change in stem and the regular **-is** ending in the genitive). **Fēlīx** is said to be an adjective of one termination since all three genders have the same form and so the same "termination" in the nominative, i.e., **fēlīx**, **fēlīx**, **fēlīx**; the principal parts of an adjective of two terminations are **tristis, triste** – sad; unhappy (usually written **tristis, -e**); in this case the masculine and feminine nominative singular are the same in form, so written in full the principal parts would be **tristis, tristis, triste**; the principal parts of adjectives of three terminations are written **ācer, ācris, ācre** – keen; sharp; in other words each of the genders has a different form in the nominative. These adjectives are declined as follows:

	SINGULAR			PLURAL		
	m.	f.	n.	m.	f.	n.
Nom.	fēlix	fēlīx	fēlīx	fēlīc-ēs	fēlīc-ēs	fēlīc-ia
Gen.	felīc-is	fēlīc-is	fēlīc-is	fēlīc-ium	fēlīc-ium	fēlīc-ium
Dat.	fēlīc-ī	fēlīc-i	fēlīc-ī	fēlīc-ibus	fēlīc-ibus	fēlīc-ibus
Acc.	fēlīc-em	fēlīc-em	fēlīx	fēlīc-ēs or -īs	fēlīc-ēs or -īs	fēlīc-ia
Abl.	fēlīc-ī	fēlīc-ī	fēlīc-ī	fēlīc-ibus	fēlīc-ibus	fēlīc-ibus
Voc.	fēlix	fēlīx	fēlīx	fēlīc-ēs	fēlīc-ēs	fēlīc-ia

Note that for adjectives of one termination the stem is derived from the second principal part.

	SINGULAR			PLURAL		
	m.	f.	n.	m.	f.	n.
Nom.	tristis	tristis	triste	trist-ēs	trist-ēs	trist-ia
Gen.	trist-is	trist-is	trist-is	trist-ium	trist-ium	trist-ium
Dat.	trist-ī	trist-ī	trist-ī	trist-ibus	trist-ibus	trist-ibus
Acc.	trist-em	trist-em	triste	trist-es or -īs	trist-ēs or -īs	trist-ia
Abl.	trist-ī	trist-ī	trist-ī	trist-ibus	trist-ibus	trist-ibus
Voc.	tristis	tristis	triste	trist-es	trist-ēs	trist-ia

	SINGULAR			PLURAL		
	m.	f.	n.	m.	f.	n.
Nom.	ācer	ācris	ācre	ācr-ēs	ācr-ēs	ācr-ia
Gen.	ācr-is	ācr-is	ācr-is	ācr-ium	ācr-ium	ācr-ium
Dat.	ācr-ī	ācr-ī	ācr-ī	ācr-ibus	ācr-ibus	ācr-ibus
Acc.	ācr-em	ācr-em	ācre	ācr-ēs or -īs	ācr-ēs or -īs	ācr-ia
Abl.	ācr-ī	ācr-ī	ācr-ī	ācr-ibus	ācr-ibus	ācr-ibus
Voc.	ācer	ācris	ācre	ācr-ēs	ācr-ēs	ācr-ia

Note that for adjectives of three terminations the stem is derived from the second principal part.

Find the correct form of the adjective [in brackets] to agree with the noun, e.g., *puella* [*bonus*] will be *puella bona*, and then decline either in the singular (*puella bona, puellae bonae* etc.) or in the plural (*puellae bonae, puellarum bonarum* etc.).

In the singular:
(i) *animal* [*sapiens*]
(ii) *urbs* [*felix*]
(iii) *civis* [*liber*]
(iv) *corpus* [*longus*]
(v) *civitas* [*novus*]

In the plural:
(i) *fatum* [*tristis*]
(ii) *imperator* [*acer*]
(iii) *homo* [*doctus*]
(iv) *consul* [*fortis*]
(v) *caput* [*omnis*]

4.2 USES OF THE CASES

4.2.1 Dative of Possessor

As we have seen, the dative case is used for the indirect object of a verb (translated *to* or *for*). It is also used, most frequently with **est** or **sunt**, to express possession:

est mihi namque domī pater (Virgil *Eclogue* 3.33): *for **there is** a father **to me** at home* (i.e., ***I have** a father at home*).

SOUND BITE   Seneca on goodness (Seneca *De Beneficiis* 7.31)

vincit malos pertinax bonitas.

TRANSLATION FROM LATIN

1. sunt mihi intus ... nummi aurei. (Plautus *Poenulus* 345)

2. Romani Sabinique in media convalle duorum montium redintegrant proelium. (Livy *Ab Urbe Condita* 1.12.10)

3. invidiam posteritatis times? (Cicero *In Catilinam* 1.28)

HINT! As sentences become more complicated you need to consider the uses of the cases: for example, why is this word in the dative? How does Latin use the dative? Which use works best for your translation?

4. est locus extremis Scythiae glacialis in oris,
   triste solum, sterilis, sine fruge, sine arbore tellus.

   (Ovid *Metamorphoses* 8.788–9)

5. sed quis hic est homo? (Plautus *Amphitruo* 292)

6. haec urbs est Thebae. (Plautus *Amphitruo* 97)

7. cui dono lepidum novum libellum? (Catullus 1.1)

8. nam neque turpis mors forti viro potest accidere neque immatura consulari nec misera sapienti. (Cicero *In Catilinam* 4.3)

9. te exspectamus, te desideramus, te iam etiam arcessimus. (Cicero *Epistulae ad Atticum* 1.18.1)

> **THE BIGGER PICTURE**
>
> *Epistulae ad Atticum* (*Letters to Atticus*): this collection of letters to his friend Atticus (without replies) was not published in the form we have it until the time of Nero. A shorter version in 11 books had existed earlier. Atticus had been a friend of Cicero from boyhood and spent much of his time (until the mid-sixties BC) studying philosophy in Athens, hence his cognomen, Atticus. He advised Cicero on political matters and acted as his publisher.

TRANSLATION INTO LATIN

1. Caesar is sending ambassadors to him with these orders. (Caesar *De Bello Gallico* 1.35.2)

2. There is also piety among the unhappy. (Ovid *Tristia* 1.9.35)

3. Caesar orders the soldiers and horsemen to go on board the ships. (Caesar *De Bello Gallico* 5.7.4)

4. But where is this man? (Plautus *Aulularia* 243)

5. Thus he leads . . . the soldiers back into the camp. (Caesar *De Bello Gallico* 7.19.6)

6. Who is breaking our door down in this way? (Plautus *Asinaria* 384)

7. He had a plan suited to the crime. (Cicero *In Catilinam* 3.16)

8. We are waiting every day for my brother, Quintus. (Cicero *Epistulae ad Atticum* 1.5.8)

9. Why do you remain seated? Why do you not get up and leave in the middle of [use the adjective *medius*; see #2 Latin to English] my speech? (Cicero *In Verrem* 2.3.208)

FIGURE 4.2 Silver denarius, Castor and Pollux. Castor and Pollux, also called the Dioscuri (= sons of Zeus) were the brothers of Helen (of Troy). The Dioscuri were saviors of sailors in trouble at sea and there was a temple to them in the Forum at Rome. © *Leeds Museums and Galleries (Discovery Centre)*

VOCABULARY TO LEARN

Nouns; Pronouns

animal, -ālis (n.) – animal
caput, -itis (n.) – head
celeritās, celeritātis – speed; swiftness
cīvis, -is (m.) – citizen
cīvitās, cīvitātis (f.) – citizenship; state
consul, -is (m.) – consul
fātum, -ī (n.) – fate (in pl. the Fates)
frāter, -tris (m.) – brother
homō, -inis (m.) – man; human
ille, illa, illud – that; that man; that woman; that thing
imperātor, -ōris (m.) – general; emperor
labor, -ōris (m.) – labor; toil
lībertās, -ātis (f.) – freedom
magnitūdō, -inis (f.) – size; importance; extent
mare, maris (n.) – sea
māter, -tris (f.) – mother
mīles, -itis (m.) – soldier

mōns, montis (m.) – mountain
mors, mortis (f.) – death
mulier, -eris (f.) – woman
nōmen, -inis (n.) – name; noun
oppidum, -ī (n.) – town
pars, partis (f.) – part
pater, -tris (m.) – father
proelium, -iī (n.) – battle
rex, rēgis (m.) – king
soror, -ōris (f.) – sister
tempus, -oris (n.) – time
urbs, urbis (f.) – city

Verbs

dūcō, dūcere, dūxī, ductum – lead
gerō, gerere, gessī, gestum – wage; carry on
mittō, mittere, mīsī, missum – send
moneō, monēre, monuī, monitum – warn
relinquō, relinquere, relīquī, relictum – leave

respondeō, respondēre, respondī, respōnsum – reply

scrībō, scrībere, scrīpsī, scrīptum – write

vincō, vincere, vīcī, victum – defeat

Adjectives

ācer, -cris, -cre – keen; sharp

fēlīx, -īcis – happy

fortis, -e – brave

omnis, -e – all

sapiens, sapientis – sensible; wise; as noun = wise man

tristis, -e – sad

Adverbs; Prepositions; Conjunctions

ab (+ abl.) – away from

dē (+ abl.) – down from; out of; about (concerning)

in (+ abl.) – among

ita – in this way; so; thus

per (+ acc.) – through

quia – since; because

quod – because

sīc – thus

sine (+ abl.) – without

tamen – however; nevertheless

> **HINT!** Helpful mnemonic device: *ex, cum, ab, pro, in, sine, de* take the ablative, they say (and sometimes *sub*).

FIGURE 4.3 Statue of Apollo, Pompeii. Son of Zeus, Apollo was the god associated with (among other things) healing, poetry, and music. A Greek god, he was adopted by the Romans and after the battle of Actium, the emperor Augustus dedicated a temple to him in 28 BC. *Source: courtesy Sam Penberthy*

VOCABULARY SPECIFICALLY FOR CHAPTER 4 PASSAGES

Nouns

arbor, -oris (f.) – tree

avunculus, -ī (m.) – uncle

convallis, -is (f.) – valley

custōs, -ōdis (m.) – guard

facinus, -oris (n.) – deed; crime

fīnis, -is (m.) – end

frux, frūgis (f.) – fruit; grain

invidia, -ae (f.) – envy; ill-will; hatred

iter, itineris (n.) – road

libellus, -ī (m.) – little book

līmen, -inis (n.) – threshold

lītus, -oris (n.) – shore

mandātum, -ī (n.) – order

nummus, -ī (m.) – coin

occāsiō, -ōnis (f.) – occasion; opportunity

opus, -eris (n.) – work

ōra, -ae (f.) – border; margin

ōrātiō, -ōnis (f.) – speech; language

pietās, -ātis (f.) – piety; loyalty; respect

posteritās, -ātis (f.) – future generations; posterity

Sabīnī, -ōrum (m. pl.) – Sabines (an Italian tribe)

Scythia, -ae (f.) – Scythia (an area in the north beyond the Black Sea)

solum, -ī (n.) – ground; soil; region

tellūs, -ūris (f.) – earth; region; land

Thēbae, -ārum (f. pl.) – Thebes

Verbs

accidō, accīdere, accīdī (+ dat.) – happen (to someone); befall (someone)

arcessō, arcessere, arcessīvī, arcessītum – send for

castra pōnō, pōnere, posuī, positum – pitch camp

cōgō, cōgere, coēgī, coactum – compel

consurgō, consurgere, consurrēxī, consurrēctum – rise; get up

dēsīderō, dēsīderāre, dēsīderāvī, dēsīderātum – desire; long for

discēdō, discēdere, discessī, discessum – leave

dōnō, dōnāre, dōnāvī, dōnātum – give; present (with)

exspectō, exspectāre, exspectāvī, exspectātum (+ acc.) – wait for

pellō, pellere, pepulī, pulsum – repel

prohibeō, prohibēre, prohibuī, prohibitum – prevent

redintegrō, redintegrāre, redintegrāvī, redintegrātum – renew; start again

redūcō, redūcere, redūxī, reductum – lead back

regō, regere, rēxī, rēctum – rule

sedeō, sedēre, sēdī, sessum – sit; remain seated

trādō, trādere, trādidī, trāditum – hand over

Adjectives

aptus, -a, -um – suited

aureus, -a, -um – golden; gold

consulāris, -e – of a consul; of consular rank

duo, duae, duo – two (see Appendix 2)

extrēmus, -a, -um – farthest

glaciālis, -e – icy; frozen

immātūrus, -a, -um – unripe; untimely

immortālis, -e – immortal

lepidus, -a, -um – fine; charming

medius, -a, -um – in the middle; middle

sānus, -a, -um – sane

sterilis, -e – sterile; barren

turpis, -e – foul; disgraceful; shameful

Adverbs; Prepositions

etiam – even; also

iam – now

intus – inside

nam – for

neque . . . nec – neither . . . nor

prō (+ abl.) – on behalf of

quoque – also

trans (+ acc.) – across

English Derivations

From which Latin roots do the following English words derive?

(i) fate
(ii) fraternal
(iii) capital
(iv) regal

CHAPTER 5

FIGURE 5.1 Romano-British bronze figurine, thought to be a soldier. Under Augustus a professional standing army was created made up of Roman citizens and non-citizens (called *auxilia*). Garrisons were stationed in provinces around the empire. © *Leeds Museums and Galleries (Discovery Centre)*

Wiley's Real Latin: Learning Latin from the Source, First Edition.
Robert Maltby and Kenneth Belcher.
© 2014 John Wiley & Sons, Inc. Published 2014 by John Wiley & Sons, Inc.

5.1 FOURTH AND FIFTH DECLENSION NOUNS

5.1.1 Fourth Declension

The characteristic identifying feature of fourth declension nouns is that the second principal part (genitive singular) ends in -**ūs** (the **ū** in the genitive is long): **exercitus, -ūs** (m.) – army; **manus, -ūs** (f.) – hand; **cornū, -ūs** (n.) – horn. The only other neuter noun of this declension that you are likely to encounter is **genū, -ūs** (n.) – knee.

The rule for forming the cases (stem + endings) is the same as for the second and third declensions and the stem is found by removing the -**ūs** from the second principal part; masculine and feminine nouns have the same endings.

> **HINT!** Remember that for all nouns the stem is found by removing the ending from the second principal part.

Masculine and feminine nouns of this declension decline as follows:

	SINGULAR	PLURAL
Nom.	manus	man-ūs
Gen.	man-ūs	man-uum
Dat.	man-uī	man-ibus
Acc.	man-um	man-ūs
Abl.	man-ū	man-ibus
Voc.	manus	man-ūs

Neuter nouns of this declension decline as follows:

	SINGULAR	PLURAL
Nom.	cornū	corn-ua
Gen.	corn-ūs	corn-uum
Dat.	corn-ū	corn-ibus
Acc.	cornū	corn-ua
Abl.	corn-ū	corn-ibus
Voc.	cornū	corn-ua

Notice that again the nominative, vocative, and accusative of neuter nouns have the same ending.

The declension of the noun **domus, -ūs** (f.) – home; house has some variations in its declension:

	SINGULAR	PLURAL
Nom.	domus	dom-ūs
Gen.	dom-ūs (or dom-ī)	dom-ōrum
Dat.	dom-uī (or dom-ō)	dom-ibus
Acc.	dom-um	dom-ōs (or dom-ūs)
Abl.	dom-u (or dom-ō)	dom-ibus
Voc.	domus	dom-ūs

5.1.2 Fifth Declension

The characteristic identifying feature of fifth declension nouns is that the second principal part (genitive singular) ends in -ēī (except **rēes**, -eiī). All nouns of this declension are feminine except **diēs**, -ēī (m.) – day; there are no fifth declension neuter nouns. The most important noun of the fifth declension is **rēs**, -eī (f.) – thing.

FYI As you will see, in some cases there is an alternative ending (e.g., domūs and domī). The less common forms are in brackets.

The rule for forming the cases (stem + endings) is the same as for the second and third declensions and the stem is found by removing the -eī (or -ēī) from the second principal part; masculine and feminine nouns have the same endings.

The declension of **rēs**, -eī is as follows:

	SINGULAR	PLURAL
Nom.	rēs	rēs
Gen.	r-eī	r-ērum
Dat.	r-eī	r-ēbus
Acc.	r-em	rēs
Abl.	r-ē	r-ēbus
Voc.	rēs	rēs

And for **diēs**, -ēī:

	SINGULAR	PLURAL
Nom.	diēs	diēs
Gen.	di-ēī	di-ērum
Dat.	di-ēī	di-ēbus
Acc.	di-em	diēs
Abl.	di-ē	di-ēbus
Voc.	diēs	diēs

HINT! Once you have the principal parts of a noun, you can immediately tell the declension to which it belongs; e.g., second principal part in -ae = first declension; in -i = second declension, and so on.

TRY THIS

Decline in full the following noun + adjective pairs, which may be either singular or plural; identify the declension to which the noun belongs:

(i) *res publica*	(vi) *dies mali*
(ii) *exercitus noster*	(vii) *manus mea*
(iii) *gloria vetus*	(viii) *corpora tota*
(iv) *duces felices*	(ix) *domus universa*
(v) *genu tuum*	(x) *cornua longa*

5.2 FOURTH AND MIXED CONJUGATIONS: PRESENT AND IMPERFECT INDICATIVE ACTIVE

5.2.1 Fourth Conjugation

The defining feature of verbs of the fourth conjugation is that the second principal part (the present infinitive active) ends in -**īre**, for example **inveniō, -īre** – come upon; find.

In order to conjugate a verb of the fourth conjugation in the present indicative active, begin by removing the -**ō** from the first principal part then add the following endings: -**ō**, -**s**, -**t**, -**mus**, -**tis**, -**unt**:

	SINGULAR	PLURAL
1st person	inveni-ō – I find, am finding, do find	invenī-mus – we find, etc.
2nd person	invenī-s – you find, etc.	invenī-tis – you find, etc.
3rd person	inveni-t – he, she, it finds, etc.	inveni-unt – they find, etc.

In order to conjugate verbs of the fourth conjugation in the imperfect indicative active, simply remove the -**o** from the first principal part and add the letter **ē** then the regular imperfect endings: -**bam**, -**bās**, -**bat**, -**bāmus**, -**bātis**, -**bant**:

	SINGULAR	PLURAL
1st person	inveni-ē-bam – I was finding	inveni-ē-bāmus – we were finding
2nd person	inveni-ē-bās – you were finding	inveni-ē-bātis – you were finding
3rd person	inveni-ē-bat – he, she, it was finding	inveni-ē-bant – they were finding

5.2.2 Mixed Conjugation

The defining features of verbs of the mixed conjugation are that the first principal part ends in -**iō** (as in the fourth conjugation), while the second principal part (the present infinitive active) ends in -**ere** (as in the third conjugation: for example **faciō, -ere** – do; make).

In order to conjugate a verb of the mixed conjugation in the present indicative active, begin by removing the -**ō** from the first principal part then add the following endings: -**ō**, -**s**, -**t**, -**mus**, -**tis**, -**unt**:

	SINGULAR	PLURAL
1st person	capi-ō – I capture, am capturing	capi-mus – we capture, etc.
2nd person	capi-s – you capture, etc.	capi-tis – you capture, etc.
3rd person	capi-t – he, she, it captures, etc.	capi-unt – they capture, etc.

In order to conjugate verbs of the mixed conjugation in the imperfect indicative active, simply remove the -**ō** from the first principal part and add the letter **ē** then the regular imperfect endings: -**bam**, -**bās**, -**bat**, -**bāmus**, -**bātis**, -**bant**.

	SINGULAR	PLURAL
1st person	capi-ē-bam – I was capturing	capi-ē-bāmus – we were capturing
2nd person	capi-ē -bās – you were capturing	capi-ē-bātis – you were capturing
3rd person	capi-ē-bat – he, she, it was capturing	capi-ē-bant – they were capturing

5.3 FUTURE INDICATIVE ACTIVE

5.3.1 First and Second Conjugations

The future tense in Latin is used to denote an action occurring in the future and may be translated, for example, I shall/will do or I shall/will be doing. In order to conjugate verbs of the first and second conjugations in the future indicative active, simply remove the -**re** from the second principal part and add the following endings: -**bō**, -**bis**, -**bit**, -**bimus**, -**bitis**, -**bunt**.

	SINGULAR	PLURAL
1st person	amā-bō – I shall love	amā-bimus – we shall love
2nd person	amā-bis – you will love	amā-bitis – you will love
3rd person	amā-bit – he, she, it will love	amā-bunt – they will love

	SINGULAR	PLURAL
1st person	vidē-bō– I shall see	vidē-bimus – we shall see
2nd person	vidē-bis – you will see	vidē-bitis – you will see
3rd person	vidē-bit – he, she, it will see	vidē-bunt – they will see

5.3.2 Third, Fourth, and Mixed Conjugations

However, in order to conjugate verbs of the third, fourth, and mixed conjugations in the future indicative active different endings are used. Here it is necessary to remove the **-ō** from the first principal part and add the following endings: **-am**, **-ēs**, **-et**, **-ēmus**, **-ētis**, **-ent**.

	SINGULAR	PLURAL
1st person	pōn-am – I shall place	pōn-ēmus – we shall place
2nd person	pōn-ēs – you will place	pōn-ētis – you will place
3rd person	pōn-et – he, she, it will place	pōn-ent – they will place

	SINGULAR	PLURAL
1st person	inveni-am – I shall find	inveni-ēmus – we shall find
2nd person	inveni-ēs – you will find	inveni-ētis – you will find
3rd person	inveni-et – he, she, it will find	inveni-ent – they will find

	SINGULAR	PLURAL
1st person	capi-am – I shall capture	capi-ēmus – we shall capture
2nd person	capi-ēs – you will capture	capi-ētis – you will capture
3rd person	capi-et – he, she, it will capture	capi-ent – they will capture

5.3.3 Irregular Verbs: *Sum, Esse; Possum, Posse*

	SINGULAR	PLURAL
1st person	erō – I shall be	erimus – we shall be
2nd person	eris – you will be	eritis – you will be
3rd person	erit – he, she, it will be	erunt – they will be

	SINGULAR	PLURAL
1st person	poterō – I shall be able	poterimus – we shall be able
2nd person	poteris – you will be able	poteritis – you will be able
3rd person	poterit – he, she, it will be able	poterunt – they will be able

HINT! Here the endings are the same as the future indicative of *sum*.

TRY THIS

Supply the verb forms requested:

(i) *capio* – 2nd person sing. imperfect indicative active

(ii) *invenio* – 3rd person pl. present indicative active

(iii) *amo* – 1st person pl. future indicative active

(iv) *video* – 3rd person sing. future indicative active

(v) *pono* – 1st person sing. future indicative active

(vi) *sum* – 3rd person pl. future indicative

(vii) *possum* – 2nd person sing. future indicative

(viii) *audio* – 3rd person sing. imperfect indicative active

(ix) *facio* – 1st person pl. future indicative active

(x) *venio* – 3rd person pl. present indicative active

5.4 USES OF THE CASES

5.4.1 Adverbial Accusative

The neuter singular of certain pronouns and adjectives may be used adverbially. The commonest examples of this are **nihil** – not at all; **quid?** – why?:

quid tacēs? (Cicero *In Catilinam* 1.8): **why are you silent?**

SOUND BITE   Seneca on deceptive appearances (Seneca *De Beneficiis* 4.34)

fallaces enim sunt rerum species.

 # TRANSLATION FROM LATIN

1. senatus haec intellegit, consul videt; hic tamen vivit. vivit? immo vero etiam in senatum venit. (Cicero *In Catilinam* 1.2)

   HINT! Look at punctuation as this is usually a guide to the way the clauses/parts of the sentence divide up. Also check if the sentence is a question.

2. nunc iam aperte rem publicam universam petis; templa deorum immortalium, tecta urbis, vitam omnium civium, Italiam totam ad exitium et vastitatem vocas. (Cicero *In Catilinam* 1.12)

3. exercitus nostri . . . crebras ex oppido excursiones faciebant. (Caesar *De Bello Gallico* 2.30.2)

4. ille miser defensorem reperire neminem poterat. (Cicero *In Verrem* 2.1.74)

5. rem publicam . . . vitamque omnium, bona, fortunas, coniuges liberosque vestros vobis conservatam ac restitutam videtis. (Cicero *In Catilinam* 3.1–2)

6. contentus eram . . . tua gloria satisque ex ea magnam laetitiam voluptatemque capiebam. (Cicero *Epistulae ad Familiares* 9.14.1)

HINT! Word order: as noted word order is flexible but often the subject (nominative) is at the beginning with the verb at the end.

7. manent istae litterae Mileti [at Miletus], manent, et dum erit, illa civitas manebunt. (Cicero *In Verrem* 2.1.89)

8. me . . . tuarum actionum, sententiarum, voluntatum, rerum denique omnium socium comitemque habebis. (Cicero *Epistulae ad Familiares* 1.9.22)

9. castra sunt in Italia contra populum Romanum . . ., crescit in dies singulos [day by day] hostium numerus; eorum autem castrorum imperatorem ducemque hostium intra moenia atque . . . in senatu videtis. (Cicero *In Catilinam* 1.5)

FIGURE 5.2 Statue of Cicero, 1st century BC. For a biography of Cicero, see Appendix 6. *Source: Ashmolean Museum, University of Oxford, UK/The Bridgeman Art Library*

TRANSLATION INTO LATIN

1. Why shall I repeat old matters? (Cicero *In Verrem* 2.3.182)

2. You will find that crime born from greed. (Cicero *In Verrem* 2.2.82)

3. I was eager to be with you. (Cicero *Epistulae ad Atticum* 8.11d.6)

4. They take up arms and occupy the entire forum. (Cicero *In Verrem* 2.5.95)

5. That man's sheep are not far from the wolves. (Plautus *Truculentus* 657)

6. They were placing all hope of safety in courage. (Caesar *De Bello Gallico* 5.34.2)

7. The Helvetii move their camp from that place. Caesar does the same thing and sends forward all the cavalry. (Caesar *De Bello Gallico* 1.15.1)

8. Will you hesitate, judges, to punish this man's great recklessness, great cruelty, great injustice? (Cicero *In Verrem* 2.2.109)

9. There was a swamp, not large, between our army and the army of the enemy. (Caesar *De Bello Gallico* 2.9.1)

FIGURE 5.3 Temple of Jupiter at the northern end of the forum in Pompeii. Mt Vesuvius is in the background. *Source: courtesy Sally Baume*

VOCABULARY TO LEARN

Nouns; Pronouns

consul, -sulis (m.) – consul

cornū, -ūs (n.) – horn; flank (of army)

corpus, -oris (n.) – body

diēs, -ēī (m.) – day

dux, dūcis (m.) – leader; commander; general

excursiō, -ōnis (f.) – assault; sally

exercitus, -ūs (m.) – army

gloria, -ae (f.) – glory

hostis, -is (m.) – enemy

Ītalia, -ae (f.) – Italy

manus, -ūs (f.) – hand

populus, -ī (m.) – people

rēs, -eī (f.) – thing; matter; event

rēs pūblica, reī pūblicae (f.) – state; republic
(sometimes written as one word)

senātus, -ūs (m.) – senate

spēs, -eī (f.) – hope

templum, -ī (n.) – temple

virtus, -ūtis (f.) – virtue; courage

Verbs

audiō, audīre, audīvī, audītum – hear

capiō, capere, cēpī, captum – take; capture
(arma capiō – take up arms)

faciō, facere, fēcī, factum – do; make

interficiō, interficere, interfēcī, interfectum – kill

inveniō, invenīre, invēnī, inventum – find

petō, petere, petīvī, petītum – seek; seek out;
attack

veniō, venīre, vēnī, ventum – come

Adjectives

malus, -a, -um – bad

meus, -a, -um – my

noster, -stra, -strum – our

pūblicus, -a, -um – public

tōtus, -a, -um – the whole of; all

tuus, -a, -um – your (sing.)

ūniversus, -a, -um – entire

vester, -stra, -strum – your (pl.)

vetus, -eris – old

Adverbs; Prepositions; Conjunctions

autem – however; moreover

iam – already

VOCABULARY SPECIFICALLY FOR CHAPTER 5 PASSAGES

Nouns; Pronouns

actiō, -ōnis (f.) – action
comes, -itis (m.) – companion; friend
coniunx, -iugis (f.) – wife; spouse
dēfensor, -ōris (m.) – defender
equitātus, -ūs (m.) – cavalry
excursiō, -ōnis (f.) – assault; sally
exitium, exitiī (n.) – destruction
facinus, -oris (n.) – deed; crime
iniūria, -ae (f.) – injury; injustice
iste, ista, istud – that (of you/of yours); (pl. those) (for declension, see Appendix 2)
laetitia, -ae (f.) – joy
libellus, -ī (m.) – book
littera, -ae (f.) – letter; (pl. letters, letter (i.e., epistle); written records)
Milētus, -ī (m.) – a city in Asia Minor
moenia, -ium (n. pl.) – walls (of the city)
nēmō, nūllius (m. and f.) – no (one)
numerus, -ī (m.) – number
porta, -ae (f.) – gate
sententia, -ae (f.) – opinion; feeling; purpose
splendor, -ōris (m.) – splendor; brilliance
tectum, -ī (n.) – roof; house
vastitās, -ātis (f.) – waste; devastation
voluntās, -ātis (f.) – wish; desire
voluptās, -ātis (f.) – pleasure

Verbs

compleō, complēre, complēvī, complētum – fill; occupy
crescō, crescere, crēvī, crētum – grow
intelligō, intelligere, intellēxī, intellēctum – understand
reperiō, reperīre, repperī, repertum – find; discover
vīvō, vīvere, vīxī, vīctum – live

Adjectives

conservātus, -a, -um – preserved
contentus, -a, -um (+ abl.) – happy with
crēber, -bra, -brum – frequent
restitūtus, -a, -um – restored
ūniversus, -a, -um – whole; entire

Adverbs; Prepositions; Conjunctions

apertē – openly
contrā (+ acc.) – against
dēnique – finally; in short
dum – while; as long as
haud – not
immō vērō – no indeed
intrā (+ acc.) – within
vērō – but; in truth

> **FYI** In classical Latin the genitive and ablative cases of nēmō are usually replaced by *nūllius* and *nullō/ā*. The accusative and dative forms are *nēminem* and *nēminī* as expected.

English Derivations

From which Latin roots do the following English words derive?

(i) invidious
(ii) avuncular
(iii) mandate
(iv) fine

CHAPTER 6

FIGURE 6.1 Romano-British bowl (1st–2nd century AD) made in Gaul. Transalpine Gaul (Gaul "across the Alps") was completely subdued by Caesar during the "Gallic Wars" (58–51 BC). It became a Roman province, famed for its food and pottery industries (especially for Samian ware). © *Leeds Museums and Galleries (Discovery Centre)*

CHAPTER CONTENTS

Wiley's Real Latin: Learning Latin from the Source, First Edition.
Robert Maltby and Kenneth Belcher.
© 2014 John Wiley & Sons, Inc. Published 2014 by John Wiley & Sons, Inc.

6.1 PERFECT INDICATIVE ACTIVE

FYI There is an alternative 3rd person plural ending: *-ēre*.

The perfect indicative active of regular verbs is formed from the third principal part and is made up of the perfect stem + endings. In order to find the perfect stem, simply remove the **-ī** from the third principal part; to the stem add the endings **-ī, -istī, -it, -imus, -istis, -ērunt**.

Particularly striking about the perfect tenses in Latin is that they are extremely regular in their formation: even the perfect of the verb **sum** is quite regular. The perfect in Latin may be translated as, for example, **I saw**, **I did see** or **I have seen**; whereas English has various ways to express the perfect tense, Latin has only one form (compare the present indicative).

dēfendī rem pūblicam adulescens, non dēseram senex (Cicero *Philippicae* 2.118): **I defended** *the Republic when I was a young man; I will not desert it now that I am an old man.*

THE BIGGER PICTURE

*P*hilippicae (*The Philippics*), a series of speeches made by Cicero in the years after the assassination of Caesar, 44–43 BC, against M. Antonius (Shakespeare's Mark Antony). The speeches were given the name *Philippics* from those delivered by the Athenian orator Demosthenes in the fourth century BC against the Macedonian King Philip, the father of Alexander the Great.

	SINGULAR	PLURAL
1st person	amāv-ī – I loved, have loved, etc.	amāv-imus – we loved, etc.
2nd person	amāv-istī – you loved, etc.	amāv-istis – you loved, etc.
3rd person	amāv-it – he, she, it loved, etc.	amāv-ērunt – they loved, etc.

	SINGULAR	PLURAL
1st person	posu-ī – I placed, have placed, etc.	posu-imus – we placed, etc.
2nd person	posu-istī – you placed, etc.	posu-istis – you placed, etc.
3rd person	posu-it – he, she, it placed, etc.	posu-ērunt – they placed, etc.

Notice that in all of the above, the perfect indicative active is formed by adding the perfect endings to the perfect stem.

6.2 FUTURE PERFECT INDICATIVE ACTIVE

The future perfect indicative active defines an action as complete in the future, for example, **I will have read** *this book by tomorrow.* The forms of the future perfect, as is the case with the perfect, consist of the stem + endings. The endings of the future perfect (with the exception of the third person plural) are the same as the future indicative of the verb **sum** (see Chapter 5). Again the formation of the future perfect in Latin is strikingly regular:

	SINGULAR	PLURAL
1st person	invēn-erō – I will have found	invēn-erimus – we will have found
2nd person	invēn-eris – you will have found	invēn-eritis – you will have found
3rd person	invēn-erit – he (etc.) will have found	invēn-erint – they will have found

NOTE: the third person plural ending is **-erint**, not **-ērunt**.

6.3 PLUPERFECT INDICATIVE ACTIVE

The third and final perfect tense is the pluperfect indicative active. This tense describes an action as completed in the past. The Latin pluperfect, therefore, is more or less the same as the pluperfect in English: *I had seen*. The pluperfect is also built on the perfect stem and the endings are the same in form as the imperfect indicative of the verb **sum** (see Chapter 2):

	SINGULAR	PLURAL
1st person	vīd-eram – I had seen	vīd-erāmus – we had seen
2nd person	vīd-erās – you had seen	vīd-erātis – you had seen
3rd person	vīd-erat – he, she, it had seen	vīd-erant – they had seen

6.4 IRREGULAR VERBS: *SUM* AND *POSSUM*

The perfect tenses of **sum** and **possum** are not, in fact, irregular. They are formed in exactly the same way as other verbs: perfect stem + endings and the stem is derived from the third principal part.

6.4.1 Perfect Indicative

	SINGULAR	PLURAL
1st person	fu-ī – I was	fu-imus – we were
2nd person	fu-istī – you were	fu-istis – you were
3rd person	fu-it – he, she, it was	fu-ērunt – they were

	SINGULAR	PLURAL
1st person	potu-ī – I was able	potu-imus – we were able
2nd person	potu-istī – you were able	potu-istis – you were able
3rd person	potu-it – he, she, it was able	potu-ērunt – they were able

6.4.2 Future Perfect Indicative

	SINGULAR	PLURAL
1st person	fu-erō – I will have been	fu-erimus – we will have been
2nd person	fu-eris – you will have been	fu-eritis – you will have been
3rd person	fu-erit – he, she, it will have been	fu-erint – they will have been

	SINGULAR	PLURAL
1st person	potu-erō – I will have been able	potu-erimus – we will have been able
2nd person	potu-eris – you will have been able	potu-eritis – you will have been able
3rd person	potu-erit – he, she, it will have been able	potu-erint – they will have been able

6.4.3 Pluperfect Indicative

	SINGULAR	PLURAL
1st person	fu-eram – I had been	fu-erāmus – we had been
2nd person	fu-erās – you had been	fu-erātis – you had been
3rd person	fu-erat – he, she, it had been	fu-erant – they had been

	SINGULAR	PLURAL
1st person	potu-eram – I had been able	potu-erāmus – we had been able
2nd person	potu-erās – you had been able	potu-erātis – you had been able
3rd person	potu-erat – he, she, it had been able	potu-erant – they had been able

TRY THIS

Perfect tenses. Translate into Latin:

(i) they had left

(ii) we have been able

(iii) you (sing.) have been

(iv) they will have surrendered

(v) he has made

(vi) she had ordered

(vii) I will have defended

(viii) he has deterred

(ix) they had seen

(x) we have found

6.5 USES OF THE CASES

6.5.1 Ablative of Means/Instrument

So far most of the examples in the text have demonstrated the basic uses of the cases as outlined in Chapter 1. However, as will become clear, the cases in Latin, especially the accusative, genitive, dative, and ablative have various grammatical functions. For example, the ablative is used without a preposition to indicate the instrument or means by which an action is carried out:

> **gladiīs** rem gerunt (Caesar *De Bello Gallico* 7.88.3): *they accomplish the matter **by means of/with swords**.*

> tum vir optimus Sex. Naevius hominem **multīs verbīs** dēterret (Cicero *Pro Quinctio* 16): *then that most excellent man, Sextus Naevius, deters the man **with/by means of many words**.*

THE BIGGER PICTURE

*P*ro Quinctio (*On behalf of Quinctius*), Cicero's first extant speech from 81 BC, on behalf of Gaius Qunctius, accused by Sextus Naevius, a business partner of Qinctius' recently deceased brother, of failure to pay a debt.

SOUND BITE   Tacitus on the Roman Empire (Tacitus *Agricola* 30.6)

ubi solitudinem faciunt, pacem appellant.

TRANSLATION FROM LATIN

1. facinus fecit audax. (Plautus *Miles Gloriosus* 309)

2. de navi timidae desiluerunt in scapham. (Plautus *Rudens* 75)

> **HINT!** *Navi* is an alternative form of the ablative singular in the early Latin of Plautus.

3. ab saxo avertit fluctus ad litus scapham. (Plautus *Rudens* 165)

4. non argentum, non aurum, non vestem, non mancipia repetunt. (Cicero *In Verrem* 2.5.126)

5. sunt autem duo crimina, auri et veneni. (Cicero *Pro Caelio* 30)

6. O, immoderata mulier, . . . tu aurum ad facinus dedisti? (Cicero *Pro Caelio* 53)

7. Hammonius, regis legatus, aperte pecunia nos oppugnat. (Cicero *Epistulae Ad Familiares* 1.1.1)

8. horum duorum criminum video auctorem, video fontem, video certum nomen et caput. auro opus fuit; sumpsit a Clodia, sumpsit sine teste, habuit quamdiu voluit. (Cicero *Pro Caelio* 31)

9. Caesar . . . a dextro cornu, quod eam partem minime firmam hostium esse animadverterat, proelium commisit. nostri acriter in hostes . . . impetum fecerunt, atque hostes repente celeriterque procurrerunt. (Caesar *De Bello Gallico* 1.52.4)

FIGURE 6.2 Gold aureus, AD 164–9, inscription: VOTA PUBLICA. The aureus was the standard Roman gold coin. The inscription "VOTA PUBLICA" translates as "Public Prayers," that is to say, an official or religious ceremony in response to a state of emergency. © *Leeds Museums and Galleries (Discovery Centre)*

TRANSLATION INTO LATIN

1. I defied the swords of Catiline and I will not fear yours. (Cicero *Philippicae* 2.118)

2. Why did you not come to the barber's shop as I had ordered? (Plautus *Asinaria* 413)

3. I have written carefully before about my reasons. (Cicero *Epistulae ad Atticum* 1.2.1)

4. He [Caesar] fortified that place with a rampart and a ditch. (Caesar *De Bello Gallico* 3.1.6)

5. They could not withstand the large number of javelins and worn out by their wounds, they abandoned their position. (Caesar *Bellum Civile* 3.95)

6. From that time he began to seek praise from states and not only to frighten off witnesses with his words, but also to prevent them by force. (Cicero *In Verrem* 2.2.64)

7. Caesar himself, our friend, had sent threatening and harsh letters to the senate. (Cicero *Epistulae ad Familiares* 16.11.2)

8. Marcus Bibulus and I were commanders in the neighboring and nearby provinces. (Cicero *Philippicae* 11.34)

9. Our ancestors have left this land to us. (Cicero *De Lege Agraria* 2.84)

FIGURE 6.3 The Baths of Neptune at Ostia. The corner of the room containing the mosaic of Neptune which gives the baths their name, with the next room (more the focus of the picture) thought to be the *frigidarium*. *Source: courtesy Sally Baume*

VOCABULARY TO LEARN

Nouns; Pronouns

adulescens, -entis (m.) – young man
argentum, -ī (n.) – silver
aurum, -ī (n.) – gold
caput, -itis (n.) – head; face
crīmen, -inis (n.) – crime
flūmen, -inis (n.) – river
gladius, gladiī (m.) – sword
impetus, -ūs (m.) – attack
legātus, -ī (m.) – ambassador; envoy
līberī, -ōrum (m.) – children
lītus, -oris (n.) – shore
maiōrēs, -um (m.) – ancestors
nāvis, -is (f.) – ship
nōmen, -inis (n.) – name
opus est (+ abl.) – there is need of
ratiō, -ōnis (f.) – reason; account
vīs, vis (f.) – power; force
vulnus, -eris (n.) – wound

> **FYI** *Vis* in the singular commonly occurs only in the nominative, accusative, and ablative: *vis, vim, vi.* In the plural it has the meaning *strength; military forces* and declines as follows: *vires, vires (virīs), virium, viribus, viribus.*

Verbs

coepit – he began (occurs only in the perfect tenses)

dēdō, dēdere, dēdidī, dēditum – surrender; hand over
dēfendō, dēfendere, dēfendī, dēfensum – defend
dēterreō, dēterrēre, dēterruī, dēterritum – frighten off; deter
faciō, facere, fēcī, factum – do; make
iubeō, iubēre, iussī, iussum – order
relinquō, relinquere, relīquī, relictum – leave (behind); abandon

Adjectives

audax, -ācis – brave
certus, -a, -um – certain
dexter, -tra, -trum – right
duo, duae, duo – two (see Appendix 3)
propinquus, -a, -um – neighboring
pūblicus, -a, -um – public
sex (indeclinable) – six (see Appendix 3)
timidus, -a, -um – fearful; frightened

Adverbs; Prepositions

anteā – before
celeriter – swiftly
nōn sōlum . . . sed etiam – not only . . . but also
repentē – suddenly

VOCABULARY SPECIFICALLY FOR CHAPTER 6 PASSAGES

Nouns; Pronouns

auctor, -ōris (m.) – author; perpetrator
Clōdia, -ae (f.) – Clodia (identified by some as Catullus' "Lesbia")
cohors, -hortis (f.) – cohort
fluctus, -ūs (m.) – wave
fons, fontis (f.) – spring; fountain; source
ipse, ipsa, ipsum – himself, herself, itself etc. (for declension, see Appendix 2)
laudātiō, -ōnis (f.) – praise
liber, -brī (m.) – book
mancipium, mancipiī (n.) – slave
pons, pontis (m.) – bridge
praesidium, praesidiī (n.) – guard
Quintus, -ī (m.) – Quintus (abbreviated Q.)
saxum, -ī (n.) – rock
scapha, -ae (f.) – boat
senex, senis (m.) – old man
tēlum, -ī (n.) – javelin
testis, -is (m.) – witness
vallum, -ī (n.) – rampart
venēnum, -ī (n.) – poison
vestis, vestis (f.) – clothes

Verbs

animadvertō, animadvertere, animadvertī, animadversum – notice
āvertō, āvertere, āvertī, āversum – turn aside; turn away

dēserō, dēserere, dēseruī, dēsertum – desert
dēsiliō, dēsilere, dēsiluī – leap down
mūniō, mūnīre, mūnīvī, mūnītum – build a wall around; fortify
oppugnō, -āre, -āvī, -ātum – attack
prōcurrō, prōcurrere, prōcurrī, prōcursum – run forward
proelium (acc. n. sing.) committō, committere, commīsī, commissum – join battle
repetō, repere, repetīvī, repetītum – ask back
sūmō, sūmere, sumpsī, sumptum – take
voluit – perfect indicative – he wished; he wanted

Adjectives

acerbus, -a, -um – harsh
alter, -tera, -terum – other
firmus, -a, -um – firm; strong
immoderātus, -a, -um – wanton; unbridled

Adverbs; Prepositions

acriter – keenly
ad (+ acc.) – for
apertē – openly
autem – however; moreover
minimē – least
quamdiū – for as long as

English Derivations

From which Latin roots do the following English words derive?

(i) adolescent
(ii) navy
(iii) rational
(iv) audacious

FIGURE R.1 The right hand of the Colossal Statue of the emperor Constantine (AD 272–337), currently adorning the courtyard of the Capitoline Museum in Rome. Constantine was responsible for the rise of Christianity in the Roman world. *Photo © javarman/Shutterstock*

(A) Change the tense of the verbs from present to imperfect:
1. castra in Italia sunt.
2. id ubi vident, mutant consilium.
3. bellum parat administrare.
4. Ennius sanctos appellat poetas.
5. quam rem publicam habemus?

(B) Change the verb from singular to plural:
1. iubes me bona cogitare.
2. multa miser timeo.
3. cui dono novum libellum.
4. magnam capies voluptatem.
5. defensorem reperire neminem poterat.

(C) Identify the case, number, and gender of the nouns underlined:
1. <u>castra</u> sunt in Italia.
2. me tuarum <u>actionum</u> socium habebis.
3. <u>exercitus</u> nostri crebras excursiones faciebat.
4. Romani in media <u>convalle</u> redintegrant proelium.
5. quem das finem, <u>rex</u> magne, laborum?

(D) Identify the person, number, and tense of the verbs underlined:
1. <u>sunt</u> mihi intus nummi aurei.
2. consul castra Aequorum <u>oppugnabat</u>.
3. me socium comitemque <u>habebis</u>.
4. <u>manent</u> istaec litterae Mileti.
5. Italiam totam ad exitium et vastitatem <u>vocas</u>.

(E) Translate into English:
1. stabant Romano pila Sabina foro. (Propertius, 4.4.12)
2. iubes me bona cogitare. (Cicero *Tusculanae Disputationes* 3.35)
3. quem das finem, rex magne, laborum? (Virgil *Aeneid* 1.242)
4. magnam ex eorum splendore . . . capies voluptatem. (Cicero *Epistulae ad Familiares* 12.26.2)
5. in eo flumine pons erat. ibi praesidium ponit et in altera parte fluminis Q. Titurium Sabinum legatum cum sex cohortibus relinquit. (Caesar *De Bello Gallico* 2.5.6)

HINT! As sentences become more complex, it is even more important to parse every word and consider its function in the sentence.

(F) Translate into Latin:
1. This man is not sane. (Plautus *Amphitruo* 402)
2. I am speaking the truth [translate as *true things*]. (Plautus *Asinaria* 186)
3. He is the uncle of that young man. (Plautus *Aulularia* 35)
4. They were repairing the walls, the gates, and the fleet. (Caesar *Bellum Civile* 1.34.5)
5. You have written nothing to me about it. (Cicero *Epistulae ad Atticum* 1.3.2)

CHAPTER 7

▶

FIGURE 7.1 Silver denarius (130 BC), Jupiter in chariot. The denarius was a Roman silver coin. Jupiter, the Roman equivalent of Zeus, is depicted carrying a thunderbolt. He was a sky god; hence the thunderbolt is an appropriate symbol of his power. © *Leeds Museums and Galleries (Discovery Centre)*

Wiley's Real Latin: Learning Latin from the Source, First Edition.
Robert Maltby and Kenneth Belcher.
© 2014 John Wiley & Sons, Inc. Published 2014 by John Wiley & Sons, Inc.

7.1 THE PASSIVE VOICE

Recall that one of the qualities of a finite verb is voice (also of some non-finite forms such as infinitives and participles): active and passive. In the active voice, the subject performs the action of the verb; in the passive voice the subject is the "recipient" of the action: *Caesar **was killed** by Brutus.*

It may not come as a surprise to learn that once again in Latin it is the endings of verb forms that change to indicate that the verb form is passive. The basic endings for all five conjugations are: **-r**, **-ris**, **-tur**, **-mur**, **-mini**, **-ntur**; however, there are differences in the forms to which these endings are added. For first conjugation verbs, the first person singular ending is simply added to the first principal part but for the other forms, remove the **-o** from the first principal part and add the letter **a**, then the endings.

7.1.1 Present Indicative Passive

	SINGULAR	PLURAL
1ˢᵗ **person**	amo-r – I am loved, being loved	am-ā-mur – we are loved, etc.
2ⁿᵈ **person**	am-ā-ris – you are loved, etc.	am-ā-mini – you are loved, etc.
3ʳᵈ **person**	am-ā-tur – he, she, it is loved, etc.	am-a-ntur – they are loved, etc.

FYI An alternative 2ⁿᵈ person singular ending for the present, future, and imperfect of all conjugations is *-re*; e.g., *amare* = "you are loved"; *vidēbere; capiēbēre.* Be careful not to confuse the forms of the present with the present infinitive active.

For second conjugation verbs, the first person singular ending is simply added to the first principal part, but for the other forms, remove the **-ō** from the first principal part and add the endings.

	SINGULAR	PLURAL
1ˢᵗ **person**	video-r – I am seen, being seen	vid-ē-mur – we are seen, etc.
2ⁿᵈ **person**	vid-ē-ris – you are seen, etc.	vid-ē-mini – you are seen, etc.
3ʳᵈ **person**	vid-ē-tur – he, she, it is seen, etc.	vid-e-ntur – they are seen, etc.

The treatment of third conjugation verbs is a bit more complicated: the first person singular ending is simply added to the first principal part but for the other forms, remove the -**ō** from the first principal part and add the letter **e** in the second person singular **i** in the third person singular and first and second person plural, and **u** in the third person plural:

HINT! *Video* in the passive also has the meaning "seem."

	SINGULAR	PLURAL
1st person	pōno-r – I am placed, being placed	pōn-i-mur – we are placed, etc.
2nd person	pōn-e-ris – you are placed, etc.	pōn-i-minī – you are placed, etc.
3rd person	pōn-i-tur – he, she, it is placed, etc.	pōn-u-ntur – they are placed, etc.

For fourth conjugation verbs, the first person singular ending is simply added to the first principal part but for the other forms, remove the -**ō** from the first principal part and add the endings (for the third person plural add the letter **u** before the ending).

	SINGULAR	PLURAL
1st person	invenio-r – I am found, being found	inven-ī-mur – we are found
2nd person	inven-ī-ris – you are found, etc.	inven-ī-minī – you are found
3rd person	inven-ī-tur – he, she, it is found, etc.	inven-i-**u**ntur – they are found

For mixed conjugation verbs the passive is formed in the same way as for fourth conjugation verbs with one exception – the second person singular, which, like the third conjugation, has an **e** in the second person singular.

	SINGULAR	PLURAL
1st person	capio-r – I am captured, being captured	cap-i-mur – we are captured
2nd person	cap-e-ris – you are captured, etc.	cap-i-minī – you are captured
3rd person	cap-i-tur – he, she, it is captured, etc.	cap-i-**u**ntur – they are captured

7.1.2 Future Indicative Passive: First and Second Conjugations

To form the future indicative passive, first remove the -**re** ending from the infinitive. The future indicative passive uses the endings -**r**, -**ris**, -**tur**, -**mur**, -**minī**, -**ntur** and the familiar **b** of the future active occurs here as well; however, the vowel before the ending is **o** in the first person singular, **e** in the second person singular, **i** in the third person singular and first and second person plural, and **u** in the third person plural.

	SINGULAR	PLURAL
1st person	amā-bo-r – I shall be loved	amā-bi-mur – we shall be loved
2nd person	amā-be-ris – you will be loved	amā-bi-minī – you will be loved
3rd person	amā-bi-tur – he, she, it will be loved	amā-bu-ntur – they will be loved

	SINGULAR	PLURAL
1ˢᵗ person	vidē-bo-r – I shall be seen	vidē-bi-mur – we shall be seen
2ⁿᵈ person	vidē-be-ris – you will be seen	vidē-bi-minī – you will be seen
3ʳᵈ person	vidē-bi-tur – he, she, it will be seen	vidē-bu-ntur – they will be seen

7.1.3 Future Indicative Passive: Third, Fourth, and Mixed Conjugations

	SINGULAR	PLURAL
1ˢᵗ person	pōn-ar – I shall be placed	pōn-ē-mur – we shall be placed
2ⁿᵈ person	pōn-ē-ris – you will be placed	pōn-ē-minī – you will be placed
3ʳᵈ person	pōn-ē-tur – he, she, it will be placed	pōn-e-ntur – they will be placed

	SINGULAR	PLURAL
1ˢᵗ person	inveni-ar – I shall be found	inveni-ē-mur – we shall be found
2ⁿᵈ person	inveni-ē-ris – you will be found	inveni-ē-minī – you will be found
3ʳᵈ person	inveni-ē-tur – he, she, it will be found	inveni-e-ntur – they will be found

	SINGULAR	PLURAL
1ˢᵗ person	capi-ar– I shall be taken	capi-ē-mur – we shall be taken
2ⁿᵈ person	capi-ē-ris – you will be taken	capi-ē-minī – you will be taken
3ʳᵈ person	capi-ē-tur – he, she, it will be taken	capi-e-ntur – they will be taken

7.1.4 Imperfect Indicative Passive

To form the imperfect indicative passive, simply change the active endings (-**m**, -**s**, -**t**, etc.) to the passive (-**r**, -**ris**, -**tur**, etc.):

	SINGULAR	PLURAL
1ˢᵗ person	am-ā-bar – I was being loved	am-ā-bāmur – we were being loved
2ⁿᵈ person	am-ā-bāris – you were being loved	am-ā-bāminī – you were being loved
3ʳᵈ person	am-ā-bātur – he, she, it was being loved	am-ā-bantur – they were being loved

	SINGULAR	PLURAL
1ˢᵗ person	vid-ē-bar – I was being seen	vid-ē-bāmur – we were being seen
2ⁿᵈ person	vid-ē-bāris – you were being seen	vid-ē-bāminī – you were being seen
3ʳᵈ person	vid-ē-bātur – he, she, it was being seen	vid-ē-bantur – they were being seen

	SINGULAR	PLURAL
1st person	pōn-ē-bar – I was being placed	pōn-ē-bāmur – we were being placed
2nd person	pōn-ē-bāris – you were being placed	pōn-ē-bāminī – you were being placed
3rd person	pōn-ē-bātur – he, she, it was being placed	pōn-ē-bantur – they were being placed

	SINGULAR	PLURAL
1st person	capi-ē-bar – I was being taken	capi-ē-bāmur – we were being taken
2nd person	capi-ē-bāris – you were being taken	capi-ē-bāminī – you were being taken
3rd person	capi-ē-bātur – he, she, it was being taken	capi-ē-bantur – they were being taken

	SINGULAR	PLURAL
1st person	inveni-ē-bar – I was being found	inveni-ē-bāmur – we were being found
2nd person	inveni-ē-bāris – you were being found	inveni-ē-bāminī – you were being found
3rd person	inveni-ē-bātur – he, she, it was being found	inveni-ē-bantur – they were being found

TRY THIS

Present, future, and imperfect passive forms.

Translate into English:
(i) *poneris*
(ii) *inveniemur*
(iii) *videbor*
(iv) *capiuntur*
(v) *ponebatur*

Translate into Latin:
(i) I am wounded
(ii) they will seem
(iii) you (sing.) were being accused
(iv) I shall be condemned
(v) he will be ordered

7.2 RELATIVE PRONOUN

The Latin relative pronoun translates as "who," "which," or "that." It introduces a subordinate relative clause: *The man **whom** I saw was my friend*. Notice that this sentence has two finite verbs: *was* is the main verb in the sentence; *saw* is the finite verb in the subordinate relative clause. In this English example *whom* is a relative pronoun (and direct object of the verb). In Latin the form will be accusative, masculine, and singular. In Latin a relative pronoun regularly gets its gender and number from its antecedent and its case from its

HINT! Notice that the declension of the relative pronoun is the same as that of the interrogative adjective; however, the context usually will make clear which is being used and so there is little chance of confusion.

grammatical function in its own clause. The antecedent is the word in the main clause to which the relative pronoun refers (or relates). Here the antecedent is "man," so in Latin masculine and singular; it is the direct object in its clause and so accusative case. In English the relative pronoun may be omitted (*The man I saw was my friend*); however, it is never omitted in Latin.

The relative pronoun declines as follows:

	SINGULAR			PLURAL		
	m.	**f.**	**n.**	**m.**	**f.**	**n.**
Nom.	quī	quae	quod	quī	quae	quae
Gen.	cuius	cuius	cuius	quōrum	quārum	quōrum
Dat.	cui	cui	cui	quibus	quibus	quibus
Acc.	quem	quam	quod	quōs	quās	quae
Abl.	quō	quā	quō	quibus	quibus	quibus
Voc.	NO VOCATIVE			NO VOCATIVE		

ego in ūnō homine omnia vitia **quae** possunt in homine perditō nefāriōque esse reprehendō (Cicero *In Verrem* 2.3.5): *in one person I find fault with all the vices **that** can exist in a ruined and wicked man.*

TRY THIS

Relative pronoun practice.

Supply the correct form of the relative pronoun to agree with the following antecedents:

e.g., *consilium* (relative in nom. sing.) – *quod*

puella (relative in acc. pl.) – *quas*

(i) *casus* (gen. sing.)   (vi) *dignitas* (nom. sing.)

(ii) *poena* (acc. pl.)   (vii) *virtus* (dat. pl.)

(iii) *regnum* (abl. sing.)   (viii) *sensus* (nom. pl.)

(iv) *memoria* (gen. pl.)   (ix) *proelium* (dat. sing.)

(v) *mulier* (acc. sing.)   (x) *opinio* (nom. pl.)

7.3 CONNECTING OR DEMONSTRATIVE RELATIVE

Because the Romans liked to connect the beginning of a new sentence with the end of the previous one, a relative is sometimes used at the beginning of a sentence referring back to an earlier noun. This is called a connecting or demonstrative relative and is usually translated in English as a demonstrative "this" or "that": statuit <exspectāre> classem. **quae** ubi convēnit . . . (Caesar *De Bello Gallico* 3.14.11): *he decided to wait for the fleet;* ***and when this arrived . . .*** The word *quae* translated "this" is actually the nominative (subject of *convēnit*) feminine singular of the relative agreeing with *classis*.

7.4 USES OF THE CASES

7.4.1 Accusative

Place

We have seen that the accusative case is used with the prepositions **in** and **ad** to express motion towards: **ad urbem**: to the city; however, with the names of cities, towns, small islands, **domus** – home, and **rus** – countryside, normally no preposition is used:

> ut **Rōmam** vēnit . . . (Cicero *In Verrem* 2.1.101): *when he came **to Rome** . . .*; numquam **domum** revertērunt (Cicero *Tusculanae Disputationes* 5.107): *they never returned* ***home***.

Compare the English: *I returned **home**.* The construction in Latin is exactly the same as in English.

Space

The accusative is used usually without a preposition to express distance or extent of space:

> Mīlites aggerem lātum **pedēs trecentōs trīgintā**, altum **pedēs octōgintā** extrūxērunt (Caesar *De Bello Gallico* 7.24.1): *the soldiers constructed an embankment **three hundred and thirty feet** wide, and **eighty feet** high.*

In the sentence "The camp was about one mile away" the expression "one mile" in Latin goes into the accusative. The Latin for a mile is *mille passus*, literally "a thousand paces." *Mille* is an indeclinable adjective/numeral and the word *passus* remains in the accusative: locus erat castrorum . . . ab imo acclivis **circiter passus mille** (Caesar *De Bello Gallico* 3.19.1): *the position of the camp . . . was **about a mile** from the base of the hill.*

If the distance is more than one mile, Latin uses the plural i-stem noun *milia* and *passus* goes into the partitive genitive, *passuum*. So two miles is *duo milia passuum*, literally "two thousands of paces." In expressions of extent of space the "two, three etc. thousands" remains in the accusative: **milia passuum tria** ab eorum castris castra ponit (Caesar *De Bello Gallico* 1.22.5): *he placed his camp **three miles (literally: three thousands of paces)** from their camp.*

> **FYI** For *mille* and the declension of *milia*, see Appendix 3.

Time

The accusative is also used (usually without a preposition – though the preposition **per** is sometimes used) to express time how long:

annōs multōs legātus fuit (Cicero *Pro Murena* 85): *he was an ambassador **for many years**.*

---

*P*ro Murena (*On behalf of Murena*), a speech for Lucius Licinius Murena, a candidate, along with Catiline, for the consulship of 62 BC. He was charged with electoral bribery. The speech was made in November 63 BC between the second and third speeches against Catiline. Murena was acquitted and held the consulship for 62 BC.

THE BIGGER PICTURE

7.4.2 Ablative

Time

The ablative is used (again usually without a preposition) to express time when:

eō tempore Galli castra munīre instituērunt (Caesar *De Bello Gallico* 7.30.4): ***at that time** the Gauls began to fortify their camp.*

The ablative is also used (again usually without a preposition) to express

time within which:

paucīs diēbus opus efficitur (Caesar *De Bello Gallico* 6.9.4): *the work is [was] accomplished **within a few days**.*

Place

We have seen that the ablative case is used with the prepositions **ex** and **ab** to express motion from: **ex urbe**: from the city; however with the names of cities, towns, small islands, **domus** – home, and **rus** – countryside, normally no preposition is used:

mē **domō** meā per vim expūlistis (Cicero *Pro S. Roscio Amerino* 32): *you have driven me by force **from my home**.*

[terrent] eōs quī **domō** exīre nolēbant (Cicero *Pro Flacco* 14): *[they frighten] those who were unwilling to leave **home**.*

Agent

The person by whom the action of a passive verb is done is called the agent. To express this relationship Latin regularly uses **ab** + ablative case:

circumveniēbantur atque interficiēbantur **ab nostrīs** (Caesar *De Bello Gallico* 2.34.3): *they were being surrounded and killed **by our men**.*

FIGURE 7.2 Section of painted wall plaster from a Romano-British villa (*c.* AD 200–25). The decoration of walls of houses with paintings was extremely common. For example, almost every house in Pompeii was decorated with wall paintings. © *Leeds Museums and Galleries (Discovery Centre)*

TRANSLATION FROM LATIN

1. veni Athenas, inquit Democritus, neque me quisquam ibi agnovit. (Cicero *Tusculanae Disputationes* 5.104)

2. in eo itinere persuadet Castico . . . Sequano, cuius pater regnum in Sequanis multos annos obtinuerat. (Caesar *De Bello Gallico* 1.3.5)

3. magna est hominum opinio de te, magna commendatio liberalitatis, magna memoria consulatus tui. (Cicero *Epistulae ad Familiares* 1.7.9)

4. ego eo die casu apud Pompeium cenavi. (Cicero *Epistulae ad Familiares* 1.2.3)

5. de litterarum missione sine causa abs te accusor. (Cicero *Epistulae ad Atticum* 1.5.3)

   HINT! *Abs* is simply a variant spelling of the preposition *ab*.

6. hic locus aequum fere spatium a castris . . . Ariovisti et Caesaris aberat. (Caesar *De Bello Gallico* 1.43.2)

7. omnia tela totius accusationis in Oppianicum coniciebantur, aperiebatur causa insidiarum, Fabriciorum familiaritas commemorabatur. (Cicero *Pro Cluentio* 50).

8. proximique <Belgae> sunt Germanis, qui trans Rhenum incolunt, quibuscum continenter bellum gerunt. qua de causa Helvetii quoque reliquos Gallos virtute praecedunt, quod fere cotidianis proeliis cum Germanis contendunt. (Caesar *De Bello Gallico* 1.1.3–4)

9. nostri milites facile superabant . . . quod in conspectu Caesaris atque omnis exercitus res gerebatur . . . omnes enim colles ac loca superiora, unde erat propinquus despectus in mare, ab exercitu tenebantur. (Caesar *De Bello Gallico* 3.14.8–9)

TRANSLATION INTO LATIN

1. Everything will be done carefully by us. (Cicero *Epistulae ad Familiares* 1.5.3)

2. That opinion of men is confirmed more and more day by day. (Cicero *Epistulae ad Familiares* 6.4.1)

3. On the following days the senate is held outside the city. (Caesar *Bellum Civile* 1.6.1)

4. The Aduatuci, about whom we have written above . . . returned home from their march. (Caesar *De Bello Gallico* 2.29.1)

5. By what penalty, now at last, will he be punished or with what sentence will he be condemned? (Cicero *Pro S. Roscio Amerino* 113)

6. Do you hesitate to avoid the sight and presence of those whose minds and feelings you are wounding? (Cicero *In Catilinam* 1.17)

7. I had completed what you had directed as soon as I came to Rome following your departure. (Cicero *Epistulae ad Atticum* 1.5.4)

8. Therefore will the wretched man go [he will go = **ibit**] in exile? Where? To those parts of the East in which for many years he was lieutenant-general, led armies and accomplished very great things? (Cicero *Pro Murena* 89)

9. I shall say nothing about the man's frugality, virtue, and diligence and I shall leave out that about which I spoke before. (Cicero *In Verrem* 2.5.20)

FIGURE 7.3 Gold aureus, *c.*
AD 113. Standing eagle,
inscription: CONSECRATIO.
Consecratio means dedication;
the eagle was the principal
standard of a Roman legion of
soldiers. © *Leeds Museums and
Galleries (Discovery Centre)*

VOCABULARY TO LEARN

Nouns; Pronouns

annus, -ī (m.) – year

cāsus, -ūs (m.) – chance; casū – by chance

causa, -ae (f.) – reason; cause

dignitās, -ātis (f.) – dignity; excellence

locus, -ī (m.) – place; position; (in the plural the
    gender is neuter – loca, locorum)

memoria, -ae (f.) – memory; remembering;
    recollection

mulier, -eris (f.) – woman

opīniō, -ōnis (f.) – opinion; belief

pars, partis (f.) – part

poena, -ae (f.) – punishment; penalty

proelium, proeliī (n.) – battle

quī, quae, quod – who; which; that

regnum, -ī (n.) – rule; power; kingdom

sensus, -ūs (m.) – sense; feeling

virtus, -ūtis (f.) – courage

Verbs

absum, abesse, āfuī – be distant from; away
    from

accūsō, accūsāre, accūsāvī, accūsātum – accuse

agō, agere, ēgī, actum – do

cēnō, cēnāre, cēnāvī, cēnātum – dine

damnō, damnāre, damnāvī, damnātum –
    condemn

mandō, mandāre, mandāvī, mandātum – order;
    direct

persuādeō, persuādēre, persuāsī, persuāsum (+
    dat.) – persuade

superō, superāre, superāvī, superātum –
    overcome; be victorious

vendō, vendere, vendidī, venditum – sell

vulnerō (*or* volnerō), vulnerāre, vulnerāvī,
   vulnerātum – wound

Adjectives

aequus, -a, -um – equal; fair

alius, -a, -um – other

proximus, -a, -um – next to; following

tertius, -a, -um – third (see Appendix 3)

tres, tria – three (see Appendix 3)

ūnus, -a, -um – one (see Appendix 3)

Adverbs; Prepositions

ab – from (of time); following

aperte – openly

apud (+ acc.) – at the house of

atque – and

dē (+ abl.) – about; concerning

facile – easily

inter (+ acc.) – between

magis – more

quō – where (to)?

quoque – also

sine (+ abl.) – without

tamen – however

tandem – at last; (in questions) pray; now

trans (+ acc.) – across

FIGURE 7.4 Aeneas and Anchises (17th century). After the fall of Troy, Aeneas, whose descendants were destined to found Rome, carried his aged father from the burning city on his shoulders. See Virgil *Aeneid* 2.707–8: "Come, dear father, set yourself upon my neck. I will support you on my shoulders; that task will not be too great a burden for me." *Source: Galleria Borghese, Rome, Italy/Alinari/ The Bridgeman Art Library*

VOCABULARY SPECIFICALLY FOR CHAPTER 7 PASSAGES

Nouns; Pronouns

accūsātiō, -ōnis (f.) – accusation; prosecution

Aquitānī, -ōrum (m. pl.) – Aquitanians

Ariovistus, -ī (m.) – ruler of a tribe in Germany

aspectus, -ūs (m.) – sight

Athēnae, -ārum (f. pl.) – Athens

Belgae, -ārum (m. pl.) – Belgae (a Gallic tribe)

Casticus, -ī (m.) – Casticus, one of the Sequani

Celtae, -ārum (m. pl.) – Celts

collis, -is (m.) – hill

commendātiō, -ōnis (f.) – praise; commendation

conspectus, -ūs (m.) – view

consulātus, -ūs (m.) – consulship

Democritus, -ī (m.) – Democritus (a Greek philosopher, *c.* 460 BC)

dēspectus, -ūs (m.) – view down

exilium, -iī (n.) – exile

Fabriciī, -ōrum (m. pl.) – the Fabricii, an aristocratic Roman family

familiāritās, -ātis (f.) – familiarity; friendship

Germānī, -ōrum (m. pl.) – the Germans

Helvetiī, -ōrum (m. pl.) – the Helvetii (a people of Gaul)

insidiae, -ārum (f. pl.) – ambush; plot

institūtum, -ī (n.) – custom

iūdicium, -iī (n.) – judgment; sentence

līberālitās, -ātis (f.) – generosity; kindness

lingua, -ae (f.) – language

missiō, -ōnis (f.) – sending

Oppianicus, -ī (m.) – Oppianicus (step-father of Cluentius whom Cluentius was accused of poisoning)

Pompeius, -ī (m.) – Pompey, a Roman general, opponent of Julius Caesar

quisquam – anyone

Rhēnus, -ī (m.) – the Rhine

sē – themselves

Sēquanus, -a, -um – belonging to the Sequani, a Gallic tribe from the Seine area

spatium, -iī (n.) – distance; space

status, -ūs (m.) – state; condition

tēlum, -ī (n.) – weapon

Verbs

afficiō, afficere, affēcī, affectum – inflict upon; punish

agnōscō, agnōscere, agnōvī, agnitum – recognize

aperiō, aperīre, aperuī, apertum – open; reveal

commemorō, commemorāre, commemorāvī, commemorātum – mention

conficiō, conficere, confēcī, confectum – complete

coniciō, conicere, coniēcī, coniectum – throw at

contendō, contendere, contendī, contentum – compete with; strive against

dēlectō, delectāre, delectāvī, delectātum – please

differō, differre, distūlī, dīlātum – differ

dissimulō, dissimulāre, dissimulāvī, dissimulātum – dissimulate; pretend

incolō, incolere, incoluī – inhabit

inquit – he (she, it) says

obtineō, obtinēre, obtinuī, obtentum – hold; obtain; acquire

praecēdō, praecēdere, praecessī, praecessum – excel; precede

remaneō, remanēre, remansī – remain

reprehendō, reprehendere, reprehendī, reprehensum – find fault with; blame

retineō, retinēre, retinuī, retentum – retain

vītō, vītāre, vītāvī, vītātum – avoid

Adjectives

cotīdiānus, -a, -um – daily

divīsus, -a, -um – divided

nefārius, -a, -um – wicked
perditus, -a, -um – ruined; broken
propinquus, -a, -um – nearby; (+ dat.) near (to)
superior (gen.), superiōris – higher
totus, -a, -um (gen. *totius*, dative *toti* – for full
    declension, see Chapter 16) – whole

Adverbs; Prepositions; Conjunctions

continenter – continually
ferē – almost
unde – from where

ENGLISH DERIVATIONS

From which Latin roots do the following English words derive?

(i) territory
(ii) absent
(iii) persuasive
(iv) act

CHAPTER 8

FIGURE 8.1 Roman glass bowl, AD 1–200. Wall paintings depict bowls of this type filled with fruit such as pomegranates. These were expensive items whose use was restricted to the relatively well-off. © *Leeds Museums and Galleries (Discovery Centre)*

Wiley's Real Latin: Learning Latin from the Source, First Edition.
Robert Maltby and Kenneth Belcher.
© 2014 John Wiley & Sons, Inc. Published 2014 by John Wiley & Sons, Inc.

8.1 PARTICIPLES

A participle is a verbal adjective. That is to say it has qualities of a verb (tense and voice) and qualities of an adjective (gender, number, and case). Like a verb it is modified by an adverb and can take an object in the appropriate case; like an adjective it agrees with the noun or pronoun that it modifies in gender, case, and number and like an adjective may be used by itself as a noun.

8.1.1 Present Participle

The present participle in Latin corresponds to the English present participle, which ends in -ing. It is always active (NB: there is no present participle passive in Latin). It describes an action that takes place at the same time as the main verb of the sentence. It is formed by taking the imperfect stem (this can be found by removing **-bam** from the first person singular) and adding **-ns** in the nominative singular. The present participle is a third declension adjective of one termination.

amāns, amantis – (while) loving

vidēns, videntis – (while) seeing

pōnēns, pōnentis – (while) placing

inveniēns, invenientis – (while) finding

capiēns, capientis – (while) capturing

Notice that the present participle is an adjective of the third declension (one-termination) and so declines as follows:

	SINGULAR			PLURAL		
	m.	**f.**	**n.**	**m.**	**f.**	**n.**
Nom.	amāns	amāns	amāns	amant-ēs	amant-ēs	amant-ia
Gen.	amant-is	amant-is	amant-is	amant-ium	amant-ium	amant-ium
Dat.	amant-ī	amant-ī	amant-ī	amant-ibus	amant-ibus	amant-ibus
Acc.	amant-em	amant-em	amāns	amant-ēs	amant-ēs	amant-ia
Abl.	amant-e	amant-e	amant-e	amant-ibus	amant-ibus	amant-ibus
Voc.	amāns	amāns	amāns	amant-ēs	amant-ēs	amant-ia

FYI The form *amantīs* (long *ī*) occurs in the accusative plural (masculine or feminine). *Amant-ī* also occurs in the ablative singular. This form is used when the participle acts as an adjective; the form *amante* is used in all other contexts.

Notice that the stem ends in **-nt**. This is true for all present participles and all decline in the same way (it does not matter to which conjugation the verb belongs).

8.1.2 Perfect Participle

The perfect participle of all regular verbs in Latin is passive in meaning (NB: the verbs we have been treating so far have no perfect participle active). The perfect participle describes an action prior to the action of the main verb in the sentence. It is formed from the supine (the fourth principal part). To form the perfect participle passive remove the **-um** ending and, for the nominative masculine, feminine, and neuter singular add **-us**, **-a**, **-um** respectively.

amātus, -a, -um – having been loved; loved

vīsus, -a, -um – having been seen; seen

positus, -a, -um – having been placed; placed

inventus, -a, -um – having been found; found

captus, -a, -um – having been captured; captured

The perfect participle passive is a first/second declension adjective and so declines in exactly the same way as **bonus, -a, -um**.

	SINGULAR			PLURAL		
	m.	f.	n.	m.	f.	n.
Nom.	vīs-us	vīs-a	vīs-um	vīs-ī	vīs-ae	vīs-a
Gen.	vīs-ī	vīs-ae	vīs-ī	vīs-ōrum	vīs-arum	vīs-ōrum
Dat.	vīs-ō	vīs-ae	vīs-ō	vīs-īs	vīs-īs	vīs-īs
Acc.	vīs-um	vīs-am	vīs-um	vīs-ōs	vīs-ās	vīs-a
Abl.	vīs-ō	vīs-ā	vīs-ō	vīs-īs	vīs-īs	vīs-īs
Voc.	vīs-e	vīs-a	vīs-um	vīs-ī	vīs-ae	vīs-a

8.1.3 Future Participle

The future participle is active (there is no future participle passive in Latin). Like the perfect participle it is formed by using the supine stem; for example, to form the future participle of the verb **amō** you take the supine stem **amāt-** and add **-ūrus**, **-ūra**, **-ūrum**. The basic translations are *(being) about to love, going to love, intending to love*. The future participle is a first/second declension adjective and so declines in exactly the same way as **bonus, -a, -um**. This participle may be used with forms of the verb **sum** as an alternative way of expressing future action with the sense of "having the intention to do something" (the so-called active periphrastic construction):

ipse hanc **acturus est** Iuppiter comoediam (Plautus *Amphitruo* 88): *Jupiter himself **is about to act** this comedy.*

	SINGULAR			PLURAL		
	m.	f.	n.	m.	f.	n.
Nom.	amātūr-us	amātūr-a	amātūr-um	amātūr-ī	amātūr-ae	amātūr-a
Gen.	amātūr-ī	amātūr-ae	amātūr-ī	amātūr-ōrum	amātūr-ārum	amātūr-ōrum
Dat.	amātūr-ō	amātūr-ae	amātūr-ō	amātūr-īs	amātūr-īs	amātūr-īs
Acc.	amātūr-um	amatur-am	amātūr-um	amātūr-ōs	amātūr-ās	amātūr-a
Abl.	amātūr-ō	amātur-ā	amātūr-ō	amātūr-īs	amātūr-īs	amātūr-īs
Voc.	amātūr-e	amātūr-a	amātūr-um	amātūr-ī	amātūr-ae	amātūr-a

Similarly **visurus, -a, -um**; **positurus, -a, -um**; **inventurus, -a, -um**; **capturus, -a, -um**.

Note: although the verb **sum** has neither a present nor perfect participle, it does have a future participle: **futūrus, -a, -um** – (being) about to be, going to be, etc.

TRY THIS

Provide the form of the participle requested:

e.g., *habeo* (perfect participle passive, nom. pl. m.) – *habiti*

(i) *doceo* (perfect participle passive, acc. pl. f.)
(ii) *fugio* (present participle active, nom. sing. m.)
(iii) *interficio* (perfect participle passive, abl. pl. m.)
(iv) *moveo* (perfect participle passive, abl. sing. m.)
(v) *occido* (present participle active, acc. sing. m.)
(vi) *pervenio* (future participle active, nom. pl. m.)
(vii) *capio* (perfect participle passive, acc. pl. n.)
(viii) *video* (future participle active, nom. sing. f.)
(ix) *amo* (present participle active, abl. sing. f.)
(x) *pono* (perfect participle passive, acc. pl. m.)

8.2 USE OF PARTICIPLES

Participles occur more frequently in Latin than in English and are used in constructions where there is no obvious English equivalent.

8.2.1 Attributive

FYI For the term "attributive adjective," see Introduction: Parts of Speech, Adjectives.

(1) Some participles are used simply as adjectives.
From **occidō, occidere, occidī, occāsum** – fall down; set:

alterum [lātus] vergit ad Hispaniam atque **occidentem sōlem** (Caesar *De Bello Gallico* 5.13.2): *the other side [of Britain] is situated facing towards Spain and* **the setting sun**.

From **doceō, docēre, docuī, doctum** – teach: **doctus, -a, -um** – learned (literally having been taught):

sunt tamen et **doctae** . . . puellae (Ovid *Ars Amatoria* 2.281): *however, there are also* **learned** *girls*.

(2)   And like other adjectives, the participle itself may be used as a noun:
amans, amantis – the/a lover.

dicit: sed mulier cupidō quod dīcit **amantī** / omnia in ventō et rapidā scribere oportet aquā (Catullus 70.3–4): *she says so, but everything a woman says to her eager* **lover** *should be written on the wind and swift-flowing water*.

fugientēs ab equitātū interficiuntur (Caesar *Bellum Civile* 2.42.2): **the fugitives** *are killed by the cavalry*.

When the present participle is used as a noun it ends in **-e** rather than **-ī** in the ablative singular:

atque ā **sollicitō** multus **amante** legar! (Ovid *Amores* 1.15.38): *I will be much read* **by an anxious lover!**

(3)   Related to this is the fact that Latin may use a participle where English uses a relative clause:

moritūra puella (Virgil *Georgics* 4.458): *the girl* **who is about to die.**

8.2.2 Circumstantial

Also, Latin uses a participle where English uses two co-ordinate clauses (i.e., clauses joined by "and"):

Pan deus Arcadiae **captam tē**, Lūna, fefēllit (Virgil *Georgics* 3.392): *Pan, the god of Arcadia,* **captured and deceived you**, *Luna* [literally: *deceived* **you having been captured**].

8.2.3 Temporal

Latin may also use a participle where English uses a subordinate clause. A participle may indicate a temporal relationship between two actions and so it is often appropriate to translate a participle as a temporal clause introduced by a conjunction such as "when," "after," or "while":

FIGURE 8.2 Roman bust of Pan, date unknown. Pan was a rustic god, half man, half goat. He came to be associated with irrational fear and it is from his name that we get the word "panic." © *Leeds Museums and Galleries (Discovery Centre)*

<mihi> **cogitantī** autem haec fere succurrēbant (Cicero *Epistulae ad Atticum* 2.16.1): *as I was pondering, however, something like this occurred to me.*

8.2.4 Causal

Again it may be more appropriate to the context to translate a participle as a causal clause introduced by "since" or "because":

et portūs omnes **timēns** . . . ad eum locum quī appellābātur Palaeste . . . mīlites exposuit (Caesar *Bellum Civile* 3.6.3): *since he feared all the ports, he put his soldiers ashore at that place which is called Palaeste.*

Otacilius . . . **timēns** oppidō fugit et ad Pompeium pervēnit (Caesar *Bellum Civile* 3.6.3): *since he was afraid, Otacilius fled the town and came to Pompey.*

8.2.5 Concessive

Sometimes a participle is best translated as a concessive clause, i.e., one introduced by "although":

vehementissime **perturbātus** Lentulus tamen et signum et manum suam cognōvit (Cicero *In Catilinam* 3.12): ***although he was greatly shaken****, nevertheless Lentulus identified his own seal and handwriting.*

 TRANSLATION FROM LATIN

1. ibi casu rex erat Ptolomaeus, puer aetate, magnis copiis cum sorore Cleopatra bellum gerens, quam . . . per suos propinquos atque amicos regno expulerat. (Caesar *Bellum Civile* 3.103.2)

2. talia dicentem nervosque ad verba moventem
    exsangues flebant animae; nec Tantalus undam
    captavit refugam, stupuitque Ixionis orbis,
    nec carpsere iecur volucres, urnisque vacarunt
    Belides, inque tuo sedisti, Sisyphe, saxo.

    (Ovid *Metamorphoses* 10.40–44)

3. hi primum cum gladiis non in regnum appetentem, sed in regnantem impetum fecerunt. (Cicero *Philippicae* 2.114)

4. libenter Caesar petentibus Haeduis dat veniam excusationemque accipit. (Caesar *De Bello Gallico* 6.4.3)

5. multa praeterea spolia praeferebantur, capti homines equitesque producebantur. (Caesar *Bellum Civile* 2.39.5)

6. duo Numidae cum litteris missi ad Hannibalem . . . a vagis per agros pabulatoribus Romanis ad Q. Clodium propraetorem deducuntur. (Livy *Ab Urbe Condita* 27.43.1)

7. delectatur audiens multitudo et ducitur oratione et quasi voluptate quadam perfunditur. (Cicero *Brutus* 188)

8. mortem igitur omnibus horis impendentem timens, qui poterit animo consistere? (Cicero *De Senectute* 74)

9. reliquos frequenter audiens acerrimo studio tenebar cotidieque et scribens et legens . . . oratoriis tantum exercitationibus contentus non eram. (Cicero *Brutus* 305)

> THE BIGGER PICTURE
>
> *D*e Senectute (*On Old Age*), a philosophical work on the nature of old age, completed in 44 BC and addressed to his aging friend Atticus. The discussion takes the form of a dialogue set in the year 150 BC between the aged Cato (then 84), and two younger aristocrats, Scipio (then 35) and Laelius (then 36), in which Cato sets out the advantages of growing old.

TRANSLATION INTO LATIN

1. You have handed over to me a state troubled by suspicion, anxious with fear, and thrown into chaos by your laws, your assemblies, and your evictions. (Cicero *De Lege Agraria* 1.23)

2. I consider nothing difficult for one who loves, and I love and have always loved your spirit, enthusiasm, and character. (Cicero *Orator* 33)

3. Sopater, weeping again, reports the matter to the senate and makes clear to them that man's <Verres'> greed and threats. The senate gives Sopater no reply, but he leaves upset and perturbed. (Cicero *In Verrem* 2.4.85)

4. The enemy turn their backs; our cavalry runs after those fleeing; there is a great massacre. Sedulius, the general and prince of the Lemovices, is killed. (Caesar *De Bello Gallico* 7.88.3)

5. But I say this about the whole race of the Greeks: I grant them their literature, I allow them their knowledge of many skills, I do not deny them the charm of their language . . . but that nation has never cultivated respect for evidence and good faith. (Cicero *Pro Flacco* 9)

6. Caesar, at first light, ordered all those who had camped on the mountain to descend from the higher ground onto the plain and to throw down their weapons. (Caesar *Bellum Civile* 3.98.1)

7. Although Caesar was being called back to Italy by many pressing matters, nevertheless he had decided not to abandon any part of the war in Spain. (Caesar *Bellum Civile* 2.18.7)

8. Caesar was considered great because of his good deeds and generosity, Cato because of the integrity of his life. The former was made famous because of his gentleness and pity, the severity of the latter lent him dignity. (Sallust *Catiline* 54.2)

9. There is no severity in the courts, no respect . . . And so we are belittled and despised by the Roman people. (Cicero *In Verrem* 1.1.43)

O *rator* (*The Orator*), written in 46 BC, is the last of Cicero's rhetorical works after *De Oratore* in 55 BC and *Brutus* earlier in 46 BC. Addressed to Brutus, the dialogue discusses in some technical detail the characteristics of the ideal orator.

THE BIGGER PICTURE

FIGURE 8.3 Dying Gaul: a Roman copy of a Greek original. In his work *De Bello Gallico*, Caesar recounts his campaigns in Gaul (58–51 BC) to complete Rome's conquest of the region. *Source: Musei Capitolini, Rome, Italy/Photo © BEBA/ AISA/The Bridgeman Art Library*

VOCABULARY TO LEARN

Nouns

auctoritās, -ātis (f.) – authority; influence
cāsus, -ūs (m.) – chance
deus, deī (m.) – god
eques, equitis (m.) – horseman; member of the cavalry
equitātus, -ūs (m.) – cavalry
fātum, -ī (n.) – fate
gladius, gladiī (m.) – sword
impetus, -ūs (m.) – attack; charge

latus, lateris (n.) – side
lūna, -ae (f.) – moon
mundus, -ī (m.) – world
portus, -ūs (m.) – port
pretium, pretiī (n.) – price
regnum, -ī (n.) – reign
saxum, -ī (n.) – rock
scelus, sceleris (n.) – crime
sōl, sōlis (m.) – sun
soror, sorōris (f.) – sister

spolia, -ōrum (n. pl.) – spoils
unda, -ae (f.) – wave; water (in poetry)
vultus, -ūs (m.) – face; expression

Verbs

doceō, docēre, docuī, doctum – teach
fugiō, fugere, fūgī, fugitum – flee
interficiō, interficere, interfēcī, interfectum – kill
moveō, movēre, mōvī, mōtum – move; (of strings) pluck
occidō, occidere, occidī, occāsum – fall down; set (of sun)
perveniō, pervenīre, pervēnī, perventum – come to

Adjectives

alter, altera, alterum – other (of two)
cupidus, -a, -um – desirous; eager
idōneus, -a, -um – suitable
propinquus, -a, -um – related
reliquus, -a, -um – remaining; (pl. the rest; the others)
suus, -a, -um – his own; her own; their own
tālis, -e – such; of such a kind
tōtus, -a, -um (gen. tōtius, dat. tōtī) – whole

Adverbs

aliquandō – at some time
igitur – therefore; accordingly

VOCABULARY SPECIFICALLY FOR CHAPTER 8 PASSAGES

Nouns

aetās, aetātis (f.) – age; time of life
anima, -ae (f.) – spirit; ghost
Belides, -um (f. pl.) – the 50 granddaughters of Belus, i.e., the Danaids (of whom 49 killed their husbands on their wedding night)
Cleopātra, -ae (f.) – Cleopatra, Queen of Egypt, lover of Julius Caesar and then Marc Antony
Clōdius, -iī, Q. (m.) – Quintus Clodius, propraetor 207 BC, during the Second Punic War
excūsātiō, -ōnis (f.) – excuse
exercitatiō, exercitatiōnis (f.) – exercise; practice
familiāris, -is (m.) – family member; acquaintance; friend
Haeduī, -ōrum (m. pl.) – Haedui (a people of Gaul)
Hannibal, Hannibalis (m.) – Carthaginian leader during the Second Punic War (218–201 BC)

Hispania, -ae (f.) – Spain
hōra, -ae (f.) – hour
iecur, iecinoris (n.) – liver
Ixīon, -onis (m.) – Ixion, punished in the Underworld, attached to an eternally revolving wheel
lacrima, -ae (f.) – tear
manus, -ūs (f.) – (usually) hand; (here) hand-writing
moenia, -ium (n. pl.) – walls
monstrum, -ī (n.) – monster
multitūdō, -inis (f.) – large number; crowd
nervus, -ī (m.) – string (of a musical instrument)
Numida, -ae (m.) – Numidian
orbis, orbis (m.) – wheel
pābulātor, -ōris (m.) – forager
Pān (gen. Pānos; acc. Pāna) (m.) – Pan
perniciēs, -eī (f.) – disaster; destruction
pestis, -is (m.) – plague

prōdigium, prōdigiī (n.) – monster; prodigy

propinquus, -i (m.) – relative

prōpraetor, -ōris (m.) – propraetor (a Roman magistrate)

Ptolomaeus, -i (m.) (also Ptolemaeus) – ruler of Egypt; brother of Cleopatra

signum, -ī (n.) – (usually) sign; (here) seal

tabernaculum, -ī (n.) – tent

Tantalus, -i (m.) – punished in the Underworld – he stands in water and fruit trees are just above his head; however, when he tries to drink the water flows away and the fruit remains just beyond his grasp.

urna, -ae (f.) – urn

venia, -ae (f.) – forgiveness; veniam dō = grant forgiveness

ventus, -ī (m.) – wind

volucer, volucris (m. and f.) – bird

Verbs

abdō, abdere, abdidī, abditum – hide

abeō, abīre, abīvī (see Chapter 12) – go away

accipiō, accipere, accēpī; acceptum – receive; accept

agō, agere, ēgī, actum – act (in a play)

anhelō, anhelāre, anhelāvī, anhelātum – breath (out); exhale

appetō, appetere, appetīvī, appetītum – aim at; make for

captō, captāre, captāvī, captātum – catch

carpō, carpere, carpsī, carptum – pluck at; feed on

comparō, comparāre, comparāvī, comparātum – furnish; provide

consisto, consistere (animō) – stand firm (in one's mind)

dēdūcō, dēdūcere, dēdūxī, dēductum – lead

dēlectō, dēlectāre, dēlectāvi, dēlectātum – please; delight

ērumpō, ērumpere, ērūpī, ēruptum – burst out

ēvādō, ēvādere, ēvāsī – get away; escape

excēdō, excēdere, excessī, excessum – leave; walk out of

expellō, expellere, expulsī, expulsum – expel

expōnō, expōnere, exposuī, expositum – put (troops) ashore

fallō, fallere, fefellī, falsum – deceive

fingō, fingere, finxī, fictum – compose; arrange

fleō, flēre, flēvī, flētum – weep; cry

furō, furere, furuī – rage; be mad

impellō, impellere, impulsī, impulsum – urge; impel

impendeō, impendēre, impendī, impensum – hang over; threaten

inserō, inserere, insēvī, insitum – implant

legō, legere, lēgī, lectum – read

oportet, oportuit (occurs only in 3rd person singular + infinitive) – one ought to; it is necessary to

perfundō, perfundere, perfūdī, perfūsum – moisten; bathe; fill

perturbō, perturbāre, perturbāvī, perturbātum – perturb; frighten; throw into confusion

praeferō, praeferre, praetulī, praelātum – carry in front; put on display

prōdūcō, prōdūcere, prōdūxī, prōductum – lead forward

regnō, regnāre, regnāvī, regnātum – rule; reign

stupeō, stupēre, stupuī – stop; stand still

succurrō, succurrere, succurrī, succursum – come to mind; occur

vacō, vacāre, vacāvī, vacātum (+ dat.) – be at leisure for; rest from

vergō, vergere – lie; be situated

Adjectives

acerrimus, -a, -um – most eager; most passionate

Athēnienis, -e – Athenian

commūnis, -e – common

exsanguis, -e – bloodless; pale

moritūrus, -a, -um – being about to die

quīdam, quaedam, quoddam – a certain

rapidus, -a, -um – rapid; swift
refugus, -a, -um – fleeing back
vagus, -a, -um – scattered; wandering

Adverbs; Conjunctions

cotīdiē – daily
etsi – although
frequenter – often

interdum – from time to time
libenter – willingly
nefāriē – evilly; impiously
praetereā – besides
prīmum – in the first place; first
quasi – as if; as it were
qui? – how?
tantum – only
vehementissimē – very greatly

English Derivations

From which Latin roots do the following English words derive?

(i) authority
(ii) lateral
(iii) motion
(iv) fugitive

CHAPTER 9

FIGURE 9.1 Gladiators mosaic (3rd century AD). Gladiatorial contests became increasingly popular at Rome. Emperors, for example, gained favor with the people of Rome by staging elaborate games where gladiators were part of the entertainment. *Source: Bignor Roman Villa, West Sussex, UK/Ancient Art and Architecture Collection Ltd/The Bridgeman Art Library*

Wiley's Real Latin: Learning Latin from the Source, First Edition.
Robert Maltby and Kenneth Belcher.
© 2014 John Wiley & Sons, Inc. Published 2014 by John Wiley & Sons, Inc.

9.1 THE PASSIVE VOICE CONTINUED

The perfect, pluperfect, and future perfect tenses are also used in the passive. To form the passive voice of these tenses the perfect participle and appropriate forms of the verb **sum** are used. The perfect indicative passive is formed by using the present indicative of the verb **sum** with the perfect participle passive.

9.1.1 Perfect Indicative Passive

HINT! As with the perfect active, Latin has only one form of the perfect passive and may mean, for example, "I have been placed."

SINGULAR	PLURAL
positus, -a, -um sum – I was placed	positī, -ae, -a sumus – we were placed
positus, -a, -um es – you were placed	positī, -ae, -a estis – you were placed
positus, -a, -um est – he, she, it was placed	positī, -ae, -a sunt – they were placed

9.1.2 Pluperfect Indicative Passive

Similarly, the pluperfect indicative passive is formed using the imperfect indicative of the verb **sum** with the perfect participle passive.

HINT! Because the participle is an adjective, it must agree with the subject. If the subject is feminine, singular, the participle must have feminine singular endings, etc.

SINGULAR	PLURAL
positus, -a, -um eram – I had been placed	positī, -ae, -a erāmus – we had been placed
positus, -a, -um erās – you had been placed	positī, -ae, -a erātis – you had been placed
positus, -a, -um erat – he, etc. had been placed	positī, -ae, -a erant – they had been placed

9.1.3 Future Perfect Indicative Passive

The future perfect indicative passive is formed using the future indicative of the verb **sum** with the perfect participle passive.

SINGULAR	PLURAL
vīsus, -a, -um erō – I will have been seen	vīsī, -ae, -a erimus – we will have been seen
vīsus, -a, -um eris – you will have been seen	vīsī, -ae, -a eritis – you will have been seen
vīsus, -a, -um erit – he, etc. will have been seen	vīsī, -ae, -a erunt – they will have been seen

TRY THIS

Perfect tenses of the passive.

Translate the following into Latin:

e.g., they had been taught – *docti erant*

(i) it had been decided

(ii) they will have been destroyed

(iii) it had been felt

(iv) these things will have been changed

(v) the city had been defeated

(vi) they will have been seen

(vii) you (sing.) had been killed

(viii) we shall have been captured

(ix) you (pl.) have been moved

(x) I had been loved

9.2 USES OF THE CASES

9.2.1 Ablative Absolute

The participle is frequently used in Latin with a noun or pronoun in the ablative case. This construction occurs when there is no grammatical connection between the ablative absolute phrase and the rest of the sentence. The ablative absolute occurs especially with the present and perfect participles and may be translated in various ways: temporal clause; causal clause; concessive clause; by a phrase introduced by *with* (which is one of the original meanings of the ablative case); sometimes even as a main clause.

> **hīs rēbus gestīs** . . . **superātīs Belgīs, expulsīs Germānīs, victīs in Alpibus Sedūnīs** . . . Caesar in Illyrium contendit (Caesar *De Bello Gallico* 3.7.1): *after these things **had been accomplished and the Belgae had been defeated, the Germans driven out and the Seduni in the Alps conquered*** . . . Caesar hastened to Illyrium.

> **nullō hoste prohibente aut iter demorante** incolumem legiōnem in Nantuātēs, inde in Allobrōgēs perdūxit ibique hiemāvit (Caesar *De Bello Gallico* 3.6.5): *as no enemy was hindering or delaying the march,* he led the legion in safety into the territory of the Nantuates, and from there into that of the Allobroges and he wintered there.

Notice that in the ablative absolute construction the present participle ends in -**e**, not -**i**.

The ablative absolute is also used to indicate the year in which events occur (i.e., in whose consulship). There is no present participle from the verb **sum**:

> Romam vēnit **Mariō consule** (Cicero *Pro Archia* 5): *he came to Rome in the **consulship of Marius (i.e., when Marius was consul)**.*

HINT! If you see a noun or pronoun with a participle in the ablative case, your first thought should be ablative absolute. Consider all the possible ways to translate.

9.2.2 Ablative of Cause

The ablative of a noun is used without a preposition to express cause:

sunt in culpā, qui officia dēserunt **mollitiā** animī, id est labōrum et dolōrum **fugā** (Cicero *De Finibus* 1.33): *they are to blame who abandon their duties **because of a weakness** of spirit, that is **because of avoidance** of work and pains.*

SOUND BITE	Ovid on when to apply drink (Ovid *Remedia Amoris* 131–2)

data tempore prosunt
et data non apto tempore vina nocent.

TRANSLATION FROM LATIN

1. Idibus Ianuariis in senatu nihil est confectum, propterea quod dies magna ex parte consumptus est altercatione Lentuli consulis et Canini tribuni plebis. (Cicero *Epistulae ad Familiares* 1.2.1)

2. de ceteris rebus quicquid erit actum, scribam ad te. (Cicero *Epistulae ad Familiares* 1.2.4)

3. ceteris iniuriis, quae propositae sunt a Catone, facile, ut spero, resistemus. (Cicero *Epistulae ad Familiares* 1.5b.2)

4. hic Sulpicius temporibus floruit iis, quibus inter profectionem reditumque L. Sullae sine iure fuit et sine ulla dignitate res publica. (Cicero *Brutus* 227)

5. ubi de eius adventu Helvetii certiores facti sunt, legatos ad eum mittunt. (Caesar *De Bello Gallico* 1.7)

6. Vercingetorix . . . cuius pater principatum totius Galliae obtinuerat et ob eam causam, quod regnum appetebat, a civibus erat interfectus, convocatis suis clientibus, facile incendit. (Caesar *De Bello Gallico* 7.4.1)

7. sic cum suis fugientibus permixti, quos non silvae montesque texerunt, ab equitatu sunt interfecti. (Caesar *De Bello Gallico* 7.62.9)

8. M. Metius repertus et ad eum reductus est. (Caesar *De Bello Gallico* 1.53.8)

9. reus in iudicium adductus est C. Verres, homo vita atque factis omnium iam opinione damnatus. (Cicero *In Verrem* 1.1.2)

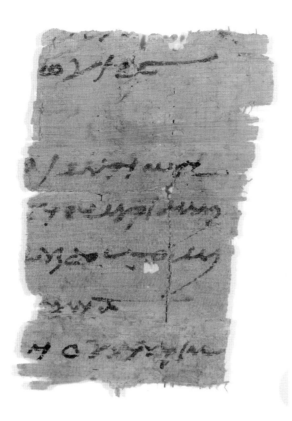

FIGURE 9.2 Roman papyrus fragment. The papyrus plant grew mainly in Egypt. It was processed to make a kind of writing surface; often a number of sheets were glued together to form a roll (usually 20–26 feet long). © *Leeds Museums and Galleries (Discovery Centre)*

TRANSLATION INTO LATIN

1. The Helvetii, induced by a lack of all things, sent envoys to him concerning surrender. (Caesar *De Bello Gallico* 1.27.1)

2. Having learned these things Caesar encouraged the spirits of the Gauls with his words. (Caesar *De Bello Gallico* 1.33.1)

3. However, having read the letters of Philotimus I changed my plan about the women whom, as I had written to you, I was sending back to Rome. (Cicero *Epistulae ad Atticum* 7.23.2)

4. Having learned of the arrival of Caesar, <Pompey> departed from that place and in a few days came to Mitylene. (Caesar *Bellum Civile* 3.102.4)

5. With these men as our advisers and leaders, if the gods help, if we are watchful and exercise much forethought for the future, if the Roman people agree, we will surely be free in a short time. (Cicero *Philippicae* 3.36)

6. Publius Servilius brought back for the Roman people those statues and ornaments which had been captured from the city of the enemy by force and courage and which he removed by the law of war and his right as a general. (Cicero *In Verrem* 2.1.57)

7. I had decided not, by Hercules, because of idleness but because of regret for my former authority, to keep silent forever. (Cicero *Epistulae ad Familiares* 4.4.4)

8. A boy, sent by your sister from Rome, gave a letter to me from you. (Cicero *Epistulae ad Atticum* 1.10.1)

9. They suddenly rushed from the woods and, having made an attack on those who had been placed on guard in front of the camp, they fought fiercely. (Caesar *De Bello Gallico* 5.15.3)

VOCABULARY TO LEARN

Nouns; Pronouns

aciēs, aciēī (f.) – battle-line
adventus, -ūs (m.) – arrival
aetās, aetātis (f.) – age
iniūria, -ae (f.) – injustice
iūs, iūris (n.) – right; law; custom
mulier, -eris (f.) – woman
plebs, plēbis (m.) – the people
portus, -ūs (m.) – port
sapientia, -ae (f.) – wisdom
signum, -ī (n.) – sign; banner; statue
silva, -ae (f.) – forest; wood

Verbs

cōgitō, cōgitāre, cōgitāvī, cōgitātum – think
cognōscō, cognōscere, cognōvī, cognitum – come to know; learn (about)
dēleō, dēlēre, dēlēvī, dēlētum – destroy
discēdō, discēdere, discessī, discessum – depart; leave
iuvō, iuvāre, iūvī, iūtum – help

mūtō, mūtāre, mūtāvī, mūtātum – change
regnō, regnāre, regnāvī, regnātum – reign
reputō, reputāre, reputāvī, reputātum – think; consider
resistō, resistere, restitī (+ dat.) – resist
sentiō, sentīre, sēnsī, sēnsum – sense; feel
statuō, statuere, statuī, statūtum – decide
taceō, tacēre, tacuī, tacitum – be silent

Adjectives

brevis, -e – short; brief
cēterus, -a, -um – rest; remaining
cupidus, -a, -um – eager; desirous
iucundus, -a, -um – sweet
vērus, -a, -um – true

Adverbs; Prepositions; Conjunctions

non modō – not only
sed etiam – but also
ut – as

VOCABULARY SPECIFICALLY FOR CHAPTER 9 PASSAGES

Nouns; Pronouns

agger, aggeris (m.) – earthwork; ramp

altercātiō, -ōnis (f.) – argument

auctor, -ōris (m.) – author; adviser

auctoritās, -tātis (f.) – authority

Canīnius, -iī (m.) – Caninius Gallus, tribune 56 BC

Cato, -ōnis (m.) – Gaius Porcius Cato, tribune 56 BC

cliens, -entis (m.) – client; follower

dēsiderium, dēsideriī (n.) – desire; (+ gen.) regret (for)

equitātus, -ūs (m.) – cavalry

excūsātiō, -ōnis (f.) – excuse

Īdus, -uum (f. pl.) – Ides (March, May, July, October 15; 13 of other months)

inertia, -ae (f.) – idleness

inopia, -ae (f.) – scarcity; lack

iūdicium, iūdiciī (n.) – court

Lentulus, -ī (m.) – Gnaeus Cornelius Lentulus Marcellinus, consul 56 BC

Metius – Marcus Metius, an envoy sent by Caesar to the German king, Ariovistus

Mitylēnae, -ārum (f. pl.) – Mytilene (capital city of Lesbos)

oppugnātiō, -ōnis (f.) – attack

ornamentum, -ī (n.) – equipment; ornament

praedicātiō, -ōnis (f.) – proclamation

principātus, -ūs (m.) – position of commander-in-chief

profectiō, -ōnis (f.) – setting out

provincia, -ae (f.) – province

quaestor, -ōris (m.) – quaestor (public official; magistrate)

quicquid (nom. n. sing.) – whatever

quiēs, -ētis (f.) – quiet

ratiō, -ōnis (f.) – reason

reditus, -ūs (m.) – return

reus, -ī (m.) – defendant (in court)

sententia, -ae (f.) – opinion

Sulla, -ae (m.) – Lucius Cornelius Sulla; Roman dictator 81–79 BC

Sulpicius, -iī (m.) – Publius Sulpicius Rufus; an orator, tribune 88 BC; put to death by Sulla in 88

tranquillitās, -ātis (f.) – tranquillity

tribūnus, -ī (m.) – tribune

turris, turris (f.) – siege-tower

venia, -ae (f.) – favor; forgiveness

Vercingetorix, -igis (m.) – Vercingetorix, commander of the Gauls in the Gallic War

vinea, -ae (f.) – siege-shelter

Verbs

absolvō, absolvere, absolvī, absolūtum – absolve; free; acquit

addūcō, addūcere, addūxī, adductum – lead to; induce

appetō, appetere, appetī(v)ī, appetītum – seek for

apportō, apportāre, apportāvī, apportātum – carry to; bring to

certiōrem faciō, facere, fēcī, factum – inform

conficiō, conficere, confēcī, confectum – complete

confirmō, confirmāre, confirmāvī, confirmātum – strengthen; encourage

consentiō, consentīre, consēnsī, consēnsum – agree

constituō, constituere, constituī, constitūtum – set up

consumō, consumere, consumpsī, consumptum – take up; consume

convocō, convocāre, convocāvī, convocātum – call together; assemble

damnō, damnāre, damnāvī, damnātum –
   condemn
expōnō, expōnere, exposuī, expositum –
   disembark
flōreō, flōrēre, flōruī – flourish; be in good
   repute
incendō, incendere, incendī, incensum – set fire
   to; rouse
legō, legere, lēgī, lectum – read
permisceō, permiscēre, permiscuī, permixtum
   – mix
prōpōnō, prōpōnere, prōposuī, prōpositum – set
   out; threaten
prōvideō, prōvidēre, prōvīdī, prōvīsum – take
   thought for; exercise foresight
redūcō, redūcere, redūxī, reductum – lead back
reperiō, reperīre, reperrī, repertum – find;
   discover
succurrō, succurrere, succurrī, succursum (+
   dat.) – come to the help of; occur to
tegō, tegere, tēxī, tēctum – cover; protect
tollō, tollere, sustulī, sublātum – take away
vigilō, vigilāre, vigilāvī, vigilātum – be watchful

Adjectives

admirābilis, -e – admirable
Iānuarius, -a, -um – of (belonging to) January

īdem, eadem, idem – same
idōneus, -a, -um – suitable
imperātōrius, -a, -um – of a general; belonging
   to a general
pristīnus, -a, -um – former
rapidus, -a, -um – swift; swift-flowing
summus, -a, -um – greatest

Adverbs; Prepositions; Conjunctions

cāsū – by chance
fērē – almost
in perpetuum – forever
in posterum – for the future
libenter – willingly
mehercule – by Hercules
multum – much
potissimum – especially
profectō – surely
propterea quod – because

English Derivations

From which Latin roots do the following English words derive?

   (i) sylvan
   (ii) delete
   (iii) sense
   (iv) tacit

CHAPTER 10

FIGURE 10.1 Romano-British oil lamp, date unknown. Lamps were made from various materials, including gold, lead, bronze, and ceramic. They were used in a variety of contexts and most obviously for lighting. The usual fuel was olive oil. © *Leeds Museums and Galleries (Discovery Centre)*

CHAPTER CONTENTS

Wiley's Real Latin: Learning Latin from the Source, First Edition.
Robert Maltby and Kenneth Belcher.
© 2014 John Wiley & Sons, Inc. Published 2014 by John Wiley & Sons, Inc.

10.1 INFINITIVES

The infinitive is a verbal noun; that is to say it has qualities of a verb (tense and voice) and qualities of a noun (gender – neuter, number – singular, and case – nominative or accusative). Latin infinitives occur in three tenses: present, perfect, and future. As we have already seen, the present infinitive active is the second principal part: **amāre**, **vidēre**, **pōnere**, **invenīre**, **capere**. These forms we have already met. The following table contains all infinitives of non-deponent verbs (deponent verbs will be introduced in the next chapter).

	ACTIVE	PASSIVE
Present	amāre – to love	amārī – to be loved
	vidēre – to see	vidērī – to be seen
	pōnere – to place	pōnī – to be placed
	invenīre – to find	invenīrī – to be found
	capere – to take	capī – to be taken
	esse – to be	
	posse – to be able	
Perfect	amāvisse – to have loved	amātus, -a, -um esse – to have been loved
	vīdisse – to have seen	vīsus, -a, -um esse – to have been seen
	posuisse – to have placed	positus, -a, -um esse – to have been placed
	invēnisse – to have found	inventus, -a, -um esse – to have been found
	cēpisse – to have taken	captus, -a, -um esse – to have been taken
	fuisse – to have been	
	potuisse – to have been able	
Future	amātūrus, -a, -um esse – to be going to love	
	vīsūrus, -a, -um esse – to be going to see	
	positūrus, -a, -um esse – to be going to place	
	inventūrus, -a, -um esse – to be going to find	
	captūrus, -a, -um esse – to be going to take	
	futūrus, -a, -um esse – to be going to be	

FYI An alternative form of the future infinitive of esse is *fore*.

The future infinitive passive is formed using the supine + the present infinitive passive of the verb **eō, īre**, e.g., **amātum īrī** – to be going to be loved, but it is not the most common construction. To avoid this unusual form Latin authors regularly use a different construction (see Chapter 21).

10.1.1 Formation of Infinitives

The present infinitive active is the second principal part; the present infinitive passive is formed from the present infinitive active as follows: for the 1st, 2nd, and 4th conjugations change the final **-e** to **-ī**; for the 3rd and mixed conjugations remove the ending **-ere** and simply add **-ī**.

The perfect infinitive active is formed by adding **-isse** to the perfect stem (from the third principal part); the perfect infinitive passive is made up of two parts: the perfect participle passive and the present infinitive of the verb **sum**. It is important to note that the perfect participle, as an adjective, will agree in gender, number, and case with the subject of an infinitive; hence, if the subject is masculine the participle will have masculine endings, if the subject is feminine the participle will have feminine endings and if the subject is neuter the participle will have neuter endings.

The future infinitive active is also made up of two parts: the future participle and the present infinitive of **sum**. It is important to note that the future participle, as an adjective, will agree in gender, number, and case with the subject of an infinitive; hence, if the subject is masculine the participle will have masculine endings, if the subject is feminine the participle will have feminine endings, and if the subject is neuter the participle will have neuter endings.

TRY THIS

Infinitive practice.

Translate into English:
  (i) *prohiberi*
  (ii) *deliberavisse*
  (iii) *coactum iri*
  (iv) *iuraturus esse*
  (v) *fore*

Translate into Latin:
  (i) to be about to betray
  (ii) to be about to be ruined
  (iii) to free
  (iv) to have been found
  (v) to be about to be far away

10.2 REPORTED/INDIRECT STATEMENT; ACCUSATIVE AND INFINITIVE

One of the most common constructions in Latin involves indirect or reported speech. Consider the following: *I am afraid* (direct speech); *he says that he is afraid* (indirect speech). To report someone's words, thoughts, or feelings English frequently uses a subordinate clause, introduced by the conjunction "that" and containing a finite verb. Here Latin uses a construction that is quite different from English. Instead of a "that" clause, Latin uses the accusative and infinitive construction. What in English is the finite verb of the clause becomes in Latin an infinitive and the subject of the infinitive goes into the accusative case.

The same construction is used after verbs of "saying" (e.g., **dīcō**; **respondeō**), "thinking" (e.g., **putō**), "knowing" (e.g., **sciō**; **intellegō**) and "perceiving" (e.g., **videō**; **sentiō**; **audiō**).

> **HINT!** English also uses the accusative and infintive construction; for example, "I consider him to be pompous."

> **dīcit montem** . . . ab hostibus **tenērī** (*Caesar De Bello Gallico* 1.22.3): ***he says that the mountain is being held*** *by the enemy.*

> **audīvī Dolabellam** in Ciliciam **vēnisse** cum suīs copiīs (Cicero *Epistulae ad Familiares* 12.12.5): ***I have heard that Dolabella has come*** *into Cilicia with his forces.*

After verbs of "hoping" (**spērō**), "promising" (**promittō**), and "swearing" (**iūrō**), the accusative and future infinitive is the commonest construction.

> **iūrāvit sē** nisi victōrem in castra **non reversūrum** <esse> (Caesar *Bellum Civile* 3.87.6): ***he swore that he would not return*** *to camp except as a victor.*

> **HINT!** Anticipate the sentence structure/grammar. If, for example, you find a verb of "saying," "thinking," "knowing," or "perceiving," look for an accusative followed by an infinitive.

Note that in the accusative and infinitive construction the **esse** of the perfect passive and of the future infinitive is frequently omitted.

10.3 REFLEXIVE PRONOUN

Reflexive pronouns occur in the predicate of the sentence and refer back to the subject (e.g., in English: I see myself; he sees himself), and therefore cannot occur in the nominative case. For the first and second persons, singular and plural, the forms of the reflexive in Latin are exactly the same as the non-reflexive forms (e.g., **mē** = me or myself, depending on the context). For the third person reflexive pronoun himself, herself, itself, and themselves Latin has separate forms but uses the same forms in the singular and plural:

Nom.	NO NOMINATIVE
Gen.	suī
Dat.	sibi
Acc.	sē
Abl.	sē
Voc.	NO VOCATIVE

Notice that in the accusative and infinitive construction, Latin uses **se** when the subject of the infinitive is the same as the subject of the verb of saying, thinking, etc.; however, if a third person subject of an infinitive is different from the subject of the introductory verb, the forms **eum**, **eam**, **id** in the singular and in the plural **eōs**, **eās**, **ea** are used.

> consulēs **sē** aut dictatōrēs aut etiam regēs spērant **futūrōs**? (Cicero *In Catilinam* 2.19): *do the consuls hope that **they will be** either dictators or even kings?*

> homo disertus non intellegit **eum** quem contrā dīcit **laudārī ā sē** (Cicero *Philippicae* 2.18): *the eloquent gentleman does not realize that **he** whom he is speaking against [i.e., his opponent] **is being praised by himself**.*

There is a corresponding reflexive adjective of the first/second declension, **suus, sua, suum** – his, hers, its, their. This declines in exactly the same way as **bonus, -a, -um**. To show possession in third person non-reflexive contexts Latin uses the genitive singular or plural of **is, ea, id**.

> **HINT!** The adjectives *meus, -a, -um* – my, and *tuus, -a, -um* – your (sing.) may be used reflexively or non-reflexively.

> aut **suīs fīnibus eōs** prohibent aut ipsī **in eōrum fīnibus** bellum gerunt (Caesar *De Bello Gallico* 1.1.4): *either they are keeping **them out of their own territory** or waging war themselves **in the territory of those men**.*

10.4 SYNCOPATED FORMS OF THE PERFECT

Perfects ending -**āvī**, -**ēvī**, -**ōvī**, or -**īvī** have alternative syncopated forms where the -**vī** or -**vē** drop out. For example, instead of **amāvistī** the form **amāstī** may occur (or **dēlērunt** for **dēlēverunt**). Similarly in the pluperfect: **amāram** for **amāveram**; **nōram** for **nōveram**; **audīssem** for **audīvissem**. These forms occur in prose and especially in poetry where they are used to fit the meter.

> simul ad sē Valerium mittī **audiērunt** (Caesar *Bellum Civile* 1.30.3): *as soon as **they heard** that Valerius was being sent to them.*

TRANSLATION FROM LATIN

1. palam iam cum hoste nullo impediente bellum iustum geremus. sine dubio perdidimus hominem magnificeque vicimus. (Cicero *In Catilinam* 2.1)

2. ille dixit . . . a P. Lentulo se habere ad Catilinam mandata et litteras. (Cicero *In Catilinam* 3.8)

3. nominat ille servum . . . eum dicit coniuravisse et familias concitavisse (is omnino servus in familia non erat) eum statim exhiberi iubet. (Cicero *In Verrem* 2.5.17)

4. L. Opimius eiectus est e patria, is qui praetor et consul maximis rem publicam periculis liberarat. (Cicero *In Pisonem* 95)

5. iuravit se nisi victorem in castra non reversum . . . hoc laudans Pompeius idem iuravit. (Caesar *Bellum Civile* 3.86.5–87.6)

6. confirmo vobis nullum posthac malum civile ac domesticum ad ullam rei publicae partem esse venturum. (Cicero *In Catilinam* 4.15)

7. audiverat Pompeium per Mauretaniam cum legionibus iter in Hispaniam facere confestimque esse venturum. (Caesar *Bellum Civile* 1.39.4)

8. his datis mandatis eum ab se dimittit. postquam omnes Belgarum copias in unum locum coactas ad se venire vidit neque iam longe abesse ab eis quos miserat exploratoribus et ab Remis cognovit, flumen Axonam, quod est in extremis Remorum finibus, exercitum traducere maturavit atque ibi castra posuit. (Caesar *De Bello Gallico* 2.5.5)

9. horum omnium fortissimi sunt Belgae . . . proximique sunt Germanis, qui trans Rhenum incolunt, quibuscum continenter bellum gerunt. qua de causa Helvetii quoque reliquos Gallos virtute praecedunt, quod fere cotidianis proeliis cum Germanis contendunt, cum aut suis finibus eos prohibent aut ipsi in eorum finibus bellum gerunt. eorum una pars, quam Gallos obtinere dictum est, initium capit a flumine Rhodano, continetur Garunna flumine, Oceano, finibus Belgarum. (Caesar *De Bello Gallico* 1.1.4)

TRANSLATION INTO LATIN

1. He says that he is doing this for the sake of his own protection. (Cicero *Philippicae* 2.112)

2. They handed over to Caesar themselves and all their goods. (Caesar *De Bello Gallico* 3.16.4)

3. While you were listening, he said that he would come to my house with workmen. (Cicero *Philippicae* 1.12)

4. He was most troubled when he heard that the consuls had fled from Italy. (Cicero *Pro Rege Deiotaro* 11)

5. Which of these things does he say that he has not done? (Cicero *In Verrem* 2.2.80)

6. When he had swiftly taken care of these things, as soon as he was able . . . , he himself hastened to his army. (Caesar *De Bello Gallico* 3.9.2)

7. I hope that you and your children will see many good things in the republic. (Cicero *Pro Milone* 78)

8. They say that they were deserted and betrayed by you and they make mention of your former oath. (Caesar *Bellum Civile* 2.32.7)

9. I certainly know that I can easily be defeated by you. (Cicero *De Natura Deorum* 3.95)

THE BIGGER PICTURE

*D*e Natura Deorum (*On the Nature of the Gods*), a philosophical work in dialogue form on the nature of the gods, completed in 44 BC. Epicurean theory is set out in book I by Velleius, Stoic theory in book II by Balbus, and the Academic position, with which Cicero sympathizes, is given in book III by Cotta.

FIGURE 10.2 Silver denarius, 46–45 BC. Trophy with seated captives. Victorious Roman generals could be granted the honor of a "triumph," a procession to the Temple of Jupiter where the spoils of war, including captives, were paraded through the streets. © *Leeds Museums and Galleries (Discovery Centre)*

VOCABULARY TO LEARN

Nouns; Pronouns

familia, -ae (f.) – (often plural) household; household slaves
fīnēs, -ium (m. pl.) – territory
perīculum, -ī (n.) - danger
praesidium, praesidiī (n.) – defense; protection
servus, -ī (m.) – slave
—, suī – himself; herself; themselves

Verbs

absum, abesse, āfuī – be far away
cognōscō, cognōscere, cognōvī, cognitum – find out
cōgō, cōgere, coēgī, coactum – collect; compel
contendō, contendere, contendī, contentum – hasten; fight (with)
dēlīberō, dēlīberāre, dēlīberāvī, dēlīberātum – consider; deliberate
incolō, incolere, incoluī – dwell
iūrō, iūrāre, iūrāvī, iūrātum – swear (an oath)
līberō, līberāre, līberāvī, līberātum – free (from + abl.)
perdō, perdere, perdidī, perditum – destroy; ruin
prōdō, prōdere, prōdidī, prōditum – betray
prōhibeō, prōhibēre, prōhibuī, prōhibitum – keep out; prevent

Adjectives

cīvīlis, -e – civil; public
dubius, -a, -um – doubtful; sine dubiō – without doubt
iustus, -a, -um – just
māximus, -a, -um – greatest
reliquus, -a, -um – remaining

Adverbs; Prepositions; Conjunctions

facile – easily
ferē – almost
maximē – very much; most
postquam – after
statim – immediately
ut (+ indicative) – when

FIGURE 10.3 Ruins of a *thermopolium* in Herculaneum, Italy. *Thermopolia* are thought to be a type of ancient fast food cafe. The large terracotta containers (*dolia*) sunk into a masonry counter are thought to have contained hot food which was sold to customers. *Photo © Alain Lauga/Shutterstock*

VOCABULARY SPECIFICALLY FOR CHAPTER 10 PASSAGES

Nouns; Pronouns

Axōna, -ae (m.) – a river in Gaul

causa, -ae – cause; reason (abl. *causā* + gen. – for the sake of)

explorātor, -ōris (m.) – scout; spy

faber, -brī (m.) – workman

Garunna, -ae (m.) – a river in Gaul

initium, initiī (n.) – beginning

ipse, ipsa, ipsum – -self; -selves (for declension of *ipse*, see Appendix 2)

legātus, -ī (m.) – envoy; ambassador

mandātum, -ī (n.) – order

Maurītānia, -ae (f.) – Mauritania (a country of Africa)

mentiō, -ōnis (f.) – mention

Oceanus, -ī (m.) – Ocean

L. Opimius, -iī – Lucius Opimius, consul 121 BC; put Gaius Gracchus to death

praetor, -ōris (m.) – praetor (Roman official)

Rēmī, -ōrum (m. pl.) – a people of Gaul

Rhodanus, -ī (m.) – the river Rhône

sacramentum, -ī (n.) – oath

victor, -ōris (m.) – victor

Verbs

concitō, concitāre, concitāvī, concitātum – stir up

confirmō, confirmāre, confirmāvī, confirmātum – confirm; encourage; assure

coniūrō, coniūrāre, coniūrāvī, coniūrātum – conspire

contineō, continēre, continuī, contentum – bound; limit

dīmittō, dīmittere, dīmīsī, dīmissum – dismiss

ēiciō, ēicere, ēiēcī, ēiectum – drive out

exhibeō, exhibēre, exhibuī, exhibitum – show; produce; give up

impediō, impedīre, impedīvī, impedītum – impede; hinder

mātūrō, mātūrāre, mātūrāvī, mātūrātum (+ inf.) – hurry (to do something)

nōminō, nōmināre, nōmināvī, nōminātum – name; call

praecēdō, praecēdere, praecēssī, praecēssum – surpass

obtineō, obtinēre, obtinuī, obtentum – possess

referō, referre, retulī (or rettulī), relātum – report

revertō, revertere, revertī, reversum – return

tradūcō, tradūcere, tradūxī, traductum – lead across

Adjectives

cotīdiānus, -a, -um – daily

domesticus, -a, -um – belonging to one's home; domestic

extrēmus, -a, -um – most distant

fortissimus, -a, -um – strongest; bravest

perturbātus, -a, -um – troubled

prior, -ōris – former

Adverbs; Prepositions; Conjunctions

certō – certainly

confestim – hurriedly; quickly

continenter – continuously

longē – far; a long way

magnificē – magnificently

omnīnō – completely; altogether

palam – openly

posthāc – in future

English Derivations

From which Latin roots do the following English words derive?

(i) perdition
(ii) contention
(iii) relic
(iv) content

CHAPTER 11

FIGURE 11.1 Greco-Roman figurine of a slave carrying a yoke supporting an amphora and shopping basket. Slaves were, for the most part, captives of war. They were involved in all aspects of Roman life, both public and private. Some estimates put the number of slaves in Italy at 2,000,000 by around 30 BC. © *Leeds Museums and Galleries (Discovery Centre)*

Wiley's Real Latin: Learning Latin from the Source, First Edition.
Robert Maltby and Kenneth Belcher.
© 2014 John Wiley & Sons, Inc. Published 2014 by John Wiley & Sons, Inc.

CHAPTER CONTENTS

11.1 DEPONENT VERBS

In Latin there are some verbs for which in many instances there are no active forms, only passive; however, these verbs, although passive in form are active in meaning. They are called deponent verbs because they have "laid aside" (**dēpōnō**) their active forms. Some deponent verbs are very common.

The good news here is that there are no new forms to learn: deponent verbs are formed in exactly the same way as the passives of the verbs we have met so far. They have only three principal parts: **arbitror** (present indicative, 1st person singular), **arbitrārī** (present infinitive), **arbitrātus sum** (perfect indicative, 1st person singular). So **arbitror** – I think; I judge; **arbitrārī** – to think; to judge; **arbitrātus sum** – I thought, I judged.

11.1.1 Present Indicative

First Conjugation

	SINGULAR	PLURAL
1st **person**	arbitror – I think, am thinking, do think	arbitr-ā-mur – we think, etc.
2nd **person**	arbitr-ā-ris – you think, etc.	arbitr-ā-minī – you think, etc.
3rd **person**	arbitr-ā-tur – he, she, it thinks etc.	arbitr-a-ntur – they think, etc.

The endings **-r**, **-ris**, **-tur**, **-mur**, **-minī**, **-ntur** are exactly the same as the passive endings learnt in Chapter 7.

Second Conjugation

vereor, -ērī, veritus sum – I am afraid; I fear

	SINGULAR	PLURAL
1st **person**	vereor – I fear, am fearing, do fear	ver-ē-mur – we fear, etc.
2nd **person**	ver-ē-ris – you fear, etc.	ver-ē-minī – you fear, etc.
3rd **person**	ver-ē-tur – he, she, it fears, etc.	ver-e-ntur – they fear, etc.

Third Conjugation

sequor, sequī, secūtus sum – I follow

	SINGULAR	PLURAL
1st person	sequor – I follow, am following, do follow	sequ-i-mur – we follow, etc.
2nd person	sequ-e-ris – you follow, etc.	sequ-i-minī – you follow, etc.
3rd person	sequ-i-tur – he, she, it follows, etc.	sequ-u-ntur – they follow, etc.

Fourth Conjugation

mentior, mentīrī, mentītus sum – deceive; lie

	SINGULAR	PLURAL
1st person	mentior – I lie, am lying, do lie	ment-ī-mur – we lie, etc.
2nd person	ment-ī-ris – you lie, etc.	ment-ī-minī – you lie, etc.
3rd person	ment-ī-tur – he, she, it lies, etc.	ment-i-untur – they lie, etc.

Mixed Conjugation

prōgredior, prōgredī, prōgessus sum – go forward; advance

	SINGULAR	PLURAL
1st person	prōgredior – I advance, am advancing	prōgred-i-mur – we advance, etc.
2nd person	prōgred-e-ris – you advance, etc.	prōgred-i-minī– you advance, etc.
3rd person	prōgred-i-tur – he, she, it advances, etc.	prōgred-i-u-ntur – they advance, etc.

The other tenses of deponent verbs are also passive in form, but active in meaning.

11.1.2 Future Indicative

First and Second Conjugations

	SINGULAR	PLURAL
1st person	verēbor – I shall fear	ver-ē-bimur – we shall fear
2nd person	ver-ē-beris – you will fear	ver-ē-biminī – you will fear
3rd person	ver-ē-bitur – he, she, it will fear	ver-ē-buntur – they will fear

Third, Fourth, and Mixed Conjugations

	SINGULAR	PLURAL
1st person	sequar – I shall follow	sequ-ē-mur – we shall follow
2nd person	sequ-ē-ris – you will follow	sequ-ē-minī – you will follow
3rd person	sequ-ē-tur – he, she, it will follow	sequ-e-ntur – they will follow

11.1.3 Imperfect Indicative

	SINGULAR	PLURAL
1st person	menti-ē-bar – I was lying	menti-ē-bāmur – we were lying
2nd person	menti-ē-bāris – you were lying	menti-ē-bāminī – you were lying
3rd person	menti-ē-bātur – he, she, it was lying	menti-ē -bantur – they were lying

11.1.4 Perfect Indicative

	SINGULAR	PLURAL
1st person	secūtus, -a, -um sum – I followed	secūtī, -ae, -a sumus – we followed
2nd person	secūtus, -a, -um es – you followed	secūtī, -ae, -a estis – you followed
3rd person	secūtus, -a, -um est – he, she, it followed	secūtī, -ae, -a sunt – they followed

HINT! The perfect of deponent verbs may also be translated, for example, "I have followed" or "I did follow."

11.1.5 Future Perfect Indicative

	SINGULAR	PLURAL
1st person	secūtus, -a, -um erō	secūtī, -ae, -a erimus
2nd person	secūtus, -a, -um eris	secūtī, -ae, -a eritis
3rd person	secūtus, -a, -um erit	secūtī, -ae, -a erunt

Translations: I shall have followed; you will have followed, etc.

11.1.6 Pluperfect Indicative

	SINGULAR	PLURAL
1st person	secūtus, -a, -um eram	secūtī, -ae, -a erāmus
2nd person	secūtus, -a, -um erās	secūtī, -ae, -a erātis
3rd person	secūtus, -a, -um erat	secūtī, -ae, -a erant

HINT! Remember for forms of the perfect tenses, the participle has to agree with the subject.

Translations: I had followed; you had followed, etc.

11.2 PARTICIPLES OF DEPONENT VERBS

Deponent verbs have only three forms of participles: the present, which is active; the future, which is also active; the perfect, which is *active*. Participles of deponents are formed in the same way as those of non-deponent verbs.

11.2.1 Present Active

arbitrāns, arbitrantis – (while) thinking

verēns, verentis – (while) fearing

sequēns, sequentis – (while) following

mentiēns, mentientis – (while) lying

prōgrediēns, prōgredientis – (while) advancing

The present participles of deponent verbs, like those of non-deponent verbs, decline and belong to the third declension.

11.2.2 Perfect Active

arbitrātus, -a, -um – having thought

veritus, -a, -um – having feared

secūtus, -a, -um – having followed

mentītus, -a, -um – having lied

prōgressus, -a, -um – having advanced

11.2.3 Future Active

arbitrātūrus, -a, -um – (being) about to think; going to think

veritūrus, -a, -um – (being) about to fear; going to fear

secūtūrus, -a, -um – (being) about to follow; going to follow

mentītūrus, -a, -um – (being) about to lie; going to lie

prōgressūrus, -a, -um – (being) about to advance; going to advance

11.3 INFINITIVES OF DEPONENT VERBS

As might be expected, the infinitives of deponent verbs are rather different. For the present infinitive the form is the same as the present infinitive passive of non-deponent verbs, but as with other deponent forms, it is passive in form but active in meaning. Also it is the second principal part. Similarly, the perfect infinitive is passive in form but active in meaning. It is made up of two parts: the perfect participle and the present infinitive of the verb **sum**. The future infinitive is, perhaps surprisingly, active in form and active in meaning. It is made up of two parts: the future participle active and the present infinitive of the verb **sum**.

11.3.1 Present

arbitrārī – to think; to judge

verērī – to fear

sequī – to follow

mentīrī – to lie

progredī – to advance

11.3.2 Perfect

arbitrātus, -a, -um esse – to have thought; to have judged

veritus, -a, -um esse – to have feared

secūtus, -a, -um esse – to have followed

mentītus, -a, -um esse – to have risen

prōgressus, -a, -um esse – to have advanced

11.3.3 Future

arbitrātūrus, -a, -um esse – to be going to think; to be going to judge

veritūrus, -a, -um esse – to be going to fear

secutūrus esse – to be going to follow

mentītūrus, -a, -um esse – to be going to lie

prōgressūrus esse – to be going to advance

TRY THIS

Practice with deponent verbs.

Translate into Latin, using deponent verbs:

(i) to have promised

(ii) they will follow

(iii) I had died

(iv) to be about to delay

(v) they rose

(vi) we shall suffer

(vii) we shall have set out

(viii) to use

(ix) you (pl.) will pursue

(x) you (sing.) had feared

FIGURE 11.2 Pompeii: the Marina Gate, situated on the western limit of the city on the Via Marina. Cities were walled for protection with gates, usually at the four corners to allow entrance to the city. *Source: courtesy Sally Baume*

11.4 CAUSAL CLAUSES

Latin has a number of ways of expressing cause. We have already met one of these: the participle may have a causal force (including the ablative absolute construction). Latin also uses subordinate clauses with a finite verb regularly in the indicative. These may be introduced by **quia, quoniam** – since; because, or **quod** – because.

> M'. Aquilium patrēs nostrī . . . , **quia** cum fugitīvīs **fortiter bellum gesserat**, iūdiciō līberāvērunt (Cicero *Pro Flacco* 98): *our fathers acquitted Manlius Aquilius . . . **since he had bravely waged war** with the runaway slaves.*

11.5 USES OF CASES

11.5.1 Genitive of Characteristic

The genitive is also used (especially with the verb **sum**) to express ideas such as "characteristic of," "the mark of," and "the duty of":

> omnēs virī bonī . . . ius ipsum amant, **nec est virī bonī errāre** (Cicero *De Legibus* 1.48): *all good men love the law itself, **nor is it the mark of/characteristic of a good man to err**.*

*D*e Legibus (*On the Laws*), a philosophical work, probably composed in 51 BC, but perhaps unfinished in the form we have it. It is written in dialogue form and concerns the nature of law and justice and the kind of laws that would be necessary in an ideal state.

SOUND BITE   Horace on the passing of time (Horace *Odes* 2.14.1–2)

eheu fugaces, Postume, Postume,
labuntur anni.

TRANSLATION FROM LATIN

1. quoniam id non <facere> poterat, harum rerum actorem quem idoneum esse arbitrata est ipsa delegit. (Cicero *In Q. Caecilium* 20)

2. quo in genere quia praestat omnibus Demosthenes, idcirco a doctis oratorum est princeps iudicatus. (Cicero *Brutus* 141)

3. institutas turres, testudines munitionesque hostium admiratur. (Caesar *De Bello Gallico* 5.52.2)

4. Caesar his de causis quas commemoravi Rhenum transire decreverat; sed navibus transire neque satis tutum esse arbitrabatur neque suae neque populi Romani dignitatis esse statuebat. (Caesar *De Bello Gallico* 4.17.1)

5. fateor me homines coegisse, fateor armasse, fateor tibi mortem esse minitatum, fateor hoc interdicto praetoris vindicari. (Cicero *Pro Caecina* 66)

6. hic primum ortus est a tribunis militum, praefectis reliquisque, qui ex urbe amicitiae causa Caesarem secuti non magnum in re militari usum habebant. (Caesar *De Bello Gallico* 1.39.3)

7. eo tempore tu non modo non ad C. Aquilium aut L. Lucilium rettulisti, sed ne ipse quidem te consuluisti, ne hoc quidem tecum locutus es: "Horae duae fuerunt; Quinctius ad vadimonium non venit." (Cicero *Pro Quinctio* 53)

8. ii posteaquam temporibus rei publicae exclusi per senatum agere quae voluerant non potuerunt, in Syriam in regnum patrium profecti sunt. eorum alter, qui Antiochus vocatur, iter per Siciliam facere voluit, itaque isto praetore venit Syracusas. hic Verres hereditatem sibi venisse arbitratus est, quod in eius regnum ac manus venerat is quem

iste et audierat multa secum praeclara habere e suspicabatur. (Cicero *In Verrem* 2.4.61–2)

9. aliis illud indignum, aliis ridiculum videbatur: ridiculum iis qui istius causam in testium fide, in criminum ratione, in iudicum potestate, non in comitiis consularibus positam arbitrabantur, indignum iis qui altius perspiciebant . . . etenim sic ratiocinabantur, sic honestissimi homines inter se et mecum loquebantur, aperte iam et perspicue nulla esse iudicia. (Cicero *In Verrem* 1.1.19–20)

THE BIGGER PICTURE

*I*n Q. Caecilium (*Against Q. Caecilius*), a speech made by Cicero before the senate in 70 BC, arguing that he, rather than Q. Caecilius, should be in charge of the prosecution of Verres. Caecilius had been an alternative candidate put up by Verres' supporters, thinking that his incompetence would lead to an acquittal. Cicero, of course, succeeded in being given the prosecution of the case.

TRANSLATION INTO LATIN

1. It is not characteristic of a man, least of all of a Roman, to hesitate to give up his life breath for his homeland. (Cicero *Philippicae* 10.20)

2. I promise that I will carry out all these things diligently and strictly. (Cicero *In Verrem* 1.1.40)

3. The forces of the Gauls had filled all this place under the wall – the part of the hill which looked towards the rising sun. (Caesar *De Bello Gallico* 7.69.5)

4. He placed Quintus Atrius in charge of the garrison and the ships. He himself having advanced about 12 miles by night he caught sight of the forces of the enemy. (Caesar *De Bello Gallico* 5.9.2)

5. The envoys said that they would report these things to their people and, having considered the matter, would return to Caesar after the third day. (Caesar *De Bello Gallico* 4.9.1)

6. And so when nearly 40 days have elapsed, then at last they think they will respond to those things which have been said by us. (Cicero *In Verrem* 1.1.31)

7. Having decided these things . . . around the third watch he set sail and ordered the cavalry to advance to the further harbour, to embark and to follow him. (Caesar *De Bello Gallico* 4.23.1)

8. Did you try to lay your impious and sacrilegious hands upon that temple, so ancient, so holy, so sacred? (Cicero *In Verrem* 2.1.47)

9. In the meantime he ordered the baggage to be collected into one place and that the place be fortified by those troops who had halted on the higher flank. The Helvetii having followed with all their carts collected their equipment in one place. (Caesar *De Bello Gallico* 1.24.3–4)

FIGURE 11.3 Romano-British stone altar. The altar is dedicated to the goddess Brigantia. Brigantia was a goddess associated with the Brigantes, a tribe of people living in northern England. The Romans generally did not forbid the worship of local divinities. © *Leeds Museums and Galleries (Discovery Centre)*

VOCABULARY TO LEARN

Nouns; Pronouns

crīmen, crīminis (n.) – crime; charge
fidēs, fideī (f.) – faith; honesty; credibility
hōra, -ae (f.) – hour
iūdex, iūdicis (m.) – judge
manus, manūs (f.) – hand (in sentence 10 in the
    sense "power")
nāvis, -is (f.) – ship
ōrātor, -ōris (m.) – orator
ratiō, ratiōnis (f.) – reason; manner; motive
tempus, temporis (n.) – time; (pl.
    circumstances; troubles)
ūsus, ūsūs (m.) – use; experience

Deponent Verbs

admīror, admīrārī, admīrātus sum – admire;
    marvel at
arbitror, arbitrārī, arbitrātus sum – think; judge;
    suppose
ēgredior, ēgredī, ēgressus sum – march out; set
    out
fateor, fatērī, fassus sum – admit; confess
loquor, loquī, locūtus sum – speak
minitor, minitārī, minitātus sum (+ acc. of the
    thing threatened; dat. of person) – threaten
morior, morī, mortuus sum – die
moror, morārī, morātus sum – delay
orior, orīrī, ortus sum – rise; originate; begin
patior, patī, passus sum – put up with; suffer
persequor, persequī, persecūtus sum – pursue
polliceor, pollicērī, pollicitus sum – promise
proficiscor, proficiscī, profectus sum – set out
sequor, sequī, secūtus sum – follow
ūtor, ūtī, ūsus sum (+ abl.) – use
vereor, verērī, veritus sum – fear
versor, versārī, versātus sum – spend one's time

Other Verbs

armō, armāre, armāvī, armātum – arm
cōgō, cogere, coēgī, coactum – assemble; bring
    together
consulō, consulere, consuluī, consultum –
    consult; question
dēcernō, dēcernere, dēcrēvī, dēcrētum – decide
praemittō, praemittere, praemīsī, praemissum
    – send ahead; send in advance
praestō, praestāre, praestitī, praestātum – be
    superior to; surpass
statuō, statuere, statuī, statūtum – establish;
    decide; consider

Adjectives

duo, duae, duo – two
idōneus, -a, -um – suitable
indignus, -a, -um – unworthy; intolerable
posterus, -a, -um – next; following
praeclārus, -a, -um – magnificent; opulent;
    valuable
princeps, -cipis – first; most eminent
rīdiculus, -a, -um – ridiculous; amusing;
    laughable
tūtus, -a, -um – safe

Adverbs; Prepositions; Conjunctions

idcirco – for this reason
nē . . . quidem – not even
nōn modo – not only
posteāquam – after that
similiter – in a like manner; similarly

VOCABULARY SPECIFICALLY FOR CHAPTER 11 PASSAGES

Nouns; Pronouns

actor, -ōris (m.) – actor; orator; advocate

Antiochus, -i (m.) – a Syrian prince

C. Aquilius, -iī (m.) – Gaius Aquilius, a Roman jurist and contemporary of Cicero

comitia, -orum (n. pl.) – assembly

Demosthenes, -is (m.) – Demosthenes, the most famous Greek orator

hērēditās, hērēditātis (f.) – inheritance

impedimentum, -ī (n.) – (in pl. baggage; (military) equipment)

interdictum, -ī (n.) – provisional decree

Lūcīlius, -ii (m.) – Lucius Lucilius, an assistant to Aquilius (above)

mūnītiō, mūnītiōnis (f.) – fortification

praefectus, -ī (m.) – commander

P. Quinctius, -ii (m.) – Publius Quinctius, defended by Cicero

testūdō, testūdinis (f.) – tortoise; shelter (to protect besiegers)

turris, turris (f.) – tower

Sicilia, -ae (f.) – Sicily

Syrācūsae, -ārum (f. pl.) – Syracuse, a city in Sicily

Syria, -ae (f.) – Syria, country in Asia

vadimōnium vadimōniī (n.) – appearance in court; hearing

vigilia, -ae (f.) – watch (time of keeping watch at night – four watches per night)

Verbs

commemorō, commemorāre, commemorāvī, commemorātum – remind of; mention

dēligō, dēligere, dēlēgī, dēlectum – choose

exclūdō, exclūdere, exclūdī, exclūsum – shut out; hinder; prevent

insector, insectārī, insectātus sum – pursue

instituō, instituere, instituī, institūtum – build

perspiciō, perspicere, perspexī, perspectum – look at; examine

ratiōcinor, ratiōcinārī, ratiōcinātus sum – reckon; argue

referō, referre, rettulī, relātum – refer (to) (see *fero*, Chapter 12)

suspicor, suspicārī, suspicātus sum – suspect; believe; suppose

transeō, transīre, transīvī (or transiī), transitum – cross

vindicō, vindicāre, vindicāvī, vindicātum – punish

volō, velle, voluī – want; wish (see Chapter 12)

Adjectives

alius, -a, -ud – other; another; aliī . . . aliī – some . . . others

alter, -tera, -terum – one (of two)

consulāris, -e – consular

honestissimus, -a, -um – most honest; most honorable

patrius, -a, -um – belonging to one's father; belonging to one's forefathers; ancestral

quartus, -a, -um – fourth

Adverbs; Prepositions; Conjunctions

altius – more deeply

perspicuē – clearly; manifestly

English Derivations

From which Latin roots do the following English words derive?

(i) temporary
(ii) locution
(iii) patient
(iv) sequel

CHAPTER 12

FIGURE 12.1 Roman mosaic, 3rd century AD. Virgil and the Muses. The Muses were goddesses, nine in number. Each was associated with a specific sphere; for example, Calliope was the muse of epic poetry, Terpsichore of dancing. *Source: Musée National du Bardo, Le Bardo, Tunisia/Giraudon/The Bridgeman Art Library*

Wiley's Real Latin: Learning Latin from the Source, First Edition.
Robert Maltby and Kenneth Belcher.
© 2014 John Wiley & Sons, Inc. Published 2014 by John Wiley & Sons, Inc.

12.1 IRREGULAR VERBS: *FERŌ, VOLŌ, NŌLŌ, MĀLŌ, EŌ, FĪŌ*

FYI See Appendix 4 for the conjugation of *nōlō* and *mālō*.

The following verbs are irregular: **ferō** – carry; bear; endure; **volō** – wish; **nōlō** – be unwilling; **mālō** – prefer; **eō** – go. Of these, only **ferō** has a full set of passive forms.

The verb **fīō** is used in the present tense as the passive of **faciō** and so means *be made*, *be done* or, often, *happen*. They are conjugated in the present indicative as follows:

FYI The verb *eō* has three passive forms: *itur* (present indicative 3rd person singular), *itum est* (perfect indicative 3rd person singular), and *īrī* (present infinitive passive). The use of these forms is discussed in Chapter 17.

	ACTIVE		PASSIVE	
	SINGULAR	**PLURAL**	**SINGULAR**	**PLURAL**
1st person	ferō	ferimus	feror	ferimur
2nd person	fers	fertis	ferris	feriminī
3rd person	fert	ferunt	fertur	feruntur
1st person	volō	volumus		
2nd person	vīs	vultis		
3rd person	vult	volunt		
1st person	eō	īmus		
2nd person	īs	ītis		
3rd person	it	eunt		
1st person	fīō	(fīmus)		
2nd person	fīs	(fītis)		
3rd person	fit	fiunt		

The principal parts are as follows:

ferō, ferre, tulī, lātum

volō, velle, volui

eō, ire, i(v)i, itum

fīō, fierī, factus sum

The future forms are **feram** (passive **ferar**), **volam**, and **ībō**. Here **ferō** and **volō** follow the third conjugation pattern in **-am, -ēs, -et, -ēmus, -ētis, -ent**, and **eō** follows the first and second conjugation pattern **ībō, ībis, ībit, ībimus, ībitis, ībunt**. The perfect active forms (including perfect active infinitives) are derived regularly from the third principal part, which for **eō** may be the full form **īvī** or the contracted form **iī**. The perfect passive forms of **ferō** (including the perfect passive infinitive **latus esse**) and its future participle **lātūrus** are derived regularly from the fourth principal part (e.g., **lātus, -a, -um sum**; **lātus, -a, -um eram**; **lātus, -a, -um erō**).

TRY THIS

Irregular verbs

Translate into Latin:

(i) I was unwilling

(ii) they have preferred

(iii) it will happen

(iv) we carry

(v) she wishes

(vi) we are going

(vii) they are carried

(viii) we were brought

(ix) you (sing.) will approach

(x) they became

12.2 USES OF THE CASES

12.2.1 Ablative of Description

The ablative is used (regularly without a preposition) to describe a quality or characteristic of a person. In this use the ablative phrase must include an adjective:

ipsī clam consiliō initō Achillam, praefectum rēgium, **singulārī hominem audāciā**, . . . mīserunt (Caesar *Bellum Civile* 3.104.3): *they themselves, having formed a plot in secret, sent Achillas, a prefect of the king, **a man of singular audacity.***

mē . . . canō capite atque albā barbā . . . vidēs (Plautus *Bacchides* 1101): *you see **me with my grey head and white beard.***

Notice that the ablative of description is most frequently used to describe physical characteristics.

12.2.2 Genitive of Quality/Description

The genitive is used also used to describe the quality of a person:

sed quid ego Socrātem aut Theramēnem, **praestantis virōs virtūtis** . . . commemorō? (Cicero *Tusculanae Disputationes* 1.100): *but why do I mention Socrates or Theramenes, **men of outstanding virtue?***

C. Volusēnus, tribūnus mīlitum, **vir et consiliī magnī et virtūtis**, ad Galbam accurrit (Caesar *De Bello Gallico* 3.5.2): *Gaius Volusenus, a military tribune, **a man of great wisdom and courage**, hastened to Galba.*

Notice that the genitive is most frequently used to describe what may be described as inherent characteristics.

TRANSLATION FROM LATIN

1. nam ut Brundisio profectus es, nullae mihi abs te sunt redditae litterae. (Cicero *Epistulae ad Atticum* 1.15.2)

   HINT! *Abs* is an alternative form of the preposition *ab*.

2. nobiscum versari iam diutius non potes; non feram, non patiar, non sinam. (Cicero *In Catilinam* 1.11)

3. L. Catilina, nobili genere natus, fuit magna vi et animi et corporis, sed ingenio malo pravoque. (Sallust *Catiline* 5.1)

4. erat una cum ceteris Dumnorix ... de quo a nobis antea dictum est. hunc secum habere in primis <Caesar> constituerat, quod eum cupidum rerum novarum, cupidum imperii, magni animi, magnae inter Gallos auctoritatis cognoverat. (Caesar *De Bello Gallico* 5.6.1)

5. quis nunc te adibit? cui videberis bella?
   quem nunc amabis? cuius esse diceris?
   quem basiabis?

   (Catullus 8.16–18)

6. hostes paulisper morati militum nostrorum impetum non tulerunt seseque alia ex parte oppidi eiecerunt. (Caesar *De Bello Gallico* 5.21.5)

7. atque ille Tarquinius, quem maiores nostri non tulerunt, non crudelis, non impius, sed superbus est habitus et dictus: quod nos vitium in privatis saepe tulimus, id maiores nostri ne in rege quidem ferre potuerunt. (Cicero *Philippicae* 3.9)

8. hostes postero die multo maioribus coactis copiis castra oppugnant, fossam complent ... hoc idem reliquis deinceps fit diebus. nulla pars nocturni temporis ad laborem intermittitur. (Caesar *De Bello Gallico* 5.40.3–4)

9. rem publicam, Quirites, vitamque omnium, bona, fortunas, coniuges liberosque vestros atque hoc domicilium clarissimi imperi, fortunatissimam pulcherrimamque urbem, hodierno die deorum immortalium summo erga vos amore, laboribus, consiliis, periculis meis e flamma atque ferro ac paene ex faucibus fati ereptam et vobis con-servatam ac restitutam videtis. (Cicero *In Catilinam* 3.1)

FIGURE 12.2 Silver denarius, 47–46 BC. Aeneas carrying the Palladium and Anchises. The Palladium was a statue of the goddess Pallas Athene (Roman Minerva). As long as it was in Troy, the city was safe; however, it was stolen by Odysseus and Diomedes and Troy fell. © *Leeds Museums and Galleries (Discovery Centre)*

TRANSLATION INTO LATIN

1. There is present a man of utmost authority, reverence, and honesty, Marcus Lucullus. (Cicero *Pro Archia* 8)

2. The remaining crowd of women and children (for they had left home with all their possessions and had crossed the Rhine) began to flee in all directions. (Caesar *De Bello Gallico* 4.14.5)

3. Caesar himself, starting at the fourth watch, marched against the enemy by the same route that they had gone. (Caesar *De Bello Gallico* 1.21.3)

4. Caesar himself, because he had noticed that this part of the enemy was least strong, joined battle from the right flank. (Caesar *De Bello Gallico* 1.52.2)

5. Those men, because they feared the punishments and tortures of the Gauls, whose lands they had harassed, said that they wanted to remain with him [i.e., Caesar]. (Caesar *De Bello Gallico* 4.15.5)

6. At this point I do not suppose that that man will deny that he has a great many statues and countless paintings. (Cicero *In Verrem* 2.1.60)

7. Caesar brought assistance to our men at the most opportune time: for the enemy halted at his arrival and our men recovered from their fear. (Caesar *De Bello Gallico* 4.34.1)

8. \<Caesar\> himself, having advanced a little with the legion from the place where he had halted, awaited the outcome of the battle. (Caesar *De Bello Gallico* 7.49.3)

9. You have heard these things, judges; and now I pass over and leave them all. I say nothing about the luxury of Apronius, nothing about his insolence . . . nothing about his unparalleled baseness and depravity. (Cicero *In Verrem* 2.3.106)

VOCABULARY TO LEARN

Nouns

dolor, dolōris (m.) – pain; sorrow
ferrum, -ī (n.) – iron; sword
genus, generis (n.) – race; family
ingenium, -iī (n.) – quality; nature; character
officium, officiī (n.) – duty
ratiō, ratiōnis (f.) – method; manner
signum, -ī (n.) – sign; statue
virtus, -ūtis (f.) – courage
vitium, -iī (n.) – vice; fault

Verbs

adeō, adīre, adiī, aditum – approach
adferō, adferre, attulī, allātum – bring to; carry to
cōgō, cōgere, coēgī, coactum – bring together; gather
constituō, constituere, constituī, constitūtum – arrange; determine
cupiō, cupere, cupīvī, cupītum – desire
existimō, existimāre, existimāvī, existimātum – think; consider
ferō, ferre, tulī, lātum – carry; bear; endure; allow; molestē ferō, ferre, tulī, lātum – take badly; be annoyed at
habeō, habēre, habuī, habitum – have; hold; consider
moror, morārī, morātus sum – delay
negō, negāre, negāvī, negātum – say . . . not; deny

patior, patī, passus sum – put up with; suffer
reddō, reddere, reddidī, redditum – return; give back; give up
resistō, resistere, restitī (+ dat.) – resist
restituō, restituere, restituī, restitūtum – restore
sinō, sinere, sīvī, situm – allow
transeō, transīre, transiī, transitum – cross over

Adjectives

aliquis, aliquid – someone; anyone
cupidus, -a, -um – (+ gen.) desirous (of)
difficilis, -e – difficult
gravis, -e – serious
immortālis, -e – immortal
infirmus, -a, -um – weak
nocturnus, -a, -um – belonging to the night; nocturnal
nullus, -a, -um – no
summus, -a, -um – highest; greatest
superbus, -a, -um – proud
tōtus, -a, -um – whole

Adverbs; Prepositions; Conjunctions

molestē – with annoyance
paene – almost; scarcely
prīdiē – on the day before
ūnā – together

VOCABULARY SPECIFICALLY FOR CHAPTER 12 PASSAGES

Nouns; Pronouns

auctoritās, -tātis (f.) – authority
Brundisium, Brundisiī (n.) – Brundisium (town in Italy)
domicilium, domiciliī (n.) – home
Dumnorix, -igis (m.) – Dumnorix, a Gallic leader
faucēs, -ium (f. pl.) – throat; jaws
fossa, -ae (f.) – ditch; trench
īdem . . . quī – the same . . . as
maiōres, -um (m. pl.) – ancestors
prīvātus, -ī (m.) – private citizen
rēs novae, rērum novārum (f. pl.) – revolution; rebellion
Tarquinius, -iī (m.) – Tarquinius Superbus, the last king of Rome
vultus, -ūs (m.) – expression; face

Verbs

bāsiō, bāsiāre, bāsiāvī, bāsiātum – kiss
compleō, complēre, complēvī, complētum – fill
conservō, conservāre, conservāvī, conservātum – save
dissimulō, dissimulāre, dissimulāvī, dissimulātum – dissimulate; hide
ēiciō, ēicere, ēiēcī, ēiectum – with sē: rush out
ēripiō, ēripere, ēripuī, ēreptum – snatch
intermittō, intermittere, intermīsī, intermissum – leave out; discontinue; interrupt
molestē ferō, ferre, tulī, lātum – take badly; be annoyed at
nascor, nascī, nātus sum – be born
subsum, subesse – underlie
tegō, tegere, tēxī, tēctum – cover; conceal
versor, versārī, versātus sum – dwell; remain

Adjectives

bellus, -a, -um – beautiful
cānus, -a, -um – white (of hair)
clārissimus, -a, -um – most famous
fortūnātissimus, -a, -um – most fortunate
hodiernus, -a, -um – of today; hodiernō diē – on this very day
muliebris, -e – of a woman
necessārius, -a, -um – necessary
opportūnissimus, -a, -um – most opportune
plūrimus, -a, -um – most; a great many
posterus, -a, -um – next
praestans, -antis – outstanding
prāvus, -a, -um – crooked; vicious; depraved
prīmus, -a, -um – first; early
propinquus, -a, -um (+ dat.) – neighboring; nearby
pulcherrimus, -a, -um – most beautiful
rēgius, -a, -um – royal; of the king
singulāris, -e – outstanding

Adverbs; Prepositions

deinceps – next; following
diūtius – longer
ergā (+ acc.) – towards; in respect of
hīc – here; at this point
in prīmīs, also written as one word imprīmīs – especially; above all
insolenter – unusually; immoderately; insolently
minimē – least of all
paulisper – for a little while
prīmā nocte – at nightfall

English
Derivations

From which Latin roots do the following English words derive?

(i) total
(ii) eject
(iii) grave
(iv) habit

(A) Identify and explain the case of the nouns underlined:
1. paucis <u>diebus</u> opus efficitur.
2. officia deserunt <u>mollitia</u> animi.
3. me <u>domo</u> mea per vim expulisitis.
4. nullo <u>hoste</u> prohibente legionem in Allobriges perduxit.
5. <u>annos</u> multos legatus fuit.
6. praestantis viros <u>virtutis</u> commemoro.
7. Roman venit <u>Mario</u> consule.
8. nec est <u>viri</u> boni errare.
9. me cano <u>capite</u> vides.

(B) Identify the person, number, tense, and voice of the verbs underlined:
1. nullae mihi abs te <u>sunt redditae</u> litterae.
2. Lentulus naves suas <u>pollicetur</u>.
3. <u>audiverat</u> Popeium esse venturum.
4. rem publicam periculis <u>liberarat</u>.
5. cum fugitivis fortiter bellum <u>gesserat</u>.

(C) Supply the part of the verb specified:
1. facio: future infinitive active
2. teneo: present participle active (nominative plural masculine)
3. appeto: present infinitive active
4. confirmo: present infinitive passive
5. damno: perfect participle passive (accusative singular feminine)
6. voco: perfect infinitive passive
7. volo: present infinitive active
8. duco: future infinitive passive
9. fingo: future participle active (dative singular neuter)

(D) Translate into English:
1. vix a te videor posse tenere manus! (Ovid *Amores* 1.4.10)
2. eius ergo auctoritate impulsi Athenienses copias ex urbe eduxerunt locoque idoneo castra fecerunt. (Nepos *Miltiades* 5.3)
3. omnibus rebus ad Britannicum bellum comparatis, Indutiomarum ad se cum ducentis obsidibus venire iussit. (Caesar *De Bello Gallico* 5.4)
4. legati haec se ad suos relaturos dixerunt et re deliberata post diem tertium ad Caesarem reversuros. (Caesar *De Bello Gallico* 4.9.2)
5. postero die Caesar similiter praemissis prima nocte impedimentis de quarta vigilia ipse egreditur. (Caesar *Bellum Civile* 3.77.1)
6. cupiebam dissimulare me id moleste ferre, cupiebam animi dolorem vultu tegere. (Cicero *In Verrem* 1.1.21)

(E) Translate into Latin:

1. On that day the military tribune, Q. Laberius Durus, is killed. (Caesar *De Bello Gallico* 5.15.5)

2. They cut down a large number of those fleeing. (Caesar *De Bello Gallico* 2.11.4)

3. When he had learnt these things Caesar strengthened the minds of the Gauls with his words. (Caesar *De Bello Gallico* 1.33.1)

4. I certainly know that I can easily be defeated by you. (Cicero *De Natura Deorum* 3.95)

5. The records are just as you see, judges. What are you waiting for? What more do you seek? And you yourself, Verres, why are you lingering? Why do you delay? (Cicero *In Verrem* 2.2.191)

6. The senate wanted you to give me cash and me to give you corn. You will have the cash yourself which the senate wanted you to give to me. (Cicero *In Verrem* 2.3.197)

CHAPTER 13

FIGURE 13.1 Head of youthful Bacchus, date unknown. Bacchus was the god of wine (also called Dionysus; both names occur, although Bacchus is more common in Latin poets). He was also associated with poetic inspiration. © *Leeds Museums and Galleries (Discovery Centre)*

Wiley's Real Latin: Learning Latin from the Source, First Edition.
Robert Maltby and Kenneth Belcher.
© 2014 John Wiley & Sons, Inc. Published 2014 by John Wiley & Sons, Inc.

13.1 SUBJUNCTIVE MOOD

We have now examined all forms of the indicative mood. Only the subjunctive and imperative remain. In this chapter we meet the forms of the subjunctive. In addition some of the so-called independent uses of the subjunctive are introduced: that is, where the subjunctive mood is used as the main verb in its sentence. However, the subjunctive appears most normally in a number of subordinate clauses and we will be looking at the various uses of the subjunctive in the coming chapters. There are only four tenses of the subjunctive: present, imperfect, perfect, and pluperfect.

13.1.1 Present Subjunctive Active

First Conjugation

	SINGULAR	PLURAL
1st person	amem	amēmus
2nd person	amēs	amētis
3rd person	amet	ament

The easiest way to remember how to conjugate a first conjugation verb in the present subjunctive in all forms except the first person singular is: take the present indicative and change the -a before the ending to -e; the first person singular also has -e before the ending, but here the ending is -m (compare the ending of the imperfect indicative -ba**m**).

All first conjugation verbs form the present subjunctive in this way. There are no "formulaic" translations for the subjunctive. The meaning is determined by the type of clause in which the subjunctive appears. This will become clearer as we proceed.

Second Conjugation

	SINGULAR	PLURAL
1st person	videam	videāmus
2nd person	videās	videātis
3rd person	videat	videant

The easiest way to remember the forms of the present subjunctive of second conjugation verbs is: take the present indicative and add the letter -**a** before the ending; as in the first conjugation the first person singular ends in -**m**.

Third Conjugation

	SINGULAR	PLURAL
1st person	ponam	ponāmus
2nd person	ponās	ponātis
3rd person	ponat	ponant

Once again the first person singular ends in -**m**. The best way to remember the forms here is: take the present indicative and except for the first person singular change the letter before the ending to -**a**.

Fourth Conjugation

	SINGULAR	PLURAL
1st person	inveniam	inveniāmus
2nd person	inveniās	inveniātis
3rd person	inveniat	inveniant

Once again the first person singular ends in -**m**. The easiest way to remember the forms of the present subjunctive of fourth conjugation verbs is: take the present indicative and add the letter -**a** before the ending.

Mixed Conjugation

	SINGULAR	PLURAL
1st person	capiam	capiāmus
2nd person	capiās	capiātis
3rd person	capiat	capiant

Once again the first person singular ends in -**m**. The easiest way to remember the forms of the present subjunctive of mixed conjugation verbs is: take the present indicative and add the letter -**a** before the ending.

13.1.2 Imperfect Subjunctive Active

The simplest way to remember how to construct the imperfect subjunctive for all conjugations is: take the present infinitive and add the endings -**m**, -**s**, -**t**, -**mus**, -**tis**, -**nt**.

First Conjugation

	SINGULAR	PLURAL
1st person	amārem	amārēmus
2nd person	amārēs	amārētis
3rd person	amāret	amārent

Second Conjugation

	SINGULAR	PLURAL
1st person	vidērem	vidērēmus
2nd person	vidērēs	vidērētis
3rd person	vidēret	vidērent

Third Conjugation

	SINGULAR	PLURAL
1st person	ponerem	ponerēmus
2nd person	ponerēs	ponerētis
3rd person	poneret	ponerent

Fourth Conjugation

	SINGULAR	PLURAL
1st person	invenīrem	invenīrēmus
2nd person	invenīrēs	invenīrētis
3rd person	invenīret	invenīrent

Mixed Conjugation

	SINGULAR	PLURAL
1st person	caperem	caperēmus
2nd person	caperēs	caperētis
3rd person	caperet	caperent

13.1.3 Perfect Subjunctive Active

The perfect subjunctive is built on the perfect stem. The simplest way to remember how to form the perfect subjunctive for all conjugations is: take the perfect stem and add the endings **-erim**, **-erīs**, **-erit**, **-erīmus**, **-erītis**, **-erint**.

FYI For the perfect subjunctive of all conjugations, see Appendix 5.

First Conjugation

HINT! These endings appear to be the same as the future perfect indicative (with the exception of the first person singular). In fact there are differences in pronunciation which need not concern us here. However, because of the way the subjunctive is used, the context almost always makes it clear which is being used.

	SINGULAR	PLURAL
1st person	amāverim	amāverīmus
2nd person	amāverīs	amāverītis
3rd person	amāverit	amāverint

13.1.4 Pluperfect Subjunctive Active

The pluperfect subjunctive is technically also built on the perfect stem. However, the simplest way to remember how to form the pluperfect subjunctive active for all conjugations is: take the perfect infinitive and add the endings **-m**, **-s**, **-t**, **-mus**, **-tis**, **-nt**.

First Conjugation

FYI For the pluperfect subjunctive of all conjugations, see Appendix 5.

	SINGULAR	PLURAL
1st person	amāvissem	amāvissēmus
2nd person	amāvissēs	amāvissētis
3rd person	amāvisset	amāvissent

TRY THIS

Parse the following subjunctive forms:

e.g., *decertet* – 3rd person singular present subjunctive active of decerto – fight

(i) *servias*   (vi) *redidissem*

(ii) *cognoscerent*   (vii) *remanserit*

(iii) *optet*   (viii) *vertisset*

(iv) *pareamus*   (ix) *stabiliat*

(v) *placaverim*   (x) *dissimulent*

13.2 SUBJUNCTIVE OF IRREGULAR VERBS

13.2.1 Sum

Present Subjunctive

	SINGULAR	PLURAL
1st person	sim	sīmus
2nd person	sīs	sītis
3rd person	sit	sint

Imperfect Subjunctive

	SINGULAR	PLURAL
1st person	essem	essēmus
2nd person	essēs	essētis
3rd person	esset	essent

Note that the imperfect of **sum** follows the pattern of all imperfect subjunctives: present infinitive plus endings.

Perfect Subjunctive

	SINGULAR	PLURAL
1st person	fuerim	fuerīmus
2nd person	fuerīs	fuerītis
3rd person	fuerit	fuerint

Note again that the perfect subjunctive follows the pattern of all perfect subjunctives.

Pluperfect Subjunctive

	SINGULAR	PLURAL
1st person	fuissem	fuissēmus
2nd person	fuissēs	fuissētis
3rd person	fuisset	fuissent

Note again that the pluperfect subjunctive follows the pattern of all pluperfect subjunctives.

13.2.2 Possum

Present Subjunctive

	SINGULAR	PLURAL
1st person	possim	possīmus
2nd person	possīs	possītis
3rd person	possit	possint

HINT! To remember, note that the conjugation is simply *pos* + the present subjunctive of *sum*.

The subjunctive forms of **possum** are regular in all tenses except the present. Imperfect subjunctive: **possem, possēs, posset**, etc. Perfect subjunctive: **potuerim, potuerīs, potuerit**, etc. Pluperfect subjunctive: **potuissem, potuissēs, potuisset**, etc.

13.2.3 *Eō*

Present Subjunctive

	SINGULAR	PLURAL
1st person	eam	eāmus
2nd person	eās	eātis
3rd person	eat	eant

The subjunctive forms are regular in all tenses except the present. Imperfect subjunctive: **īrem, īrēs, īret**, etc. Perfect subjunctive: **ierim, ierīs, ierit**, etc. (or **iverim, iverīs, iverit**, etc.). Pluperfect subjunctive: **īssem, īssēs, īsset**, etc. (or **īvissem, īvissēs, īvisset**, etc; in compounds, the forms -**īissem**, -**īissēs**, -**īisset** are occasionally found).

13.2.4 *Ferō*

Present Subjunctive Active

	SINGULAR	PLURAL
1st person	feram	ferāmus
2nd person	ferās	ferātis
3rd person	ferat	ferant

The subjunctive forms of these verbs are regular in all tenses except the present. Imperfect subjunctive: **ferrem, ferrēs, ferret**, etc. Perfect subjunctive: **tulerim, tulerīs, tulerit**, etc. Pluperfect subjunctive: **tulissem, tulissēs, tulisset**, etc.

13.2.5 *Volō*

Present Subjunctive

	SINGULAR	PLURAL
1st person	velim	velīmus
2nd person	velīs	velītis
3rd person	velit	velint

The subjunctive forms of these verbs are regular in all tenses except the present. Imperfect subjunctive: **vellem, vellēs, vellet**, etc. Perfect subjunctive: **voluerim, voluerīs, voluerit**, etc. Pluperfect subjunctive: **voluissem, voluissēs, voluisset**, etc.

13.2.6 The Verb *Fīō*

Recall that the verb **faciō** is not used in the present, future, and imperfect indicative passive. Instead the verb **fīō, fierī, factus sum** – be made; happen is used. We met the conjugation of the present indicative in Chapter 12; the present subjunctive is conjugated as follows:

Present Subjunctive

	SINGULAR	PLURAL
1st person	fīam	fīāmus
2nd person	fīās	fīātis
3rd person	fīat	fīant

For forms of **fio**, see Appendix 4.

FIGURE 13.2 Roman figurine bottle (date unknown). The bottle is in the shape of a woman seated between two birds. It could have contained an ointment or unguent. Oils and suchlike were very popular in antiquity – for example, they were used in medicine and as a luxury item. © *Leeds Museums and Galleries (Discovery Centre)*

Active subjunctive of irregular verbs.
Supply the subjunctive form requested:

e.g., *sum* (1ˢᵗ person singular present subjunctive) – *sim*

(i) *sum* (1ˢᵗ person singular imperfect subjunctive)

(ii) *possum* (2ⁿᵈ person singular perfect subjunctive)

(iii) *eo* (3ʳᵈ person singular pluperfect subjunctive)

(iv) *fero* (3ʳᵈ person plural present subjunctive active)

(v) *volo* (1ˢᵗ person plural present subjunctive)

(vi) *fio* (2ⁿᵈ person singular imperfect subjunctive)

(vii) *sum* (2ⁿᵈ person plural present subjunctive)

(viii) *volo* (3ʳᵈ person plural pluperfect subjunctive)

(ix) *fero* (2ⁿᵈ person present subjunctive active)

(x) *eo* (3ʳᵈ person perfect subjunctive)

13.3 INDEPENDENT USES OF THE SUBJUNCTIVE

As noted above the subjunctive most frequently occurs in subordinate clauses. However, there are instances where the subjunctive is used as the main verb in its sentence. The present subjunctive is most commonly used in this way.

13.3.1 Jussive Subjunctive

The present subjunctive may be used to express commands in the third person singular or plural of the type: *let him/her/it/them do something* (often referred to as a jussive subjunctive – from the Latin **iubeō, -ēre, iussī, iussum** – order).

> Dīvitiās alius fulvō sibi **congerat** aurō
> Et **teneat** cultī iūgera multa solī (Tibullus 1.1–2):
> **Let another gather up** wealth for himself in yellow gold
> And **let him possess** many acres of cultivated land.

The present subjunctive is also used, most frequently in the first person plural, to express commands of the type: *let us do something*. This is referred to in some grammars as jussive in others as hortatory subjunctive (from the Latin **hortor, -āri, hortātus sum** – encourage).

vīvāmus, mea Lesbia, atque **amēmus** (Catullus 5.1): **let us live**, *my Lesbia, and let us love*.

In each case the negative is not **non**, but **ne**.

sed acta **ne agamus**, reliqua paremus (Cicero *Epistulae ad Atticum* 9.6.7): **let us not consider** *past actions but let us prepare for that which remains <to be done>*.

13.3.2 Deliberative Subjunctive

The subjunctive is also used in questions where the speaker is or appears to be uncertain what action to take; hence, deliberative subjunctive because the speaker is deliberating what to do, what to say, etc. Compare the English: *What am I doing?* (simple question) and *What am I to do?* For past deliberative questions, the imperfect subjunctive is used.

> sed quid **faciāmus**? victī, oppressī, captī plānē sumus (Cicero *Epistulae ad Atticum* 7.23.2): *but what **are we to do**? we are quite clearly conquered, held in check, and captured.*

> quid **faciam**? **roger** anne **rogem**? (Ovid *Metamorphoses* 3.465): *what **am I to do**? **am I to be sought** or **am I to seek**?*

FYI For the form **roger**, see Chapter 14.

> quid **dīcerem**? (Cicero *Epistulae ad Atticum* 6.3.9): *what **was I to say**?*

Negative deliberative questions use **nōn** rather than **nē**.

> an ego **nōn venīrem**? (Cicero *Philippicae* 2.3): ***should I not have come**?*

13.3.3 Potential Subjunctive

The subjunctive is also used to express what may happen; that is to express not a fact, but a possibility. The potential subjunctive may be translated as *may* or *would* as in English *someone **may say*** or *if I should see you, **I would be happy**.*

> nunc aliquis **dīcat** mihi "quid tu?
> nullane habēs vitia?" (Horace *Satires* 1.3.19–20):
> *now someone **may say** to me, "What about you?*
> *Have you no vices?"*

The present subjunctive is commonly used to express potentiality; however, the perfect subjunctive also occurs:

> ut aliquis fortasse **dixerit** (Cicero *De Officiis* 3.97): *as someone perhaps **may say**.*

THE BIGGER PICTURE

*D*e Officiis (On Duties), a philosophical work in the form of a letter addressed to his son Marcus, completed in 44 BC. The work is a practical discussion of ethics and the way moral duties should guide the life of a Roman politician. It is dependent to a large extent on Greek philosophical thought, especially that of the Stoic Panaetius.

The negative is rare, but in this instance **nōn** would be used.

The construction with some verbs is slightly different. For example, **velim – *I would wish*** may be followed by a complementary infinitive or by another subjunctive without the subordinating conjunction **ut**:

> **velim** mihi **dīcās** (Cicero *Philippicae* 2.41): *I would wish that you tell me*.

13.3.4 Optative Subjunctive

The present subjunctive is used (sometimes with the word **utinam**) to express a wish for the future as in English *May you be happy*:

> **valeant** cīvēs meī; **sint** incolumēs, **sint** florentēs, **sint** beātī (Cicero *Pro Milone* 93): *may my fellow citizens be strong; may they be safe, may they flourish, may they be fortunate*.

For a wish that something may not be happening Latin uses the imperfect subjunctive (unfulfilled wish for the present); for a wish that something might not have happened (unfulfilled wish for the past) Latin uses the pluperfect subjunctive. Here **nē** (sometimes with **utinam**) is used:

> illud **utinam nē** vērē **scrīberem** (Cicero *Epistulae ad Familiares* 5.17.3): *how I wish that I were not writing this truly*.

13.4 MORE USES OF THE CASES

13.4.1 Locative

A few nouns (especially the names of cities, towns, small islands, **domus** and **rus**) have a locative case which is used without a preposition to express place where. For first and second declension nouns, the locative singular has the same form as the genitive singular (e.g., **Rōmae**); plural nouns have the same form as the ablative (e.g., **Athēnīs**); for third declension nouns, the locative normally has the same form as the ablative (e.g., **Carthāgine**; the form **Carthāginī** also occurs). So **domī** – *at home*; **domī mīlitiaeque** – *at home and on the field of battle* (i.e., in peace and in war); **rūre** – *in the country*.

> Marcellus . . . duo templa sē **Rōmae** dedicātūrum vōverat (Cicero *In Verrem* 2.4.123): *Marcellus had vowed that he would dedicate two temples at Rome*.

FIGURE 13.3 Temple of Saturn, Roman Forum. Saturn was an older god who ruled before Jupiter in the time of the Golden Age. He was identified with the Greek god Cronus. His temple was located on the Capitoline Hill in Rome. *Source: courtesy Sam Penberthy*

TRANSLATION FROM LATIN

1. non est iam lenitati locus; severitatem res ipsa flagitat. unum etiam nunc concedam: exeant, proficiscantur . . . demonstrabo iter: Aurelia via profectus est. (Cicero *In Catilinam* 2.6)

2. quo me igitur vertam? rem tam improbam, crimen tantae audaciae tantaeque impudentiae propter inopiam testium ac litterarum praetermittam? (Cicero *In Verrem* 2.3.166)

3. nos modum aliquem et finem orationi nostrae criminibusque faciamus. (Cicero *In Verrem* 2.2.118)

4. de his qui dissimulant, qui Romae remanent, qui nobiscum sunt nihil dicimus? (Cicero *In Catilinam* 2.17)

5. Athenis audistis ex aede Minervae grande auri pondus ablatum; dictum est hoc in Cn. Dolabellae iudicio. dictum? etiam aestimatum. huius consili non participem C. Verrem, sed principem fuisse reperietis. (Cicero *In Verrem* 2.1.45)

6. hoc agitemus convivium/vino et sermoni suavi. (Plautus *Asinaria* 834–5)

7. utinam ille omnis secum suas copias eduxisset! (Cicero *In Catilinam* 2.4)

8. quid ego vetera repetam aut quid eorum scribarum mentionem faciam quos constat sanctissimos homines atque innocentissimos fuisse? non me fugit, iudices, vetera exempla pro fictis fabulis iam audiri atque haberi: in his temporibus versabor miseris ac perditis. (Cicero *In Verrem* 2.3.182)

9. quis Carthaginiensium pluris fuit Hannibale [pluris . . . Hannibale = greater than Hannibal] consilio, virtute, rebus gestis, qui unus cum tot imperatoribus nostris per tot annos de imperio et de gloria decertavit? hunc sui cives e civitate eiecerunt: nos etiam hostem litteris nostris et memoria videmus esse celebratum. qua re imitemur nostros Brutos, Camillos, Ahalas, Decios, Curios, Fabricios, Maximos, Scipiones, Lentulos, Aemilios, innumerabilis alios qui hanc rem publicam stabiliverunt; quos equidem in deorum immortalium coetu ac numero repono. amemus patriam, pareamus senatui, consulamus bonis; praesentis fructus neglegamus, posteritatis gloriae serviamus; id esse optimum putemus quod erit rectissimum; speremus quae volumus, sed quod acciderit feramus; cogitemus denique corpus virorum fortium magnorum hominum esse mortale, animi vero motus et virtutis gloriam sempiternam. (Cicero *Pro Sestio* 142–3)

HINT! Famous Roman families. Translate: Bruti, Camilli, etc. For details, see, for example, *Oxford Classical Dictionary*.

TRANSLATION INTO LATIN

1. What am I to say about the extraordinary greatness of his spirit and about his incredible courage? (Cicero *Pro Sestio* 62)

2. Who was the judge in this matter? How I wish that he were in Rome. He is in Rome. How I wish that he were present at the trial. (Cicero *Pro Q. Roscio Comoedo* 12)

3. Are we to give in to the man? Are we to listen to this man's conditions? Are we to believe that peace can be made with this man? (Cicero *Philippicae* 13.16)

4. How I wish, Quirites, that you had such a supply of brave and innocent men. (Cicero *Pro Lege Manilia* 27)

5. Let the wicked not dare to appease the gods with gifts. (Cicero *De Legibus* 2.41)

6. I would wish you to consider me not only a friend to you but also the greatest friend. (Cicero *Epistulae ad Familiares* 3.7.6)

7. By all means, let him come. Let him declare war on the Cretans. Let him set free the Byzantines. Let him call Ptolemy king. (Cicero *In Verrem* 2.2.76)

8. When these reports became known at Rome, a public thanksgiving of 20 days was granted. (Caesar *De Bello Gallico* 7.90.8)

9. When this battle had been reported across the Rhine, the Suebi, who had come to the banks of the Rhine, began to return home. (Caesar *De Bello Gallico* 1.54.1)

THE BIGGER PICTURE

*P*ro Roscio Comoedo (*On behalf of Roscius the Actor*), a speech, probably from the year 66 BC, in defense of the famous actor Quintus Roscius, whose agent Fannius is claiming half the value of a farm which he had won for Roscius in settlement of an earlier case.

THE BIGGER PICTURE

*P*ro Lege Manilia (*On behalf of the Manilian Law*), a speech made by Cicero before the popular assembly in 66 BC, supporting legislation proposed by G. Manilius, to give supreme command to Pompey, after his defeat of the pirates in 67 BC.

EXTRA PASSAGE

The hunter, Actaeon, has come upon the goddess, Diana, bathing and because he has seen her naked, she turns him into a stag. In this passage his metamorphosis is described. First Diana sprinkles water on Actaeon's head and then she brings about his metamorphosis.

dat[1] sparso capiti vivacis cornua cervi,
dat spatium collo summasque cacuminat aures
cum pedibusque manus, cum longis bracchia mutat
cruribus et velat maculoso vellere corpus;
additus et pavor est: fugit Autonoeius heros
et se tam celerem cursu miratur in ipso.
ut vero vultus et cornua vidit in unda,
"me miserum!"[2] dicturus erat: vox nulla secuta est!
ingemuit: vox illa fuit, lacrimaeque per ora
non sua fluxerunt; mens tantum pristina mansit.
quid faciat? repetatne domum et regalia tecta
an lateat silvis? pudor hoc, timor inpedit illud.
  Dum dubitat, videre[3] canes . . .
    Ovid *Metamorphoses* 3.194–206

[1]The subject of *dat* is Diana.

[2]This is an example of an accusative of exclamation; translate: "woe is me."

[3]*videre* is an alternative form of the perfect indicative active 3rd person plural = *viderunt*.

VOCABULARY

Nouns

aedis, -is (f.) – temple
āra, -ae (f.) – altar
arbiter, -trī (m.) – arbiter; judge
Athēnae, -ārum (f. pl.) – Athens
Aurēlia via, Aurēliae viae (f.) – the Aurelian
    Way, a coastal road from Rome to the Alps
Byzantiī, -ōrum (m. pl.) – Byzantines
coetus, -ūs (m.) – assembly; company
condiciō, -ōnis (f.) – condition
convīvium, conviviī (n.) – party; celebration
Crētensēs, -ium (m. pl.) – Cretans
crīmen, -inis (n.) – charge
Dolabella, -ae, Cn. (m.) – Gnaeus Dolabella (an
    associate of Verres)
fābula, -ae (f.) – story; fable
fructus, -ūs (m.) – enjoyment
Hannibal, Hannibalis – Hannibal, the most
    famous Carthaginian leader
impudentia, -ae (f.) – shamelessness
inopia, -ae (f.) – lack
iūdicium, iūdiciī (n.) – judgment; trial
lēnitās, -ātis (f.) – kindness; leniency
litterae, -ārum (f. pl.) – letter; document;
    report
magnitūdō, -inis (f.) – size; greatness
Minerva, -ae (f.) – Minerva, goddess of
    wisdom, handicrafts (= Greek Athena)
modus, -ī (m.) – limit
Natālis, -is (m.) – Birthday Spirit
particeps, -cipis (m.) – participant; partner
pondus, -eris (n.) – weight
princeps, -cipis (m.) – leader
rēs gestae, rērum gestārum (f. pl.) –
    accomplishments
Rhēnus, -ī (m.) – the Rhine
rīpa, -ae (f.) – bank (of a river)
scrība, -ae (m.) – clerk

sermō, -ōnis (m.) – conversation
sevēritās, -ātis (f.) – severity; seriousness
Suēbī, -ōrum (m. pl.) – the Suebi (a people of
    northeastern Germany)
supplicātiō, -ōnis (f.) – public prayer; public
    thanksgiving
testis, -is (m.) – witness
virtūs, -tūtis (f.) – virtue; courage

Verbs

accidō, -ere, accidī – happen
aestimō, -āre – value; appraise; weigh
agitō, -āre –move; drive; rouse; celebrate
appellō, -āre – call
audeō, -ēre, ausus sum – dare
auferō, auferre, abstulī, ablātum – take from
cēdō, -ere, cessī, cessum (+ dat.) – yield (to);
    give in (to)
celebrō, -āre – celebrate; honor
coepī, coepisse, coeptum – began (this verb
    occurs only in past tenses)
cognoscō, -ere, -nōvī, -nitum – become
    acquainted with
concēdō, -ere, -cessī, -cessum – depart; yield
    (to); concede
cōnstat – it is agreed
cōnsulō, -ere, -uī, consultum (+ dat.) – take
    thought for; have regard for
dēcernō, -ere, -crēvī, -crētum – decide; declare
dēcertō, -āre – fight; contend with
dēmonstrō, -āre – point out; show
dissimulō, -āre – hide; conceal
ēdūcō, -ere, -dūxī, -ductum – lead out
existimō, -āre – consider
flagitō, -āre – demand
imitor, -ārī, imitātus sum – imitate
līberō, -āre – set free
nōn mē fugit – I am not unaware

optō, -āre – desire; choose
pareō, -ēre, -uī, paritum (+ dat.) – obey
placō, -āre – calm; appease
praetermittō, -ere, -mīsī, -missum – pass over
reddō, -ere, -didī, -ditum – give back; grant
remaneō, -ēre, -mansī, -mansum – stay; remain
reperiō, -īre, repperī, repertum – perceive; find
repetō, -ere, -īvī, -ītum – return to; go back to
revertor, -ī, reversus sum – return
serviō, -īre, -īī, -ītum (+ dat.) – be devoted to;
  care for
stabiliō, -īre, -īvī, -ītum – make firm; make
  stable
versor, -ārī, versātus sum – concern oneself with
vertō, -ere, vertī, versum – turn

> **FYI** *Audeō* is one of a very few
> **semi-deponent** verbs in Latin. These
> verbs are active in the present, future,
> and imperfect tenses, but deponent in
> the perfect tenses: *ausum sum* – I dared,
> etc. *Soleō, -ēre, solitus sum* – be
> accustomed; *gaudeō, -ēre, gavīsus sum*
> – rejoice; and *fīdō, -ere, fīsus sum* –
> trust, are also semi-deponent verbs.

Adjectives

aliquī, aliqua, aliquod – some; any
amīcissimus, -a, -um – most friendly
difficilis, -e – difficult
fictus, -a, -um – (participle from *fingo*) false

grandis, -e – large; great
impius, -a, -um – wicked; impious
improbus, -a, -um – wicked
innocentissimus, -a, -um – most harmless; most
  innocent
optimus, -a, -um – best
perditus, -a, -um – (participle from *perdo*)
  degenerate
rectissimus, -a, -um – most correct; most
  appropriate
sanctissimus, -a, -um – most upright
sempiternus, -a, -um – eternal
singulāris, -e – singular; extraordinary
suāvis, -e – sweet; delightful
tantus, -a, -um – so great
tot (indeclinable) – so many
ūnus, -a, -um – one; alone
vetus, -eris – old; former
vīgintī (indeclinable) – twenty

Adverbs; Prepositions; Conjunctions

dēnique – finally
equidem – truly
nōn sōlum . . . sed etiam – not only . . . but also
plānē – clearly; completely; certainly
propter (+ acc.) – on account of
quō – where
sānē – truly; by all means
vērō – assuredly; however

English Derivations

From which Latin roots do the following English words derive?

(i) accident
(ii) agitate
(iii) scribe
(iv) fruit

CHAPTER 14

FIGURE 14.1 Undersea mosaic. Roman copy of Hellenistic original. Mosaics were made in a number of styles over many years. During the Imperial period they were mass-produced and were found in both private houses and public buildings (such as baths). *Source: Museo Archeologico Nazionale, Naples, Italy/Alinari/The Bridgeman Art Library*

Wiley's Real Latin: Learning Latin from the Source, First Edition.
Robert Maltby and Kenneth Belcher.
© 2014 John Wiley & Sons, Inc. Published 2014 by John Wiley & Sons, Inc.

14.1 SUBJUNCTIVE PASSIVE

The subjunctive mood also has passive forms. The simplest way to remember how the present and imperfect subjunctive passive are formed is: take the active forms and change the endings from **-m, -s, -t, -mus, -tis, -nt** to **-r, -ris, -tur, -mur, -mini, -ntur.**

14.1.1 Present Subjunctive Passive

First Conjugation

	SINGULAR	PLURAL
1st person	amer	amēmur
2nd person	amēris	amēminī
3rd person	amētur	amentur

> **FYI** The present and imperfect subjunctives of all conjugations have the alternative 2nd person singular ending -re; for example, *amēre, ponāre* and imperfect *vidērēre.*

Second Conjugation

	SINGULAR	PLURAL
1st person	videar	videāmur
2nd person	videāris	videāminī
3rd person	videātur	videantur

Third Conjugation

	SINGULAR	PLURAL
1st person	ponar	ponāmur
2nd person	ponāris	ponāminī
3rd person	ponātur	ponantur

Fourth Conjugation

	SINGULAR	PLURAL
1st person	inveniar	inveniāmur
2nd person	inveniāris	inveniāminī
3rd person	inveniātur	inveniantur

Mixed Conjugation

	SINGULAR	PLURAL
1st person	capiar	capiāmur
2nd person	capiāris	capiāminī
3rd person	capiātur	capiantur

14.1.2 Imperfect Subjunctive Passive

The easiest way to remember how to form the imperfect subjunctive is: take the present infinitive active and add the endings **-r**, **-ris**, **-tur**, **-mur**, **-mini**, **-ntur**.

First Conjugation

	SINGULAR	PLURAL
1st person	amārer	amārēmur
2nd person	amārēris	amārēminī
3rd person	amārētur	amārentur

Second Conjugation

	SINGULAR	PLURAL
1st person	vidērer	vidērēmur
2nd person	vidērēris	vidērēminī
3rd person	vidērētur	vidērentur

Third Conjugation

	SINGULAR	PLURAL
1st person	ponerer	ponerēmur
2nd person	ponerēris	ponerēminī
3rd person	ponerētur	ponerentur

Fourth Conjugation

	SINGULAR	PLURAL
1st person	invenīrer	invenīrēmur
2nd person	invenīrēris	invenīrēminī
3rd person	invenīrētur	invenīrentur

Mixed Conjugation

	SINGULAR	PLURAL
1st person	caperer	caperēmur
2nd person	caperēris	caperēminī
3rd person	caperētur	caperentur

14.1.3 Perfect Subjunctive Passive

The perfect subjunctive passive, like the perfect indicative passive, has two parts: the perfect participle and in this case the present subjunctive of the verb **sum**.

First Conjugation

	SINGULAR	PLURAL
1st person	amātus, -a, -um sim	amātī, -ae, -a sīmus
2nd person	amātus, -a, -um sīs	amātī, -ae, -a sītis
3rd person	amātus, -a, -um sit	amātī, -ae, -a sint

Second Conjugation

	SINGULAR	PLURAL
1st person	vīsus, -a, -um sim	vīsī, -ae, -a sīmus
2nd person	vīsus, -a, -um sīs	vīsī, -ae, -a sītis
3rd person	vīsus, -a, -um sit	vīsī, -ae, -a sint

Third Conjugation

	SINGULAR	PLURAL
1st person	positus, -a, -um sim	positī, -ae, -a sīmus
2nd person	positus, -a, -um sīs	positī, -ae, -a sītis
3rd person	positus, -a, -um sit	positī, -ae, -a sint

Fourth Conjugation

	SINGULAR	PLURAL
1st person	inventus, -a, -um sim	inventī, -ae, -a sīmus
2nd person	inventus, -a, -um sīs	inventī, -ae, -a sītis
3rd person	inventus, -a, -um sit	inventī, -ae, -a sint

Mixed Conjugation

	SINGULAR	PLURAL
1st person	captus, -a, -um sim	captī, -ae, -a sīmus
2nd person	captus, -a, -um sīs	captī, -ae, -a sītis
3rd person	captus, -a, -um sit	captī, -ae, -a sint

14.1.4 Pluperfect Subjunctive Passive

The pluperfect subjunctive passive, like the pluperfect indicative passive, has two parts: the perfect participle and in this case the imperfect subjunctive of the verb **sum**.

First Conjugation

	SINGULAR	PLURAL
1st person	amātus, -a, -um essem	amātī, -ae, -a essēmus
2nd person	amātus, -a, -um essēs	amātī, -ae, -a essētis
3rd person	amātus, -a, -um esset	amātī, -ae, -a essent

Second Conjugation

	SINGULAR	PLURAL
1st person	vīsus, -a, -um essem	vīsī, -ae, -a essēmus
2nd person	vīsus, -a, -um essēs	vīsī, -ae, -a essētis
3rd person	vīsus, -a, -um esset	vīsī, -ae, -a essent

Third Conjugation

	SINGULAR	PLURAL
1st person	positus, -a, -um essem	positī, -ae, -a essēmus
2nd person	positus, -a, -um essēs	positī, -ae, -a essētis
3rd person	positus, -a, -um esset	positī, -ae, -a essent

Fourth Conjugation

	SINGULAR	PLURAL
1st person	inventus, -a, -um essem	inventī, -ae, -a essēmus
2nd person	inventus, -a, -um essēs	inventī, -ae, -a essētis
3rd person	inventus, -a, -um esset	inventī, -ae, -a essent

Mixed Conjugation

	SINGULAR	PLURAL
1st person	captus, -a, -um essem	captī, -ae, -a essēmus
2nd person	captus, -a, -um essēs	captī, -ae, -a essētis
3rd person	captus, -a, -um esset	captī -ae, -a essent

FIGURE 14.2 Silver denarius, 41 BC. Head of Marc
Antony. Marc Antony, general, ally of Julius Caesar,
lover of Cleopatra, waged war against Octavian (later
Augustus). He was defeated by the forces of Octavian
at the battle of Actium and committed suicide in 30
BC. © *Leeds Museums and Galleries (Discovery Centre)*

14.2 SUBJUNCTIVE OF DEPONENT VERBS

14.2.1 Present Subjunctive

The present subjunctive of deponent verbs is formed in the same manner as the passive of
non-deponent verbs (again, active in meaning as with the indicative mood).

FYI The present and imperfect
subjunctives of all conjugations
have the alternative 2nd person
singular ending *-re*; for example,
arbitrēre, *sequāre* and imperfect
progrederēre.

First Conjugation

	SINGULAR	PLURAL
1st person	arbitrer	arbitrēmur
2nd person	arbitrēris	arbitrēminī
3rd person	arbitrētur	arbitrentur

Second Conjugation

	SINGULAR	PLURAL
1st person	verear	vereāmur
2nd person	vereāris	vereāminī
3rd person	vereātur	vereantur

Third Conjugation

	SINGULAR	PLURAL
1st person	sequar	sequāmur
2nd person	sequāris	sequāminī
3rd person	sequātur	sequantur

Fourth Conjugation

	SINGULAR	PLURAL
1st person	mentiar	mentiāmur
2nd person	mentiāris	mentiāminī
3rd person	mentiātur	mentiantur

Mixed Conjugation

	SINGULAR	PLURAL
1st person	prōgrediar	prōgrediāmur
2nd person	prōgrediāris	prōgrediāminī
3rd person	prōgrediātur	prōgrediantur

14.2.2 Imperfect Subjunctive

The imperfect subjunctive of deponent verbs is formed as follows: take what *would be* the present infinitive *active* and add the endings **-r**, **-ris**, **-tur**, **-mur**, **-mini**, **-ntur**.

First Conjugation

	SINGULAR	PLURAL
1st person	arbitrārer	arbitrārēmur
2nd person	arbitrārēris	arbitrārēminī
3rd person	arbitrāretur	arbitrārentur

Second Conjugation

	SINGULAR	PLURAL
1st person	verērer	verērēmur
2nd person	verērēris	verērēminī
3rd person	verērētur	verērentur

Third Conjugation

	SINGULAR	PLURAL
1st person	sequerer	sequerēmur
2nd person	sequerēris	sequerēminī
3rd person	sequerētur	sequerentur

Fourth Conjugation

	SINGULAR	PLURAL
1st person	mentīrer	mentīrēmur
2nd person	mentīrēris	mentīrēminī
3rd person	mentīrētur	mentīrentur

Mixed Conjugation

	SINGULAR	PLURAL
1st person	prōgrederer	prōgrederēmur
2nd person	prōgrederēris	prōgrederēminī
3rd person	prōgrederētur	prōgrederentur

14.2.3 Perfect Subjunctive

The perfect subjunctive of deponent verbs, like the perfect indicative, has two parts: the perfect participle and in this case the present subjunctive of the verb **sum**.

First Conjugation

	SINGULAR	PLURAL
1st person	arbitrātus, -a, -um sim	arbitrātī, -ae, -a sīmus
2nd person	arbitrātus, -a, -um sīs	arbitrātī, -ae, -a sītis
3rd person	arbitrātus, -a, -um sit	arbitrātī, -ae, -a sint

The perfect subjunctive of the other conjugations follows this pattern.

14.2.4 Pluperfect Subjunctive

The pluperfect subjunctive of deponent verbs, like the pluperfect indicative, has two parts: the perfect participle and in this case the imperfect subjunctive of **sum**.

First Conjugation

	SINGULAR	PLURAL
1st person	arbitrātus, -a, -um essem	arbitrātī, -ae, -a essēmus
2nd person	arbitrātus, -a, -um essēs	arbitrātī, -ae, -a essētis
3rd person	arbitrātus, -a, -um esset	arbitrātī, -ae, -a essent

The pluperfect subjunctive of the other conjugations follows this pattern.

TRY THIS

Deponent and passive forms of the subjunctive.

Parse the following subjunctive forms:

e.g., *deligaris* – 2nd person singular present subjunctive passive of *deligo* – choose

(i) *abitrati essetis*   (vi) *adiuveris*

(ii) *progredereris*   (vii) *aequaretur*

(iii) *sequerentur*   (viii) *cernantur*

(iv) *progrediar*   (ix) *considerentur*

(v) *abstracti essent*   (x) *corrupti sint*

14.3 SEQUENCE OF TENSES

We now come to one of the fundamental rules of Latin: the so-called sequence of tenses. It should be noted first that this deals with (1) subordinate clauses and (2) only those subordinate clauses that require the subjunctive mood (we have already seen clauses, e.g., certain causal clauses, that take the indicative – the sequence of tenses does not apply to these).

Latin sentences are defined as being in primary or secondary (also called historic) sequence. The sequence is determined by the main verb in the sentence.

Primary tenses of the indicative	Secondary tenses of the indicative
Present	Imperfect
Present Perfect (translated as "has" or "have")	Simple perfect
Future	Pluperfect
Future perfect	

If the main verb in the sentence is a primary tense, the verb in a subordinate clause must also be a primary tense of the subjunctive. These are the present and perfect subjunctive.

If the main verb in the sentence is a secondary tense, the verb in a subordinate clause must also be a secondary tense of the subjunctive. These are the imperfect and pluperfect subjunctive.

Primary tenses of the subjunctive	Secondary tenses of the subjunctive
Present	Imperfect
Perfect	Pluperfect

There is a further point to note: if the action of the subordinate clause occurs at the same time or time subsequent to the action of the main verb, in primary sequence the present subjunctive is used; whereas in secondary sequence the imperfect subjunctive is used. If the action of the verb in the subordinate clause appears before the action of the main verb, in primary sequence the perfect subjunctive is used; whereas in secondary sequence the pluperfect subjunctive is used. This will become clearer as more examples are introduced.

14.4 PURPOSE AND RESULT CLAUSES

14.4.1 Purpose Clauses (also called final clauses)

English has a number of ways to express purpose: "in order to" or by an infinitive or by a clause introduced by "that" or "in order that." Latin similarly has a number of ways to express purpose; however, the infinitive is used only very rarely in Latin to express purpose. Instead Latin may use a subordinate clause introduced by **ut** (or, if negative, **nē**) with its verb in the subjunctive. Here the rules of sequence apply, but because the purpose is usually subsequent to the action of the main verb we regularly find either present (in primary sequence) or imperfect subjunctive (in secondary/historic sequence):

mē praemīsit **ut haec nuntiem** uxōrī suae (Plautus *Amphitruo* 195): *he has sent me on ahead **so that I may report these things** to his wife.*

[Dionysius] **nē tonsōrī collum committeret**, tondere filiās suās docuit (Cicero *Tusculanae Disputationes* 5.58): *[Dionysius] had his daughters taught to cut hair **so that he might not entrust** his neck to a barber.*

THE BIGGER PICTURE

Tusculanae Disputationes (*Tusculan Disputations*), a philosophical work, taking its name from Cicero's country villa at Tusculum, written in 45 BC during a retirement from politics, after the *De Finibus* and before the *De Natura Deorum*. Composed in the form of a dialogue in five books the work takes its subject matter from earlier Greek philosophers, including Plato, and discusses such topics as death, pain, distress, and virtue.

The regular words for the indefinite pronouns *anyone*, *someone* and *anything*, *something* in Latin are **aliquis**, **aliqua**, **aliquid**; however, after the conjunctions **sī**, **nisi**, **nē**, and **num** the forms **quis**, **qua**, **quid** are used. Except for the nominative singular and accusative singular (here the forms are: **quem**, **quam**, **quid**) the declension is the same as that of the relative pronoun (see Chapter 7).

> habēs epilogum, **nē quid** praetermissum aut relictum putēs (Cicero *Tusculanae Disputationes* 1.119): *you have the epilogue **so that** you may not think that **anything** has been passed over or omitted.*

> **HINT!** Helpful mnemonic device: the Latin for someone, anyone is *aliquis, aliquid*; however, after *si, nisi, num,* and *ne,* the *ali-* "takes a holiday." That is: instead of *aliquis, aliquid,* Latin uses *quis, quid.*

14.4.2 Result Clauses (also called consecutive clauses)

There is also a class of subordinate clauses in Latin which express the result of the action of the main verb: *he was so seriously wounded (with the result) that he was not able to fight.* In Latin such clauses are introduced by **ut** and have their verb in the subjunctive mood. In result clauses the tense of the subjunctive is, generally speaking, determined by the rules of sequence. Result clauses, when negative as in the example above, are introduced not by **nē** but by **ut** followed by a negative word such as **nōn**. Often there is a word in the main clause which signals that a result clause is coming, for example, the adverbs **tam**, **ita**, **sīc**, and **adeō** (all of which mean **so**) and the adjectives **tantus, -a, -um** – so great, **tālis, -e** – of such a kind, or **tot** – so many (indeclinable adjective).

> **tantus** subitō timor omnem exercitum occupāvit, **ut nōn** mediocriter omnium mentēs animōsque **perturbāret** (Caesar *De Bello Gallico* 1.39.2): ***so great** a fear suddenly took hold of all the army **that it troubled** the minds and hearts of all **in no small way**.*

> sī **tanta** vīs probitātis est . . . **ut** in hoste etiam **dīligāmus** . . . (Cicero *De Amicitia* 29): *if the force of integrity is **so great** . . . **that we love it** even in an enemy . . .*

THE BIGGER PICTURE

*D*e Amicitia (*On Friendship*), a philosophical dialogue on friendship composed in 44 BC, after *De Senectute*. The dialogue is set in 129 BC and the interlocutors are Laelius (who also figures in the *De Senectute*) and his two sons-in-law, Quintus Mucius Scaevola and Gaius Fannius. It was possibly influenced by a now lost Greek treatise on friendship by Theophrastus.

Result clauses generally follow the rules of sequence. However, here exceptions to the rules of sequence do occur: when a primary tense of the subjunctive is used in secondary sequence if the writer wishes to stress that the result is still true at the time of writing (present subjunctive) or that the action is actually completed (perfect subjunctive):

[in Lūcullō] **tanta** prūdentia fuit . . . **tanta** aequitās, **ut hodiē stet** Asia (Cicero *Lucullus* 3): *so great* was the wisdom in Lucullus . . . *so great* his sense of justice *that Asia stands firm today.*

> L ucullus (*Lucullus*), the second of two
> philosophical works written in 45 BC and
> known later as the *Academici Libri* (*Academic Books*). The first version of this work was in two books, the first called *Catulus* and the second called *Lucullus*, after the interlocutors involved. Later Cicero changed the format of the work from two to four books, and changed the names of the interlocutors. Our copy of the *Lucullus* probably goes back to a private copy of this earlier version.
>
> **THE BIGGER PICTURE**

There is another construction you should be aware of: if the emphasis is on the fact that the result is going to occur in the future Latin uses the future participle with the subjunctive of **sum**:

in eam ratiōnem vītae nōs . . . fortūna **dēduxit ut** sempiternus sermō hominum dē nōbīs **futūrus sit** (Cicero *Epistulae ad Quintum Fratrem* 1.1.38): *fortune **has brought** us into such a position of life **that** the talk of men about us **is going to be** everlasting.*

> E pistulae ad Quintum Fratrem (*Letters to His
> Brother Quintus*), a collection of letters by
> Cicero to his younger brother Quintus (without replies), spanning the years 60–54 BC. Like the *Letters to Friends* these were collected and edited by Cicero's secretary, Tiro, and published in this case in three books.
>
> **THE BIGGER PICTURE**

14.5 NOUN CLAUSES INTRODUCED BY *UT*

There are some verbs, often impersonal, that are followed by a noun clause introduced by **ut**. Such clauses are similar to result clauses in that they take the subjunctive mood and are regularly negated not by **nē**, but **ut** plus a negative word:

accidit – it happens (that); perfect: accīdit

ēvenit – it happens (that); perfect: ēvēnit

facio, -ere – I cause; bring it about (that)

FIGURE 14.3 *Cave Canem* ("Beware of the dog"). 1st century AD from Pompeii, House of the Tragic Poet (named after a mosaic found in the *triclinium* (dining room)). *Source: Pompeii, Italy/Alinari/The Bridgeman Art Library*

fit – it happens (that)

fierī potest – it is possible (that)

casu **accidit ut** id quod Romae audierat primus nuntiaret? (Cicero *Pro S. Roscio Amerino* 96): *did **it happen** by chance **that he was the first to report** what he had heard at Rome?*

TRANSLATION FROM LATIN

1. ego Siciliam totam quinquaginta diebus sic obii ut omnium populorum privatorumque litteras iniuriasque cognoscerem. (Cicero *In Verrem* 1.1.6)

2. Iphicrates Atheniensis non tam magnitudine rerum gestarum quam disciplina militari nobilitatus est. fuit enim talis dux, ut non solum aetatis suae cum primis compararetur, sed ne de maioribus natu quidem quisquam anteponeretur. (Nepos *Iphicrates* 1.1)

3. Caesar primum suo, deinde omnium ex conspectu remotis equis, ut aequato omnium periculo spem fugae tolleret, cohortatus suos proelium commisit. (Caesar *De Bello Gallico* 1.25.1)

4. ceteros iam nosti; qui ita sunt stulti ut amissa re publica piscinas suas fore salvas sperare videantur. (Cicero *Epistulae ad Atticum* 1.18.6)

5. neque dixi quicquam pro testimonio nisi quod erat ita notum atque testatum ut non possem praeterire. (Cicero *Epistulae ad Atticum* 1.16.2)

6. nunc vero quae tua est ista vita? sic enim iam tecum loquar, non ut odio permotus esse videar, quo debeo, sed ut misericordia, quae tibi nulla debetur. venisti paulo ante in senatum. quis te ex hac tanta frequentia, tot ex tuis amicis ac necessariis salutavit? (Cicero *In Catilinam* 1.16)

7. ubi eum castris se tenere Caesar intellexit, ne diutius commeatu prohiberetur, ultra eum locum quo in loco Germani consederant, . . . castris idoneum locum delegit. (Caesar *De Bello Gallico* 1.49.1)

8. haec ad Antonium statim per Graecos deferuntur. ille missis ad Caesarem nuntiis unum diem sese castris tenuit, altero die ad eum pervenit Caesar. cuius adventu cognito Pompeius, ne duobus circumcluderetur exercitibus, ex eo loco discedit omnibusque copiis ad Asparagium Dyrrachinorum pervenit atque ibi idoneo loco castra ponit. (Caesar *Bellum Civile* 3.30.6–7)

9. sed plane nec precibus nostris nec admonitionibus relinquit locum, nam cum in sermone cotidiano tum in senatu palam sic egit causam tuam, ut neque eloquentia maiore quisquam nec gravitate nec studio nec contentione agere potuerit, cum summa testificatione tuorum in se officiorum et amoris erga te sui. (Cicero *Epistulae ad Familiares* 1.1.2)

 # TRANSLATION INTO LATIN

1. On the same night it happened that there was a full moon. (Caesar *De Bello Gallico* 4.29.1)

2. Our men, in order that they might attack the enemy in difficulty, were ready in arms. (Caesar *De Bello Gallico* 2.9.2)

3. With a clear voice so that the whole assembly might be able to hear, he said that he knew that that man had committed perjury. (Cicero *Pro Cluentio* 134)

4. All these things, citizens, have been administered by me in such a way that they seem to have been done and looked after by the will and purpose of the immortal gods. (Cicero *In Catilinam* 3.18)

5. I shall make all these things which have lain hidden in long-lasting obscurity so clear that you may seem to see them with your own eyes. (Cicero *Pro Cluentio* 66)

6. Vercingetorix ordered the gates to be closed in order that the camp not be left defense-less. After many were killed, and many horses captured the Germans retreated. (Caesar *De Bello Gallico* 7.70.7)

7. No one at that time offended in such a way that he did not leave grounds for a defense; no one lived in such a way that no part of his life was free from the greatest shameful-ness. (Cicero *In Verrem* 2.2.191)

8. When this battle had ended, in order that he might be able to pursue the remaining forces of the Helvetii, he built a bridge on the Arar and led his army across in this way. (Caesar *De Bello Gallico* 1.13.1)

9. Have you come into this city for this reason: in order that you may corrupt the laws and examples of this city? (Cicero *Pro Rege Deiotaro* 32)

THE BIGGER PICTURE

Pro Rege Deiotaro (*On behalf of King Deiotarus*) – Deiotarus was king of *Armenia Minor* who had helped Cicero with troops in 51 BC during an expected Parthian invasion of the Roman province of Cilicia (in modern Turkey). He had fought for Pompey against Caesar at Pharsalia, but had later been pardoned by Caesar in 47 BC, who helped him regain his kingdom from Mithradates' son, Pharnaces, at the battle of Zama. Two years later Deiotarus was accused by his grandson, Castor, of plotting to murder Caesar after the battle of Zama. Cicero defends him before Caesar, but Caesar was assassinated before he made a decision on the matter.

EXTRA PASSAGE

Catullus addresses a poem to Lesbia's pet sparrow. Poems addressed to pets became popular in the Hellenistic period (following the death of Alexander the Great in 323 BC).

FIGURE 14.4 *Lesbia and Her Sparrow*, Sir Edward John Poynter (1836–1919). Lesbia was the pseudonym that the poet Catullus (c. 95 BC–c. 55 BC) gave to his mistress. A number of poems in his collection deal with his apparent affair with her. *Source: Christie's Images/Photo © Christie's Images/ The Bridgeman Art Library*

Passer, deliciae meae puellae,
quicum[1] ludere, quem in sinu tenere,
cui primum digitum dare appetenti
et acres solet incitare morsus
cum[2] desiderio meo nitenti
carum nescioquid libet iocari,
credo, ut, cum gravis acquiescet ardor,
sit solaciolum sui doloris:
tecum ludere, sicut ipsa, possem[3]
et tristes animi levare curas.

Catullus 2

[1]*quicum = quocum.*

[2]*cum* here (and in line 7 below) = when, introducing a temporal clause.

[3]an optative subjunctive.

VOCABULARY

Nouns; Pronouns

admonitiō, -ōnis (f.) – suggestion; admonition

aetās, -ātis (f.) – life; age; generation

Antōnius, -iī (m.) – Marc Antony, a Roman general

Arar, Araris (m.) – the Arar, a river in Gaul (abl. Arari in Caesar)

Asparāgium, -iī (n.) – a town in Illyria

commeātus, -ūs (m.) – provisions; supplies

consilium, consiliī (n.) – counsel; purpose

cōnspectus, -ūs (m.) – view; sight

contentiō, -ōnis (f.) – exertion; effort

cursus, -ūs (m.) – course

dēfensiō, -ōnis (f.) – defense

Dyrrachīnī, -orum (m. pl.) – the Dyrrachini, a people of Illyria

frequentia, -ae (f.) throng; assembly

gravitās, -tātis (f.) – seriousness; dignity

iniūria, -ae (f.) – injury; injustice

Īphicrates, -is (m.) – Iphicrates, a famous Athenian general (fourth century BC)

locus, -ī (m.) – place; opportunity

lūna, -ae (f.) – moon

maiōrēs, -um natu – ancestors; previous generations

misericordia, -ae (f.) – pity

nāvis, -is (f.) – ship

necessārius, -iī (m.) – friend; relation; close associate

nēmō, nullius – no one

nūtus, -ūs (m.) – nod; will

obscūritās, -tātis (f.) – darkness; obscurity

oculus, -ī (m.) – eye

piscīna, -ae (f.) – fish-pond

quisquam, quaequam, quidquam (or quicquam) – anyone; (with negative) no one

remulcum, -ī (n.) – tow-rope

sēsē = sē (acc. m. sing.)

Sicilia, -ae (f.) – the island of Sicily

tempestās, -tātis (f.) – storm

testificātiō, -ōnis (f.) – testimony

testimōnium, -iī (n.) – evidence

turpitūdō, -inis (f.) – disgrace; shamefulness

Vercingetorix, -igis (m.) – Vercingetorix, a commander of the Gauls

Verbs

abstrahō, -ere, -traxī, -tractum – drag away

adiuvō, adiuvāre, adiūvī, adiūtum – help

aequō, -āre – make equal

antepōnō, -ere, -posuī, -positum – place before

aperiō, -īre, -eruī, -ertum – reveal; make clear

cernō, -ere, crēvī, crētum – perceive; see

claudō, -ere, clausī, clausum – close

cohortor, -ārī, cohortātus sum – encourage

cōnsequor, -ī, consecūtus sum – pursue

cōnsīdō, -ere, -sēdi, -sessum – establish a position; encamp

coorior, -īrī, coortus sum – arise

corrumpō, -ere, -rūpī, -ruptum – break; corrupt

dēferō, -ferre, -tulī, -lātum – announce; report

dēligō, -ere, -lēgi, -lectum – choose

lateō, -ēre, -uī – lie hidden

loquor, -ī, locūtus sum – speak

nōbilitō, -āre – (passive) be famous

noscō, -ere, nōvi, nōtum – come to know; in the perfect = know

nūdō, -āre – strip; lay bare; leave defenseless

obeō, -īre, -iī, -itum – travel through

peccō, -āre – commit an offense

permoveō, -ēre, -mōvi, -mōtum – move deeply; influence

praetereō, -īre, -iī, -itum – pass over; omit

prōvideō, -ēre, -vīdī, -vīsum – act with foresight; look after

relinquō, -ere, -līquī, -lictum – abandon; leave
  behind; give up
salūtō, -āre – greet
sē recipiō, -ere, -cēpī, -ceptum – retreat
teneō, -ēre, -uī, tentum – hold; maintain
tollō, -ere, sustulī, sublātum – take away;
  remove
trādūcō, -ere, -dūxī, -ductum – lead across

Adjectives

alter, -tera, -terum – the other (of two); second
Athēniensis, -e – Athenian
clārus, -a, -um – clear
diūturnus, -a, -um – long-lasting
expers, expertis – without; free from
idōneus, -a, -um (+ dat.) – suitable (for)
impedītus, -a, -um – weighed down; in
  difficulty
nullus, -a, -um – not any; none (translate as
  "not")
onerārius, -a, -um – carrying freight
parātior, -ōris – more ready

plēnus, -a, -um – full
quīnquāgintā (indeclinable) – fifty
summus, -a, -um – greatest
testātus, -a, -um – manifest; attested

Adverbs; Conjunctions; Prepositions

ante = anteā – before
cum . . . tum – not only . . . but also
dē (+ abl.) – from; of (here replacing a partitive
  genitive)
diūtius – longer
ergā (+ acc.) – towards
idcircō – for this reason
nē . . . quidem – not even
nōn sōlum – not only
paulō – a little
statim – at once
subitō – suddenly
tam . . . quam – so (much) . . . as
ultra (+ acc.) – beyond

English Derivations

From which Latin roots do the following English words derive?

(i) contention
(ii) gravity
(iii) oculist
(iv) abstract

CHAPTER 15

FIGURE 15.1 Mosaic from the House of Neptune and Amphitrite (Herculaneum). Neptune was the god of water and, through his association with the Greek god Poseidon, god of the sea. Amphitrite, his wife, was a sea goddess. He was the brother of Jupiter. *Source:* © *Peter Phipp/Travelshots/The Bridgeman Art Library*

Wiley's Real Latin: Learning Latin from the Source, First Edition.
Robert Maltby and Kenneth Belcher.
© 2014 John Wiley & Sons, Inc. Published 2014 by John Wiley & Sons, Inc.

15.1 GERUNDS AND GERUNDIVES

15.1.1 Definitions

The gerund is a verbal noun. In Latin it occurs only in the singular and only in the accusative, genitive, dative, and ablative cases; for the nominative Latin uses the infinitive. Gerunds are active; gerunds occur in English with the ending *-ing* and so it is necessary to distinguish between a gerund and a present participle. Compare ***singing*** *is fun* (gerund) and ***while singing*** *that man was also dancing* (present participle).

The gerundive is a verbal adjective; it occurs in all cases, has gender and number. It declines as an adjective of the first/second declension. As an adjective a gerundive agrees with the noun that it modifies in gender, number, and case; gerundives are passive (even those formed from deponent verbs); there is no English equivalent.

15.1.2 Formation

Both are formed on what may be called the imperfect stem (i.e., remove the ending from the imperfect: inveniē-**bam**) and adding -**nd** before the endings. The gerund has second declension endings:

Nom.	the gerund does not have a nominative form; Latin uses the infinitive: invenīre
Gen.	inveniendī – of finding
Dat.	inveniendō – to/for finding
Acc.	inveniendum – finding
Abl.	inveniendō – by finding

TRY THIS

Give the required case of the gerund for the following verbs:

e.g., *eo* (acc.) – *eundum*

(i) *ceno* (gen.)

(ii) *conficio* (acc.)

(iii) *comparo* (abl.)

(iv) *abdico* (acc.)

(v) *commoneo* (dat.)

(vi) *contemno* (gen.)

(vii) *deligo* (abl.)

(viii) *conicio* (abl.)

(ix) *cunctor* (abl.)

(x) *dico* (gen.)

The gerundive is formed in exactly the same way but has a full declension as a first/second declension adjective:

SINGULAR

	m.	f.	n.
Nom.	inveniendus	invenienda	inveniendum
Gen.	inveniendī	inveniendae	inveniendī
Dat.	inveniendō	inveniendae	inveniendō
Acc.	inveniendum	inveniendam	inveniendum
Abl.	inveniendō	inveniendā	inveniendō
Voc.	inveniende	invenienda	inveniendum

PLURAL

	m.	f.	n.
Nom.	inveniendī	inveniendae	invenienda
Gen.	inveniendōrum	inveniendārum	inveniendōrum
Dat.	inveniendīs	inveniendīs	inveniendīs
Acc.	inveniendōs	inveniendās	invenienda
Abl.	inveniendīs	inveniendīs	inveniendīs
Voc.	inveniendī	inveniendae	invenienda

15.1.3 Uses

Gerund

As noted above there is no nominative of the gerund; instead the infinitive is used:

nōn est bonum **vīvere**, sed bene **vīvere** (Seneca *De Beneficiis* 3.31.4): **living** *(literally:* **to live***) is not a good thing, but* **living** *well <is>.*

The **accusative** is used with the preposition **ad** to express purpose.

quae est enim aut ūtilior aut **ad bene vīvendum** aptior partitio quam illa, quā est ūsus Epicūrus? (Cicero *De Finibus* 1.45): *for what is more useful or more fitting inheritance* **for the purpose of living well** *than that which Epicurus enjoyed?*

Note that although the gerund has certain qualities of a noun, like a verb it is modified by an adverb not an adjective.

The **genitive** is used: (1) with **causā** or **grātiā** to show purpose (both ~ for the sake of):

insimulant hominem **fraudandī causā** discessisse (Cicero *In Verrem* 2.2.59): *they allege that the man absconded* **in order to cheat** *<his creditors>.*

(2) with adjectives such as **cupidus, -a, -um** – desirous (of); eager (for); **memor, -oris** – mindful (of); **perītus, -a, -um** – experienced, skilled (in); **imperītus, -a, -um** – inexperienced, unskilled (in); and nouns such as **cupiditās, -tātis** – desire; **memoria, -ae** – memory; recollection (in this instance the genitive is objective).

> dē impetū animī loquor, **dē cupiditāte vincendī**, dē ardōre mentis ad gloriam (Cicero *Pro Caelio* 76): *I am speaking about the passion of his spirit, **about his desire for winning**, about the eagerness of his mind for glory.*

The **dative** is not particularly common; however, the dative does occur with certain verbs, adjectives, and phrases, for example, **praeficio** – place in charge (of); **operam dare** – pay attention to; **pār, paris** – equal. For an example, see below under gerundives replacing gerunds.

The **ablative** is used: (1) with prepositions; **ex, in, dē** being the commonest:

> nunc nihil dē mē dīcō, sed dē eīs quī **in dīcendō** magnī sunt aut fuērunt (Cicero *Pro Murena* 29): *now I am not speaking at all about myself, but about those who are and have been great **in speaking**.*

(2) as an ablative of means/instrument:

> ad eamque feruntur omnī impetū, hominis autem mens **discendō** alitur et **cogitandō** (Cicero *De Officiis* 1.105): *and they are carried along by every impulse to this [i.e., pleasure]; however, the mind of a person is nurtured **by learning** and **by meditating**.*

Gerundive

The gerundive has a variety of uses. It may be used simply as an attributive adjective. This is not particularly common (e.g., **amandus, -a, -um** – to be loved; loveable; **metuendus, -a, -um** – to be feared; frightening).

> in augendō in ornandō in refellendō magis existumātor **metuendus** quam **admirandus** orātor (Cicero *Brutus* 146): *in praising, in embellishing, in refuting he is a critic **to be feared (frightening)** rather than an orator **to be admired (admirable)**.*

A second and more common use of the gerundive is to replace a gerund followed by a direct object. So, for example, instead of saying **ab spē urbem . . . capiendī** – *from the hope of capturing the city*, Latin more commonly uses a gerundive in agreement with the noun: **ab spē capiendae . . . urbis** (Livy *Ab Urbe Condita* 8.23.12): (literally) *from the hope of the city being captured*.

In the first version **capiendī** is a gerund (noun, active) in the genitive case (genitive after **spē**: hope *of capturing*); **urbem** is accusative, direct object of the gerund. In the second (more idiomatic) version **urbis** is genitive case (again after **spē**: hope *of the city*); **capiendae** is a gerundive (adjective, passive), genitive feminine singular, agreeing with the noun **urbis**. This may seem strange, but it is just one of the various instances where Latin idiom differs from English idiom.

It is perhaps worth noting here that there are examples of gerunds taking a direct object, but this is not the common construction in Classical Latin (except in very specific circumstances).

omnis autem cogitātio mōtusque animī aut **in consiliīs capiendīs** dē rēbus honestīs et pertinentibus ad bene beātēque vīvendum aut in studiīs scientiae cognitiōnisque versābitur (Cicero *De Officiis* 1.19): *moreover all our thought and activity of the mind will be involved either **in making plans** about things that are honorable and related to living well and happily or in the pursuits of knowledge and learning.*

T. Maenium **dilectuī habendō** praefēcērunt (Livy *Ab Urbe Condita* 39.20.5): *they placed Titus Maenius in charge of **carrying out a recruitment**.*

The second passage above is an example of the rare dative (see above under uses of the gerund).

Some Exceptions

The gerund may be used with a direct object with neuter pronouns/adjectives:

consilium est **aliquid faciendī** aut **nōn faciendī** excogitāta ratiō (Cicero *De Inventione* 1.36): *consilium is a reasoned plan **of doing** or **of not doing something**.*

THE BIGGER PICTURE

De Inventione (*On Invention*), an early work of Cicero's on the art of rhetoric, of uncertain date, but written when he was a young man, long before the main rhetorical works *De Oratore*, *Brutus*, and *Orator*. It represents one of the first attempts, along with the un-Ciceronian *Rhetorica ad Herrenium*, to write a systematic rhetorical handbook in Latin.

It may also be used to avoid **-ōrum** . . . **-ōrum**: i.e., to avoid expressions such as *amicōrum vīsendōrum* (although this is not always avoided).

itaque hostēs repentē celeriterque prōcurrērunt, ut spatium **pīla in hostēs coniciendī** nōn darētur (Caesar *Dē Bellō Gallicō* 1.52.4): *and the enemy ran forward so suddenly and so swiftly that no opportunity was given **for throwing javelins against the enemy**.*

Gerundive Expressing Obligation or Necessity

The gerundive is used with forms of the verb **sum** (in any tense) to express necessity (sometimes called the passive periphrastic construction). It is important to note that the construction is always passive; however, the agent, when it occurs in this construction, is expressed not by the ablative, but by the dative case – the so-called **dative of agent**:

quid igitur **nōbīs faciendum est**? (Cicero *In Verrem* 2.4.11): *therefore what **must be done by us** (i.e., **must we do**)?*

quamquam omnia **sunt metuenda**, nihil magis quam perfidiam timēmus (Cicero *Epistulae ad Familiares* 1.5a.2): *although everything **must be feared**, we fear nothing more than treachery.*

TRY THIS

Give the required case and gender of the gerundive from the following verbs:

e.g., *porto* (acc. pl. f.) – *portandas*

(i) *emo* (nom. sing. m.)

(ii) *patefacio* (acc. sing. f.)

(iii) *faveo* (gen. sing. n.)

(iv) *loquor* (gen. pl. m.)

(v) *molior* (nom. pl. n.)

(vi) *luo* (acc. pl. n.)

(vii) *fraudo* (nom. sing. m.)

(viii) *exprobo* (abl. pl. n.)

(ix) *tango* (acc. pl. f.)

(x) *praetereo* (nom. sing. n.)

15.2 SUPINE

We have met the supine as the fourth principal part of regular verbs.

In fact the supine is another type of verbal noun. It does decline but only in the singular and only in the accusative and ablative. So, for, example:

Acc.	dictum	Acc.	audītum
Abl.	dictū	Abl.	audītū

The accusative is the fourth principal part; the ablative has the fourth declension ablative ending.

15.2.1 Uses of the Supine

Accusative

So far we have seen a number of ways in which Latin can express purpose: by means of a clause introduced by **ut** or **nē** having its verb in the subjunctive; **ad** + the gerund or gerundive; **causā** or **grātiā** + the gerund or gerundive. There is yet another construction: the accusative of the supine, without a preposition. This occurs most frequently with verbs of motion (or verbs that imply motion): **eō**; **veniō**; **mittō**:

> **admonitum** venimus tē, nōn **flagitātum** (Cicero *De Oratore* 3.17): *we come **to advise** you, not **to make demands**.*

THE BIGGER PICTURE

*D*e Oratore (*On the Orator*), written in 55 BC, is the first of Cicero's main rhetorical works, to be followed in 46 BC by *Brutus* and *Orator*. The speech takes the form of a dialogue in which notable orators from the present and previous generations discuss the theory of rhetoric at Rome.

Ablative

The use of the ablative is similarly restricted. It is used as an ablative of respect (see below: Uses of Cases) with certain adjectives, for example, **facilis, -e** – easy; **difficilis, -e** – difficult; **mīrābilis, -e** – marvellous; **crēdibilis, -e** – credible; **incrēdibilis, -e** – incredible; **turpis, -e** – shameful; **gravis, -e** – serious; painful. Only a few verbs have ablative supines in common use and the most common are : **dictū**; **audītū**; **vīsū**; **tactū**. The literal translation is *in respect of the saying*; however, the best translation is often simply the English infinitive, for example *to say*:

> accessī viridemque ab humō convellere silvam
> cōnātus, rāmīs tegerem ut frondentibus ārās,
> horrendum et **dictū** videō **mīrābile** monstrum.
>
> (Virgil *Aeneid* 3.24–6):
>
> *I approached and as I attempted to tear from the earth green foliage so that I might cover the altars with leafy branches I saw a monster horrifying and **marvellous to tell**.*

15.3 USES OF CASES

15.3.1 Ablative of Price

The ablative case is used without a preposition with verbs of buying (**emō, -ere**), selling (**vendō, -ere**), etc. to express the price paid.

FIGURE 15.2 Gold aureus AD 96, inscription: CONCORDIA EXERCITUUM. Following the death of the emperor Domitian (who was murdered in September AD 96 and died without an heir), there was the very real danger of another civil war; however, the senate chose Nerva to serve as emperor and his "election" was approved by the armies stationed around the empire. © *Leeds Museums and Galleries (Discovery Centre)*

remissior aliquantō eius fuit aestimatiō quam annōna; nam aestimāvit **dēnāriīs iii** (Cicero *In Verrem* 2.3.214): *the price was somewhat less than the market price; for he placed the value at **three denarii**.*

Note also **magnō** – at a great price; **plūrimō** – at a very great price; **parvō** – at a small price; **minimō** – at a very small price.

condūxit in Palātio **nōn magnō** domum (Cicero *Pro Caelio* 18): ***he rented** a house on the Palatine **at no great price**.*

15.3.2 Ablative of Respect

The ablative is used regularly without a preposition to express the point in respect of which something is measured.

Ennius **ingeniō** maximus, **arte** rudis (Ovid *Tristia* 2.424): *Ennius mightiest **in (respect of) his genius** but rough **in (respect of) his art**.*

[Ennius] qui fuit māior **natū** quam Plautus et Naevius (Cicero *Tusculanae Disputationes* 1.3): *[Ennius] who was older **in (respect of birth) age** than Plautus and Naevius.*

15.3.3 Genitive of Value

The genitive of value is used with verbs of buying, selling, and **esse** and **aestimō** when the precise cost is not given. For example **magnī**, **parvī**, and **tantī**:

magnī enim aestimābat pecūniam (Cicero *De Finibus* 2.55): *for he was accustomed to value money **highly**.*

SOUND BITE   Juvenal on health (Juvenal 10.356)

orandum est ut sit mens sana in corpora sano.

TRANSLATION FROM LATIN

1. loquor enim de docto homine et erudito, cui vivere est cogitare. (Cicero *Tusculanae Disputationes* 5.111)

2. magnopere sibi praecavendum Caesar existimabat. (Caesar *De Bello Gallico* 1.38.2)

3. tum quoque inter tantas fortunae minas metuendus magis quam metuens, "Romanus sum" inquit, "civis; C. Mucium vocant." (Livy *Ab Urbe Condita* 2.12.9)

4. omnia praeteribo quae mihi turpia dictu videbuntur. (Cicero *In Verrem* 2.1.32)

5. Aedui . . . legatos ad Caesarem mittunt rogatum auxilium. (Caesar *De Bello Gallico* 1.11.2)

6. atque illud quod faciendum primum fuit factum atque transactum est. nam P. Lentulus, quamquam patefactis indiciis, confessionibus suis, iudicio senatus non modo praetoris ius verum etiam civis amiserat, tamen magistratu se abdicavit . . . (Cicero *In Catilinam* 3.15)

7. cunctandi causa erat metus undique imminentium discriminum, ut saepe lupum se auribus tenere diceret. nam et servus Agrippae Clemens nomine non contemnendam manum in ultionem domini compararat et L. Scribonius Libo vir nobilis res novas clam moliebatur. (Suetonius *Tiberius* 25.1)

8. ego enim, quam diu senatus auctoritas mihi defendenda fuit, sic acriter et vehementer proeliatus sum ut clamor concursusque maxima cum mea laude fierent. (Cicero *Epistulae ad Atticum* 1.16.1)

   HINT! In Cicero's speeches look for synonyms. He will often say things like "this is a terrible crime and a horrible deed." Note "*acriter et vehementer.*"

9. Gallia est omnis divisa in partes tres, quarum unam incolunt Belgae, aliam Aquitani tertiam qui ipsorum lingua Celtae, nostra Galli appellantur. hi omnes lingua, institutis, legibus inter se differunt. (Caesar *De Bello Gallico* 1.1)

TRANSLATION INTO LATIN

1. Oregetorix is chosen for the purpose of completing these things. (Caesar *De Bello Gallico* 1.3.3)

2. I cannot forget that this is my homeland and that I am the consul of these men, and that I must live with these men or die for them. (Cicero *In Catilinam* 2.27)

3. I have replied to the greatest charges; now I must also reply to those remaining. (Cicero *Philippicae* 2.36)

4. The German war completed, Caesar decided for many reasons that it was necessary for him to cross the Rhine. (Caesar *De Bello Gallico* 4.16.1)

5. When the signal had been given, our men attacked so fiercely and the enemy ran forward so suddenly and swiftly that no opportunity of throwing javelins against the enemy was given. (Caesar *De Bello Gallico* 1.52.3)

6. Caesar made an end of speaking and withdrew to his own men. (Caesar *De Bello Gallico* 1.46.2)

7. It is painful to say but nevertheless it must be said. (Cicero *Philippicae* 9.8)

8. Will this man even now dare to tell me that he sold the tithes for a great price? (Cicero *In Verrem* 2.3.117)

9. Was Verres of such importance to you that you were willing that his lust be satisfied by the blood of innocent people? (Cicero *In Verrem* 2.1.77)

EXTRA PASSAGE

Icarus flies too close to the sun.

> et iam Iunonia laeva
> parte Samos (fuerant Delosque Parosque relictae)
> dextra Lebinthos erat fecundaque melle Calymne,
> cum puer audaci coepit gaudere volatu
> deseruitque ducem caelique cupidine tractus
> altius[1] egit iter. rapidi vicinia solis
> mollit odoratas, pennarum vincula, ceras;
> tabuerant cerae: nudos quatit ille lacertos,
> remigioque[2] carens non ullas percipit auras,
> oraque caerulea patrium clamantia nomen
> excipiuntur aqua,[3] quae nomen traxit ab illo.
> at pater infelix, nec iam pater, "Icare," dixit,
> "Icare," dixit "ubi es? qua te regione requiram?"
> "Icare" dicebat: pennas aspexit in undis
> devovitque suas artes corpusque sepulcro
> condidit, et tellus a nomine dicta sepulti.
>   Ovid *Metamorphoses* 8.220–35

[1] *altius* is a comparative form of the adjective *altus*; here it is neuter and modifies *iter* (i.e., "a loftier path").

[2] literally = oars; also used of wings.

[3] *caerulea* and *aqua* go together – both ablative singular.

FIGURE 15.3 *Icarus Falling*, Paul Ambroise Slodtz (1702–58). Daedalus was a renowned craftsman; among his many creations he built the labyrinth that housed the Minotaur. In order to escape from King Minos of Crete he fashioned wings for himself and his son Icarus (with tragic results). *Source: Louvre, Paris, France/ Giraudon/The Bridgeman Art Library*

VOCABULARY

Nouns; Pronouns

Aeduī, -ōrum (m. pl.; also spelled Haeduī, see
  Chapter 8) – the Aedui, a Gallic tribe
Agrippa, -ae (m.) – Marcus Vipsanius Agrippa,
  a Roman general
auctoritas, -ātis (f.) – authority
auris, -is (f.) – ear
auxilium, auxiliī (n.) – help
C. Mūcius, -iī (m.) – Gaius Mucius (see Chapter
  2)
clāmor, -ōris (m.) – shout
concursus, -ūs (m.) – running; rush
contiō, -ōnis (f.) – meeting
decima, -ae (f.) or decuma, -ae (f.) – tax on
  landholders; tithe
discrīmen, -inis (n.) – crisis
fīnis, -is (m.) – end
indicium, indiciī (n.) – evidence
laus, laudis (f.) – praise
libīdō, -inis (f.) – lust
lupus, -ī (m.) – wolf
magistrātus, -ūs (m.) – magistracy; public office
metus, -ūs (m.) – fear
P. Lentulus, -ī (m.) – Publius Lentulus, a
  fellow-conspirator with Catiline
pīlum, -ī (n.) – javelin
Rhēnus, -ī (m.) – Rhine
sanguis, -inis (m.) – blood
spatium, -iī (n.) – space; space (of time);
  opportunity
ultiō, -ōnis (f.) – act of revenge

Verbs

abdicō, -āre – (with *sē*) resign
cēnō, -āre – dine
commoneō, -ēre, -uī, -itum – remind
comparō, -āre – prepare
conficiō, -ere, -fēcī, -fectum – finish; complete

cōniciō, -ere, -iēcī, -iectum – hurl; throw
contemnō -ere, -tempsī, -temptum – consider
  unimportant; despise
cunctor, -ārī, cunctātus sum – delay
deligō, -ere, -lēgī, -lectum – choose
differō, -ferre, distulī, dīlātum – be different
emō, -ere, ēmī, emptum – buy
exprobō, -are – reproach; charge
faveō, -ēre, fāvī, fautum – be favorable
fraudō, -āre – act illegally; defraud
immineō, -ēre – hang over; threaten
loquor, -ī, locūtus sum – speak
luō, -ere, luī – satisfy
molior, -īrī, molītus sum – undertake; set in
  motion
patefaciō, -ere, -fēcī, -factum – reveal
praecaveō, -ēre – to take care (in advance)
praestō, -āre, praestitī, praestitum – be superior;
  surpass; guarantee
praetereō, -īre, -iī, -itum – pass over; omit
proelior, -ārī, proeliātus sum – battle
sē recipiō, -ere, -cēpī, -ceptum – withdraw
vendō, -ere, -didī, -ditum – sell

Adjectives

ērudītus, -a, -um – clever; skilled; erudite
innocens, -entis – innocent
melior, -iōris – better
probābilior, -iōris – more likely
turpis, -e – foul; disgraceful

Adverbs; Conjunctions; Prepositions

acriter – fiercely
apud (+ acc.) – in the house of
celeriter – swiftly
disertē – eloquently
etiam – and also; even now

fermē – almost; for the most part
magnoperē – greatly
maximus, -a, -um – greatest
nōn modo . . . sed etiam – not only . . . but also

plūrimum – greatest; most
reliquus, -a, -um – remaining
vehementer – vehemently
vērē – truly

English Derivations

From which Latin roots do the following English words derive?

(i) concourse
(ii) magistrate
(iii) sanguine
(iv) laudable

CHAPTER 16

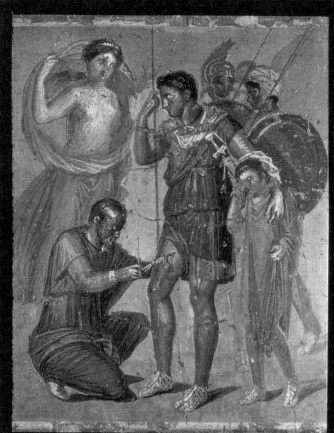

FIGURE 16.1 Wounded Aeneas, fresco from Pompeii, 1st century BC. As described in Book 12 of the *Aeneid*, Aeneas is wounded by an arrow and withdraws from battle. In Virgil's account when the physician Iapyx is unable to remove the arrow-head, Venus provides supernatural potions and the wound is healed. *Source: Museo Archeologico Nazionale, Naples, Italy/The Bridgeman Art Library*

Wiley's Real Latin: Learning Latin from the Source, First Edition.
Robert Maltby and Kenneth Belcher.
© 2014 John Wiley & Sons, Inc. Published 2014 by John Wiley & Sons, Inc.

CHAPTER CONTENTS

We have already seen that Latin has a number of ways to express subordinate temporal clauses, causal clauses, and concessive clauses. Various conjunctions may be used with the indicative mood, for example: **ubi** – when; **postquam** – after; **quia** – since; **quamquam** – although; **simulac** (**simul atque**) – as soon as. Participles may also be used to express these ideas. Perhaps even more common is the conjunction **cum** (not to be confused with the preposition).

16.1 *CUM* CLAUSES

16.1.1 Temporal: Present and Future

Cum is followed by the indicative mood when the reference is to the present or future time. In the latter case, the future perfect commonly occurs in the **cum**-clause. This is especially true when the action of the subordinate clause occurs before the action of the main verb. Consider the following English example: *When he comes/has come, I will see him.* Notice that English rather illogically uses the present tense or the perfect tense in the "when" clause even though his arrival is in the future. Here Latin would use the future perfect because the action of the **cum**-clause is in the future but is completed before the action of the main verb.

Present

dē tē autem, Catilīna, **cum quiescunt**, probant (Cicero *In Catilinam* 1.21): *however, when they are silent about you, Catiline, they show their approval.*

Future

scrībam ad tē **cum** Caesarem **vīderō** (Cicero *Epistulae ad Atticum* 2.1.10): *I shall write to you when I have seen (will have seen) Caesar.*

cum vīderō tē, sciēs (Cicero *Epistulae ad Atticum* 13.22.4): **When I have seen (will have seen)** *you, you will know.*

16.1.2 *Cum* Temporal: Past Time

Temporal clauses introduced by **cum** and referring to past time regularly take the subjunctive. Since by definition the sequence of such sentences is secondary/historic, the imperfect or pluperfect subjunctive is used.

sed merīdiē **cum** Caesar pābulandī causā trēs legiōnēs atque omnem equitātum cum C. Trebōniō legātō **mīsisset**, repentē ex omnibus partibus ad pābulatōrēs advolāvērunt (Caesar *De Bello Gallico* 5.17.3): *but at midday* **when Caesar had sent** *three legions and all the cavalry with Gaius Trebonius, the lieutenant-general, to forage, suddenly <the enemy> rushed from all sides at those foraging.*

However, when the main clause contains **tum** – then, or a similar word, the **cum**-clause regularly takes the indicative, even when the reference is to past time.

tum scripsimus **cum** gubernācula reī pūblicae **tenēbāmus** (Cicero *De Divinatione* 2.3): *we wrote [this]* **at the time when we controlled** *the government of the state.*

16.1.3 *Cum* Causal

Cum may also have a causal force = "since." It is not always easy to tell the difference between **cum**-causal and **cum**-temporal and in fact it often makes little difference to the sense. However, unlike **cum**-temporal, **cum**-causal clauses regularly take the subjunctive in both primary and secondary sequence: **quae cum ita sint**, Catilīna, dubitās . . . abīre in aliquās terrās? (Cicero *In Catilinam* 1.20): **and since these things are so**, *Catiline, do you hesitate to depart to other lands?*

16.1.4 *Cum* Concessive

Cum may also have a concessive force = "although." A concessive sense is usually very easy to recognize from the context. Consider the following English examples: *Since he was a brave leader, the soldiers fought bravely; Although he was a good leader, the soldiers fought bravely.* There is an obvious difference in meaning and the context in Latin is equally useful in deciding the sense of **cum**. For example, the word **tamen** "nevertheless" often appears in the main clause.

cum prīmī ordinēs hostium transfīxī pīlīs **concidissent**, **tamen** acerrimē reliquī resistēbant (Caesar *De Bello Gallico* 7.62.4): **although** *the first ranks of the enemy* **had fallen**, *pierced by the missiles*, **nevertheless** *those who were left resisted most keenly.*

16.2 SUBJUNCTIVE IN RELATIVE CLAUSES

To review: relative clauses are introduced by the relative pronoun, **quī**, **quae**, **quod**. The relative pronoun gets its gender and number from its antecedent (the word in the main clause to which it refers or "relates"); it gets its case from its grammatical function in its own clause. Regularly the verb in the relative clause is in the indicative mood. However, there are a number of specific instances where the subjunctive is used. Two of the commonest examples of this are relative clauses of purpose (final clauses) and the so-called generic subjunctive (sometimes called relative clause of characteristic).

16.2.1 Relative Clause of Purpose

The relative clause of purpose occurs most frequently with verbs of motion, verbs of "sending," and the like. Here the relative clause is more than simply descriptive. Compare the following English examples: *He sent the messengers who knew the region* (descriptive; verb in the indicative); *He sent messengers who might report what had happened* (= to report what had happened; purpose; verb in the subjunctive). The verb in relative clauses of purpose goes into the subjunctive mood and the tense of the subjunctive is determined, as is regularly the case, by the Rules of sequence.

> Agrigentīnī ad istum lēgātōs mittunt **quī** eum lēgēs **doceant** consuētūdinemque omnium annōrum **dēmonstrent** (Cicero *In Verrem* 2.2.124): *The Agrigentines send envoys to him to (literally: who may)* **explain** *to him their laws and to* **indicate** *<to him> the customary usage of all years past.*

16.2.2 Generic Subjunctive/Relative Clause of Characteristic

The generic subjunctive occurs in relative clauses where once again the clause is more than simply descriptive. Compare the following English examples: *There are those who say the world is flat; There are those (of the type) who would say that the world is flat.* Notice that the first example is merely descriptive whereas the second describes a "class" or "type" of individual. The difference is between those who actually say that the world is flat and those who would or may say that the world is flat. In the second type of clause Latin uses the subjunctive and the tense of the subjunctive is regularly determined by the rules of sequence.

There are a number of phrases in Latin which are frequently followed by this type of clause:

Sunt (erant, etc.) quī

Nēmō est quī

Quis est quī?

Nihil est quod

Is est (tu es; ego sum, etc.) quī

Multī sunt quī

Notice that any tense may be used in these expressions and not all of these phrases occur only in the 3rd person.

> **Quis est quī** fraudātiōnis causā latuisse **dīcat, quis quī** absentem dēfensum **neget** esse Quinctium? (Cicero *Pro Quinctio* 74): **who is there who would say** *that Quinctius remained hidden for the sake of fraud;* **who is there who would deny** *that he was defended while he was absent?*

16.2.3 Relative Clause of Result

Sometimes a relative clause is used to express result. Such clauses regularly take the subjunctive; often **tam**, **ita**, or **sīc** will appear in the main clause:

> quis enim est **tam excors, quem** ista moveant? (Cicero *Tusculanae Disputationes* 1.11): *for who is* **so foolish that** *(literally: whom) these things influence* **him?**

Identify the verbs in the following passage (including participles, infinitives, gerunds, and gerundives) and parse them (you will need to use a dictionary to complete this exercise):

e.g., *cano* 1st person singular, present indicative active of *cano, canere, cecini, cantum* – sing

Arma virumque cano, Troiae qui primus ab oris
Italiam fato profugus Laviniaque venit
litora, multum ille et terris iactatus et alto
vi superum, saevae memorem Iunonis ob iram,
multa quoque et bello passus, dum conderet urbem
inferretque deos Latio; genus unde Latinum
Albanique patres atque altae moenia Romae.
Musa, mihi causas memora, quo numine laeso
quidve dolens regina deum tot volvere casus
insignem pietate virum, tot adire labores
impulerit. tantaene animis caelestibus irae?

(Virgil *Aeneid* 1.1–11)

16.3 PRONOMINAL ADJECTIVES

The following adjectives in Latin show certain variations in their declension: **alter, altera, alterum** – one (of two); **alius, alia, aliud** – other, another (genitive here is **alterius, alterius, alterius**); **neuter, neutra, neutrum** – neither; **nullus, -a, -um** – no, none; **sōlus, -a, -um** – alone, only; **tōtus, -a, -um** – whole; **ullus, -a, -um** – any; **ūnus, -a, -um** – one; **uter, utra, utrum** – which (of two).

The variations occur only in the singular: the genitive singular ends in **-ius** (for all three genders) and the dative singular regularly in **-i** (again for all three genders. For example:

	m.	f.	n.
Nom.	tōtus	tōta	tōtum
Acc.	tōtum	tōtam	tōtum
Gen.	**tōtius**	**tōtius**	**tōtius**
Dat.	**tōtī**	**tōtī**	**tōtī**
Abl.	tōtō	tōtā	tōtō

All of the adjectives listed regularly decline this way in the singular (and some naturally occur only in the singular), with one exception: the genitive of **alius** is regularly replaced by the adjective **alienus** – *belonging to* another – or the genitive of **alter** (**alterius**).

[Caesar] post eās **tōtius exercitūs** impedimenta conlocāverat (Caesar *De Bello Gallico* 2.19): *after them he had placed the baggage **of the whole army**.*

FIGURE 16.2 Romano-British Samian ware shard, date unknown. Samian ware, or *terra sigillata*, refers to good quality ceramic table ware, with a smooth red/orange glossy surface. It was at its most common in the time of Augustus. Plautus refers to it as easily breakable: *Bacchides* 200 "confringi vas cito Samium solet" (a Samian vessel is easily broken). © *Leeds Museums and Galleries (Discovery Centre)*

TRANSLATION FROM LATIN

1. ille cum exercitum nullum habuisset, repente conflavit: hic eum exercitum quem accepit amisit. (Cicero *Philippicae* 4.15)

2. bello Helvetiorum confecto totius fere Galliae legati principes civitatum ad Caesarem gratulatum convenerunt. (Caesar *De Bello Gallico* 1.30.1)

3. huic officio praepositus erat Fufius Calenus legatus, qui celeritatem in transportandis legionibus adhiberet. (Caesar *Bellum Civile* 3.8.2)

4. equites a Q. Atrio ad Caesarem venerunt, qui nuntiarent superiore nocte maxima coorta tempestate prope omnes naves adflictas atque in litus eiectas esse. (Caesar *De Bello Gallico* 5.10.2)

5. nemo erat videlicet aratorum qui iniuriam sibi factam queri posset, nemo decumanorum qui grano amplius sibi quam deberetur deberi professus esset. (Cicero *In Verrem* 2.3.29)

6. Caesari cum id nuntiatum esset eos per provinciam nostram iter facere conari, maturat ab urbe proficisci et quam maximis potest itineribus in Galliam ulteriorem contendit et ad Genavam pervenit. (Caesar *De Bello Gallico* 1.7.1)

7. Caesar cum in Asiam venisset, reperiebat T. Ampium conatum esse pecunias tollere Epheso ex fano Dianae eiusque rei causa senatores omnes ex provincia evocavisse ut his testibus . . . uteretur. (Caesar *Bellum Civile* 3.105.1)

8. quod ad me saepe scripsisti de nostro amico placando, feci, et expertus sum omnia, . . . ; quibus de suspicionibus, etsi audisse te arbitror, tamen ex me cum veneris cognosces. (Cicero *Epistulae ad Atticum* 1.3.3)

9. Quid tempestates autumni et sidera dicam,
atque, ubi iam breviorque dies et mollior aestas,
quae vigilanda viris? vel cum ruit imbriferum ver,
spicea iam campis cum messis inhorruit et cum
frumenta in viridi stipula lactentia turgent?

(Virgil *Georgics* 1.311–16)

FIGURE 16.3 Plowing mosaic, 3rd century AD. Originally Roman plows just worked the soil without turning it. By the time of Pliny the Elder in the late first century AD a wheeled plow with a coulter (blade to cut through the soil) was introduced, which was usually pulled by oxen. The fallow soil was first plowed in spring, followed by later plowings with a lighter blade to prepare the seed bed. Virgil recommends plowing and sowing in the warm seasons of the year: *Georgics* 1.299 "nudus ara, sere nudus" (plow and sow while lightly clad). *Source: Musée des Antiquités Nationales, St. Germain-en-Laye, France/Giraudon/The Bridgeman Art Library*

TRANSLATION INTO LATIN

1. I see nothing which I may hope or may now suppose could happen. (Cicero *Epistulae ad Atticum* 10.1.3)

2. Now arguments must be sought by which this may be refuted. How I wish that I may be able to find the truth as easily as show the false. (Cicero *De Natura Deorum* 1.91)

3. There is no one who would think that there is any hope of safety remaining. (Cicero *In Verrem* 2.5.12)

4. Pompey, although he had not in any way indicated to me that he was offended, set out for Sardinia and Africa. (Cicero *Epistulae ad Familiares* 1.9.9)

5. Having heard a noise behind and when they saw that their own men were being killed, the Germans threw away their weapons, abandoned their military standards and rushed out of the camp. (Caesar *De Bello Gallico* 4.15.1)

6. Although the first ranks of the enemy had fallen pierced by javelins, nevertheless the remainder were resisting most eagerly. (Caesar *De Bello Gallico* 7.62.4)

7. The Aedui, since they were not able to defend themselves and their property from these men, sent envoys to Caesar to ask for help. (Caesar *De Bello Gallico* 1.11.2)

8. I have a certain way and means whereby I can investigate and pursue all the endeavors of those men. (Cicero *In Verrem* 1.1.48)

9. Compelled by these things the Menapii send legates to him for the sake of seeking peace. (Caesar *De Bello Gallico* 6.6.2)

EXTRA PASSAGE

Tibullus describes the Golden Age when there was no sailing and no fighting.

Quam bene Saturno vivebant rege, priusquam
   tellus in longas est patefacta vias!
nondum caeruleas pinus contempserat undas,
   effusum ventis praebueratque sinum,
nec vagus ignotis repetens conpendia terris
   presserat externa navita merce ratem.
illo non validus subiit iuga tempore taurus,
   non domito frenos ore momordit equus,
non domus ulla fores habuit, non fixus in agris,
   qui regeret certis finibus arva, lapis.
ipsae mella dabant quercus, ultroque ferebant
   obvia securis ubera lactis oves.
non acies, non ira fuit, non bella, nec ensem
   immiti saevus duxerat arte faber.
nunc Iove sub domino caedes et vulnera semper,
   nunc mare, nunc leti mille repente viae.
                    (Tibullus 1.3.35–50)

Ovid also describes the Golden Age.

Aurea prima sata est aetas, quae vindice nullo,
sponte sua, sine lege fidem rectumque colebat.
poena metusque aberant, nec verba minantia fixo
aere legebantur, nec supplex turba timebat
iudicis ora sui, sed erant sine vindice tuti.
nondum caesa suis, peregrinum ut viseret orbem,
montibus in liquidas pinus descenderat undas,
nullaque mortales praeter sua litora norant;
nondum praecipites cingebant oppida fossae;
non tuba derecti, non aeris cornua flexi,
non galeae, non ensis erat: sine militis usu
mollia securae peragebant otia gentes.
ipsa quoque inmunis rastroque intacta nec ullis
saucia vomeribus per se dabat omnia tellus,
contentique cibis nullo cogente creatis
arbuteos fetus montanaque fraga legebant
cornaque et in duris haerentia mora rubetis
et quae deciderant patula Iovis arbore glandes.
                    (Ovid *Metamorphoses* 1.89–106)

Compare the two passages.

VOCABULARY

Nouns

aedis, -is (f.) – building; temple

aestās, -ātis (f.) – summer

Africa, -ae (f.) – Africa

arātor, -ōris (m.) – ploughman; cultivator

argūmentum, -ī (n.) – argument

autumnus, -ī (m.) – autumn

auxilium, auxiliī (n.) – help

clāmor, -ōris (m.) – shout; noise

decumānus, -ī (m.) – tax gatherer

fānum, -ī (n.) – temple

frūmentum, -ī (n.) – corn; grain; ear of corn

Fūfius Calēnus, -ī (m.) – Fufius Calenus, a tribune of the plebs

Gallia ulterior, Galliae ulterioris (f.) – further Gaul (the area of Gaul across the Alps)

Genāva, -ae (f.) – Geneva

impedimenta, -ōrum (n.) – baggage

legātus, -ī (m.) – ambassador; envoy

messis, -is (f.) – harvest

ordo, -inis (m.) – rank

pābulātor, -ōris (m.) – forager

pīlum, -ī (n.) – javelin

Pompeius, -ī (m.) – Pompey

princeps, principis (m.) – prince; chief

Sardinia, -ae (f.) – Sardinia

sīdus, -eris (n.) – star

signum, -ī (n.) – military standard

stipula, -ae (f.) – stalk

tempestās, -ātis (f.) – time; weather; storm

tergum, -ī (n.) – back; in tergum – in the rear; behind

vēr, vēris (n.) – spring

vetustās, -ātis (f.) – long duration; great age

Verbs

abiciō, -ere, -iēcī, -iectum – throw away

adflīgō, -ere, -flīxī, -flictum – strike; batter; wreck

adhibeō, -ēre, -uī, -itum – show; display

āmittō, -ere, -mīsī, -missum – send away; lose

concidō, -ere, -cidī – fall in battle; fall

conflō, -āre – bring together; raise (an army)

conlocō, -āre – place; station

contendō, -ere, contendī, contentum – make for; hasten to; march

convincō, -ere, -vīcī, -victum – win over; demonstrate; show

experior, -īrī, expertus sum – try

grātulor, -ārī, grātulātus sum – congratulate

inhorreō, -ēre – grow spiky

iter faciō, -ere – march

lateō, -ēre, latuī – lie hidden

maturō, -āre – hasten

moveō, -ēre, mōvī, mōtum – move

neglegō, -ere, -lēxī, -lectum – neglect; disregard

offendō, -ere, offendī, offensum – displease; offend

ostendō, -ere, ostendī, ostensum – show; indicate

pābulō, -āre – forage (for food)

plācō, -āre – placate

praepōnō, -ere, -posuī, -positum – (+ dat.) put in charge (of)

profiteor, -ērī, professus sum – declare; confess; admit

quaerō, -ere, quaesīvī, quaesītum – seek

refellō, -ere, -fellī – disprove; refute

ruō, ruere, ruī, rutum – rush

taceō, -ēre, -uī, -itum – keep silent

transfīgō, -ere, -fīxī, -fīxum – transfix

turgeō, -ēre, tursī – swell

vigilō, -āre – watch; be vigilant

Adjectives

alius, alia, aliud – other; another

alter, altera, alterum – one (of two); the other (of two)

brevior, -ōris – shorter

dissolūtus, -a, -um – careless; dissolute

excors, -cordis – senseless; stupid
falsus, -a, -um – false
imbrifer, -era, -erum – rain-bringing
lactēns, -entis – milky
militāris, -e – belonging to a soldier; military
mollior, -ōris – milder
neuter, neutra, neutrum – neither (of two)
nullus, -a, -um – no; none
sōlus, -a, -um – alone; only
spīceus, -a, -um – made of ears of corn
superior, -ius – (of time) previous
tōtus, -a, -um – whole
ullus, -a, -um – any

uter, utra, utrum – which (of two)
viridis, -e – green

Adverbs; Prepositions; Conjunctions

acerrimē – most eagerly
facilē – easily
illuc – to that place
repentē – suddenly
tam . . . quam – as . . . as
vidēlicet – evidently; clearly (literally = "it is
    plain to see")

English Derivations

From which Latin roots do the following English words derive?

(i) vernal
(ii) principle
(iii) tempestuous
(iv) offense

FIGURE R.2 Silver denarius, 32–28 BC. Head of Augustus. Born in 63 BC, Octavius was adopted by Julius Caesar and, following the assassination of Caesar in 44 BC, took the name Gaius Julius Caesar Octavianus. He defeated Antony at the battle of Actium and in 27 BC was given the title of Augustus, becoming in effect, the first "emperor" of the Roman world. © *Leeds Museums and Galleries (Discovery Centre)*

(A) Explain the case of the noun underlined:
1. duo templa se <u>Romae</u> dedicaturum voverat.
2. tanta <u>prudentia</u> fuit ut hodie stet Asia.
3. Ennius <u>ingenio</u> maximus, arte rudis.
4. legatos ad Caesarem mittunt rogatum <u>auxilium</u>.
5. ut lupum se <u>auribus</u> tenere diceret.

(B) Identify and explain the verb/verb form underlined:
1. legatos ad Caesarem mittunt <u>rogatum</u> auxilium.
2. omnia praeteribo quae mihi turpia <u>dictu</u> videbantur.
3. magnopere sibi <u>praecavendum</u> Caesar existimabat.
4. <u>vivere</u> est cogitare.
5. <u>admonitum</u> venimus te.
6. quid nobis <u>faciendum est?</u>
7. tanta prudentia fuit ut hodie <u>stet</u> Asia.
8. me praemisit ut haec <u>nuntiem</u>.
9. habes epilogum ne quid relictum <u>putes</u>.

(C) Supply the following verb parts:
1. cognosco – 3rd person plural imperfect subjunctive passive
2. imitor – 2nd person singular perfect indicative active
3. decerno – ablative gerund
4. consulo – supine (accusative)
5. pareo – genitive gerund
6. libero – 1st person singular pluperfect subjunctive active
7. repeto – present passive infinitive
8. revertor – 2nd person singular future indicative active
9. reperio – 3rd person singular perfect subjunctive passive

(D) Translate into English:
1. dicamus bona verba: venit Natalis ad aras. (Tibullus 2.2.1)
2. post hoc proelium classem LXX navium Athenienses eidem Miltiadi dederunt, ut insulas, quae barbaros adiuverant, bello persequeretur. (Nepos *Miltiades* 7.1)
3. tanta enim erat auctoritas et vetustas illius religionis ut, cum illuc irent, non ad aedem Cereris sed ad ipsam Cererem proficisci viderentur. (Cicero *In Verrem* 2.4.108)
4. satis id est magnum, quod potes praestare, ut in iudiciis ea causa, quamcumque tu dicis, melior et probabilior esse videatur, ut in contionibus et in sententiis dicendis ad persuadendum tua plurimum valeat oratio, denique ut prudentibus diserte, stultis etiam vere videare dicere. (Cicero *De Oratore* 1.44)

(E) Translate into Latin:
1. Let us not choose what is difficult. (Cicero *In Verrem* 2.4.15)
2. Such a great storm suddenly arose that no ship could maintain its course. (Caesar *De Bello Gallico* 4.28.2)
3. I shall say this not for the sake of reproaching you but to remind you. (Cicero *Pro S. Roscio Amerino* 45)
4. Who is of such dissolute spirit that he is able to keep silent and disregard these things when he sees them? (Cicero *Pro S. Roscio Amerino* 32)

CHAPTER 17

FIGURE 17.1 Foot in sandal, fragment of a statue (75–25 BC). Footwear and sandals came in various shapes and styles. Different materials were used, including leather and cork. As happens today, styles of sandals changed over the years but often came back into fashion. © *Leeds Museums and Galleries (Discovery Centre)*

Wiley's Real Latin: Learning Latin from the Source, First Edition.
Robert Maltby and Kenneth Belcher.
© 2014 John Wiley & Sons, Inc. Published 2014 by John Wiley & Sons, Inc.

17.1 DIRECT QUESTIONS

Latin has a number of ways to pose a question. We have already met the interrogative pronoun **quis**, **quid** and adverbs such as **cur** – why?; **quōmodo** – how?; **ubi** where? Here the indicative mood is regularly used:

> sed **cur** tam diū dē ūnō hoste **loquimur**? (Cicero *In Catilinam* 2.17): *but **why are we speaking** for so long about one enemy?*

English frequently poses a question by inverting the subject and verb (statement: *You can say this*; question: *Can you say this?*); however, Latin clearly cannot do this. Even if the subject is expressed and follows the verb, the Latin sentence is not necessarily a question. In order to make clear that a question is intended, Latin frequently attaches **-ne** to the end of the first (or rarely the second or third) word in the sentence:

> **potesne** dīcere? (Cicero *Tusculanae Disputationes* 1.67): ***can you (are you able to) say?***

However, sometimes simple questions have no word to indicate that a question is being posed. Here context makes it clear that a question is being asked:

> patēre tua consilia non sentis? (Cicero *In Catilinam* 1.1): *do you not realize that your plans are revealed?*

For questions of the type *Surely you remember, don't you?* where the answer "yes" is expected, Latin uses the word **nōnne**:

> **nōnne** senatūs consultum dē Vatiniō **vidēs**? (Cicero *De Natura Deorum* 3.13): ***surely you see** the decree of the senate concerning Vatinius, **don't you?***

For questions of the type *Surely you do not believe him, do you?* where the answer "no" is expected, Latin uses the word **num**:

> **num** negāre **audēs**? (Cicero *In Catilinam* 1.8) ***surely you do not dare** to deny <it>, **do you?***

17.1.1 Alternative Direct Questions

Alternative questions offer a choice: *Do you love this man or do you hate him?* In Latin, there are three different ways of expressing the first type where a true alternative is given:

> **ūtrum** tandem abstulistī **an** ēmistī? (Cicero *In Verrem* 2.4.29): *did you take them, I ask, **or** did you buy them?*

> **vōsne** vērō L. Domitium, **an** vōs Domitius dēseruit? (Caesar *Bellum Civile* 2.32.8): *did you desert Lucius Domitius **or** did Domitius desert you?*

> ēloquar **an** sileam? (Virgil *Aeneid* 3.39): *am I to speak out **or** am I to be silent?*

That is **ūtrum . . . an; -ne . . . an; (no word to introduce first alternative) . . . an**.

Where the alternative is merely the negative of the first, e.g., *Do you love this man or not?* the words **an nōn** are used (sometimes written as one word: **annōn**). The first part may be introduced by **ūtrum**, or **-ne** or no introductory word:

> **isne** est quem quaerō **an nōn**? (Terence *Phormio* 852): *Is he the man whom I am seeking or not?*

17.2 INDIRECT QUESTIONS

As we have seen, Latin expresses indirect statements differently from English: the accusative and infinitive construction. Indirect questions also have a different construction. In English the indicative mood is regularly used: *You ask **why I am** an enemy to one against whom the Roman people are opposed*. In Latin the verb in an indirect question is in the subjunctive and the tense of the subjunctive is regularly determined by the rules of sequence:

> **quaeris cūr** eī **sim** inimīcus cuī populus Rōmānus infestus est? (Cicero *In Verrem* 2.3.7): *do you ask **why I am** an enemy to this man to whom the Roman people is hostile?*

> Verres **quaerēbātur ubi esset** Cleomenes (Cicero *In Verrem* 2.5.107): *Verres **was asked where** Cleomenes **was**.*

Indirect questions follow the rules of sequence; however, if the indirect question refers to future time, the future participle is used with the subjunctive of **sum** (compare result clauses – see Chapter 14). In primary sequence, the present subjunctive is used with the participle; in secondary/historic sequence, the imperfect subjunctive:

> <cōnsiderābimus> quid **factūrus sit**, quid ipsī **cāsūrum sit**, quā sit **ūsūrus ōrātiōne** (Cicero *De Inventione* 1.36): *<we will consider> what **he will/is going to do**, what will/ is going to happen to him, what speech **he will/is going to use**.*

It should be noted that when **num** introduces an indirect question, it no longer suggests a question expecting the answer "no"; rather it means "if" or "whether":

> quaerendum, crēdo, est Heius iste **num** aes aliēnum habuerit (Cicero *In Verrem* 2.4.11): *we must ask, I suppose, **if** this man, Heius, was in debt.*

Note that the introductory verb need not be a verb of "asking":

> **exspectābant** omnes . . . **quidnam actūrus esset** (Cicero *In Verrem* 2.5.161): *all **were awaiting** <to see> . . . **what he was going to do**.*

17.2.1 Alternative Indirect Questions

The same options apply as for direct alternative questions: **ūtrum . . . an; -ne . . . an; (no word to introduce first alternative) . . . an**. However, if the second is merely a negative of the first **necne** is used and not **an non**.

> **quaesīvī** ā Catilīnā in nocturnō conventū **fuisset necne** (Cicero *In Catilinam* 2.13): *I asked Catiline **whether he had been** at the meeting at night **or not**.*

17.3 VERBS WITH THE DATIVE

HINT! A transitive verb, by definition, is followed by a direct object in the accusative case. By this definition all verbs that are followed by the genitive, dative, or ablative are intransitive.

A number of verbs in Latin are followed by the dative case (and so may be called intransitive verbs):

> **credet hīs equitibus Rōmānīs** populus Rōmānus (Cicero *In Verrem* 2.1.13): *the Roman people **will believe these Roman knights**.*

It is important to note that the English verb *believe* is transitive, that is, takes a direct object. Many of the verbs that take the dative in Latin have an English translation that is transitive. See the vocabulary for a partial list of verbs that take the dative case.

17.4 IMPERSONAL PASSIVE

Verbs followed by the genitive, dative, or ablative (intransitive verbs) present a problem when one tries to make them passive. Latin, however, has a way of getting around this problem: the impersonal third person singular is used in the passive voice and the genitive, dative, or ablative is retained:

> **omnibus hīs resistitur** (Caesar *Bellum Civile* 1.4.1): ***all these are resisted*** *(literally: there is resistance to all these).*

> **Manilio** et **Luscio** negas **esse credendum**? (Cicero *Pro Q. Roscio Comoedo* 43): *are you saying that **Manilius** and **Luscio must not be believed**?*

Notice here that *credendum* is neuter singular (impersonal) and that the dative is retained (literally: "are you saying that there must not be belief to Manilius and Luscius?"). In this construction, if the agent is expressed *ab* + ablative is used instead of the dative of agent in order to avoid confusion.

In addition there are a number of other intransitive verbs that are used impersonally; for example, **itur** – there is movement/people are coming, and **curritur** – there is a rush, and **concurritur** – there is a rushing together/men come together.

Identify the verbs in the following passage (including participles, infinitives, gerunds, and gerundives) and parse them (you will need to use a dictionary to complete this exercise):

> Cynthia prima suis miserum me cepit ocellis,
> contactum nullis ante cupidinibus.
> tum mihi constantis deiecit lumina fastus
> et caput impositis pressit Amor pedibus,
> donec me docuit castas odisse puellas
> improbus, et nullo vivere consilio.
> ei mihi, iam toto furor hic non deficit anno,
> cum tamen adversos cogor habere deos.
> Milanion nullos fugiendo, Tulle, labores
> saevitiam durae contudit Iasidos.
> nam modo Partheniis amens errabat in antris,
> rursus in hirsutas ibat et ille feras.
> (Propertius 1.1.1–12)

17.5 USES OF THE CASES

17.5.1 Predicative/Interest/Double Dative

The dative is also used in certain expressions in place of a nominative or accusative. This use occurs especially with forms of the verb **sum** as well as **dūcō** and **habeō** (both used in the sense *consider*). This dative is called predicative and almost invariably occurs with a second dative indicating the person interested (dative of interest). This construction with two datives is often called the double dative construction.

Some examples:

(alicuī) odiō esse – to be a source of hatred (to someone)

(alicuī) impedimentō esse – to be a hindrance

(alicuī) honōrī esse – to be honorable

(alicuī) dolōrī esse – to be a source of sorrow

(alicuī) bonō esse – to be profitable

(alicuī) labōrī esse – to be a burden

(alicuī) quaestuī esse/habēre – to be/to consider as a source of gain

neminī meus adventus **labōrī** aut **sumptuī fuit** (Cicero *In Verrem* 2.1.16): *my arrival caused labor or expense to no one.*

in Asiam īre nōluī quod et **celebritās mihi odiō est** et . . . abesse longē nōlēbam (Cicero *Epistulae ad Atticum* 3.19.1): *I was unwilling to go to Asia because **a large crowd is a source of hatred to me** . . . and I was unwilling to be far away <from Rome>.*

TRANSLATION FROM LATIN

1. quaesivi quae causa fuisset cur bona non venissent, cum ex edicto possiderentur. (Cicero *Pro Quinctio* 88)

2. at quaerebat etiam paulo ante de me quid suo mihi opus fuisset auxilio. (Cicero *In Pisonem* 18)

3. utrum cetera nomina in codicem accepti et expensi digesta habes an non? (Cicero *Pro Q. Roscio Comoedo* 9)

4. non enim utrum indignum sit an non, sed factumne sit, quaeritur. (Cicero *Rhetorica ad Herennium* 2.46)

5. Hirtius noster tardius convalescit. quid futurum sit plane nescio; spes tamen una est aliquando populum Romanum maiorum similem fore. (Cicero *Epistulae ad Familiares* 12.22.2)

6. quaero enim cur Licinium titubantem, haesitantem, cedentem, fugere conantem mulieraria manus ista de manibus emiserit, cur non comprenderint, cur non ipsius confessione, multorum oculis, facinoris denique voce tanti sceleris crimen expresserint. (Cicero *Pro Caelio* 66)

7. hoc cum ceterae gentes sic arbitrantur, tum ipsis Siculis ita persuasum est ut in animis eorum insitum atque innatum esse videatur. (Cicero *In Verrem* 2.4.106)

8. tertium est genus eorum qui uri appellantur. hi sunt magnitudine paulo infra elephantos, specie et colore et figura tauri. magna vis eorum est et magna velocitas; neque homini neque ferae, quam conspexerunt, parcunt. (Caesar *De Bello Gallico* 6.28.3)

9. multa enim falsa de me audiverunt; multa ad eos improbi detulerunt, quorum commoda, ut vos optimi testes estis, semper ego sententia, auctoritate, oratione firmavi: sed credunt improbis, credunt turbulentis, credunt suis. (Cicero *Philippicae* 12.29)

TRANSLATION INTO LATIN

1. He also asked why I had returned from that very journey so suddenly. I have recently explained, Conscript Fathers, the cause of my return. (Cicero *Philippicae* 2.76)

2. When I know on what day I am going to come, I will see that you know. (Cicero *Epistulae ad Atticum* 16.8.1)

3. We are not acquainted with you; we do not know who you are; we have never seen you before. (Cicero *In Q. Caecilium* 20)

4. But I am asking whether we think something was accomplished in the past days or nothing. (Cicero *Tusculanae Disputationes* 5.15)

5. Perhaps this which I am about to say may seem wondrous to hear but surely I shall say what I feel. (Cicero *In Pisonem* 32)

6. Whom of us do you think does not know what you did last night, what you did on the night before last, where you were, and whom you summoned together? (Cicero *In Catilinam* 1.1)

7. In general those are believed who are experts. (Cicero *Topica* 74)

8. If you have been persuaded, why would you want to learn from me? (Cicero *De Natura Deorum* 3.7)

9. I know that these new things brought forward and invented by you have been a source of gain for you. (Cicero *In Verrem* 2.3.16)

THE BIGGER PICTURE

Topica (*The Topics*), a short work on rhetoric, similar to the *De Inventione*, dedicated to the lawyer Trebatius. Cicero claims it is a translation of Aristotle's *Topics*, but it bears little resemblance to this treatise and is probably derived from a later Hellenistic rhetorical work that Cicero adapts from memory.

FIGURE 17.2 Romano-British copper alloy buckle, 2nd century AD. Minerals came to Rome from a number of areas as the empire expanded. Different mining techniques were employed and mine shafts as deep as 1115 feet have been discovered. Oil lamps were used to light the mine. Mine workers were often slaves but prisoners of war and convicts were also used. © *Leeds Museums and Galleries (Discovery Centre)*

EXTRA PASSAGES

A love poem to Lesbia

Vivamus, mea Lesbia, atque amemus,
rumoresque senum severiorum[1]
omnes unius aestimemus assis.
soles occidere et redire possunt:
nobis, cum semel occidit brevis lux,
nox est perpetua una dormienda.
da mi basia mille, deinde centum,
dein mille altera, dein secunda centum,
deinde usque altera mille, deinde centum.
dein, cum milia multa fecerimus,
conturbabimus illa, ne sciamus,
aut nequis malus invidere possit,
cum tantum sciat esse basiorum.

(Catullus 5)

[1]Comparative form of the adjective *severus*, genitive masculine plural; translate "rather severe" or "stricter."

A response to Lesbia's reply

Quaeris, quot mihi basiationes
tuae, Lesbia, sint satis superque.
quam magnus numerus Libyssae harenae
laserpiciferis[2] iacet Cyrenis,
oraclum Iovis inter aestuosi
et Batti veteris sacrum sepulcrum;
aut quam sidera multa, cum tacet nox,
furtivos hominum vident amores:
tam te basia multa basiare
vesano satis et super Catullo est,
quae nec pernumerare curiosi
possint nec mala fascinare lingua.

(Catullus 7)

[2]"producing silphium," which was used in medicine.

VOCABULARY

Nouns; Pronouns

acceptum, -ī (n.) – credit; income

aes aliēnum, aeris aliēnī (n.) – debt; loan

aliquis, aliquid – someone; something; anyone; anything

cōdex, -icis (m.) – book; account book

color, -ōris (m.) – color

commodum, -ī – advantage; interest

conventus, -ūs (m.) – meeting

elephantus, -ī (m.) – elephant

expensum, -ī (n.) – payment; expense

figūra, -ae (f.) – figure; shape

Hirtius, -iī (m.) – Aulus Hirtius, an acquaintance of Cicero

Licinius, -iī – Publius Licinius, a friend of Caelius

nōmen, -inis (n.) – name; item (in an account book)

reditus, -ūs (m.) – return

senātūs consultum, -ī (n.) – decree of the senate

speciēs, -ēī (f.) – appearance

sumptus, -ūs (m.) – expense

taurus, -ī (m.) – bull

testis, -is (m.) – witness; (testicle)

urus, -ī (m.) – wild ox; ure-ox

Verbs Taking the Dative

crēdō, -ere, crēdidī, crēditum – believe; entrust

dēferō, -ferre, -tulī, -lātum – report; denounce; accuse

faveō, -ēre, fāvī, fautum – favor

firmō, -āre – confirm; support

haesitō, -āre – hesitate

ignoscō, -ere, ignōvī, ignōtum – forgive

imperō, -āre – (+ dat.) order

invideō, -ēre, invīdī, invīsum – envy

irascor, irascī, irātus sum – be angry with

noceō, -ēre, nocuī, nocitum – harm

obsequor, obsequī, obsecūtus sum – submit to; obey

obstō, -stāre, -stitī, -stātum – stand in the way of; hinder

parcō, -ere, pepercī, parsum – spare

pāreō, pārēre, pāruī, pāritum – obey

persuādeō, -ēre, persuāsī, persuāsum – persuade

placeō, -ēre, placuī, placitum – please

resistō, -ere, restitī – resist

serviō, -īre, servi(v)ī, servitum – serve

studeō, -ēre, studuī – be eager; apply onself to; study

suādeō, -ēre, suāsī, suāsum – advise

subveniō, -īre, subvēnī, subventum – help

Other Verbs

agō, -ere, ēgī, actum – do; accomplish

audeō, -ēre, ausus sum – dare

auferō, auferre, abstulī, ablātum – steal; take away

cadō, -ere, cecidī, cāsum – fall; happen

dēserō, -ere, dēseruī, dēsertum – desert

dīgerō, -ere, -gessī, -gestum – separate; arrange

discō, -ere, didicī – learn

expōnō, -ere, -posuī, -positum – explain

noscō, -ere, nōvī, notum – become acquainted with; (in perfect) know; be acquainted with

possideō, -ēre, -sēdī, -sessum – hold; possess

prōferō, -ferre, -tulī, -lātum – bring forward

quaerō, -ere, quaesīvī, quaesītum – ask; inquire

revertō, -ere, -vertī, -versum – return

sentiō, -īre, sēnsī, sensum – perceive; feel

sileō, -ēre, -uī – be silent

titubō, -āre – totter; stagger; be in doubt; waver

veneō, -īre, -iī (or īvī), -ītum – be sold

Adjectives

conscriptus, -a, -um – elected; conscript (title for senators)

improbus, -a, -um – bad; wicked

infestus, -a, -um – hostile

innātus, -a, -um – inborn; innate

insitus, -a, -um – implanted; fixed

mulierārius, -a, -um – belonging to a woman;
    sent by a woman

superior, -ius – past; previous

tertius, -a, -um – third

turbulentus, -a, -um – restless; troublesome

Adverbs; Conjunctions

certē – certainly; surely

forsitan – perhaps

plānē – clearly; entirely

tardius – more slowly

English Derivations

From which Latin roots do the following English words derive?

(i) sumptuary

(ii) imperative

(iii) credit

(iv) irate

FIGURE 17.3 Temple of Mithras, Carrawburgh, Hadrian's Wall, Northumberland, England. Founded in the 3rd century AD near a military base. Mithras was an Indo-Iranian god, adopted by the Romans. For the Romans, Mithras was a sun-god and his cult flourished especially in the 2nd and 3rd centuries AD. *Source: courtesy Sally Baume*

CHAPTER 18

FIGURE 18.1 Fragment of stone sculpture, horse's muzzle. 75–25 BC. There are references in literature to horses being ridden. They were used in warfare, racing, and hunting and there is evidence they were used as a mode of travel by wealthy Romans (including women). © *Leeds Museums and Galleries (Discovery Centre)*

Wiley's Real Latin: Learning Latin from the Source, First Edition.
Robert Maltby and Kenneth Belcher.
© 2014 John Wiley & Sons, Inc. Published 2014 by John Wiley & Sons, Inc.

18.1 IMPERATIVE MOOD

Recall that the term "mood" refers to the type of action described by the verb. So far we have dealt with two moods: the indicative (the mood of "fact") and the subjunctive (the mood of "potentiality," etc.). In this chapter the imperative mood, the mood of command, is introduced.

The only forms commonly in use are 2nd person singular and 2nd person plural. There is a certain logic to this inasmuch as commands are usually directed to someone in the second person: *(you) do this!* Active and passive forms occur; however, with a few exceptions, passive forms are common only with deponent verbs (passive in form but active in meaning).

18.1.1 Active

SINGULAR	PLURAL
amā	amāte
vidē	vidēte
pone	ponite
cape	capite

There are three verbs that have a slightly different form in the 2nd person singular: from **dīco** – **dīc**; from **dūco** – **dūc**; from **facio** – **fac** (and their compounds; for example **educ**); however, their plural forms are regular (for example **dicite**). The 2nd person singular imperative of the verb **fero** is **fer** and the plural **ferte**.

FYI For the so-called future imperative, see Appendix 7.

audīte relīqua et diligenter **attendite** (Cicero *In Verrem* 2.3.72): **listen to** *the rest and* **pay** *careful* **attention**.

18.1.2 Passive

SINGULAR	PLURAL
amāre	amāminī
vidēre	vidēminī
ponere	poniminī
invenīre	invenīminī
capere	capiminī

Notice that the 2nd person singular is the same form as the alternative form of the present indicative 2nd person singular (see Chapter 7). You can see that the forms **amare** and **amāminī** – be loved, are rather unlikely to occur; rather these passive forms occur for the most part with deponent verbs.

18.1.3 *Sum*

SINGULAR	PLURAL
es	este

18.1.4 Deponents

As you would expect, the imperatives of deponent verbs are passive in form but active in meaning.

SINGULAR	PLURAL
arbitrāre	arbitrāminī
verēre	verēminī
sequere	sequiminī
mentīre	mentīminī
prōgredere	prōgrediminī

> signō datō "**sequiminī** mē" inquit (Caesar *Bellum Civile* 3.91.2): *when the signal had been given, "**Follow** me," he said.*

18.2 NEGATIVE COMMANDS (PROHIBITIONS)

In prose negative commands are expressed by the imperative of the verb **nōlō** (literally = be unwilling) followed by an infinitive. The singular is **nōlī** and the plural is **nōlīte**:

> aude hoc saltem dīcere quod necesse est; **nōlī metuere**, Hortensī (Cicero *In Verrem* 2.5.45): *dare to say this at least since it is necessary; **do not be afraid**, Hortensius.*

Sometimes a negative command is expressed by **nē** followed by the perfect subjunctive:

> **nē transiēris** Hibērum (Livy *Ab Urbe Condita* 21.44.6): ***do not cross** the Ebro.*

18.3 INDIRECT/REPORTED COMMANDS

We have examined constructions such as indirect/reported statement and indirect/reported questions and now we come to indirect commands. Indirect commands are introduced by **ut** (for a positive indirect command) or **nē** (for a negative indirect command). The verb is in the subjunctive mood and the tense is determined by the rules of sequence. However, since it is unlikely someone will be ordered to do something he or she has already done, the command is always subsequent to the main verb and so only the present subjunctive or imperfect subjunctive is used: the present in primary sequence; the imperfect in secondary/historic sequence. Many verbs take this construction: **imperō** – order; **persuādeō** – persuade; **petō** – ask; beg; **rogō** – ask; **moneō** – warn; **hortor** – encourage, to name a few. The one verb of "ordering" that does not take this construction is **iubeō**, which regularly takes an accusative and infinitive construction:

> **HINT!** *Rogo* can mean *ask a question* (and therefore may be followed by an indirect question) or *ask* in the sense of demand (in which case it is followed by an indirect command).

> **petis ā** mē **ut** Bibulō tē quam dīligentissimē **commendem** (Cicero *Epistulae ad Familiares* 2.17.6): ***you beg** of me **that I recommend** you to Bibulus as strongly as possible.*

> sub vesperum Caesar **portās claudī militēsque** ex oppidō **exīre iussit** (Caesar *De Bello Gallico* 2.33.1): *towards evening Caesar **ordered the gates to be closed** and **the soldiers to leave** the town.*

TRY THIS

Identify the verbs in the following passage (including participles, infinitives, gerunds, and gerundives) and parse them (you will need to use a dictionary to complete this exercise):

> Arma gravi numero violentaque bella parabam
>   edere, materia conveniente modis.
> par erat inferior versus – risisse Cupido
>   dicitur atque unum surripuisse pedem.
> "Quis tibi, saeve puer, dedit hoc in carmina iuris?
>   Pieridum vates, non tua turba sumus.
> quid, si praeripiat flavae Venus arma Minervae,
>   ventilet accensas flava Minerva faces?
> quis probet in silvis Cererem regnare iugosis,
>   lege pharetratae Virginis arva coli?
> crinibus insignem quis acuta cuspide Phoebum
>   instruat, Aoniam Marte movente lyram?"
>   (Ovid *Amores* 1.1–12)

18.4 USES OF CASES

18.4.1 Verbs Governing the Genitive

We have seen that some Latin verbs are followed by the dative case even though their English equivalents take a direct object. There are also verbs in Latin that are followed by the genitive, for example: verbs of **condemning**, **accusing**, and **acquitting** (**condemnāre**, **accūsāre**, **absolvere**) take the genitive of the charge; verbs of remembering, forgetting, and pitying (**meminī, oblīviscor, misereor**); certain impersonal verbs, such as **pudet** – it shames; **piget** – it troubles; **paenitet** – it repents; **taedet** – it wearies, take the *accusative of the person* and the *genitive of what causes the feeling*.

Note also the construction with **refert** – it concerns, and **interest** – it matters, which are followed by the *genitive of the person* or the *ablative feminine singular of the possessive adjective* (*meā, tuā*, etc.).

> **nihil** enim **meā** iam **refert** (Cicero *In Pisonem* 39): *for **it does not** now **concern me at all**.*

> audīte, quaeso, iūdicēs, et aliquandō **miserēminī sociōrum** (Cicero *In Verrem* 2.1.72): *listen, please, judges, and at last **take pity on your allies***

> Crasse, **pudet mē tuī** (Cicero *In Pisonem* 58): *Crassus, **I am ashamed of you**.*

18.4.2 Verbs Governing the Ablative

There are also verbs that are followed by the ablative, for example: **fungor** – perform; fulfil; **fruor** – enjoy; **ūtor** – use; **potior** – win; gain; **careō** – lack; **egeō** – need:

> **pecūniā meā** tot annōs **ūtitur** P. Quinctius (Cicero *Pro Quinctio* 43): *Publius Quinctius **has used** (literally: uses) **my money** for so many years.*

> quamquam abest ā culpā, **suspiciōne** tamen **nōn caret** (Cicero *Pro S. Roscio Amerino* 56): *although he is without guilt, nevertheless **he is not free from suspicion**.*

 # TRANSLATION FROM LATIN

1. peto abs te, ut haec cures diligenter. (Cicero *Epistulae ad Atticum* 1.9.2)

2. recita Cn. Fanni testimonium. nolite Cn. Fannio dicenti credere, noli, inquam, tu, Q. Titini, Cn. Fannio, fratri tuo, credere; dicit enim rem incredibilem. (Cicero *In Verrem* 2.1.128)

3. Pompeium et hortari et orare etiam liberius accusare et monere, ut magnam infamiam fugiat, non desistimus. (Cicero *Epistulae ad Familiares* 1.1.2)

4. regni cupiditate inductus coniurationem nobilitatis fecit, et civitati persuasit ut de finibus suis cum omnibus copiis exirent. (Caesar *De Bello Gallico* 1.2.1)

5. commoda quibus utimur lucemque qua fruimur spiritumque quem ducimus ab eo Iove Optimo Maximo dari videmus. (Cicero *Pro S. Roscio Amerino* 131)

6. primum a Chrysogono peto ut pecunia fortunisque nostris contentus sit, sanguinem et vitam ne petat. (Cicero *Pro S. Roscio Amerino* 7)

7. nonne aut in tabulis aut in testibus omnis exspectatio iudicum est? (Cicero *In Verrem* 2.1.27)

8. si adfinitatis inter vos, si conubii piget, in nos vertite iras; nos causa belli, nos vulnerum ac caedium viris ac parentibus sumus. (Livy *Ab Urbe Condita* 1.13.3)

9. quae cum ita sint, Catilina, perge quo coepisti: egredere aliquando ex urbe; patent portae; proficiscere. nimium diu te imperatorem tua illa Manliana castra desiderant. educ tecum etiam omnis tuos, si minus, quam plurimos; purga urbem. (Cicero *In Catilinam* 1.10)

TRANSLATION INTO LATIN

1. He ordered these men to learn what Ariovistus was saying and report back to him. (Caesar *De Bello Gallico* 1.47.)

2. Look and consider closely what defense you are going to use; for you will realize that you must confess this about the statues. (Cicero *In Verrem* 2.2.149)

3. Do not then wish for that which cannot happen and by the immortal gods, take care, Conscript Fathers, that you do not lose a lasting peace because of the hope of present peace. (Cicero *Philippicae* 7.25)

4. I am ashamed to write more things to you about this matter. (Cicero *Epistulae ad Familiares* 4.5.6)

5. Ariovistus demanded that Caesar not bring any infantry to the meeting. (Caesar *De Bello Gallico* 1.42.4)

6. Gnaeus Domitius, prefect of the cavalry, surrounding Curio with a few horsemen, urges him to seek safety by flight and to hurry to the camp and he promises that he will not leave him. (Caesar *Bellum Civile* 2.42.3)

7. These are great things that I am speaking about, believe me. Do not make light of them. Everything must be stated; everything must be demonstrated; everything must be explained. (Cicero *In Caecilium* 39)

8. Who of us can forget what great moderation he [Lepidus] exercised in the crisis of the state that followed the death of Caesar? (Cicero *Philippicae* 5.38)

9. If we want to enjoy peace, it is necessary to wage war; if we reject war, we shall never enjoy peace. (Cicero *Philippicae* 7.19)

FIGURE 18.2 Romano-British pottery beaker, 3rd century AD. Roman pottery was made throughout the empire. By the 2nd century AD local industry was flourishing in various centers in Britain. © *Leeds Museums and Galleries (Discovery Centre)*

EXTRA PASSAGE

Catullus writes on the death of Lesbia's sparrow.

Lugete, o Veneres Cupidinesque,
et quantumst[1] hominum venustiorum!
passer mortuus est meae puellae,
passer, deliciae meae puellae,
quem plus illa oculis suis amabat:
nam mellitus erat suamque norat
ipsam tam bene quam puella matrem,
nec sese a gremio illius movebat,
sed circumsiliens modo huc modo illuc
ad solam dominam usque pipiabat.
qui nunc it per iter tenebricosum
illuc, unde negant redire quemquam.
at vobis male sit, malae tenebrae
Orci, quae omnia bella devoratis:
tam bellum mihi passerem abstulistis.
o factum male, quod, miselle passer,
tua nunc opera meae puellae
flendo turgiduli rubent ocelli!
                         (Catullus 3)

[1] *quantumst = quantum est*;
translate "all there are."

VOCABULARY

Nouns

adfīnitās, -ātis (f.) – relationship; family ties

caedēs, -is (f.) – slaughter

Chrysogonus, -ī (m.) – Lucius Cornelius Chrysogonus, Roscius' accuser

Cn. Fannius, -iī (m.) – Gnaeus Fannius, brother of Q. Titinius

colloquium, -iī (n.) – conference; meeting

coniūrātiō, -ōnis (f.) – conspiracy

cōnūbium, cōnūbiī (n.) – marriage

cupiditās, -tātis (f.) – desire; greed

defensio, -ōnis (f.) – defense

eques, -itis (m.) – horseman; cavalry

exspectātiō, -ōnis (f.) – expectation

fīnēs, -ium (m. pl.) – territory

fraudātor, -ōris (m.) – cheat

impudentia, -ae (f.) – impudence

infāmia, -ae (f.) – disgrace

infitiātor, -ōris – bad debtor; defaulter

īra, -ae (f.) – anger

iūdex, -icis (m.) – judge

manipulāris, -is (m.) – common soldier

moderātiō, -ōnis (f.) – moderation

nōbilitās, -tātis (f.) – nobility

parens, -entis (m.) – parent

pax, pācis (f.) – peace

praeda, -ae (f.) – booty

praefectus, -ī (m.) – commander; prefect

Q. Titinius, -iī (m.) – Quintus Titinius, a jurist and Fannius' brother (see above)

reus, -ī (m.) – defendant

spīritus, -ūs (m.) – air; breath

statua, -ae (f.) – statue

tabula, -ae (f.) – written document; will

tabulae, -ārum (f. pl.) – records

tempus, -oris (n.) – time; crisis

testimōnium, testimōniī (n.) – testimony; evidence

testis, -is (m.) – witness

vulnus, -eris (n.) – wound

Verbs

absolvō, -ere, absolvī, absolūtum (+ acc. + gen.) – absolve (someone) of

accusō, -āre (+ acc. + gen.) – accuse (someone) of

careō, -ēre, caruī (+ abl.) – lack

caveō, -ēre, cavī, cautum – be on one's guard; take care

circumsistō, -ere, -stitī – surround

condemnō, -āre (+ acc. + gen.) – accuse; condemn (someone) of something

confiteor, -ērī, confessus sum – confess

contemnō, -ere, contempsī, contemptum – make light of

curō, -āre – care for; look after

dēsīderō, -āre – miss; long for

dēsistō, -ere, -stitī, -stitum – desist; give over; (+ abl.) desist (from)

discēdō, -ere, -cessī, -cessum (+ *ab* + abl.) – leave

dissimulō, -āre – pretend that something is not so

ēdūcō, -ere, -dūxī, -ductum – lead out

egeō, -ēre, eguī (+ abl.) – lack, need

explicō, -āre – explain

fruor, fruī, fructus sum (+ abl.) – enjoy

fungor, fungī, functus sum (+ abl.) – fulfill

hortor, -ārī, hortātus sum – encourage; urge

indūcō, -ere, -duxī, -ductum – induce

interest – it matters

mandō, -āre (+ dat.) – order; command

meminī, meminisse – remember

misereor, -ērī, miseritus sum (+ gen.) – pity

necō, -āre – kill

oblīviscor, oblīviscī, oblītus sum (+ gen.) – forget

omittō, -ere, -mīsī, -missum – give up; neglect;
    reject
paenitet – it repents; it displeases
pateō, -ēre, patuī – lay open
pergō, -ere, perrexī, perrectum – proceed
perspiciō, -ere, -spexī, -spectum – look into;
    consider closely
piget – it troubles
potior, -īrī, potītus sum (+ abl.) – take
    possession of
pudet – it shames
purgō, -āre – purge; cleanse
recitō, -āre – recite; read out
ūtor, ūtī, ūsus sum (+ abl.) – use; exercise

Adjectives

eximius, -a, -um – excellent; outstanding
incrēdibilis, -e – incredible

Manliānus, -a, -um – belonging to Manlius
militāris, -e – relating to the military
perpetuus, -a, -um – enduring; lasting
quantus, -a, -um – how great

Adverbs

diligenter – diligently
igitur – therefore; then
impūnē – with impunity
līberius – more freely
saltem – at least

English Derivations

From which Latin roots do the following English words derive?

(i) infamy
(ii) predator
(iii) absolution
(iv) circumstance

FIGURE 18.3 Close-up of
the Colosseum, Rome.
Source: courtesy Anna Reeve

CHAPTER 19

FIGURE 19.1 Gold aureus, AD 125–8. Wolf and twins (Romulus and Remus). Minted during the reign of the emperor Hadrian (AD 117–38). The motif/myth of the wolf and twins continued to be a powerful image for the Romans. © *Leeds Museums and Galleries (Discovery Centre)*

Wiley's Real Latin: Learning Latin from the Source, First Edition.
Robert Maltby and Kenneth Belcher.
© 2014 John Wiley & Sons, Inc. Published 2014 by John Wiley & Sons, Inc.

19.1 DEGREES OF COMPARISON: COMPARATIVE AND SUPERLATIVE

Latin adjectives and adverbs, like their English counterparts, exist in three degrees of comparison: positive (adjective: brave; adverb: bravely); comparative (adjective: braver, more brave, quite brave; adverb: more bravely); superlative (adjective: bravest, most brave, very brave; adverb: most bravely, very bravely).

19.1.1 Comparative Adjectives

The positive degree is the form we have already met: **dignus**, **felix**, etc. To form the masculine and feminine comparative, add -**ior** to the stem and to form the neuter add -**ius**: **dignior**, **dignius** – more worthy. Even if the positive degree belongs to the first/second declension, the comparative declines in the same way as third declension non-i-stem nouns:

	SINGULAR			PLURAL		
	m.	f.	n.	m.	f.	n.
Nom.	dignior	dignior	dignius	digniōrēs	digniōrēs	digniōra
Gen.	digniōris	digniōris	digniōris	digniōrum	digniōrum	digniōrum
Dat.	digniōrī	digniōrī	digniōrī	digniōribus	digniōribus	digniōribus
Acc.	digniōrem	digniōrem	dignius	digniōrēs	digniōrēs	digniōra
Abl.	digniōre	digniōre	digniōre	digniōribus	digniōribus	digniōribus
Voc.	dignior	dignior	dignius	digniōrēs	digniōrēs	digniōra

Notice that the stem (from the genitive singular) is **digniōr**-.

The comparative of third declension adjectives declines in exactly the same way:

	SINGULAR			PLURAL		
	m.	f.	n.	m.	f.	n.
Nom.	fēlīcior	fēlīcior	fēlīcius	fēlīciōrēs	fēlīciōrēs	fēlīciōra
Gen.	fēlīciōris	fēlīciōris	fēlīciōris	fēlīciōrum	fēlīciōrum	fēlīciōrum
Dat.	fēlīciōrī	fēlīciōrī	fēlīciōri	fēlīciōribus	fēlīciōribus	fēlīciōribus
Acc.	fēlīciōrem	fēlīciōrem	fēlīcius	fēlīciōrēs	fēlīciōrēs	fēlīciōra
Abl.	fēlīciōre	fēlīciōre	fēlīciōre	fēlīciōribus	fēlīciōribus	fēlīciōribus
Voc.	fēlīcior	fēlīcior	fēlīcius	fēlīciōrēs	fēlīciōrēs	fēlīciōra

19.1.2 Superlative Adjectives

To form the superlative find the stem of the positive degree in the normal way and add -**issimus**, -**issima**, -**issimum** for the nominative singular; the remaining forms have the same case endings as regular first/second declension adjectives:
dignus, -**a**, -**um**

	SINGULAR			PLURAL		
	m.	**f.**	**n.**	**m.**	**f.**	**n.**
Nom.	dignissimus	dignissima	dignissimum	dignissimī	dignissimae	dignissima
Gen.	dignissimī	dignissimae	dignissimī	dignissimōrum	dignissimārum	dignissimōrum
Dat.	dignissimō	dignissimae	dignissimō	dignissimīs	dignissimīs	dignissimīs
Acc.	dignissimum	dignissimam	dignissimum	dignissimōs	dignissimās	dignissima
Abl.	dignissimō	dignissimā	dignissimō	dignissimīs	dignissimīs	dignissimīs
Voc.	dignissime	dignissima	dignissimum	dignissimī	dignissimae	dignissima

The superlative of third declension adjectives declines in exactly the same way as that of first/second declension adjectives (i.e., belongs to the second declension):

fēlīx, fēlīcis

	SINGULAR			PLURAL		
	m.	**f.**	**n.**	**m.**	**f.**	**n.**
Nom.	fēlīcissimus	fēlīcissima	fēlīcissimum	fēlīcissimī	fēlīcissimae	fēlīcissima
Gen.	fēlīcissimī	fēlīcissimae	fēlīcissimi	fēlīcissimōrum	fēlīcissimārum	fēlīcissimōrum
Dat.	fēlīcissimō	fēlīcissimae	fēlīcissimo	fēlīcissimīs	fēlīcissimīs	fēlīcissimīs
Acc.	fēlīcissimum	fēlīcissimam	fēlīcissimum	fēlīcissimōs	fēlīcissimās	fēlīcissima
Abl.	fēlīcissimō	fēlīcissimā	fēlīcissimo	fēlīcissimīs	fēlīcissimīs	fēlīcissimīs
Voc.	fēlīcissime	fēlīcissima	fēlīcissimum	fēlīcissimī	fēlīcissimae	fēlīcissima

19.1.3 Adjectives in -*er*

Adjectives in -**er** form their comparatives in the regular way: stem + -**ior** (neuter -**ius**):

tener, -era, -erum

	SINGULAR			PLURAL		
	m.	**f.**	**n.**	**m.**	**f.**	**n.**
Nom.	tenerior	tenerior	tenerius	teneriōrēs	teneriōrēs	teneriōra
Gen.	teneriōris	teneriōris	teneriōris	teneriōrum	teneriōrum	teneriōrum
Dat.	teneriōrī	teneriōrī	teneriōrī	teneriōribus	teneriōribus	teneriōribus
Acc.	teneriōrem	teneriōrem	tenerius	teneriōrēs	teneriōrēs	teneriōra
Abl.	teneriōre	teneriōre	teneriōre	teneriōribus	teneriōribus	teneriōribus
Voc.	tenerior	tenerior	tenerius	teneriōrēs	teneriōrēs	teneriōra

ācer, -cris, -cre

	SINGULAR			PLURAL		
	m.	f.	n.	m.	f.	n.
Nom.	ācrior	ācrior	ācrius	ācriōrēs	ācriōrēs	ācriōra
Gen.	ācriōris	ācriōris	ācriōris	ācriōrum	ācriōrum	ācriōrum
Dat.	ācriōrī	ācriōrī	ācriōrī	ācriōribus	ācriōribus	ācriōribus
Acc.	ācriōrem	ācriōrem	ācrius	ācriōrēs	ācriōrēs	ācriōra
Abl.	ācriōre	ācriōre	ācriōre	ācriōribus	ācriōribus	ācriōribus
Voc.	ācrior	ācrior	ācrius	ācriōrēs	ācriōrēs	ācriōra

Notice that if the stem contains an "e," it remains throughout; however, if the "e" is dropped from the stem, it is dropped throughout.

The superlative of **-er** adjectives is formed in a slightly different way: double the "r" at the end of the masculine singular and add **-imus**:

	SINGULAR			PLURAL		
	m.	f.	n.	m.	f.	n.
Nom.	ācerrimus	ācerrima	ācerrimum	ācerrimī	ācerrimae	ācerrima
Gen.	ācerrimī	ācerrimae	ācerrimī	ācerrimōrum	ācerrimārum	ācerrimōrum
Dat.	ācerrimō	ācerrimae	ācerrimō	ācerrimīs	ācerrimīs	ācerrimīs
Acc.	ācerrimum	ācerrimam	ācerrimum	ācerrimōs	ācerrimas	ācerrima
Abl.	ācerrimō	ācerrima	ācerrimō	ācerrimīs	ācerrimīs	ācerrimīs
Voc.	ācerrime	ācerrima	ācerrimum	ācerrimī	ācerrimae	ācerrima

TRY THIS

Identify the verbs in the following passage (including participles, infinitives, gerunds, and gerundives) and parse them (you will need to use a dictionary to complete this exercise):

e.g., *cano* 1st person singular, present indicative active of *cano, canere* "to sing"

ita velut defuncti regis imperio in proxima alluvie
ubi nunc ficus Ruminalis est – Romularem vocatam ferunt –
pueros exponunt. vastae tum in his locis solitudines erant.
tenet fama cum fluitantem alveum, quo expositi erant pueri,
tenuis in sicco aqua destituisset, lupam sitientem ex montibus
qui circa sunt ad puerilem vagitum cursum flexisse; eam
submissas infantibus adeo mitem praebuisse mammas ut
lingua lambentem pueros magister regii pecoris invenerit –
Faustulo fuisse nomen ferunt – ab eo ad stabula Larentiae
uxori educandos datos.

(Livy 1.4.7)

19.1.4 Adjectives in *-ilis*

There are six fairly common adjectives of this type: **facilis, -e** – easy; **difficilis, -e** – difficult; **similis, -e** – like, similar; **dissimilis, -e** – unlike, dissimilar; **gracilis, -e** – slender; **humilis, -e** – humble, lowly. These adjectives form their comparatives in the regular way; however, to form their superlative double the "l" of the stem, then add **-imus**:

Comparative

	SINGULAR			PLURAL		
	m.	**f.**	**n.**	**m.**	**f.**	**n.**
Nom.	facilior	facilior	facilius	faciliōrēs	faciliōrēs	faciliōra
Gen.	faciliōris	faciliōris	faciliōris	faciliōrum	faciliōrum	faciliōrum
Dat.	faciliōrī	faciliōrī	faciliōrī	faciliōribus	faciliōribus	faciliōribus
Acc.	faciliōrem	faciliōrem	facilius	faciliōrēs	faciliōrēs	faciliōra
Abl.	faciliōre	faciliōre	faciliōre	faciliōribus	faciliōribus	faciliōribus
Voc.	facilior	facilior	facilius	faciliōrēs	faciliōrēs	faciliōra

Superlative

	SINGULAR			PLURAL		
	m.	**f.**	**n.**	**m.**	**f.**	**n.**
Nom.	facillimus	facillima	facillimum	facillimī	facillimae	facillima
Gen.	facillimī	facillimae	facillimī	facillimōrum	facillimārum	facillimōrum
Dat.	facillimō	facillimae	facillimō	facillimīs	facillimīs	facillimīs
Acc.	facillimum	facillimam	facillimum	facillimōs	facillimās	facillima
Abl.	facillimō	facillimā	facillimō	facillimīs	facillimīs	facillimīs
Voc.	facillime	facillima	facillimum	facillimī	facillimae	facillima

19.1.5 Adverbs

We have already met a number of adverbs that are not based upon adjectives (e.g., **tam**, **ita**, etc.); however, Latin, like English, forms a number of adverbs on the adjective stem.

The commonest form of the positive degree of adverbs based upon adjectives of the first/second declension is made up of the stem + **-e**: **dignē** – *worthily* (remember that adverbs do not decline); the comparative is the same in form as the neuter nominative singular of the comparative adjective: **dignius** – more worthily; for all superlatives, take the stem of the superlative adjective and add **-e**: **dignissimē** – most worthily; (**fēlīcissimē**, **ācerrimē**, **facillimē**, etc.). Adverbs based upon third declension adjectives are regularly formed by adding **-iter** to the stem; **fortiter** – bravely; the comparative is formed regularly: **fortius** – more bravely; the superlative is formed in the same way as for the first/second declension: **fortissimē** – most bravely.

19.1.6 Irregular Comparison

As in English (good, better, best) so in Latin some adjectives have irregular forms of the comparative and superlative. And as in English, these are often fairly common adjectives:

POSITIVE	COMPARATIVE	SUPERLATIVE
bonus	melior, melius	optimus, -a, -um
magnus	maior, maius	maximus, -a, -um
malus	peior, peius	pessimus, -a, -um
multus	plūs	plūrimus, -a, -um

All of these comparatives decline in the same way as **dignior** except **plūs** – more, which is used as a neuter noun only in the singular and is regularly followed by the genitive case (partitive genitive):

atque ego hoc **plūs oneris** habeō (Cicero *In Verrem* 2.3.4): *and I consider this **more of a burden***.

In the plural **plūrēs**, **plūra** is a regular third declension adjective:

plūrēs cīvitātēs (Caesar *De Bello Gallico* 3.10.3): ***more states***.

19.2 CONSTRUCTIONS WITH THE COMPARATIVE AND SUPERLATIVE

19.2.1 Comparative in a Purpose Clause

If a purpose clause contains a comparative adjective or adverb, the clause is introduced by **quō** (the verb is still in the subjunctive):

id **quō facilius** facere **possitis**, dabō operam (Cicero *Pro Quinctio* 11): *I shall make an effort **in order that you may be able** to do this **more easily***.

19.2.2 Ablative of Comparison/*Quam*

The ablative case is used with comparative adjectives and adverbs, generally only when the first noun/pronoun is in the nominative or accusative case; **quam** – *than* may be used at any time. If the first item in the comparison is in any case other than nominative or accusative, then **quam** must be used:

nec enim **melior** vir fuit **Africānō** quisquam nec clārior (Cicero *De Amicitia* 6): *for there was no man **better than Africanus** nor more illustrious.*

certē igitur **ignōrātiō** futūrōrum malōrum **ūtilior est quam scientia** (Cicero *De Divinatione* 2.24): *certainly, therefore, **ignorance** of future misfortunes is **more profitable than knowledge** (of them).*

De Divinatione (*On Divination*), a philosophical dialogue between Cicero and his brother Quintus in two books completed in 44 BC to serve as a supplement to his work *De Natura Deorum*. In the first book, influenced by Greek Stoic ideas, Quintus defends divination, while in the second Cicero, basing his arguments on those of the Greek founder of the New Academy, Carneades, rejects it as laughable.

THE BIGGER PICTURE

When used with the superlative **quam** means *as . . . as possible*:

petō ā tē ut **quam celerrimē** mihi librārius mittātur (Cicero *Epistulae ad Familiares* 16.21.8): *I beg of you that my secretary be sent to me **as quickly as possible**.*

19.2.3 Ablative of Degree/Measure of Difference

The ablative can accompany a comparative to express the measure of difference (e.g., by how much something is larger or smaller):

multō maior alacritās studiumque pugnandī maius exercituī iniectum est (Caesar *De Bello Gallico* 1.46.4): ***far greater** eagerness and greater enthusiasm for fighting was inspired in the army.*

19.2.4 Partitive Genitive

A partitive genitive is often found with the superlative:

hōrum omnium fortissimī sunt Belgae (Caesar *De Bello Gallico* 1.1.3): ***of all these the bravest** are the Belgae.*

19.3 VERBS OF FEARING

There are three main constructions with verbs of fearing: **timeō**, **metuō**, **vereor**. These verbs may be followed by a direct object in the accusative case:

Caesar . . . eius reī **moram** temporisque **longinquitātem timēbat** (Caesar *Bellum Civile* 1.29.1): *Caesar . . . **feared the delay** involved in this matter and **the length** of time.*

Or they may be followed by a complementary infinitive:

Caesar . . . **timēbat** tantae magnitūdinī flūminis exercitum **obicere** (Caesar *Bellum Civile* 1.64.3): *Caesar . . . **was afraid to expose** his army to such a great size of current.*

Or they may be followed by a subordinate clause whose verb is in the subjunctive. The tense of the subjunctive is determined by the rules of sequence. The only difficulty occurs with the introductory conjunction: a clause expressing the fear that something will happen is introduced by **ne**; a clause expressing a fear that something will not happen is introduced by **ut** (occasionally by **nē . . . nōn**):

Indūtiomārus **veritus nē** ab omnibus **dēsererētur**, legātōs ad Caesarem mittit (Caesar *De Bello Gallico* 5.3.6): *Indutiomarus **because he feared that he was being deserted** by all, sends envoys to Caesar.*

vereor ut Dolabella ipse satis nōbīs prodesse **possit** (Cicero *Epistulae ad Familiares* 14.14.1): *I am afraid that Dolabella himself **may not be able** to help us enough.*

SOUND BITE   Seneca on goodness – again (Seneca *Epistolae Morales* 79.11)

nec enim bonitas est pessimis esse meliorem.

TRANSLATION FROM LATIN

HINT! When translating, keep in mind the context. Is Cicero defending or prosecuting? Is he writing a letter to one of his friends or is it a more "philosophical" work?

1. non modo nihil timere sed maiora et meliora exspectare debetis. (Cicero *Philippicae* 5.51)

2. deinde sententiam meam tu facillime perspicere potuisti iam ab illo tempore cum in Cumanum mihi obviam venisti. non enim te celavi sermonem T. Ampi. vidisti quam abhorrerem ab urbe relinquenda, cum audissem. (Cicero *Epistulae ad Familiares* 2.16.3)

3. atque ego hoc plus oneris habeo quam qui ceteros accusarunt, si onus est id appellandum quod cum laetitia feras ac voluptate. (Cicero *In Verrem* 2.3.4)

4. quanto erat in dies gravior atque asperior oppugnatio et maxime, quod magna parte militum confecta vulneribus res ad paucitatem defensorum pervenerat, tanto crebriores litterae nuntiique ad Caesarem mittebantur. (Caesar *De Bello Gallico* 5.45.1)

5. in occupandis praesidiis magna vi uterque nitebatur: Caesar, ut quam angustissime Pompeium contineret, Pompeius, ut quam plurimos colles quam maximo circuitu occuparet; crebraque ob eam causam proelia fiebant. (Caesar *Bellum Civile* 3.45.1)

6. tum Scaevola comiter, ut solebat, "cetera" inquit "adsentior Crasso, ne aut de C. Laeli soceri mei aut de huius generi aut arte aut gloria detraham; sed illa duo, Crasse, vereor ut tibi possim concedere." (Cicero *De Oratore* 1.35)

7. venit enim mihi in mentem in iudicio M'. Aquili quantum auctoritatis, quantum momenti oratio M. Antoni habuisse existimata sit. (Cicero *In Verrem* 2.5.3)

8. in primam aciem processit centurionibusque nominatim appellatis reliquos cohortatus milites signa inferre et manipulos laxare iussit, quo facilius gladiis uti possent. (Caesar *De Bello Gallico* 2.25.3)

9. haec est enim, ut scis, vetus et Socratica ratio contra alterius opinionem disserendi. nam ita facillime, quid veri simillimum esset, inveniri posse Socrates arbitrabatur. sed quo commodius disputationes nostrae explicentur, sic eas exponam, quasi agatur res, non quasi narretur. (Cicero *Tusculanae Disputationes* 1.8)

FIGURE 19.2 Roman bronze lamp, 1st century AD. © *Leeds Museums and Galleries (Discovery Centre)*

TRANSLATION INTO LATIN

1. It is more difficult to find the end of this speech than its beginning. (Cicero *Pro Lege Manilia* 3)

2. Listen to the evidence in order that you may more easily be able to form a judgment about his singular shamelessness. (Cicero *In Verrem* 2.2.18)

3. I cannot pretend, judges. I fear that on account of this outstanding courage in military matters Gaius Verres has done everything that he has done with impunity. (Cicero *In Verrem* 2.5.3)

4. On the preceding days Caesar, fearing that our men might be surrounded by the fleet, had made a double rampart in this place. (Caesar *Bellum Civile* 3.63.2)

5. They send envoys to ask for assistance so that they may more easily withstand the forces of the enemy. (Caesar *De Bello Gallico* 7.5.2)

6. We ask of you, Marcus Fannius, and of you, judges, that you punish wicked deeds as severely as possible and that you resist the most reckless men as boldly as possible. (Cicero *Pro S. Roscio Amerino* 12)

7. I was afraid that my sudden arrival among my friends might arouse some degree of suspicion. [use *aliquid* + gen.] (Cicero *Philippicae* 1.7)

8. Since one was bringing aid to another and since they were not afraid that they would be surrounded by the enemy from behind, they began to resist more boldly and to fight more bravely. (Caesar *De Bello Gallico* 2.26.2)

9. Next day at dawn he broke camp and, having advanced about four miles, he caught sight of a great number of the enemy across a valley and a stream. (Caesar *De Bello Gallico* 5.49.6)

EXTRA PASSAGE

The relationship with Lesbia is now over.

Miser Catulle, desinas[1] ineptire,
et quod vides perisse perditum ducas.
fulsere quondam candidi tibi soles,
cum ventitabas quo puella ducebat,
amata nobis quantum amabitur nulla.
ibi illa multa tum iocosa fiebant,
quae tu volebas nec puella nolebat.
fulsere vere candidi tibi soles.
nunc iam illa non vult: tu quoque, impotens, noli,
nec quae fugit sectare, nec miser vive,
sed obstinata mente perfer, obdura.
vale, puella, iam Catullus obdurat,
nec te requiret nec rogabit invitam.
at tu dolebis, cum rogaberis nulla.
scelesta, vae te! quae tibi manet vita?
quis nunc te adibit? cui videberis bella?
quem nunc amabis? cuius esse diceris?
quem basiabis? cui labella mordebis?
at tu, Catulle, destinatus obdura!

(Catullus 8)

[1] Present subjunctive used here in place of 2nd person imperative; translate "you should cease."

VOCABULARY

Nouns

adventus, -ūs (m.) – arrival

alacritās, -ātis (f.) – eagerness

argūmentum, -ī (n.) – argument; evidence

C. Laelius, -iī (m.) – father-in-law of Q. Mucius
  Scaevola (see below)

circuitus, -ūs (m.) – circuit; circle

classis, -is (f.) – fleet

collis, -is (m.) – hill

Crassus, -ī (m.) – Lucius Licinius Crassus the
  most famous orator before Cicero and
  Cicero's tutor

Cūmānum, -ī (n.) – an estate belonging to
  Cicero near Cumae

disputātiō, -ōnis (f.) – argument; reasoning

laetitia, -ae (f.) – joy

M'. Aquilius, -iī (m.) – Manius Aquilius,
  defended by Marc Antony

maleficium, -iī (n.) – crime; wicked deed

manipulus, -ī (m.) – an infantry unit; a
  company

mōmentum, -ī (n.) – weight; importance

multitūdō, -inis (f.) – large number

necessārius, necessāriī (m.) – relative; friend

onus, -eris (n.) – burden; trouble

ratiō, -ōnis (f.) – method

rīvus, -ī (m.) – stream

Scaevola, -ae (m.) – Quintus Mucius Scaevola, a
  renowned lawyer (during Cicero's lifetime)

socer, -erī (m.) – father-in-law

Sōcratēs, -is (m.) – Socrates (Greek philosopher,
  5th century BC)

subsidium, subsidiī (n.) – assistance

T. Ampius, -iī (m.) – Titus Ampius, a Roman
  politician

tectum, -ī (n.) – roof; house

vallēs, -is (f.) – valley

vallum, -ī (n.) – rampart

vastitās, -ātis (f.) – waste; desert

voluptās, -ātis (f.) – pleasure

Verbs

abhorreō, -ēre, -uī – abhor; hate; not to wish

accipiō, -ere, -cēpī, -ceptum – receive; hear;
  listen to

adsentior, adsentī, adsensus sum (+ dat.) –
  agree with

celō, -āre – hide

circumveniō, -īre, -vēnī, -ventum – surround

concēdō, -ere, -cessī, -cessum – concede

conspicor, -ārī, conspicātus sum – catch sight of

dētrahō, -ere, -traxī, -tractum – take away from

disserō, -ere, -seruī, -sertum – discuss; argue

dissimulō, -āre – pretend

existimō, -āre – judge

explicō, -āre – unfold; set forth

iniciō, -ere, -iēcī, -iectum (+ dat.) – bring into;
  instill

laxō, -āre – spread out

narrō, -āre – tell; relate; report

nītor, nītī, nīsus (nixus) sum – strive

petō, -ere, petīvī, petītum – seek; (+ *ab* + abl.)
  ask of

sustineō, -ēre, -tinuī, -tentum – withstand

vindicō, -āre – punish

Adjectives

ācer, -ris, -re – harsh; severe

angustus, -a, -um – narrow

asper, -era, -erum – desperate

āversus, -a, -um – turned away; from behind

commodus, -a, -um – suitable; convenient

crēber, -bris – frequent

dūplex, -icis – double

eximius, -a, -um – outstanding

repentīnus, -a, -um – sudden

Sōcraticus, -a, -um – belonging to Socrates;
   Socratic
superior, -ius – preceding

nōminātim – by name
obviam (+ dat.) – in the way of; obviam venīre
   (+ dat.) – come to meet
quasi – as if

Adverbs; Conjunctions

angustē – narrowly
comiter – in a friendly manner

English Derivations

From which Latin roots do the following English words derive?

(i) advent
(ii) dispute
(iii) accept
(iv) narrate

FIGURE 19.3 Temple of Vesta, Rome. Vesta was the goddess of fire/the hearth. Vesta was served by six Vestal Virgins (the only female priesthood in Rome) who served the goddess for 30 years after which time they were allowed to marry (though few did).
Photo © tkachuk / Shutterstock

CHAPTER 20

FIGURE 20.1 Roman glass vase from Syria, date unknown. Pompey made Syria a Roman province in 64 BC. Under the emperors Syria was an important military command. It was known for its wine and various agricultural products such as nuts, plums and dates. © *Leeds Museums and Galleries (Discovery Centre)*

Wiley's Real Latin: Learning Latin from the Source, First Edition.
Robert Maltby and Kenneth Belcher.
© 2014 John Wiley & Sons, Inc. Published 2014 by John Wiley & Sons, Inc.

20.1 CONDITIONAL SENTENCES

Conditional sentences are made up of two clauses: a conditional clause (called the protasis) introduced by **sī** – *if*, or **nisi** (or **sī . . . nōn**) – *unless*; *if . . . not*, and a main clause (called the apodosis). Different combinations are possible and conditional sentences are presented in various ways. The following provides a simplified overview of the different types.

20.1.1 Simple Conditions

Simple conditions may be past or present. A simple condition, as the label suggests, sets forth a proposal without implying whether the proposal is true or not. Consider, for example, the English *If you believe this, you are wrong.*

20.1.2 Present

Simple present conditional sentences regularly use the present indicative in both protasis and apodosis:

> **erras**, **sī** id **crēdis** (Terence *Heauton Timorumenos* 106): *you are wrong, if you believe this.*

20.1.3 Past

Simple past conditional sentences regularly use the perfect indicative in the protasis and the perfect or imperfect in the apodosis:

> **sī** vērum tibi Caelius **dīxit**, ō immoderāta mulier, sciēns **tū** aurum ad facinus **dēdistī** (Cicero *Pro Caelio* 53): *if Caelius **told** you the truth, reckless woman, **you** knowingly **gave** the gold for the crime.*

20.1.4 Future Conditions

There are two basic types of future conditions: the first is often referred to as future definite or future more vivid. Here the condition refers to something that may happen in the future and it is called definite or future more vivid because the chance of its being true is considered probable. The second type is called future indefinite or future less vivid.

Future More Vivid

As the label suggests, these sentences refer to something happening in the future. Consider, for example, the English *If you bring a fine, large banquet with you, you will dine well at my house.* Notice that here, somewhat illogically, English uses the present tense in the protasis. In Latin, a future tense is used; regularly the future perfect because the action in the protasis has to be completed before the action in the apodosis can take place:

cēnābis bene, mī Fabulle, apud mē

. . .

sī tēcum **attuleris** bonam atque magnam
cēnam

(Catullus 13.1–4):

you will dine *well at my house, my dear Fabullus*

. . .

if you bring [literally: will have brought] *with you a fine and large
dinner.*

Future Less Vivid

As noted above, conditions of this type refer to the future, but suggest that the outcome is
less certain: *If you should/were to learn this, you would be wise.* Here Latin uses the present
subjunctive in both the protasis and apodosis:

> **sī** quis, iūdicēs, forte nunc **adsit** ignārus lēgum iūdiciōrum consuetūdinisque nostrae,
> **mīrētur** profectō quae sit tanta atrōcitās huiusce causae (Cicero *Pro Caelio* 1): ***if
> anyone, judges, by chance should be present** now who is ignorant of our laws, our
> courts, and our customs, surely **he would wonder** what great atrocity there is in this
> case.*

20.1.5 Unfulfilled, Untrue, or Contrary-to-Fact Conditions

Present Unfulfilled

Here the condition is presented as something that is not being fulfilled or cannot be true
or fulfilled. Consider the following example: *If he were inside, I would be calling him out*
(but he is not inside and so I am not – notice the tenses and moods English uses here).
Here Latin uses the imperfect subjunctive in both protasis and apodosis:

> **sī** intus **esset**, **ēvocārem** (Plautus *Pseudolus* 640): ***if he were inside, I would call him
> out**.*

You can see that the if-clause immediately suggests "but he is not," i.e., is untrue.

Past Unfulfilled

Here the reference is to the past: *If I had known you were there, I would have come myself*
(again notice how English expresses conditions of this type). In past unfulfilled conditions
Latin uses the pluperfect subjunctive in both the protasis and apodosis:

> **sī** ibi tē esse **scīvissem**, ad tē ipse **vēnissem** (Cicero *De Finibus* 3.8): ***if I had known**
> that you were there, **I would have come** to you myself.*

Mixed Unfulfilled

Sometimes you find a blend of past and present in conditions of this type. Usually in this case, the protasis refers to something in the past, the apodosis to the present:

nisi ante Rōmā **profectus essēs, nunc** eam certē **relinquerēs** (Cicero *Epistulae ad Familiares* 7.11.1): *if you had not set out from Rome before, you would certainly be leaving her now*.

A word of warning: many other combinations occur. For example, the protasis may be represented by a participle:

si latet ars, prodest; adfert **dēprēnsa** pudōrem (Ovid *Ars Amatoria* 2.313): if art is hidden, it is good; but **if <it is> detected**, it brings shame.

20.2 VERBS/EXPRESSIONS OF DOUBTING: *Dubitō, Dubium Est, Incertum Est*

If the verb/expression of doubting is positive, it is followed by an indirect question:

quid enim ille **factūrus sit incertum est** (Cicero *Epistulae ad Familiares* 9.6.2): *for it is uncertain what that man will/is going to do*.

However, if the expression of doubting is itself negative or in the form of a question, the dependent clause is introduced by **quīn**; the mood is still the subjunctive:

nec dubitārī dēbet quīn fuerint ante Homērum poētae (Cicero *Brutus* 71): *nor should it be doubted that there were poets before Homer*.

NB: **dubito** may mean *hesitate* in which case it simply takes a complementary infinitive even if it is negative:

sapiens . . . **nōn dubitat** . . . **migrāre** dē vītā (Cicero *De Finibus* 1.62): *the wise man . . . does not hesitate . . . to depart from life*.

20.3 CONSTRUCTION FOR VERBS OF HINDERING, PREVENTING, FORBIDDING

Two verbs, **vetō** – *forbid*, and **prohibeō** – *prevent*, are regularly followed by the accusative and infinitive construction:

hic **sē** lacrimīs **dēfendī vetat** (Cicero *Pro Milone* 105): *this man forbids himself to be defended* by tears.

Pompeius . . . \<eum\> **loquī** plūra **prohibuit** (Caesar *Bellum Civile* 3.18.4): *Pompey prevented \<him\> from speaking further.*

For other verbs of preventing, e.g., **impediō**, **dēterreō**, **obstō**, **obsistō**, the construction is rather different: if the introductory verb is positive, the dependent clause is introduced by **quōminus** or **nē** and has its verb in the subjunctive; if negative, the dependent clause is introduced by **quōminus** or **quīn** and has its verb in the subjunctive:

sed iam **impedior** egomet, iūdicēs, dolōre animī **nē** dē huius miseriā plūra **dīcam** (Cicero *Pro Sulla* 92): *but now **I am prevented**, judges, by the pain of my spirit **from saying** more about the misery of this man.*

nec Antiochus **sē tenuit quīn** contrā suum doctōrem librum etiam **ēderet** (Cicero *Lucullus* 12): *and Antiochus did not **hold back from publishing** a book against his own teacher.*

NB: **quīn** + subjunctive may be used instead of **ut nōn** to introduce result clauses when the main verb is negative.

nēmō est tam fortis quīn reī novitāte **perturbētur** (Caesar *De Bello Gallico* 6.39.4): ***there is no one so brave that he is not disturbed** by revolution.*

TRY THIS

Identify the verbs in the following passage (including participles, infinitives, gerunds, and gerundives) and parse them (you will need to use a dictionary to complete this exercise):

> Caelo supinas si tuleris manus
> nascente Luna, rustica Phidyle,
>   si ture placaris et horna
>   fruge Lares avidaque porca,
>
> nec pestilentem sentiet Africum
> fecunda vitis nec sterilem seges
>   robiginem aut dulces alumni
>   pomifero grave tempus anno.
>
> nam quae nivali pascitur Algido
> devota quercus inter et ilices
>   aut crescit Albanis in herbis
>   victima, pontificum securis
>
> cervice tinguet; te nihil attinet
> temptare multa caede bidentium
>   parvos coronantem marino
>   rore deos fragilique myrto.
>   (Horace *Odes* 3.23.1–16)

SOUND BITE   Ovid on the art of make-up (Ovid *Ars Amatoria* 2.313)

si latet ars, prodest.

TRANSLATION FROM LATIN

1. ferreus essem, si te non amarem. (Cicero *Epistulae ad Familiares* 15.21.3)

2. mellitos oculos tuos, Iuventi,
   si quis me sinat usque basiare,
   usque ad milia basiem trecenta.

   (Catullus 48.1–3)

3. etsi ea perturbatio est omnium rerum ut suae quemque fortunae maxime paeniteat . . . tamen mihi dubium non est quin hoc tempore bono viro Romae esse miserrimum sit. (Cicero *Epistulae ad Familiares* 6.1)

   HINT! Here *ea* is the same as *talis*. What construction follows?

4. hanc ego viam, iudices, si aut asperam atque arduam aut plenam esse periculorum aut insidiarum negem, mentiar, praesertim cum id non modo intellexerim semper, sed etiam praeter ceteros senserim. (Cicero *Pro Sestio* 100)

5. nemini video dubium esse, iudices, quin apertissime C. Verres in Sicilia sacra profanaque omnia et privatim et publice spoliaverit, versatusque sit sine ulla non modo religione verum etiam dissimulatione in omni genere furandi atque praedandi. (Cicero *In Verrem* 2.5.1)

6. nostri repentina fortuna permoti arma quae possunt arripiunt, alii ex castris sese incitant. fit in hostis impetus. sed <de> muro sagittis tormentisque fugientes persequi prohibentur. illi sub murum se recipiunt. (Caesar *Bellum Civile* 2.14.4)

7. an hic, si sese isti vitae dedidisset, consularem hominem admodum adulescens in iudicium vocavisset? hic, si laborem fugeret, si obstrictus voluptatibus teneretur, hac in acie cotidie versaretur, appeteret inimicitias, in iudicium vocaret, subiret periculum capitis, ipse inspectante populo Romano tot iam mensis aut de salute aut de gloria dimicaret? (Cicero *Pro Caelio* 47)

8. tum demum Liscus oratione Caesaris adductus, quod antea tacuerat, proponit: esse nonnullos quorum auctoritas apud plebem plurimum valeat, qui privatim plus possint quam ipsi magistratus. hos seditiosa atque improba oratione multitudinem deterrere, ne frumentum conferant, quod debeant. (Caesar *De Bello Gallico* 1.17.2)

9. urbem Syracusas elegerat, cuius hic situs atque haec natura esse loci caelique dicitur ut nullus umquam dies tam magna ac turbulenta tempestate fuerit quin aliquo tempore

eius diei solem homines viderint. hic ita vivebat iste bonus imperator hibernis mensibus ut eum non facile non modo extra tectum, sed ne extra lectum quidem quisquam viderit; ita diei brevitas conviviis, noctis longitudo stupris et flagitiis continebatur. (Cicero *In Verrem* 2.5.26)

TRANSLATION INTO LATIN

1. If you do what you indicate, I will be very grateful; if you do not do it, I will forgive you. (Cicero *Epistulae ad Familiares* 5.19.2)

2. If you had come to the army, you would have been seen by the military tribunes. But you were not seen by them. Therefore you did not set out for the army. (Cicero *De Inventione* 1.87)

3. I would not be troubling you if I were able to arrange this through another. (Cicero *Epistulae ad Atticum* 15.15.4)

4. It is easy to find fault with extravagance. The day would soon fail me if I should try to explain everything which could be said upon that topic. (Cicero *Pro Caelio* 29)

5. You have understood for a long time, judges, what I wish or rather what I do not wish to say. Even if this was done, it was certainly not done by Caelius. (Cicero *Pro Caelio* 69)

6. In no way could it happen that Cleomenus not be pardoned. (Cicero *In Verrem* 2.5.104)

7. If you are doing this, you are obtaining the great reward of the excellent studies in which I know you have always been engaged. (Cicero *Epistulae ad Familiares* 6.10b.1)

8. I would not believe this about the statues if I had not seen them lying about and torn apart. (Cicero *In Verrem* 2.2.158)

9. Death, which threatens daily on account of changing events and on account of the brevity of life can never be far away, does not deter the wise man from considering the interests of the state and his family for all time. (Cicero *Tusculanae Disputationes* 1.91)

FIGURE 20.2 Romano-British jug. Before the Roman invasion of Britain (first by Julius Caesar in 54 and 54 BC, later by the emperor Claudius in AD 43), pottery was mainly available to rulers of the various tribes. As Roman influence spread, the use of pottery became much more common. © *Leeds Museums and Galleries (Discovery Centre)*

EXTRA PASSAGES

Orpheus has descended into the Underworld to bring back his wife, Eurydice, from the dead. Tragically he turns around before they reach the world above and Eurydice is lost for a second time.

iamque pedem referens [i.e., Orpheus] casus evaserat omnis,
redditaque Eurydice superas veniebat ad auras
pone[1] sequens (namque hanc dederat Proserpina legem),   [1] This is **not** from *pono*.
cum subita incautum dementia cepit amantem,
ignoscenda quidem, scirent si ignoscere Manes:
restitit, Eurydicenque suam iam luce sub ipsa
immemor heu! victusque animi respexit. ibi omnis
effusus labor atque immitis rupta tyranni
foedera, terque fragor stagnis auditus Avernis.
illa "quis et me" inquit "miseram et te perdidit, Orpheu,
quis tantus furor? en iterum crudelia retro
fata vocant, conditque natantia lumina somnus.
iamque vale: feror ingenti circumdata nocte
invalidasque tibi tendens, heu non tua, palmas."
dixit et ex oculis subito, ceu fumus in auras
commixtus tenuis, fugit diversa, neque illum
prensantem nequiquam umbras et multa volentem
dicere praeterea vidit; nec portitor Orci
amplius obiectam passus transire paludem.

(Virgil *Georgics* 4.485–503)

Compare Ovid's version of the same story.

tunc primum lacrimis victarum carmine fama est
Eumenidum maduisse genas, nec regia coniunx
sustinet oranti nec, qui regit ima, negare,
Eurydicenque vocant: umbras erat illa recentes
inter et incessit passu de vulnere tardo.
hanc simul et legem Rhodopeius accipit heros,
ne flectat retro sua lumina, donec Avernas
exierit valles; aut inrita dona futura.
carpitur adclivis per muta silentia trames,
arduus, obscurus, caligine densus opaca,
nec procul afuerunt telluris margine summae:
hic, ne deficeret, metuens avidusque videndi
flexit amans oculos, et protinus illa relapsa est,
bracchiaque intendens prendique et prendere certans
nil nisi cedentes infelix arripit auras.

(Ovid *Metamorphoses* 10.45–59)

FIGURE 20.3 Orpheus charming animals mosaic, 2nd century AD. Orpheus was famed as a singer and his song was so enchanting as to charm animals, trees, rocks, all manner of things. *Source: Musée Archéologique, Saint-Roman-en-Gal, France/ Giraudon/The Bridgeman Art Library*

 # VOCABULARY

Nouns

acies, -ēī (f.) – battle-line; battle
bāsium, bāsiī (n.) – kiss
caput, -itis (n.) – head; life; capital punishment
cāsus, -ūs (m.) – falling down; event
cēna, -ae (f.) – dinner
consuētūdō, -inis (f.) – custom
contentiō, -ōnis (f.) – contest; argument
dolor, -ōris (m.) – grief; sorrow
facinus, -oris (n.) – deed; crime
flagitium, flagitiī (n.) – shame; disgrace
fructus, -ūs (m.) – fruit; reward
inimīcitia, -ae (f.) – enmity
insidiae, -ārum (f. pl.) – trap; ambush
lectus, -ī (m.) – bed
Liscus, -ī (m.) – Liscus, a Gallic leader (from the Haedui/Aedui)

luxuriēs, -ēī (f.) – luxury; extravagance
mansuetūdō, -inis (f.) – clemency; mercy
miseria, -ae (f.) – misery; misfortune
oculus, -ī (m.) – eye
offensiō, -ōnis (f) – offense
perīculum, -ī (n.) – danger; risk
sagitta, -ae (f.) – arrow
sententia, -ae (f.) – opinion; idea; topic
situs, -ūs (m.) – site; position
stuprum, -ī (n.) – dishonor; disgrace
tectum, -ī (n.) – roof; house
tempestās, tempestātis (f.) – time; season; weather
tormentum, -ī. (n.) – catapult

Verbs

absum, abesse, afuī – be absent; be away
accusō, -āre – blame; find fault with

arripiō, -ere, arripuī, arreptum – snatch;
  seize
bāsiō, -āre – kiss
cēnō, -āre – dine
consulō, -ere, consuluī, consultum (+ dat.) –
  take thought for
dēficiō, -ere, -fēcī, -fectum – leave; fail
dīmicō, -āre – fight; struggle
ēripiō, -ere, ēripuī, ēreptum – snatch away; take
  away
errō, -āre – err; be wrong
exprōmō, -ere, -promsī, -promptum – bring
  forth; explain
fūror, -ārī, fūratus sum – steal
ignoscō, -ere, -nōvī, -nōtum (+ dat.) – forgive
immineō, -ēre – hang over; threaten
impediō, -īre, impedī(v)ī, impedītum – impede;
  prevent
incitō, -āre – hasten; rush
mentior, -īrī, mentītus sum – lie
migrō, -āre – go; depart
obstringō, -ere, -strinxī, -strictum – bind;
  hamper
ostendō, -ere, ostendī, ostensum – show;
  indicate
percipiō, -ere, -cēpī, -ceptum – understand
praedor, -ārī, praedātus sum – plunder
sentiō, -īre, sēnsī, sensum – feel; perceive
spoliō, -āre – despoil; rob

versor, -ārī, versātus sum – engage (in)
vetō, -āre, vetuī, vetitum – forbid
vigeō, -ēre, -uī – flourish
vītō, -āre – avoid

Adjectives

arduus, -a, -um – steep; difficult
consulāris, -e – of consular rank
ferreus, -a, -um – iron-hearted
hībernus, -a, -um – (belonging to) winter
incertus, -a, -um – uncertain; changing
mellītus, -a, -um – made of honey; honeyed
molestus, -a, -um – troublesome; annoying
sēditiōsus, -a, -um – seditious; rebellious
turbulentus, -a, -um – turbulent; stormy

Adverbs; Prepositions

admodum – very
cotīdiē – every day
iam dūdum (+ present tense) – now for a long
  time
in (+ acc.) – against; upon
longē – far
plūrimum – exceedingly
potius – rather
propter (+ acc.) – on account of
usque – continuously
usque (+ *ad* + acc.) – up to

English Derivations

From which Latin roots do the following English words derive?

(i) case
(ii) sententious
(iii) incite
(iv) liberate

CHAPTER 21

FIGURE 21.1 Silver denarius, date unknown. Three military standards (*signa militaria*) within a temple. Under the emperors military standards bore the images of the reigning and deified emperors. © *Leeds Museums and Galleries (Discovery Centre)*

Wiley's Real Latin: Learning Latin from the Source, First Edition.
Robert Maltby and Kenneth Belcher.
© 2014 John Wiley & Sons, Inc. Published 2014 by John Wiley & Sons, Inc.

21.1 MORE ON TEMPORAL CLAUSES

21.1.1 *Antequam, Priusquam* – Before

We have covered a number of different types of temporal clauses, for example, those introduced by **ubi** – when, or **postquam** – after (both of which are regularly followed by the perfect indicative). Other temporal conjunctions include **antequam** and **priusquam** (both may be written as two words, e.g., **ante . . . quam**) or even separated by other words. These conjunctions may take the indicative:

> nunc **antequam** ad sententiam **redeō**, dē mē pauca dīcam (Cicero *In Catilinam* 4.20): *now **before** I return to the subject, I shall say a few things about myself.*

However, when there is an added implication of purpose, the subjunctive mood is used:

> Vercingetorix **priusquam munitiōnēs** ab Rōmānīs **perficiantur**, consilium capit omnem ab sē equitātum noctū dimittere (Caesar *De Bello Gallico* 7.71.1): *Vercingetorix adopted the plan to send away all his cavalry by night **before fortifications could be completed** by the Romans.*

When the main clause is negative, **antequam** and **priusquam** are best translated as *until*:

> **neque prius** fugere dēsistērunt **quam** ad flūmen Rhēnum mīlia passuum ex eō locō circiter quīnque pervēnērunt (Caesar *De Bello Gallico* 1.53.1): **and** *they did **not** stop fleeing **until** they arrived at the river Rhine about five miles from that place.*

FIGURE 21.2 Vercingetorix coin. Vercingetorix was ruler of a Gallic tribe. He led a revolt against Caesar but was ultimately defeated and put to death after Caesar's triumph (46 BC). *Source: Private Collection/ Giraudon/The Bridgeman Art Library*

21.1.2 *Dum* (and rarely *quoad, dōnec*) – Until; While

Like **antequam** and **priusquam** these conjunctions may take the indicative:

> **dum** in hīs locīs Caesar nāvium parandārum causā **morātur**, ex magnā parte Morīnōrum ad eum legātī vēnērunt (Caesar *De Bello Gallico* 4.22): *while Caesar was delaying in this region for the sake of preparing the ships, envoys came to him from a great part of the Morini.*

And as with **antequam** and **priusquam** the subjunctive may be used:

> **dum** reliquae nāvēs eō **convenīrent**, ad hōram nōnam in ancorīs exspectāvit (Caesar *De Bello Gallico* 4.23): *they waited at anchor up to the ninth hour **until** the remaining ships **should arrive**.*

Notes on Dum

Dum takes the logically required tense when it means while, as long as, all the time:

> **dum haec** Vēiīs **agēbantur**, interim arx Rōmae . . . in ingentī perīculō fuit (Livy *Ab Urbe Condita* 5.47.2): ***while these things were being done** at Veii, meanwhile the citadel at Rome was in great danger.*

> **dum longius ā mūnitiōne aberant Gallī**, plus multitūdine tēlōrum prōficiēbant (Caesar *De Bello Gallico* 7.82.1): ***while the Gauls were further from the fortification,** they held a greater advantage because of the number of their weapons.*

However, when **dum** means *while, during the time that* (i.e., when the clause denotes a longer period during part of which something happens), it takes the present indicative:

> **dum haec . . . Rōmae aguntur**, consulēs ambō in Liguribus gerēbant bellum (Livy *Ab Urbe Condita* 39.1.1): ***while these things were being done at Rome,** both consuls were waging war in Liguria.*

Dum (also **dummodo, modo**) may introduce a so-called clause of proviso = provided that. Here the subjunctive is used and the tense of the subjunctive is determined by the rules of sequence:

> oderint, **dum metuant** (Cicero *Philippicae* 1.34, quoting Accius): *let them hate, **provided that they fear**.*

21.2 MORE ON INDIRECT SPEECH/STATEMENT

As noted in Chapter 10 the future infinitive passive (e.g., **captum īrī**) is somewhat rare in Latin. Instead Latin uses the future infinitive of **sum** (**fore** or **futūrum esse**) followed by **ut** + subjunctive. This construction must be used with verbs that have no supine such as **possum**.

> **spērant fore ut** patris litterīs nuntiīsque fīlius ab illō furōre **revocētur** (Cicero *In Verrem* 2.2.97): ***they hope** [literally: it will be] **that the son will be brought back** from that madness by his father's letters and messengers.*

cum **vidērem** . . . **fore ut** eius sociōs invidia oppressus persequī nōn **possem** . . . (Cicero *In Catilinam* 2.4): *when **I saw that I**, being checked by ill-will, **would not be able** to pursue his allies . . .*

21.2.1 Subordinate Clauses in Indirect Speech

As a general rule, subordinate clauses in indirect discourse have their verbs in the subjunctive as a matter of course (for example, causal, relative, and temporal clauses) and the tense will generally be determined by the rules of sequence: in primary sequence, the present or perfect subjunctive is used; in secondary/historic sequence, the imperfect or pluperfect subjunctive is used. The future is replaced by the future participle + present or imperfect of *sum*, depending on sequence. The future perfect is represented by the perfect subjunctive in primary sequence and by the pluperfect subjunctive in secondary/historic sequence.

dixit sē istum pūblicē laudāre **quod sibi ita mandātum esset** (Cicero *In Verrem* 2.4.16): *he said that we was praising that man publicly **because he had been so ordered**.*

dīcit montem **quem ā Labiēnō occupārī voluerit**, ab hostibus tenērī (Caesar *De Bello Gallico* 1.22): *he says that the mountain **which he wanted to be occupied by Labienus** was being held by the enemy.*

The subjunctive is also used in subordinate clauses, in fearing clauses, purpose clauses, indirect commands, and indirect questions.

> **TRY THIS**
>
> Identify the verbs in the following passage (including participles, infinitives, gerunds, and gerundives) and parse them (you will need to use a dictionary to complete this exercise):
>
> Peliaco quondam prognatae vertice pinus
> dicuntur liquidas Neptuni nasse per undas
> Phasidos ad fluctus et fines Aeeteos,
> cum lecti iuvenes, Argivae robora pubis,
> auratam optantes Colchis avertere pellem
> ausi sunt vada salsa cita decurrere puppi,
> caerula verrentes abiegnis aequora palmis.
> diva quibus retinens in summis urbibus arces
> ipsa levi fecit volitantem flamine currum,
> pinea coniungens inflexae texta carinae.
> illa rudem cursu prima imbuit Amphitriten.
> quae simul ac rostro ventosum proscidit aequor,
> tortaque remigio spumis incanuit unda,
> emersere freti candenti e gurgite vultus
> aequoreae monstrum Nereides admirantes.
> (Catullus 64.1–15)

> **SOUND BITE**   Tacitus on Servius Galba (Tacitus *Histories* 1.49)
>
> **omnium consensu capax imperii, nisi imperasset.**

TRANSLATION FROM LATIN

1. est mihi tanti, Quirites, huius invidiae falsae atque iniquae tempestatem subire, dum modo a vobis huius horribilis belli ac nefarii periculum depellatur. (Cicero *In Catilinam* 2.15)

2. Caesar, priusquam se hostes ex terrore ac fuga reciperent, in fines Suessionum, qui proximi Remis erant, exercitum duxit et magno itinere confecto ad oppidum Noviodunum contendit. (Caesar *De Bello Gallico* 2.12.1)

3. priusquam de ceteris rebus respondeo, de amicitia quam a me violatam esse criminatus est, quod ego gravissimum crimen iudico, pauca dicam. (Cicero *Philippicae* 2.3)

4. namque <Pompeius> etiam in consilio superioribus diebus dixerat, priusquam concurrerent acies, fore uti exercitus Caesaris pelleretur. (Caesar *Bellum Civile* 3.86.1)

5. non omnis moriar multaque pars mei
   vitabit Libitinam: usque ego postera
   crescam laude recens, dum Capitolium
   scandet cum tacita virgine pontifex.

   (Horace *Odes* 3.30.6–9)

6. Lacedaemonii, Philippo minitante per litteras se omnia quae conarentur prohibiturum, quaesiverunt num se esset etiam mori prohibiturus? (Cicero *Tusculanae Disputationes* 5.42)

7. pro certo habet neminem sibi, antequam in Italiam traiecerit, armatum occursurum. (Livy *Ab Urbe Condita* 42.13.10)

8. vincat aliquando cupiditas voluptasque rationem, dum modo illa in hoc genere praescriptio moderatioque teneatur. parcat iuventus pudicitiae suae, ne spoliet alienam, ne effundat patrimonium. (Cicero *Pro Caelio* 42)

9. arma virumque cano, Troiae qui primus ab oris
   Italiam fato profugus Laviniaque venit
   litora, multum ille et terris iactatus et alto
   vi superum, saevae memorem Iunonis ob iram,
   multa quoque et bello passus, dum conderet urbem
   inferretque deos Latio; genus unde Latinum
   Albanique patres atque altae moenia Romae.

   (Virgil *Aeneid* 1.1–7)

TRANSLATION INTO LATIN

1. By all means let it be said that he was driven out by me provided that he does go into exile. But believe me. He is not going to go. (Cicero *In Catilinam* 2.15)

2. I had great hope that we would be able to establish peace in Italy (and it seemed to me that nothing was more beneficial than this) or defend the republic with the utmost honor. (Cicero *Epistulae ad Atticum* 8.11d.1)

3. While these things were being transacted at the conference, it was reported to Caesar that the cavalry of Ariovistus were approaching nearer the mound and were riding up to our men and hurling stones and spears at them. Caesar made an end and withdrew to his own men and ordered them not to throw back any weapon at all against the enemy. (Caesar *De Bello Gallico* 1.46.1–2)

4. But before we speak about the rules of oratory, it seems that it is necessary to speak about the nature of the art itself, about its function, about its end, its subject-matter, and its divisions. (Cicero *De Inventione* 1.5)

5. He was afraid that he might offend the feelings of Diviciacus by the punishment of this man. Therefore, before he should try anything, he ordered Diviciacus to be summoned to him. (Caesar *De Bello Gallico* 1.19.3)

6. Do you understand what you are saying, to whom and about whom you are saying it? You want to involve the most honorable men in your and Gabinius' crime, and you are not doing this in secret. For a little while before you said that I was contending with men whom I despised and that I was not touching those men who had more influence, men with whom I ought to be angry. (Cicero *In Pisonem* 75)

VOCABULARY

Nouns; Pronouns

animus, -ī (m.) – mind; heart; feelings

Ariovistus, -ī (m.) – Ariovistus (ruler of a German tribe)

Capitōlium, -iī – the Capitol, where a temple of Jupiter was located

colloquium, -iī (n.) – conference

concordia, -ae (f.) – harmony; peace

dignitās, -tātis (f.) – dignity; honor

Diviciācus, -ī (m.) – Diviciacus (a leader of a Gallic tribe)

Gabinius, -iī (m.) – Aulus Gabinius (a consul with Piso in 58 BC)

genus, -eris (n.) – origin; nature

equitātus, -ūs (m.) – cavalry

exilium, exiliī (n.) – exile

fīnis, -is (m.) – limit; end

invidia, -ae (f.) – envy; ill-will

Lacedaemoniī, -ōrum (m. pl.) – the Spartans

lapis, -idis (m.) – stone

Lāvīnius, -a, -um – of Lavinia; Lavinian (city in Italy, founded by Aeneas in honor of his wife, Lavinia)

Libitīna, -ae (f.) – the goddess of corpses; Death

māteria, -ae (f.) – subject-matter

moenia, -ium (n. pl.) – city walls; walls

Morīnī, -ōrum – Morini (a people of Gaul)

mūnītiō, -ōnis (f.) – fortification

Noviodūnum, -ī (n.) – Noviodunum, a town in Gaul

officium, -iī (n.) – duty; function

ōra, -ae (f.) – edge; shore

pars, partis (f.) – part; division

patrimōnium, -iī (n.) – inheritance; patrimony

pontifex, pontificis (m.) – high priest

praeceptum, -ī (n.) – precept; rule

praescriptiō, -ōnis (f.) – precept; rule

profugus, -ī (m.) – fugitive; exile

pudīcitia, -ae (f.) – modesty; virtue

quisquam, quaequam, quidquam (or quicquam) – anyone; anything

ratiō, -ōnis (f.) – reason

Rēmī, -ōrum (m. pl.) – Remi (a people of Gaul)

Suessiōnēs, -um (m. pl.) – Suessiones (a people of Gaul)

supplicium, -iī (n.) – punishment

tēlum, -ī (n.) – spear; weapon

tempestās, -tātis (f.) – storm

tumulus, -ī (m.) – hill; mound

Vercingetorix, -igis (m.) – Vercingetorix (commander of the Gauls)

vīs, vis (f.) – force; violence

voluptās, -tātis (f.) – pleasure

Verbs

accēdō, -ere, -cessī, -cessum – approach

adequitō, -āre – ride up (to)

attingō, -ere, -tigī, -tactum – touch

complector, -ī, complexus sum – embrace; (+ *ad* + acc.) involve (someone) in

concurrō, -ere, concurrī, concursum – come together; engage in combat

condō, -ere, condidī, conditum – establish; found

conflīgō, -ere, conflīxī, conflictum – contend

coniciō, -ere, -iēcī, -iectum – throw

constituō, -ere, -uī, -ūtum – establish

contendō, -ere, contendī, contentum – strive for; march

criminor, -ārī, criminātus sum – charge; allege

dēpellō, -ere, -pūlī, -pulsum – drive away; remove

dēspiciō, -ere, -spexī, -spectum – look down upon; despise

dīmittō, -ere, -mīsī, -missum – dismiss; send away

effundō, -ere, -fūdī, -fūsum – pour forth; squander

iactō, -āre – throw about; drive here and there

inferō, -ferre, intulī, illātum – bring in; introduce

occurrō, -ere, -currī, -cursum – (+ dat.) meet

patior, -ī, passus sum – suffer; endure; undergo

pellō, -ere, pepulī, pulsum – repel; drive back

possum, posse, potuī – be able; have influence

scandō, -ere – climb

sē recipiō, -ere, -cēpī, -ceptum – withdraw; retreat; recover

subeō, -īre, -iī, -itum – undergo

violō, -āre – violate

vītō, -are – avoid; escape

Adjectives

Albānus, -a, -um – Alban; relating to Alba Longa, the town traditionally founded by Aeneas' son Ascanius

aliēnus, -a, -um – belonging to another

inīquus, -a, -um – unjust

Lāvīnius, -a, -um – belonging to Lavinium; Lavinian

memor, -oris – mindful; unforgiving

nefārius, -a, -um – abominable; wicked

ōrātōrius, -a, -um – relating to oratory

posterus, -a, -um – next; future

recens, -entis – new; fresh

superī, -ōrum (or -um) – the gods above

superior, -ius – past; previous

ūtilis, -e – useful; beneficial

Adverbs; Prepositions; Conjunctions

aliquandō – sometimes

noctū – by night

occultē – in secret

propius – nearer

sānē – by all means

unde – whence; from where

usque – continuously

English Derivations

From which Latin roots do the following English words derive?

(i) recent
(ii) pulse
(iii) occurrence
(iv) conflict

(A) Explain the case of the noun underlined:
1. nemini meus adventus <u>labori</u> fuit.
2. hi sunt <u>magnitudine</u> paulo infra elephantos.
3. celebritas mihi <u>odio</u> est.
4. melior vir fuit <u>Africano</u>.
5. Caesar <u>navium</u> parandarum causa moratur.

(B) Identify and explain the verb underlined:
1. quaero cur bona non <u>venierint</u>.
2. dum reliquae naves eo <u>convenirent</u> in ancoris expectavit.
3. utrum indignum <u>sit</u> an non quaeritur.
4. dixit se istum publice <u>laudare</u>.
5. petis a me ut Bibulo te <u>commendem</u>.
6. <u>sequimini</u> me.
7. vereor ut Dolabella ipse satis nobis prodesse <u>possit</u>.
8. si intus esset <u>evocarem</u>.
9. quid enim ille <u>facturus sit</u> incertum est.

(C) Supply the following verb parts:
1. iacto: present imperative singular
2. dimitto: present imperative plural
3. rogo: supine (accusative)
4. effundo: 1st person singular pluperfect subjunctive active
5. dico: supine (ablative)
6. accedo: 3rd person plural future perfect indicative active
7. effundo: genitive gerund
8. criminor: present imperative singular

(D) Translate into English:
1. quaero cur bona non venierint, cur ceteri sponsores et creditores non convenerint. (Cicero *Pro Quinctio* 73)
2. is cum interrogaretur cur nullum supplicium constituisset in eum qui parentem necavisset, respondit se id neminem facturum putavisse. (Cicero *Pro Roscio* 70)
3. ab intitio res quem ad modum gesta sit vobis exponemus, quo facilius audaciam eius cognoscere possitis. (Cicero *Pro S. Roscio Amerino* 14)
4. in ipsa enim Graecia philosophia tanto in honore numquam fuisset, nisi doctissimorum contentionibus dissensionibusque viguisset. (Cicero *Tusculanae Disputationes* 2.4)
5. dum in his locis Caesar navium parandarum causa moratur, ex magna parte Morinorum ad eum legati venerunt, qui se de superioris temporis consilio excusarent. (Caesar *De Bello Gallico* 4.22.1)

(E) Translate into Latin:

1. He asked who he was and what he wanted. (Caesar *Bellum Civile* 2.35)
2. Do not think, judges, that the impudence of cheats and defaulters is not one and the same in all places. (Cicero *Pro Flacco* 48)
3. Much greater eagerness and enthusiasm for fighting were instilled in the army. (Caesar *De Bello Gallico* 1.46.4)
4. In these matters I do not doubt that I will not be able to avoid and escape the charge of negligence. (Cicero *In Verrem* 2.1.103)

FIGURE R.3 Concordia denarius. © *Leeds Museums and Galleries (Discovery Centre)*

EXTRA PASSAGES

Horace claims immortality because of his art.

Exegi monumentum aere perennius
regalique situ pyramidum altius,
quod non imber edax, non aquilo impotens
possit diruere aut innumerabilis
annorum series et fuga temporum.
non omnis moriar multaque pars mei
vitabit Libitinam: usque ego postera
crescam laude recens, dum Capitolium
scandet cum tacita virgine pontifex:
dicar, qua violens obstrepit Aufidus
et qua pauper aquae Daunus agrestium
regnavit populorum, ex humili potens
princeps Aeolium carmen ad Italos
deduxisse modos. sume superbiam
quaesitam meritis et mihi Delphica
lauro cinge volens, Melpomene, comam.
(Horace *Odes* 3.30)

Compare the way Ovid ends his poem, the *Metamorphoses*.

Iamque opus exegi, quod nec Iovis ira nec ignis
nec poterit ferrum nec edax abolere vetustas.
cum volet, illa dies, quae nil nisi corporis huius
ius habet, incerti spatium mihi finiat aevi:
parte tamen meliore mei super alta perennis
astra ferar, nomenque erit indelebile nostrum,
quaque patet domitis Romana potentia terris,
ore legar populi, perque omnia saecula fama,
si quid habent veri vatum praesagia, vivam.
(Ovid *Metamorphoses* 15.871–9)

CONCLUSION

At this stage you have met all the important elements of Latin grammar and word forms that you will need to tackle the reading of Latin prose and verse texts. Of course, you will need to go over the various forms and continue to build upon your knowledge of the grammatical constructions; however, one challenging and, we hope, enjoyable task remains: the best way to strengthen your knowledge and to improve vocabulary is to keep on reading Latin.

The variety of texts before you is almost infinite. First there are the poets and prose-writers of the Classical period, upon whose works this course has been based. Our emphasis in the earlier parts of the course was mainly on the prose works of Cicero and Caesar, as they illustrate most clearly and unambiguously the points you need to master. But the second half introduced the poetry of Catullus and Ovid, of which there is much more for you to enjoy. From there you could move on to Horace and Virgil (whose works are only touched upon in our examples) and the love elegists, Propertius and Tibullus, whose poems can be compared with Ovid's *Amores*. On the prose side you could look at the histories of Sallust, Livy, and Tacitus, the letters of Seneca and the younger Pliny, and even perhaps that great treasure-house of ancient scientific knowledge, the *Natural Histories* of Pliny the elder. You have already had some snippets from the comedies of Plautus and Terence, why not explore a whole play? Among the poets of the Empire you could delve into the *Satires* of Juvenal or the epigrams of Martial, both of which contain vivid insights into daily life in Rome under the emperors, the tragedies of Seneca (some of which may have influenced Shakespeare), and the epics of Lucan and Statius.

Latin has many varieties, some of which diverge considerably from the literary Classical Latin taught in our course. How did Romans actually speak? Some indications of spoken Latin can be found in the more colloquial literary genres, such as comedy, satire, and technical works such as the Roman cookery book of Apicius, or the horse-curing manual known as the *Mulomedicina Chironis*. The language of the slaves in Petronius' *Cena Trimalchionis* is peppered with the Greek loan-words and colloquialisms that must have characterized their speech in real life. From a later date we have the *Peregrinatio Aetheriae*, a colloquial account of a pilgrimage to the Holy Land undertaken by a nun around AD 400. Perhaps nearer to everyday life are the inscriptions found on the walls of Pompeii, buried in the devastating lava flow from Vesuvius in AD 79 and collected by scholars for you to read in printed collections and online. The content varies from election posters and bar menus to the sort of obscene comments that would be at home today on any washroom wall. The most recent set of inscriptions to be available online are those from Hadrian's Wall, the northernmost frontier of the Roman Empire in Britain. These

Wiley's Real Latin: Learning Latin from the Source, First Edition.
Robert Maltby and Kenneth Belcher.
© 2014 John Wiley & Sons, Inc. Published 2014 by John Wiley & Sons, Inc.

are written in ink on thin slivers of wood and contain military records about leave-rotas and supplies, as well as more personal messages, such as a letter home from a soldier to his mother, asking for warmer socks and pants, and an invitation to a birthday party written by a camp commandant's wife.

While colloquial Latin continued to exist and develop at the spoken level, eventually developing into the modern Romance languages such as French, Spanish, and Italian, written or literary Latin continued to be taught and used right through the Middle Ages and into the Renaissance. The syntax of Medieval Latin is in fact very similar to that of Classical, although in vocabulary the distinction between prose and verse features tends to break down. In fact Medieval Latin continued as the international language of science until the nineteenth century. This makes Medieval Latin an essential tool for history students of all kinds. The grammatical rules you have learnt on this course, together with a good Medieval Latin dictionary, will equip you to embark on the translation of these texts. From the time of the Latin Church Fathers, such as Augustine and Jerome, Christian Latin, as seen most clearly in the Latin Vulgate, developed its own style, adopting a number of more colloquial features and influenced, in particular, by the language of the Greek New Testament. Right up until the present day Latin is used as an international language by the Vatican, and scholars are employed there to invent Latin words for the latest items of modern technology, such as mobile phones and lap-tops.

In conclusion we hope to have whetted your appetite to take your Latin studies further. The hardest part of the task, the acquisition of the basic rules, is now behind you, and although you will find it rewarding and necessary to continue to review the forms and the grammatical rules that you have learnt, what remains is the more enjoyable prospect of applying what you have learnt to wherever your Latin explorations may lead.

APPENDICES

Wiley's Real Latin: Learning Latin from the Source, First Edition.
Robert Maltby and Kenneth Belcher.
© 2014 John Wiley & Sons, Inc. Published 2014 by John Wiley & Sons, Inc.

APPENDIX 1 SOME VERBS FOLLOWED BY A COMPLEMENTARY INFINITIVE

audeō – dare
coepī – began
cōnor – try
cōnstituō – determine; decide
cōnsuēscō – become accustomed
contendō – hasten; strive
cupiō – desire
debeō – ought
dēcernō – decide; determine
dēsinō – cease
dēsistō – cease
discō – learn; am taught
doceō – teach
dubitō – hesitate
incipiō – begin
instituō – undertake; begin
malō – prefer
nesciō – not to know how
nōlō – am unwilling; do not wish
parō – prepare
possum – am able; can
sciō – know how
soleō – am accustomed
statuō – resolve
studeō – am eager
timeō – am afraid; fear
vereor – am afraid; fear
videor – seem
volō – wish; want; am willing

APPENDIX 2 *IDEM, ISTE, IPSE*

īdem, eadem, idem – same; the same

Singular

	m.	f.	n.
Nom.	īdem	eadem	idem
Gen.	eiusdem	eiusdem	eiusdem
Dat.	eīdem	eīdem	eīdem
Acc.	eundem	eandem	idem
Abl.	eōdem	eādem	eōdem

Plural

	m.	f.	n.
Nom.	īdem*	eaedem	eadem
Gen.	eōrundem	eārundem	eōrundem
Dat.	īsdem*	īsdem	īsdem
Acc.	eōsdem	eāsdem	eadem
Abl.	īsdem*	īsdem	īsdem

*NB: the following alternative forms of the nom. masc. pl. occur: *eīdem* and *iīdem*; in the dat. and abl. plural (all genders) the forms *eīsdem* and *iīsdem* also occur. Like *is, ea, id*, *īdem* may be used as a pronoun or an adjective.

iste, ista istud – this; that: *iste*, like *hic* and *ille*, is a demonstrative pronoun; it is frequently used in legal contexts for the defendant

Singular

	m.	f.	n.
Nom.	iste	ista	istud
Gen.	istīus	istīus	istīus
Dat.	istī	istī	istī
Acc.	istum	istam	istud
Abl.	istō	istā	istō

Plural

	m.	f.	n.
Nom.	istī	istae	ista
Gen.	istōrum	istārum	istōrum
Dat.	istīs	istīs	istīs
Acc.	istōs	istās	ista
Abl.	istīs	istīs	istīs

ipse, ipsa, ipsum – -self: *ipse* is an intensive pronoun, emphasizing the word it modifies; for example *ego ipse* – I myself; *nos ipsi* – we ourselves, etc.

	Singular		
	m.	**f.**	**n.**
Nom.	ipse	ipsa	ipsum
Gen.	ipsīus	ipsīus	ipsīus
Dat.	ipsī	ipsī	ipsī
Acc.	ipsum	ipsam	ipsum
Abl.	ipsō	ipsā	ipsō

	Plural		
	m.	**f.**	**n.**
Nom.	ipsī	ipsae	ipsa
Gen.	ipsōrum	ipsārum	ipsōrum
Dat.	ipsīs	ipsīs	ipsīs
Acc.	ipsōs	ipsās	ipsa
Abl.	ipsīs	ipsīs	ipsīs

APPENDIX 3 NUMERALS

Cardinal Numbers

ūnus, -a, -um – one

duo, duae, duo – two

trēs, tria – three

quattuor – four

quīnque – five

sex – six

septem – seven

octō – eight

novem – nine

decem – ten

mīlle – one thousand

mīlia, -ium (n.) – thousands

Ordinal Numbers

prīmus, -a, -um – first

secundus, -a, -um – second

tertius, -a, -um – third

quārtus, -a, -um – fourth

quīntus,- a, -um – fifth

sextus, -a, -um – sixth

septimus, -a, -um – seventh

octāvus, -a, -um – eighth

nōnus, -a, -um – ninth

decimus, -a, um – tenth

Declension of *Mīlia*

Nom.	mīlia
Gen.	mīlium
Dat.	mīlibus
Acc.	mīlia
Abl.	mīlibus

APPENDIX 4 *NŌLŌ, MĀLŌ, FĪŌ*

Nōlō, Nōlle, Nōluī

PRESENT INDICATIVE

	SINGULAR	PLURAL
1st person	nōlō	nōlumus
2nd person	nōn vīs	nōn vultis
3rd person	nōn vult	nōlunt

FUTURE INDICATIVE

	SINGULAR	PLURAL
1st person	nōlam	nōlēmus
2nd person	nōlēs	nōlētis
3rd person	nōlet	nōlent

IMPERFECT INDICATIVE

	SINGULAR	PLURAL
1st person	nōlēbam	nōlēbāmus
2nd person	nōlēbās	nōlēbātis
3rd person	nōlēbat	nōlēbant

The forms of the perfect, pluperfect and future perfect are regular.

PRESENT SUBJUNCTIVE

	SINGULAR	PLURAL
1st person	nōlim	nōlīmus
2nd person	nōlīs	nōlītis
3rd person	nōlit	nōlint

The other tenses of the subjunctive are regular. Imperfect: *nōllem*, etc.; perfect: *nōluerim*, etc.; pluperfect: *nōluissem*, etc.

Mālō, Mālle, Māluī

PRESENT INDICATIVE

	SINGULAR	PLURAL
1st person	mālō	mālumus
2nd person	māvīs	māvultis
3rd person	māvult	mālunt

FUTURE INDICATIVE

	SINGULAR	PLURAL
1st person	mālam	mālēmus
2nd person	mālēs	mālētis
3rd person	mālet	mālent

IMPERFECT INDICATIVE

	SINGULAR	PLURAL
1st person	mālēbam	mālēbāmus
2nd person	mālēbās	mālēbātis
3rd person	mālēbat	malēbant

The forms of the perfect are regular.

PRESENT SUBJUNCTIVE

	SINGULAR	PLURAL
1st person	mālim	mālīmus
2nd person	mālīs	mālītis
3rd person	mālit	mālint

The other tenses of the subjunctive are regular. Imperfect: *māllem*, etc.; perfect: *māluerim*, etc.; pluperfect: *māluissem*, etc.

Fīō, Fierī, Factus Sum

PRESENT INDICATIVE

	SINGULAR	PLURAL
1st person	fīō	(fīmus)
2nd person	fīs	(fītis)
3rd person	fit	fīunt

FUTURE INDICATIVE

	SINGULAR	PLURAL
1st person	fīam	fīēmus
2nd person	fīēs	fīētis
3rd person	fīet	fīent

IMPERFECT INDICATIVE

	SINGULAR	PLURAL
1st person	fīēbam	fīēbāmus
2nd person	fīēbās	fīēbātis
3rd person	fīēbat	fīēbant

PRESENT SUBJUNCTIVE

	SINGULAR	PLURAL
1st person	fīam	fīāmus
2nd person	fīās	fīātis
3rd person	fīat	fiant

IMPERFECT SUBJUNCTIVE

	SINGULAR	PLURAL
1st person	fierem	fierēmus
2nd person	fierēs	fierētis
3rd person	fieret	fierent

APPENDIX 5 PERFECT AND PLUPERFECT SUBJUNCTIVE

Perfect Subjunctive Active

FIRST CONJUGATION

	SINGULAR	PLURAL
1st person	amāverim	amāverimus
2nd person	amāverīs	amāverītis
3rd person	amāverit	amāverint

SECOND CONJUGATION

	SINGULAR	PLURAL
1st person	vīderim	vīderimus
2nd person	vīderīs	vīderītis
3rd person	vīderit	vīderint

THIRD CONJUGATION

	SINGULAR	PLURAL
1st person	posuerim	posuerimus
2nd person	posuerīs	posuerītis
3rd person	posuerit	posuerint

FOURTH CONJUGATION

	SINGULAR	PLURAL
1st person	invēnerim	invēnerimus
2nd person	invēnerīs	invēnerītis
3rd person	invēnerit	invēnerint

MIXED CONJUGATION

	SINGULAR	PLURAL
1st person	cēperim	cēperimus
2nd person	cēperīs	cēperītis
3rd person	cēperit	cēperint

Pluperfect Subjunctive Active

FIRST CONJUGATION

	SINGULAR	PLURAL
1st person	amāvissem	amāvissēmus
2nd person	amāvissēs	amāvissētis
3rd person	amāvisset	amāvissent

SECOND CONJUGATION

	SINGULAR	PLURAL
1st person	vīdissem	vīdissēmus
2nd person	vīdissēs	vīdissētis
3rd person	vīdisset	vīdissent

THIRD CONJUGATION

	SINGULAR	PLURAL
1st person	posuissem	posuissēmus
2nd person	posuissēs	posuissētis
3rd person	posuisset	posuissent

FOURTH CONJUGATION

	SINGULAR	PLURAL
1st person	invēnissem	invēnissēmus
2nd person	invēnissēs	invēnissētis
3rd person	invēnisset	invēnissent

MIXED CONJUGATION

	SINGULAR	PLURAL
1st person	cēpissem	cēpissēmus
2nd person	cēpissēs	cēpissētis
3rd person	cēpisset	cēpissent

APPENDIX 6 ROMAN NOMENCLATURE

Roman citizens in the Classical period had three names, the so-called *tria nomina*, e.g., Marcus Tullius Cicero, Gaius Iulius Caesar, Publius Vergilius Maro. These were: the first name or *praenomen* e.g., Marcus, Gaius, Publius; the family name (like our surname), *nomen* or *gentilicium*, giving the *gens* or family, the *gens Tullia* in the case of Cicero, the *gens Iulia* for Caesar, and the *gens Vergilia* for Virgil; finally the cognomen, or unofficial surname, designating a branch of a larger *gens* e.g., Cicero, Caesar, Maro. These often referred to physical peculiarities, so the third name of Publius Ovidius Naso would have come from a long-nosed ancestor; Cicero, literally "chickpea," probably referred to a facial pimple in the form of a chickpea on one of the earlier Tullii. Only 18 *praenomina* were in general use and the most common of these were indicated by abbreviations: P. = Publius, M. = Marcus, Sex. = Sextus, etc. Girls did not have a praenomen in the Classical period, but were known simply by the feminine form of the gentile name, e.g., Cicero's daughter was known simply as Tullia M(arci) f(ilia), Tullia, daughter of Marcus. Women did not usually change their gentile name at marriage.

Biographies

Titus Maccius Plautus (c. 249–c. 184 BC)

The comedies of Plautus are the first works of Latin literature to survive intact. Plautus wrote up to 130 plays during his lifetime and they proved so popular at the box-office after his death that a number of plays of dubious authenticity were attributed to him in order to improve their sales potential. The 20 plays and fragments of a twenty-first which have come down to us are probably those which the late republican scholar Varro said were agreed by all to have been written by Plautus. All Plautus' comedies were based loosely on Greek originals produced over a hundred years before his time. As we have only one fragment of one of these Greek originals which we can compare with Plautus' adaptation (part of Menander's *Double Deceiver*, the model for Plautus' *Bacchides*) we do not know in detail how he adapted these plays for his Roman audience. He was clearly influenced by native Italian drama and probably increased the amount of verse that was sung to musical accompaniment, made greater use of stock comic characters such as slaves and parasites, and introduced an element of Italian farce, including topical Roman allusions, which would have clashed intentionally with the ostensible Greek setting of his plays. The final result would have been altogether livelier with much more knock-about humor, music, and jokes. In this he differs from Terence, a Roman comic playwright of the following generation, who kept closer to the style and spirit of his Greek originals. Plautus is said to have come from the town of Sarsina in Umbria, to have made his money in some kind of theatrical work, to have lost it in a business venture, and to have been forced to work in a mill to recoup his fortunes. All this is probably fiction, based loosely on some of the plots of his plays.

Cornelius Nepos (c. 110–24 BC)

The first biographer whose works survive in Latin. He came from Cisalpine Gaul and was a friend of Catullus, who dedicated a collection of poems to him. He corresponded with Cicero and, like Cicero, was a friend of Atticus. Unlike Cicero, he kept well clear of politics. He published his *De Viris Illustribus*, "On famous men," which contained some 400 lives, mostly of Romans, but including some prominent Greeks and foreigners, first in 34 BC and then in a second, expanded, edition in 27 BC. From this second edition we have his section *De Excellentibus Ducibus Exterarum Gentium*, "On eminent foreign leaders," and from his section on Roman historians the lives of M. Porcius Cato and Atticus. His lost works include a universal history in three books, *Chronica*, five books of anecdotes, *Exempla*, a work on geography, and extended lives of Cicero and Cato.

Marcus Tullius Cicero (106–43 BC)

Rome's most famous orator. He was the son of a rich Roman knight from the small hilltown of Arpinum, the eldest of two sons, who were both given an excellent education in philosophy and rhetoric in Rome and later in Greece. After military service in 90/89 he trained as a lawyer and conducted his first case (*Pro Quinctio*) in 81. His successful defense of the actor Sextus Roscius on a charge of parricide in 80 won him an immediate reputation. From 77 to 79 he studied philosophy and oratory, first in Athens and then in Rhodes. On his return to Rome he took up a public career and was elected as quaestor in western Sicily in 75 and praetor in 66. By securing the conviction of C. Verres for extortion in Sicily he won a notable victory over the chief orator of the time, Q. Hortensius Hortalus, and eventually came to replace him as the leading Roman lawyer. He was elected consul in 63

FIGURE A.1 Bust of Marcus
Tullius Cicero, 106–43 BC.
*Source: Musei Capitolini, Rome,
Italy/Giraudon/The Bridgeman Art
Library*

and in the same year persuaded the senate of the danger of Catiline and his co-conspirators. Catiline fled to Etruria, but five prominent Roman conspirators were arrested and executed on December 5, 63. Cicero was subsequently threatened with prosecution for having Roman citizens executed without trial and in 58 fled the country for Macedonia before any prosecution could take place. He was declared an exile, his house in Rome was destroyed, and his country villa at Tusculum was badly damaged. With the support of Pompey and the tribune of the people, Milo, he was eventually recalled and was welcomed back to Rome in September 57. When Caesar renewed his political alliance with Pompey and Crassus in 56 Cicero reluctantly supported the triumvirate, despite his personal distaste for Caesar. He withdrew from public life and devoted himself to writing, but was forced by Pompey and Caesar to take on cases against his will. In 53 he was rewarded with the prestigious religious office of augur. He spent the year of summer 52 to summer 51 abroad as proconsular governor of Cilicia (in modern Turkey). On his return the Civil War was well under way. He refused an offer from Caesar to join the senate in 49 and joined Pompey and the republicans in Greece. After the battle of Pharsalus he refused an offer to take over the command of the republican forces and returned instead to Rome where he was pardoned by Caesar. His political career was, however, by this stage at an end and he devoted himself to writing. He was not invited to take part in the assassination plot against Caesar in 44, but, after welcoming the murder, regained some political power under the influence of Octavian and made a number of speeches in the senate against Antony (*Philippicae*). However, he was powerless to stop the formation of the triumvirate of Octavian, Antony, and Lepidus in 43. Octavian did not oppose Antony's nomination of Cicero as a victim of the proscriptions with which this new regime started and Cicero was murdered by Antony's troops while attempting to escape by sea on December 7, 43. His works include: 58 law-court speeches; several treatises on oratory, including *De Oratore* (55), *Brutus* and *Orator* (46); some early poems; letters in 16 books to his friends (*Epistulae ad Familiares*), 16 books to Atticus (*Epistulae ad Atticum*), and smaller collections to Brutus and to his brother Quintus; philosophical works including *De Republica, De Legibus, De Natura Deorum, De Finibus*, and the *Tusculanae Disputationes*.

Gaius Iulius Caesar (100–44 BC)

Caesar was born of an aristocratic family which traced its descent from Venus and Aeneas. He married the daughter of the influential L. Cornelius Cinna (consul of 87) and was

FIGURE A.2 Bust of Julius Caesar, 100–44 BC. *Source: Galleria degli Uffizi, Florence, Italy/Alinari/The Bridgeman Art Library*

elected by his father-in-law to a prestigious priesthood, the *flamen Dialis*. This appointment was annulled by Cinna's enemy, Sulla, when he became dictator in 84. Caesar spent most of the next decade in Asia, studying philosophy and winning military distinction. In 73 he returned to Rome to take up a further religious appointment as *pontifex*. He next became military tribune and then as quaestor in 69 he spent a year in the province of Further Spain. In this year both his aunt Iulia and his wife died. On his return he married Pompeia, the granddaughter of Sulla, and made an alliance with M. Licinius Crassus, with whose financial support he was able to spend vast sums on the improvement of the Appian Way as *aedile* in 65. In 63 he won election to the chief pontificate, through bribery, and his power and importance in the state were further enhanced by his election to the praetorship in 62. Initially a supporter of Catiline, he withdrew this support when Catiline turned to conspiracy. Nevertheless he spoke against the death penalty for the conspirators proposed by Cicero in 63. In 62 he divorced his second wife, who, as priestess of the rites of the *Bona Dea*, had become involved in a scandal when P. Clodius Pulcher gained admittance to the rites, from which men were excluded, by dressing as a woman. As governor of Further Spain in 61/60 he made enough booty out of attacking the local tribes to clear his personal debts and to pay huge sums into the Roman treasury. With the support of Pompey, Crassus, and the senate he was elected consul for the year 59. In 58 Caesar married Calpurnia, whose father, L. Calpurnius Piso was elected consul in 58. Caesar was in this year voted a five-year command in Illyricum and Gaul. He started a major war against the Helvetii and this eventually led to his conquest of the whole of Gaul. In 56 Caesar renewed his compact with Pompey and Crassus and received a renewal of his command in Gaul for a further five years. After the disintegration of the alliance Caesar secured authorization to stand for the consulship in absence in 49, but the legality of this move was challenged and in the same year Caesar invaded Italy and started a civil war in order to escape conviction and exile. His campaigns in Italy (against Ahenobarbus), Spain (against Pompey's legates), and Greece and Egypt (against Pompey) are described in his work *Bellum Civile* (The Civil War). Having established Cleopatra VII (with whom he had a son, Ptolemy Caesar) on the throne in Egypt and having reorganized the eastern provinces, he returned to Italy in 47, where he had to settle serious social unrest and a mutiny in the army. He then traveled to North Africa, where he defeated the republican leaders, including Scipio and Cato and returned to Rome in the autumn of 46 to celebrate four separate triumphs. Soon after this he had to move against Pompeian forces in Spain, whom he defeated at the battle of Munda, with great loss of life on both sides. After reorganizing Spain and introducing massive colonization there he returned to Rome in 45 to celebrate a triumph over Spain. In the last decade of his life he had been given unprecedented powers by the senate. He had been dictator on four occasions between 49 and 45 before being voted a perpetual dictatorship in 44 and had repeated consulships in the years 48, 46, 45, and 44. He always refused the hated title of "king," but in the last year of his life had accepted divine honors. It is hardly surprising that the leading families of Rome began to be suspicious of the accumulation of such power in the hands of one man. An assassination plot was carefully planned and resulted in the murder of Caesar in the theater of Pompey on the Ides (15th) of March 44 BC. In his writings he favored a plain and simple style. His memoirs on the Gallic War, *De Bello Gallico*, in seven books and the Civil War, *Bellum Civile*, in three have survived. Some of his

FIGURE A.3 Bust of Pompey, 106–48 BC. c. 60 BC. *Source: Ny Carlsberg Glyptotek, Copenhagen, Denmark/The Bridgeman Art Library*

speeches and a grammatical treatise were also published in his lifetime but have not come down to us.

Sallust (Gaius Sallustius Crispus) (86–35 BC)

Sallust was born of a local aristocratic family in the Sabine town of Amiternum. He initially followed a public career in Rome, becoming tribune of the people in 52 BC. He was expelled from the senate in 50, probably because of his opposition to Cicero in 52, and joined Caesar, who put him in charge of a legion in 49. As praetor in 46 he took part in the African campaign and was made first governor of the province of Africa Nova. When he returned to Rome he was charged with malpractice as governor and only escaped with help from Caesar. Deciding that his political career was now at an end he withdrew from public life and dedicated himself to writing history. His first work *Bellum Catilinae* (The War of Catiline), completed in 42–41 BC, dealt with the conspiracy of Catiline. He sees this conspiracy as symptomatic of the moral decline of Rome, which began after the fall of Carthage. His second work, *Bellum Iugurthinum* (The War of Jugurtha), completed 41–40 BC, deals with Rome's battles against Jugurtha, a prince of Numidia in North Africa, between 112 and 104 BC. The moral is again the decline of the Roman nobility and all the Roman generals involved in the campaign, including Marius and Sulla, come in for considerable criticism. Sallust's last work, *The Histories*, survives only in fragments and continues the story of the decline of the Roman state from 78 BC, perhaps down to the mid sixties or later. Sallust's approach to history may have been somewhat unsubtle, but he was much praised as a stylist, particularly for the rhetoric of his speeches, where many have noted the influence of the Greek historian Thucydides.

Gaius Valerius Catullus (c. 84–54 BC)

Born of a wealthy family in Verona, Catullus was sent to Rome as a young man to be edu-cated in preparation for a political career. Apart from serving on the staff of Gaius Memmius, pro-praetor in Bithynia in 57–56 BC, he seems to have taken no further part in public life and, except for occasional criticism of Caesar, his poetry concerns itself little with the tur-bulent politics of the late republic. He lived in a circle of wealthy young aristocrats who turned their backs on traditional Roman values and embraced Hellenistic Greek culture. In literature, too, he was one of a whole circle of young poets, referred to as the "neoterics," who looked to Hellenistic poetry to provide them with new forms and content. The central theme of his poetry is the ups and downs of his relationship with a married aristocratic lady, whom he calls Lesbia. Apuleius tells us that her real name was Clodia. The Clodia in ques-tion has since been identified with the sister of P. Clodius Pulcher and the wife of the consul of 60 BC, Q. Caecilius Metallus Celer. His love poetry addressed to Lesbia is more serious in tone than the light-hearted love poems of the Hellenistic *Greek Anthology*. It concerns his longing for a meaningful lifetime relationship which eventually ends in disillusion. Catullus died young, at around the age of 30, and left behind only one slim volume of some 116 poems. These are arranged on metrical grounds. Sixty short poems in a variety of lyric meters are followed by eight longer poems in a variety of meters. The final section 69–116 contains shorter epigrams in elegiac meter. Both the initial mixed lyric section and the final epigrammatic section contain cycles of Lesbia poems (2, 3, 5, 7, 8, 11 and 70–87) which trace the affair from its beginnings, through the height of passion to final disillusion and break up. Further cycles deal with his friends Furius and Aurelius (15–26) and Gellius (74–91 and 116). Other themes, including his love for the boy Iuventus, invectives against Caesar, and his trip to Bithynia are distributed throughout the work. In general the short "social poetry" of 1–60 reflect the careful craftsmanship of the shorter Hellenistic forms; the longer poems include two wedding poems (61–2), a poem about a youth who castrates himself as a devotee of Cybele (63), an epyllion on the loves of Peleus and Thetis and Ariadne and Theseus (64), a translation of a poem by Callimachus on the *Lock of Berenice* (66), with its introductory poem 65, and poem 68 (often split into two), a combination of mythological love themes with Catullus' own personal experience, often seen a precursor of the Latin love elegy of Tibullus, Propertius, and Ovid. The epigrams in elegiac meter with which the col-lection ends (69–116) deal with similar personal and social themes as the opening mixed meter poems, but in a more serious and reflective analytical style.

FIGURE A.4 Virgil mosaic, 3rd century AD. *Source: Museo della Civiltà Romana, Rome, Italy/The Bridgeman Art Library*

Virgil (Publius Vergilius Maro) (70–19 BC)

Virgil was the greatest poet of the Augustan age. He was born in a village near Mantua in 70 BC. He is said to have been educated in Cremona and Milan before being sent to complete his education in Rome. It can be assumed his parents were relatively well-to-do. He may have later studied Epicurean philosophy in the Greek influenced schools of Naples. Like that of Propertius and Ovid his family suffered in Octavian's land confiscations of 41–40 BC. His first collection of poems, in which this event was hinted at, was the *Eclogues*, ten pastoral poems influenced by the *Idylls* of Theocritus, published in 39–38 BC. At some time after their appearance he entered the literary circle of the influential Maecenas, later to become a firm supporter of Augustus. Virgil's second work, the *Georgics* (Farming Poems), a didactic poem on the subject of agriculture influenced by Hesiod's *Works and Days*, appeared around 29 BC. His greatest work, the *Aeneid*, an epic on the foundation of Rome by Aeneas, a fugitive from the Trojan War, was begun in the late twenties. When Virgil died in 19 BC he had apparently left it unfinished. It was edited and published posthumously by Varius Rufus and Plotius Tuca. Virgil's epic was to become the Roman equivalent of Homer and was taught to schoolboys for centuries to come. In the Middle Ages Virgil began to be seen as a divine genius, and was so portrayed in Dante's *Inferno*.

Horace (Quintus Horatius Flaccus) (65–8 BC)

The poet Horace was born on December 8, 65 BC and died on November 27, 8 BC. He came from the town of Venusia in Apulia. His father was a freedman, perhaps enslaved in the

Social War (91–87 BC), in the course of which we know Venusia was captured by Rome. His father had a smallholding in Venusia, but earned enough money as a public auctioneer (*coactor*) to give his son a good education in Rome and later Athens. While in Athens Horace joined Brutus and fought on his side in the Civil War at the battle of Philippi in Greece in 42 BC, but with the fall of Brutus Horace's family property was confiscated. Horace was lucky to be allowed back to Italy and to earn a living there as *scriba quaestorius*, a relatively respectable government post.

His first poems, written at this period between 40 and 30 BC, were the *Epodes* and the *Satires*, which brought him into contact with the poets Virgil and Varius Rufus. They in turn introduced him to the prestigious circle of Maecenas, where he was formally accepted in 38 BC. Maecenas, the patron of Virgil and head of the most important literary circle of the period, later gave him the famous Sabine farm, which made Horace financially secure for the rest of his life. Later Horace was on good terms with the emperor Augustus himself, but in his poetry tried to maintain his independence of both these influential figures. After the publication of his satirical works the *Epodes* and *Satires* around 30 BC Horace turned to lyric poetry in his *Odes*, a collection of poems in lyric Greek meters on various topics including love, philosophy, and politics, based on the work of the Greek poets Sappho and Alcaeus. The first three books of *Odes* were published as a collection in 23 BC. This was followed in 17 BC by the *Carmen Saeculare* (a hymn to Apollo and Diana sung by a chorus of 27 boys and 27 girls), to celebrate Augustus' Secular Games of that year and then later by a fourth book of *Odes*, in which panegyric of the Augustan epoch as a period of peace and prosperity comes to the fore. The fourth book of the *Odes* was Horace's final publication.

Livy (Titus Livius) (59 BC–AD 17)

Livy was born in the prosperous city of Patavium in northern Italy. An epitaph from Padua, which may be his, records that T. Livius had a wife, Cassia Prima, and two sons. It is uncertain when he came to Rome, but it is clear that later in his career he was on good terms with Augustus and it was Livy who encouraged the future emperor Claudius to take up the writing of history. Apart from the historical work for which he is famous today, he also wrote philosophical dialogues, which have not survived. Livy's history was entitled *Ab Urbe Condita Libri* (Books from the Foundation of the City) and dealt with the history of Rome from its foundation to the present day in 142 books. Of these only books 1–10 and 21–45 survive intact. There are also summaries of the rest, an epitome summarizing books 37–40 and 48–55 and the so-called *Periochae*, which summarize all books except 136 and 137. Livy relied in his composition on earlier literary sources, such as Polybius (for books 31–145) or Licinius Macer and Quadrigarius (for books 1–10), rather than consulting historical monuments and documents directly. Livy was noted for his rich, flowing style, referred to by Quintilian in the first century AD as *lactea ubertas* (milky smoothness). He brought his history to life by a mixture of vivid narrative scenes alternating with direct speech, purporting to give the actual words of those involved in the events. In his first ten books, on the early history of Rome, he used poetic or archaic words to give added weight to his narrative, a practice avoided by Caesar, who preferred a simpler and more direct narrative style. His main aim was the patriotic one of chronicling Rome's rise to power, first over Italy and then over the rest of the Mediterranean world, and highlighting the virtues of courage and moral uprightness which enabled them to achieve this result.

Albius Tibullus (c. 50–18 BC)

Tibullus wrote two books of elegies. The first contains poems addressed to his mistress Delia (1, 2, 3, 5, 6), and the second to a mistress named Nemesis (3, 4, 6). These names were pseudonyms, as was the name Marathus of a boy addressed by Tibullus in his first book (4, 8, 9). Of the three Roman elegists, Propertius, Tibullus, and Ovid, Tibullus was the only one to include in his works amatory poems addressed to a boy. A third book which comes down to us in the manuscripts with the other two, was not composed by Tibullus, but consists of a collection of poems by later authors, one of whom was the female poet Sulpicia. Like the other elegists Tibullus expresses a preference for a life of idleness and love as opposed to the active life of the soldier, although in real life he seems to have served in military campaigns alongside his patron, Messalla Corvinus (poems 1.3, 1.7). Within his poems he makes frequent use of the images of love as a form of military service or slavery to the mistress. Mythology is not absent from his poetry (e.g., 1.3, 2.3), but plays a less important role than it does in his fellow elegists. He differs from them in his expression of reverence for traditional rustic religion (with poem 1.2, for example, depicting a rustic festival at which the poet himself officiates). An anonymous life claims he was good-looking and well-dressed, that he was of well-to-do equestrian status, and that he won military awards for his service in foreign wars. His family property probably suffered in Octavian's land confiscations of 41–40 BC (1.1.41f.). In the view of the first-century AD critic, Quintilian, Tibullus was stylistically the most elegant of the elegists. He greatly influenced Ovid, who wrote a famous lament on his death (Ovid *Amores* 3.9).

Sextus Propertius (c. 50–2 BC)

Propertius was a Roman love elegist and contemporary of Tibullus. The son of a well-to-do equestrian family from the area of Assisi, he lost his father as a young man and his family property subsequently suffered in land confiscations of 41–40 BC (4.1.127ff.), as did that of Tibullus. In the last poem of his first book he tells how his family fought against Octavian in the battle of Perusia in 41 BC. Many of his poems, in the first three books, contain some criticism of Augustus and his policies. The main subject of all four of his books is his love for his mistress Cynthia (again a literary pseudonym). His language is more convoluted than that of Tibullus and he makes much greater use of mythology. Like Tibullus he rejects the life of the statesman and soldier in favor of the life of love and shares with him the imagery of love as a form of slavery or military service. His first book, published in 28 BC, consists almost entirely of a series of poems addressed to his friends. Book 2 is probably an amalgamation of two original books and contains themes of love but also explores literary issues connected with his recent attachment to the literary circle of Maecenas. In book 3 the subject matter is widened, to include, for example, a poem on the death of Augustus' nephew. The final poems of the book are concerned with the end of the affair with Cynthia. In book 4 the mood changes and the poet devotes himself to themes connected with the

FIGURE A.5 Ovid (engraving), 19th century. *Source: Cook, J.W./ Private Collection/Ken Welsh/The Bridgeman Art Library*

history and religious traditions of Rome (1, 2, 4, 6, 9, 10). In two of the remaining poems he returns to the theme of Cynthia (7 and 8). Propertius' vivid description of the affair with Cynthia, his wide literary learning, and (at least in books 1–3), his political independence make him a poet of lasting significance.

Ovid (Publius Ovidius Naso) (43 BC–AD 17)

As he tells us in his autobiographical poem, *Tristia* 4.10, Ovid was born in the town of Sulmo in the Abruzzo region of Italy. Like Tibullus and Propertius, he belonged to the equestrian rank. He received a good education in Rome and served as a minor judicial officer before abandoning a public career for poetry. His first literary patron was Messalla Corvinus, to whose circle Tibullus also belonged, and Ovid had a prominent literary career before being banished from Rome by Augustus in AD 8 to Tomis on the Black Sea., where he languished until his death in AD 17. Ovid gives two reasons for his exile, a poem (*carmen*) and a mistake (*error*). The poem was his *Ars Amatoria* (Art of Love), which ran contrary to Augustus' conservative moral legislation and encouragement of marriage in the ruling classes. About the mistake, we have little evidence, except that it may have involved his failure to report some scandal connected with the imperial house. Ovid died in exile, leaving behind in Rome a wife, a daughter, and two grandchildren. His first book *Amores* (Loves) in three books (probably a second edition of an original five-book collection) belongs to the genre of love elegy as practiced by his predecessors Propertius and Tibullus. Published in 16 BC, or perhaps a little later, in its three-book form, it celebrates a mistress Corinna, who in many respects is a literary creation, owing much to Propertius' Cynthia and Tibullus' Delia. Ovid's use of colorful mythological illustration places him closer to Propertius. His poems provide a humorous and more detached and literary exploration of previous elegiac themes. His next work, the *Heroides* (Heroines), or perhaps more correctly *Epistulae Heroidum* (Letters of Heroines) consists in poems 1–14 of single letters from mythological heroines to absent husbands or lovers. The double *Heroides* (poems 16–21) consist of letters from heroines set alongside their replies. In these poems Ovid explores to the full the humorous possibilities of the epistolary genre. The *Ars Amatoria* (Art of Love) which follows is a mock-didactic poem in three books on the art of courtship, with the first two books being addressed to men and the third to women. The situations described owe much to the conventions of elegy. Ovid's early elegiac career ends with the publication of *Remedia Amoris* (Remedies of Love), a kind of recantation of the *Ars*, giving advice on how to fall out of love. The mythological element that had played such a key role in his elegiac works comes to the fore in his unorthodox epic in 15 books, the *Metamorphoses* (Transformations). The poem consists of a series of mythological tales connected with the theme of change of shape. The whole is loosely chronological in form, beginning with the story of creation from chaos and ending with themes from the poet's own day. The greater part of the poem, however, is taken up with mythological tales in no particular chronological sequence. The work represents perhaps the best expression of Ovid's poetic genius, with its witty verbal play and arresting visual detail. The *Fasti* (Calendar) moves on to a new topic of the Roman calendar. It was planned in 12 books, with one book representing each month, but it was left incomplete on Ovid's exile and only the first six books survive. From exile Ovid wrote the *Tristia* (Sorrows), a series of poems addressed from Tomis to his wife and friends back in Rome. These, like the later *Epistulae ex Ponto* (Letters from Pontus), serve as open letters arguing for his re-instatement back in Rome. Ovid is perhaps the most influential of the Roman poets on later western art and culture and was instrumental in passing on the myths of antiquity to the Middle Ages.

APPENDIX 7 SO-CALLED FUTURE IMPERATIVE

Active

FIRST CONJUGATION

	SINGULAR	PLURAL
2nd person	amātō	amātōte
3rd person	amātō	amāntō

SECOND CONJUGATION

	SINGULAR	PLURAL
2nd person	vidētō	vidētōte
3rd person	vidētō	videntō

THIRD CONJUGATION

	SINGULAR	PLURAL
2nd person	ponitō	ponitōte
3rd person	ponitō	ponuntō

FOURTH CONJUGATION

	SINGULAR	PLURAL
2nd person	invenītō	invenītōte
3rd person	invenītō	inveniuntō

MIXED CONJUGATION

	SINGULAR	PLURAL
2nd person	capitō	capitōte
3rd person	capitō	capiuntō

Passive (these will be the forms for deponent verbs)

FIRST CONJUGATION

	SINGULAR	PLURAL
2nd person	amātor	amāminī
3rd person	amātor	amantor

SECOND CONJUGATION

	SINGULAR	PLURAL
2nd person	vidētor	vidēminī
3rd person	vidētor	videntor

THIRD CONJUGATION

	SINGULAR	PLURAL
2nd person	ponitor	poniminī
3rd person	ponitor	ponuntor

FOURTH CONJUGATION

	SINGULAR	PLURAL
2nd person	invenītor	invenīminī
3rd person	invenītor	inveniuntor

MIXED CONJUGATION

	SINGULAR	PLURAL
2nd person	capitor	capiminī
3rd person	capitor	capiuntor

APPENDIX 8 TIMELINE

Timeline of events down to the death of Augustus

753 BC	Traditional date for the foundation of Rome
753–509	Period of the kings of Rome
509	Foundation of the Roman Republic
450	Laws of the Twelve Tables published
390	Sack of Rome by the Gauls
334–264	Roman expansion to control all Italy south of the Po
264–241	First Punic War against Carthage
240–207	Livius Andronicus, first Roman playwright
227	Sicily and Sardinia made provinces
218–201	Second Punic War against Carthage
204–184	Career of playwright Plautus
204–169	Poet Ennius active in Rome
202	Carthage becomes a dependent of Rome
202–192	Conquest of Cisalpine Gaul
166–159	The plays of Terence produced in Rome
149	Cato's history of Rome, called *Origines*
149–146	Third Carthaginian War; Carthage destroyed; Africa becomes a Roman province
148	Macedonia becomes a Roman province
136–132	First Sicilian Slave War
133–129	Attalus III of Pergamum leaves his kingdom to Rome, which becomes the Roman province of Asia
133	Tribunate of Tiberius Gracchus
123–122	Tribunate of Gaius Gracchus
121	Gallia Narbonensis becomes a Roman province
106	Birth of Cicero
104–102	Second Sicilian Slave War
100	Birth of Caesar
99	Birth of the poet Lucretius
84	Birth of the poet Catullus
82–80	Sulla dictator at Rome
73–71	Slave revolt of Spartacus
70	Trial of Verres
	Consulate of Crassus and Pompey
	Birth of Virgil

65	Birth of the poet Horace
63	Consulate of Cicero
	Catilinarian conspiracy
	Birth of Augustus (Octavian)
	Roman provinces of Bithynia, Cilicia, Syria, and Crete established
60	First triumvirate of Pompey, Crassus, and Caesar
59	Birth of Livy
59–54	Catullus writes his Lesbia poems
58–49	Caesar's campaigns in Gaul and Britain (55–54)
55	First permanent stone theater in Rome (Theatre of Pompey)
49	Caesar crosses the Rubicon and begins a civil war
49–27	M. Terentius Varro active as a scholar in Rome
48	Caesar defeats Pompey at Pharsalus
	Pompey murdered in Egypt
44	Murder of Caesar on March 15 (the Ides)
	M. Antonius (Marc Antony) in sole charge of Rome
43	Murder of Cicero
	Birth of Ovid
	Consulate of Octavia
	Second triumvirate of Antony, Lepidus, and Octavian
42	Brutus and Cassius defeated at Philippi
40	Pact of Brundisium between Octavian, Lepidus, and Antony
37	Renewal of the second triumvirate
31	Octavian defeats Antony at Actium
30	Antony and Cleopatra commit suicide
	Annexation of Egypt by Rome
29–16	Propertius *Elegies* I–IV
28–19	Tibullus *Elegies* I and II
27	Octavian becomes Augustus
25	Ovid begins work on the *Amores*
19	Death of Virgil and Tibullus
9	End of Livy's history of Rome
8	Death of Horace
AD 8	Ovid banished to the Black Sea
AD 14	Death of Augustus, succession of Tiberius

ab (+ abl.) – from; away from; from (of time); following (sometimes written *a* before a consonant)

abdicō, -āre – (with *se*) resign

abdō, abdere, abdidī, abditum – hide

abeō, abīre, abī(v)ī, abitum – go away

abhorreō, abhorrēre, abhorruī – abhor; hate; not to wish

abiciō, abicere, abiēcī, abiectum – throw away

absolvō absolvere, absolvī, absolūtum – free; (+ acc. + gen.) – absolve (someone) of

abstrahō, abstrahere, abstraxī, abstractum – drag away

absum, abesse, afuī – be absent; be away; be distant (from); be far away (from)

accedō, accēdere, accessī, accessum – approach

acceptum, -ī (n.) – credit; income

accidō, accidere, accīdī – happen; (+ dat.) happen (to someone); befall (someone)

accipiō, accipere, accēpī; acceptum – receive; accept

accūsātio, -ōnis (f.) – accusation; prosecution

accusō, -āre – blame; find fault with; (+ acc. + gen.) accuse (someone) of

ācer, ācris, ācre – keen; sharp; harsh; severe

acerbus, -a, -um – harsh

acerrimus, -a, -um – most eager; most passionate

aciēs, aciēī (f.) – battle-line; battle

acriter – fiercely; keenly

actio, -ōnis (f.) – action

actor, -ōris (m.) – actor; orator; advocate

ad (+ acc.) – to; towards; for; against

addūcō, addūcere, addūxī, adductum – lead to; induce

adeō, adīre, adī(v)ī, aditum – approach

adequitō, -āre – ride up (to)

adferō, adferre, attulī, allātum – bring to; carry to

adfīnitās, -ātis (f.) – relationship; family ties

adflīgō, adflīgere, adflīxī, adflictum – strike; batter; wreck

adhibeō, adhibēre, adhibuī, adhibitum – show; display

adiuvō, adiuvāre, adiūvī, adiūtum – help; assist

administrō, -āre – assist; take charge of

admirābilis, -e – admirable

admīror, admīrārī, admīrātus sum – admire; marvel at

admodum – very

admonitio, -ōnis (f.) – suggestion; admonition

adsentior, adsentī, adsensus sum (+ dat.) – agree with

adulescens, -entis (m.) – young man

adventus, -ūs (m.) – arrival

aedificium, aedificiī (n.) – building

aedis, -is (f.) – building; temple

Aeduī, -ōrum (m. pl.); also spelled Haeduī (see Chapter 8) – the Aedui, a Gallic tribe

Aequī, -ōrum (m. pl.) – a people of Italy

aequō, -āre – make equal

aequus, -a, -um – equal; fair

aes aliēnum, aeris aliēnī (n.) – debt; loan

aestās, -ātis (f.) – summer

aestimō, -āre – value; appraise; weigh

aetās, aetātis (f.) – age; life; time of life; generation

afficiō, afficere, affēcī, affectum – inflict upon; punish

Africa, -ae (f.) – Africa

agger, aggeris (m.) – earthwork; ramp

agitō, -āre – move; drive; rouse; celebrate

agnōscō, agnōscere, agnōvī, agnitum – recognize

agō, agere, ēgī, actum – do; accomplish; lead; act (in a play); (*quid agis*? – How are you?)

agricola, -ae (m.) – farmer

Wiley's Real Latin: Learning Latin from the Source, First Edition.
Robert Maltby and Kenneth Belcher.
© 2014 John Wiley & Sons, Inc. Published 2014 by John Wiley & Sons, Inc.

Agrippa, -ae (m.) – Marcus Vipsanius Agrippa, a
   Roman general
alacritās, -ātis (f.) – eagerness
Albānus, -a, -um – Alban; relating to Alba Longa,
   the town traditionally founded by Aeneas' son
   Ascanius
aliēnus, -a, -um – belonging to another
aliquandō – at some time; sometimes
aliquī, aliqua, aliquod – some; any
aliquis, aliquid – someone; something; anyone;
   anything
alius, -a, -ud – other; another; aliī . . . aliī –
   some . . . others
alter, altera, alterum – other (of two); one (of two);
   second
altercātio, -ōnis (f.) – argument
altius – more deeply
amīcissimus, -a, -um – most friendly
amīcus, -ī (m.) – friend
āmittō, āmittere, āmīsī, āmissum – send away; lose
amō, -āre – love
angustus, -a, -um – narrow
anhelō, -āre – breath (out); exhale
anima, -ae (f.) – spirit; ghost
animadvertō, animadvertere, animadvertī,
   animadversum – notice
animal, -ālis (n.) – animal
animus, -ī (m.) – mind; spirit; heart; feelings
annus, -ī (m.) – year
ante (+ acc.) – before; also = anteā – before
anteā – before
antepōnō, antepōnere, anteposuī, antepositum –
   place before
Antiochus, -i (m.) – a Syrian prince
antīquus, -a, -um – ancient
Antōnius, Antōniī (m.) – Marc Antony, a Roman
   general
aperiō, aperīre, aperuī, apertum – open; reveal;
   make clear
aperte – openly
appellō, -āre – address; call (by name)
appetō, appetere, appetī(v)ī, appetītum – seek for;
   aim at; make for
apportō, -āre – carry to; bring to

aptus, -a, -um – suited
apud (+ acc.) – in the house of; near
aqua, -ae (f.) – water
Aquitānī, -ōrum (m. pl.) – Aquitanians
āra, -ae (f.) – altar
Arar, Araris (m.) – the Arar, a river in Gaul (abl.
   Arari in Caesar)
arātor, -ōris (m.) – ploughman; cultivator
arbiter, -trī (m.) – arbiter; judge
arbitror, arbitrārī, arbitrātus sum – think; judge;
   suppose
arbor, -oris (f.) – tree
arcessō, arcessere, arcessīvī, arcessītum –
   send for
arduus, -a, -um – steep; difficult
argentum, -ī (n.) – silver
argūmentum, -ī (n.) – argument; evidence
Ariovistus, -ī (m.) – Ariovistus (ruler of a German
   tribe)
armō, -āre – arm
arripiō, arripere, arripuī, arreptum – snatch; seize
Asparāgium, Asparāgiī (n.) – Asparagium, a town
   in Illyria
aspectus, -ūs (m.) – sight
asper, -era, -erum – desperate
Athēnae, -ārum (f. pl.) – Athens
Athēniensis, -e – Athenian
atque – and
attingō, attingere, attigī, attactum – touch
auctor, -ōris (m.) – author; adviser; perpetrator
auctoritās, -ātis (f.) – authority, influence
audācia, -ae (f.) – boldness
audax, -ācis – brave
audeō, audēre, ausus sum – dare
audiō, audīre, audīvī, audītum – hear; listen to
auferō, auferre, abstulī, ablātum – steal; take away;
   take from
Aurēlia via, Aurēliae viae (f.) – the Aurelian Way, a
   coastal road from Rome to the Alps
aureus, -a, -um – golden; gold
auris, -is (f.) – ear
aurum, -ī (n.) – gold
autem – however; moreover
autumnus, -ī (m.) – autumn

auxilium, auxiliī (n.) – help; aid (in the plural
  – reinforcements)

āversus, -a, -um – turned away; from behind

āvertō, āvertere, āvertī, āversum – turn aside; turn
  away

avunculus, -ī (m.) – uncle

Axōna, -ae (m.) – a river in Gaul

bāsiō, -āre – kiss

bāsium, bāsiī (n.) – kiss

Belgae, -ārum (m. pl.) – Belgae (a Gallic tribe)

Belides, -um (f. pl.) – the 50 granddaughters of
  Belus, i.e., the Danaids (of whom 49 killed their
  husbands on their wedding night)

bellum, -ī (n.) – war

bellus, -a, -um – beautiful

bonus, -a, -um – good

brevis, -e – short; brief

Brundisium, Brundisiī (n.) – Brundisium, a town
  in Italy

Byzantiī, -ōrum (m. pl.) – Byzantines

C. Aquilius, -iī (m.) – Gaius Aquilius, a Roman
  jurist and contemporary of Cicero

C. Laelius, -iī (m.) – father-in-law of Q. Mucius
  Scaevola (see below)

C. Mūcius, -iī (m.) – Gaius Mucius (see Chapter 2)

cadō, cadere, cecidī, cāsum – fall; happen

caedēs, -is (f.) – slaughter

Canīnius, Canīniī (m.) – Gallus Caninius, tribune
  56 BC

cānus, -a, -um – white (of hair)

capiō, capere, cēpī, captum – take; capture (*arma
  capiō* – take up arms)

Capitōlium, Capitōliī – the Capitol, where a temple
  of Jupiter was located

captō, -āre – catch

caput, capitis (n.) – head; face; life

careō, carēre, caruī (+ abl.) – lack; be without

carpō, carpere, carpsī, carptum – pluck at; feed on

Casticus, -ī (m.) – Casticus, one of the Sequani
  (see below)

castra, -ōrum (n. pl.) – camp

castra pōnō, pōnere, posuī, positum – pitch camp

cāsū – by chance

cāsus, -ūs (m.) – chance; falling down; event

Catilīna, -ae (m.) – Lucius Sergius Catilina,
  conspirator against the Republic

Cato, -ōnis (m.) – Gaius Porcius Cato, tribune 56
  BC

causa, -ae – cause; reason (abl. *causā* + gen. – for
  the sake of)

caveō, cavēre, cavī, cautum – be on one's guard;
  take care

cēdō, cēdere, cessī, cessum (+ dat.) – yield (to);
  give in (to)

celebrō, -āre – celebrate; honor

celeriter – swiftly

celō, -āre – hide

Celtae, -ārum (m. pl.) – Celts

cēna, -ae (f.) – dinner

cēnō, -āre – dine

cernō, cernere, crēvī, crētum – perceive; see

certē – certainly; surely

certiōrem faciō, facere, fēcī, factum – inform

certō – certainly

certus, -a, -um – certain

cēterus, -a, -um – rest; remaining

Chrysogonus, -ī (m.) – Lucius Cornelius
  Chrysogonus, Roscius' accuser

circuitus, -ūs (m.) – circuit; circle

circumsistō, circumsistere, circumstetī – surround

circumveniō, circumvenīre, circumvēnī,
  circumventum – surround

cīvīlis, -e – civil; public

cīvis, -is (m.) – citizen

cīvitās, -ātis (f.) – citizenship; state

clāmor, -ōris (m.) – shout; noise

clārus, -a, -um – clear

classis, -is (f.) – fleet

claudō, claudere, clausī, clausum – close

Cleopātra, -ae (f.) – Cleopatra, Queen of Egypt,
  lover of Julius Caesar and then Marc Antony

cliens, -entis (m.) – client; follower

Clōdia, -ae (f.) – Clodia (identified by some as
  Catullus' "Lesbia")

Clōdius, -iī, Q. (m.) – Quintus Clodius, propraetor
  207 BC during the Second Punic War

Cn. Dolabella, -ae (m.) – Gnaeus Dolabella, an associate of Verres

Cn. Fannius, -iī (m.) – Gnaeus Fannius, brother of the jurist Q. Titinius

cōdex, -icis (m.) – book; account book

coepī, coepisse, coeptum – began (this verb occurs only in past tenses)

coetus, -ūs (m.) – assembly; company

cōgitō, -āre – think

cognōscō, cognōscere, cognōvī, cognitum – come to know; learn (about); find out; become acquainted with

cōgō, cōgere, coēgī, coactum – collect; compel; assemble; bring together; gather

cohors, -hortis (f.) – cohort

cohortor, cohortārī, cohortātus sum – encourage

collis, -is (m.) – hill

colloquium, colloquiī (n.) – conference; meeting

color, -ōris (m.) – color

comes, -itis (m.) – companion; friend

comiter – in a friendly manner

comitia, -orum (n. pl.) – assembly

commeātus, -ūs (m.) – provisions; supplies

commemorō, -āre – remind of; mention

commendātio, -ōnis (f.) – praise; commendation

commodum, -ī – advantage; interest

commodus, -a, -um – suitable; convenient

commoneō, commonēre, commonuī, commonitum – remind

commūnis, -e – common

comparō, -āre – furnish; provide; prepare

complector, complectī, complexus sum – embrace; (+ *ad* + acc.) involve (someone) in

compleō, complēre, complēvī, complētum – fill; occupy

concēdō, concēdere, concessī, concessum – depart; yield (to); concede

concidō, concidere, concidī – fall in battle; fall

concitō, -āre – stir up

concordia, -ae (f.) – harmony; peace

concurrō, concurrere, concurrī, concursum – come together; engage in combat

concursus, -ūs (m.) – running; rush

condemnō, -āre (+ acc. + gen.) – accuse; condemn (someone) of something

condicio, -ōnis (f.) – condition

condō, condere, condidī, conditum – establish; found

confestim – hurriedly; quickly

conficiō, conficere, confēcī, confectum – complete; finish

confirmō, -āre – strengthen; encourage; confirm

confiteor, confitērī, confessus sum – confess

conflīgō, conflīgere, conflīxī, conflictum – contend

conflō, -āre – bring together; raise (an army)

cōniciō, cōnicere, cōniēcī, cōniectum – throw; throw at; hurl

coniunx, -iugis (f.) – wife; spouse

coniūrātio, -ōnis (f.) – conspiracy

coniūrō, -āre – conspire

conlocō, -āre – place; station

cōnor, cōnārī, cōnātus sum – try; (+ inf.) try (to)

conscriptus, -a, -um – elected; conscript (title for senators)

consentiō, consentīre, consēnsī, consēnsum – agree

consequor, consequī, consecūtus sum – pursue

conservātus, -a, -um – preserved

conservō, -āre – save

consīdō, consīdere, consēdi, consessum – establish a position; encamp

consilium, consiliī (n.) – counsel; purpose

consisto, consistere, constitī, constitum (animō) – stand firm (in one's mind)

conspectus, -ūs (m.) – view; sight

conspicor, conspicārī, conspicātus sum – catch sight of

constat – it is agreed

constituō, constituere, constituī, constitūtum – arrange; set up; establish; determine

consuētūdō, -inis (f.) – custom

consul, consulis (m.) – consul

consulāris, -e – of a consul; of consular rank

consulātus, -ūs (m.) – consulship

consulō, consulere, consuluī, consultum – consult; question; (+ dat.) – take thought for; have regard for

consumō, consumere, consumpsī, consumptum –
take up; consume

consurgō, consurgere, consurrēxī, consurrēctum –
rise; get up

contemnō, contemnere, contempsī, contemptum –
consider unimportant; make light of; despise

contendō, contendere, contendī, contentum –
compete with; strive against; fight with; hasten
(to); march

contentio, -ōnis (f.) – contest; argument; exertion;
effort

contentus, -a, -um (+ abl.) – happy with

continenter – continually

contineō, continēre, continuī, contentum – limit;
keep together

contio, -ōnis (f.) – meeting

contrā (+ acc.) – against

cōnūbium, cōnūbiī (n.) – marriage

convallis, -is (f.) – valley

conventus, -ūs (m.) – meeting

convincō, convincere, convīcī, convictum – win
over; demonstrate; show

convīvium, convīviī (n.) – party; celebration

convocō, -āre – call together; assemble

coorior, coorīrī, coortus sum – arise

cōpia, -ae (f.) – supply; plenty (in the plural –
(military) forces)

cornū, -ūs (n.) – horn; flank (of army)

corpus, -oris (n.) – body

corrumpō, corrumpere, corrūpī, corruptum –
break; corrupt

cotīdiānus, -a, -um – daily

cotīdiē – daily; every day

Crassus, -ī (m.) – Lucius Licinius Crassus, the
most famous orator before Cicero and Cicero's
tutor

crēber, -bris – frequent

crēdō, crēdere, crēdidī, crēditum (+ dat.) – believe;
trust; entrust

crescō, crescere, crēvī, crētum – grow

Crētēnsēs, -ium (m. pl.) – Cretans

crīmen, crīminis (n.) – crime; charge

criminor, crimināri, criminātus sum – charge;
allege

cum (+ abl.) – with

cum (+ indicative or subjunctive) – when; since;
although

cum . . . tum – not only . . . but also

Cūmānum, -ī (n.) – an estate belonging to Cicero
near Cumae

cunctor, cunctārī, cunctātus sum – delay

cupiditās, -tātis (f.) – desire; greed

cupidus, -a, -um – (+ gen.) desirous (of); eager
(for)

cupiō, cupere, cupīvī, cupītum – desire

cūrō, -āre – look after; care for; (+ inf.) care to

cursus, -ūs (m.) – course

custōs, -ōdis (m.) – guard

damnō, -āre – condemn

dē (+ abl.) – about; concerning; down from; out of;
from

dea, -ae (f.) – goddess

dēbeō, dēbēre, dēbuī, dēbitum – owe; (+ inf.)
ought (to)

dēcernō, dēcernere, dēcrēvī, dēcrētum – decide;
declare

dēcertō, -āre – fight; contend with

decima, -ae (f.) or decuma, -ae (f.) – tax on
landholders; tithe

decumānus, -ī (m.) – tax gatherer

dēdō, dēdere, dēdidī, dēditum – surrender; hand
over

dēdūcō, dēdūcere, dēdūxī, dēductum – lead

dēfendō, dēfendere, dēfendī, dēfensum – defend

dēfensio, -ōnis (f.) – defense

dēfensor, -ōris (m.) – defender

dēferō, dēferre, dētulī, dēlātum – announce; report;
denounce; accuse

dēficiō, dēficere, dēfēcī, dēfectum – leave; fail

deinceps – next; following

dēlectō, -āre – please; delight

dēleō, dēlēre, dēlēvī, dēlētum – destroy

dēlīberō, -āre – consider; deliberate

dēligō, dēligere, dēlēgī, dēlectum – choose

Democritus, -ī (m.) – Democritus (a Greek
philosopher, *c.* 460 BC)

dēmonstrō, -āre – point out; show

Demosthenes, -is (m.) – Demosthenes, the most famous Greek orator

dēnique – finally; in short

dēpellō, dēpellere, dēpulī, dēpulsum – drive away; remove

dēserō, dēserere, dēseruī, dēsertum – abandon; desert

dēsiderium, dēsideriī (n.) – desire; (+ gen.) regret (for)

dēsīderō, -āre – desire; miss; long for

dēsiliō, dēsilere, dēsiluī – leap down

dēsistō, dēsistere, dēstitī, dēstitum – desist; give over; (+ abl.) desist (from)

dēspectus, -ūs (m.) – view down

dēspiciō, dēspicere, dēspexī, dēspectum – look down upon; despise

dēterreō, dēterrēre, dēterruī, dēterritum – frighten off; deter

dētrahō, dētrahere, dētraxī, dētractum – take away from

deus, deī (m.) – god

dexter, -tra, -trum – right

dīcō, dīcere, dīxī, dictum – say

diēs, -ēī (m.) – day

differō, differre, distulī, dīlātum – be different; differ

difficilis, -e – difficult

dīgerō, dīgerere, dīgessī, dīgestum – separate; arrange

dignitās, -ātis (f.) – dignity; excellence; honor

dignus, -a, -um – worthy

diligenter – diligently

dīmicō, -āre – fight; struggle

dīmittō, dīmittere, dīmīsī, dīmissum – dismiss; send away

discēdō, discēdere, discessī, discessum – depart; (+ *ab* + abl.) depart (from); leave (from)

discō, discere, didicī – learn

discrīmen, -inis (n.) – crisis

disertē – eloquently

disputātio, -ōnis (f.) – argument; reasoning

disserō, disserere, disseruī, dissertum – discuss; argue

dissimulō, -āre – hide; conceal; dissimulate; pretend

dissolūtus, -a, -um – careless; dissolute

diūtius – longer

diūturnus, -a, -um – long-lasting

Diviciācus, -ī (m.) – Diviciacus, a leader of a Gallic tribe

divīsus, -a, -um – divided

do, dare, dedī, datum – give

doceō, docēre, docuī, doctum – teach

doctus, -a, -um – learned

dolor, dolōris (m.) – pain; sorrow; grief

domesticus, -a, -um – belonging to one's home; domestic

domicilium, domiciliī (n.) – home

dōnō, -āre – give; present (with)

dubius, -a, -um – doubtful; sine dubiō – without doubt

dūcō, dūcere, dūxī, ductum – lead

dum – while; as long as; provided that

Dumnorix, -igis (m.) – Dumnorix, a Gallic leader

duo, duae, duo – two (see Appendix 3)

dūplex, -icis – double

dux, dūcis (m.) – leader; commander; general

Dyrrachīnī, -orum (m. pl.)– the Dyrrachini, a people of Illyria

ēdūcō, ēdūcere, ēdūxī, ēductum – lead out

effundō, effundere, effūdī, effūsum – pour forth; squander

egeō, -ēre, eguī (+ abl.) – lack, need

ego, meī – I; me

ēgredior, ēgredī, ēgressus sum – march out; set out

ēiciō, ēicere, ēiēcī, ēiectum – drive out; with *sē*: rush out

elephantus, -ī (m.) – elephant

emō, emere, ēmī, emptum – buy

enim – for

Ennius, Enniī (m.) – Ennius (a Roman poet 239–169 BC)

eques, equitis (m.) – horseman; member of the cavalry

equidem – truly

equitātus, -ūs (m.) – cavalry

equus, -ī (m.) – horse

ergā (+ acc.) – towards; in respect of

ēripiō, ēripere, ēripuī, ēreptum – snatch; snatch away; take away

errō, -āre – err; be wrong

ērudītus, -a, -um – clever; skilled; erudite

ērumpō, ērumpere, ērūpī, ēruptum – burst out

et – and

et . . . et – both . . . and

etiam – even; also

etsi – although

ēvādō, ēvādere, ēvāsī – get away; escape

ex (+ abl.) – from; out of; in accordance with (sometimes written *e* before a consonant)

excēdō, excēdere, excessī, excessum – leave; walk out of

exclūdō, exclūdere, exclūdī, exclūsum – shut out; hinder; prevent

excors, -cordis – senseless; stupid

excursio, -ōnis (f.) – assault; sally

excūsātio, -ōnis (f.) – excuse

excūsō, -āre – excuse; offer an excuse (for)

exercitatio, -ōnis (f.) – exercise; practice

exercitus, -ūs (m.) – army

exhibeō, exhibēre, exhibuī, exhibitum – show; produce; give up

exilium, exiliī (n.) – exile

eximius, -a, -um – excellent; outstanding

existimō, -āre – consider; think; judge

exitium, exitiī (n.) – destruction

expellō, expellere, expulsī, expulsum – expel

expensum, -ī (n.) – payment; expense

experior, experīrī, expertus sum – try

expers, expertis – without; free from

explicō, -āre – unfold; set forth; explain

explorātor, -ōris (m.) – scout; spy

expōnō, expōnere, exposuī, expositum – explain; disembark; put (troops) ashore

exprobō, -āre – reproach; charge

exprōmō, exprōmere, exprom(p)sī, expromptum – bring forth; explain

exsanguis, -e – bloodless, pale

exspectātio, -ōnis (f.) – expectation

exspectō, -āre (+ acc.) – wait for; await

extrēmus, -a, -um – farthest; most distant

faber, fabrī (m.) – workman

Fabriciī, -ōrum (m. pl.) – the Fabricii, an aristocratic Roman family

fābula, -ae (f.) – story; fable

facilē – easily

facinus, -oris (n.) – deed; crime

faciō, facere, fēcī, factum – do; make

fallō, fallere, fefellī, falsum – deceive

falsus, -a, -um – false

fāma, -ae (f.) – report; rumor; fame

familia, -ae (f.) – (often plural) household; household slaves

familiāris, -is (m.) – family member; acquaintance; friend

familiāritās, -ātis (f.) – familiarity; friendship

fānum, -ī (n.) – temple

fateor, fatērī, fassus sum – admit; confess

fātum, -ī (n.) – fate; (in plural) the Fates

faucēs, -ium (f. pl.) – throat; jaws

faveō, favēre, fāvī, fautum (+ dat.) – favor; be favorable (to)

fēlīx, -īcis – happy

fēmina, -ae (f.) – woman

ferē – approximately; almost

fermē – almost; for the most part

ferō, ferre, tulī, lātum – carry; bear; endure; allow

ferreus, -a, -um – iron-hearted

ferrum, -ī (n.) – iron; sword

fictus, -a, -um – (participle from fingo) false

fidēs, fideī (f.) – faith; honesty; credibility

figūra, -ae (f.) – figure; shape

fīlius, fīliī (m.) – son

fīnēs, -ium (m. pl.) – territory

fingō, fingere, finxī, fictum – compose; arrange; form

fīnis, -is (m.) – limit; end

fīō, fierī, factus sum – be made; become; happen

firmō, -āre – confirm; support

firmus, -a, -um – firm; strong

flagitium, flagitiī (n.) – shame; disgrace

flagitō, -āre – demand

fleō, flēre, flēvī, flētum – weep; cry

flōreō, flōrēre, flōruī – flourish; be in good repute

fluctus, -ūs (m.) – wave

flūmen, -inis (n.) – river

fons, fontis (f.) – spring; fountain; source

forsitan – perhaps

fortis, -e – brave

fortūna, -ae (f.) – fortune

fortūnātissimus, -a, -um – most fortunate

forum, -ī (n.) – forum; market place

fossa, -ae (f.) – ditch; trench

frāter, -tris (m.) – brother

fraudātor, -ōris (m.) – cheat

fraudō, -āre – act illegally; defraud

frequenter – often

frequentia, -ae (f.) throng; assembly

fructus, -ūs (m.) – fruit; reward; enjoyment

frūmentum, -ī (n.) – corn; grain; ear of corn

fruor, fruī, fructus sum (+ abl.) – enjoy

frux, frūgis (f.) – fruit; grain

Fūfius Calēnus, -ī (m.) – Fufius Calenus, a tribune of the plebs

fugiō, fugere, fūgī, fugitum – flee

fungor, fungī, functus sum (+ abl.) – fulfill

furō, furere, furuī – rage; be mad

fūror, fūrārī, fūratus sum – steal

Gabinius, -iī (m.) – Aulus Gabinius (a consul with Piso in 58 BC)

Gaius, Gaiī (m.) – Gaius (abbreviated C.)

Gallia, -ae (f.) – Gaul

Gallia ulterior, Galliae ulterioris (f.) – further Gaul (the area of Gaul across the Alps)

Garunna, -ae (m.) – a river in Gaul

Genāva, -ae (f.) – Geneva

genus, -eris (n.) – origin; nature; race; family

Germānī, -ōrum (m. pl.) – the Germans

gerō, gerere, gessī, gestum – wage; carry on

glaciālis, -e – icy; frozen

gladius, gladiī (m.) – sword

glōria, -ae (f.) – glory; honor

grandis, -e – large; great

grātulor, grātulārī, grātulātus sum – congratulate

gravis, -e – serious

gravitās, -tātis (f.) – seriousness; dignity

habeō, habēre, habuī, habitum – have; hold; consider

Haeduī, -ōrum (m. pl.) – the Haedui, a people of Gaul (also written Aedui)

haesitō, -āre – hesitate

Hannibal, Hannibalis (m.) – Carthaginian leader during the Second Punic War (218–201 BC)

haud – not

Helvetiī, -ōrum (m. pl.) – the Helvetii, a people of Gaul

hērēditās, hērēditātis (f.) – inheritance

hībernus, -a, -um – (belonging to) winter

hīc – here; in this place; at this point

hic, haec, hoc – this; this man; this woman; this thing

Hirtius, -iī (m.) – Aulus Hirtius, an acquaintance of Cicero

Hispania, -ae (f.) – Spain

hodiernus, -a, -um – of today; hodiernō diē – on this very day

homō, hominis (m.) – man; human

honestus, -a, -um – honorable; honest

hōra, -ae (f.) – hour

hortor, hortārī, hortātus sum – encourage; urge

hostis, -is (m.) – enemy

iactō, -āre – throw about; drive here and there

iam – now; already

iam dūdum – (+ present tense) now for a long time

Iānuarius, -a, -um – of or belonging to January

idcircō – for this reason

īdem . . . quī – the same . . . as

īdem, eadem, idem – same; the same (see Appendix 2)

idōneus, -a, -um (+ dat.) – suitable (for)

Īdus, -uum (f. pl.) – Ides (March, May, July, October 15; 13 of other months)

iecur, iecinoris (n.) – liver

igitur – therefore; then; accordingly

ignoscō, ignoscere, ignōvī, ignōtum (+ dat.) – forgive

ille, illa, illud – that; that man; that woman; that thing

illuc – to that place

imbrifer, -era, -erum – rain-bringing

imitor, imitārī, imitātus sum – imitate

immātūrus, -a, -um – unripe; untimely

immineō, imminēre – hang over; threaten

immō vērō – no indeed

immoderātus, -a, -um – wanton; unbridled

immortālis, -e – immortal

impedimenta, -ōrum (n. pl.) – baggage; (military) equipment

impediō, impedīre, impedī(v)ī, impedītum – impede; prevent; hinder

impedītus, -a, -um – weighed down; in difficulty

impellō, impellere, impulsī, impulsum – urge, impel

impendeō, impendēre, impendī, impensum – hang over; threaten

imperātor, -ōris (m.) – general; emperor

imperātōrius, -a, -um – of a general; belonging to a general

imperō, -āre – (+ dat.) order

impetus, -ūs (m.) – attack, charge

impius, -a, -um – wicked; impious

improbus, -a, -um – bad; wicked

impudentia, -ae (f.) – impudence; shamelessness

impūnē – with impunity

in (+ abl.) – in; on; among

in (+ acc.) – against; upon; into; onto

in perpetuum – forever

in posterum – for the future

in prīmīs (also written as one word *imprīmīs*) – especially; above all

incendō, incendere, incendī, incensum – set fire to; rouse

incertus, -a, -um – uncertain; changing

incitō, -āre – hasten; rush

incolō, incolere, incoluī – dwell; inhabit

incrēdibilis, -e – incredible

indicium, indiciī (n.) – evidence

indignus, -a, -um – unworthy; intolerable

indūcō, indūcere, indūxī, inductum – induce

inertia, -ae (f.) – idleness

infāmia, -ae (f.) – disgrace

inferō, inferre, intulī, illātum – bring in; introduce

infestus, -a, -um – hostile

infirmus, -a, -um – weak

infitiātor, -ōris – bad debtor; defaulter

ingenium, ingeniī (n.) – quality; nature; character

inhorreō, inhorrēre – grow spiky

iniciō, inicere, iniēcī, iniectum (+ dat.) – bring into; instill

inimīcitia, -ae (f.) – enmity

inīquus, -a, -um – unjust

initium, initiī (n.) – beginning

iniūria, -ae (f.) – injury; injustice

innātus, -a, -um – inborn; innate

innocens, -entis – innocent; harmless

inopia, -ae (f.) – scarcity; lack

inquit – he (she, it) says

insector, insectārī, insectātus sum – pursue

inserō, inserere, insēvī, insitum – implant

insidiae, -ārum (f. pl.) – trap; ambush; plot

insitus, -a, -um – implanted; fixed

insolenter – unusually; immoderately; insolently

instituō, instituere, instituī, institūtum – build; set up; establish

institūtum, -ī (n.) – custom

insula, -ae (f.) – island

intelligō, intelligere, intellēxī, intellēctum – understand

inter (+ acc.) – between

interdictum, -ī (n.) – provisional decree

interdum – from time to time

interest – it matters (see Chapter 18)

interficiō, interficere, interfēcī, interfectum – kill

intermittō, intermittere, intermīsī, intermissum – leave out; discontinue; interrupt

intrā (+ acc.) – within

intus – inside

inveniō, invenīre, invēnī, inventum – find

invideō, invidēre, invīdī, invīsum – envy

invidia, -ae (f.) – envy; ill-will; hatred

Īphicrates, -is (m.) – Iphicrates, a famous Athenian general (4th century BC)

ipse, ipsa, ipsum – -self; -selves (see Appendix 2)

īra, -ae (f.) – anger

irascor, irascī, irātus sum – be angry with

is, ea, id – he; she; it; this; that, etc.

iste, ista, istud – that (of you/of yours); (pl.) those (for declension, see Appendix 2)

ita – in this way; so; thus

Ītalia, -ae (f.) – Italy

iter, itineris (n.) – road; journey

iter faciō, -ere – march

iubeō, iubēre, iussī, iussum – order; bid

iucundus, -a, -um – sweet

iūdex, -icis (m.) – judge

iūdicium, iūdiciī (n.) – judgment; trial; sentence; court

iūrō, -āre – swear (an oath)

iūs, iūris (n.) – right; law; custom

iustus, -a, -um – just

iuvō, iuvāre, iūvī, iūtum – help

Ixīon, -onis (m.) – Ixion, punished in the Underworld, attached to an eternally revolving wheel

L. Opimius, -iī – Lucius Opimius, consul 121 BC

labor, -ōris (m.) – labor; toil

Lacedaemoniī, -ōrum (m. pl.) – the Spartans

lacrima, -ae (f.) – tear

lactēns, -entis – milky

laetitia, -ae (f.) – joy

laetus, -a, -um – happy; joyful

lapis, -idis (m.) – stone

lateō, latēre, latuī – lie hidden

latus, lateris (n.) – side

laudātio, -ōnis (f.) – praise

laudō, -āre – praise

laus, laudis (f.) – praise

Lāvīnius, -a, -um – belonging to Lavinia; Lavinian (city in Italy, founded by Aeneas in honor of his wife, Lavinia)

laxō, -āre – spread out

lectus, -ī (m.) – bed

legātus, -ī (m.) – ambassador; envoy

legō, legere, lēgī, lectum – read

lēnitās, -ātis (f.) – kindness; leniency

Lentulus, -ī (m.) – Gnaeus Cornelius Lentulus Marcellinus, consul 56 BC

lepidus, -a, -um – fine; charming

libellus, -ī (m.) – little book

libenter – willingly

līber, -era, -erum – free; (m. pl.) līberī, -ōrum – children

liber, librī (m.) – book

līberālitās, -ātis (f.) – generosity; kindness

līberius – more freely

līberō, -āre – set free; (+ abl.) free (from)

lībertās, -ātis (f.) – freedom

libīdō, -inis (f.) – lust

Libitīna, -ae (f.) – the goddess of corpses; Death

Licinius, Liciniī – Publius Licinius, a friend of Caelius

lignum, -ī (n.) – wood; (pl.) logs; firewood

līmen, -inis (n.) – threshold

lingua, -ae (f.) – language

Liscus, -ī (m.) – Liscus, a Gallic leader (from the Haedui/Aedui)

littera, -ae (f.) – letter; (pl.) letters, letter (i.e., epistle); written records; document; report

lītus, -oris (n.) – shore

locus, -ī (m.) place; position; opportunity; in the plural the gender is neuter – loca, locorum

longē – far; a long way

longus, -a, -um – long

loquor, loquī, locūtus sum – speak

Lūcīlius, -ii (m.) – Lucius Lucilius, an assistant to Aquilius (above)

lūna, -ae (f.) – moon

luō, luere, luī – satisfy; pay (a debt); atone for

lupus, -ī (m.) – wolf

luxuriēs, -ēī (f.) – luxury; extravagance

M'. Aquilius, -iī (m.) – Manius Aquilius, defended by Marc Antony

magis – more

magister, magistrī (m.) – teacher

magistrātus, -ūs (m.) – magistracy; public office

magnificē – magnificently

magnitūdō, -inis (f.) – size; greatness; importance; extent

magnoperē – greatly

magnus, -a, -um – great; big

maiōrēs, -um (m. pl.) – ancestors

maiōrēs, -um natu – ancestors; previous generations

maleficium, -iī (n.) – crime; wicked deed

malus, -a, -um – bad

mancipium, mancipiī (n.) – slave

mandātum, -ī (n.) – order

mandō, -āre (+ dat.) – order; command

manipulāris, -is (m.) – common soldier

manipulus, -ī (m.) – an infantry unit; a company

Manliānus, -a, -um – belonging to Manlius

mansuetūdō, -inis (f.) – clemency; mercy

manus, -ūs (f.) – hand; hand-writing; band (of men)

mare, maris (n.) – sea

māter, -tris (f.) – mother

māteria, -ae (f.) – subject-matter

mātūrō, -āre (+ inf.) – hurry (to do something)

Maurītānia, -ae (f.) – Mauritania (a country of Africa)

maximē – very much; most

maximus, -a, -um – greatest

medius, -a, -um – in the middle; middle

mehercule – by Hercules

melior, -ōris – better

mellītus, -a, -um – made of honey; honeyed

meminī, meminisse – remember (occurs only in the perfect with present meaning)

memor, -oris – mindful; unforgiving

memoria, -ae (f.) – memory; remembering; recollection

mentio, -ōnis (f.) – mention

mentior, mentīrī, mentītus sum – lie

messis, -is (f.) – harvest

Metius – Marcus Metius, an envoy sent by Caesar to the German king, Ariovistus

metus, -ūs (m.) – fear

meus, -a, -um – my

migrō, -āre – go; depart

mīles, mīlitis (m.) – soldier

Milētus, -ī (m.) – a city in Asia Minor

militāris, -e – belonging to a soldier; relating to the military; military

Minerva, -ae (f.) – Minerva, goddess of wisdom, handicrafts (= Greek Athena)

minimē – least; least of all; not at all

minitor, minitārī, minitātus sum (+ acc. of the thing threatened + dat. of person) – threaten

miser, -era, -erum – wretched; unhappy; unfortunate

misereor, miserērī, miseritus sum (+ gen.) – pity

miseria, -ae (f.) – misery; misfortune

misericordia, -ae (f.) – pity

missio, -ōnis (f.) – sending

mittō, mittere, mīsī, missum – send

Mitylēnae, -ārum (f. pl.) – Mytilene (capital city of Lesbos)

moderātio, -ōnis (f.) – moderation

modus, -ī (m.) – limit

moenia, -ium (n. pl.) – city walls; walls

molestē – with annoyance

molestē ferō, ferre, tulī, lātum – take badly; be annoyed at

molestus, -a, -um – troublesome; annoying

molior, molīrī, molītus sum – undertake; set in motion

mollior, -ōris – milder

mōmentum, -ī (n.) – weight; importance

moneō, monēre, monuī, monitum – warn

mōns, montis (m.) – mountain

monstrum, -ī (n.) – monster

Morīnī, -ōrum – Morini (a people of Gaul)

morior, morī, mortuus sum – die

moror, morārī, morātus sum – delay

mors, mortis (f.) – death

moveō, movēre, mōvī, mōtum – move; influence; (of strings) pluck

muliebris, -e – of a woman

mulier, -eris (f.) – woman

mulierārius, -a, -um – belonging to a woman; sent by a woman

multitūdō, -inis (f.) – large number; crowd

multus, -a, -um – much; (pl.) many

mundus, -ī (m.) – world

mūniō, mūnīre, mūnīvī, mūnītum – build a wall around; fortify mūnītio, -ōnis (f.) – fortification

Murgentīnus, -a, -um – Murgentian (Murgentia – a city in Sicily)

mūtō, -āre – change

nam – for

narrō, -āre – tell; relate; report

nascor, nascī, nātus sum – be born

Natālis, -is (m.) – Birthday Spirit

nātūra, -ae (f.) – nature

nātus, -ūs (m.) – birth; age (occurs only in the abl. sing.)

nāvis, nāvis (f.) – ship

nē . . . quidem – not even

necessārius, -a, -um – necessary

necessārius, necessāriī (m.) – friend; relation; close associate

necō, -āre – kill

nefārius, -a, -um – abominable; wicked

neglegō, neglegere, neglēxī, neglectum – neglect; disregard

negō, -āre – say . . . not; deny

nēmō, nūllius (m. and f.) – no (one)

neque . . . nec – neither . . . nor

nervus, -ī (m.) – string (of a musical instrument)

neuter, neutra, neutrum – neither (of two)

nisi – unless; if . . . not; except

nītor, nītī, nīsus (or nixus) sum – strive

nōbilitās, -ātis (f.) – nobility

nōbilitō, -āre – (passive) be famous

noceō, nocēre, nocuī, nocitum – harm

noctū – by night

nocturnus, -a, -um – beloging to the night; nocturnal

nōmen, -inis (n.) – name; noun; item (in an account book)

nōminātim – by name

nōminō, -āre – name; call

nōn – not

nōn mē fugit – I am not unaware

nōn modo – not only

nōn modo . . . sed etiam – not only . . . but also

nōn sōlum – not only

nōn sōlum . . . sed etiam – not only . . . but also

nōs, nostrī (nostrum) – we

noscō, noscere, nōvī, nōtum – come to know; become acquainted with; in the perfect = know

noster, -stra, -strum – our

Noviodūnum, -ī (n.) – Noviodunum, a town in Gaul

novus, -a, -um – new

nūdō, -āre – strip; lay bare; leave defenseless

nullus, -a, -um – not any; none (sometimes best translated as "not")

numerus, -ī (m.) – number

Numida, -ae (m.) – Numidian

nummus, -ī (m.) – coin

nunc – now

nūtus, -ūs (m.) – nod; will

ob (+ acc.) – on account of; because of

obeō, obīre, obī(v)ī, obitum – travel through

oblīviscor, oblīviscī, oblītus sum (+ gen.) – forget

obscūritās, -ātis (f.) – darkness; obscurity

obsequor, obsequī, obsecūtus sum – submit to; obey

obstō, obstāre, obstitī, obstātum – stand in the way of; hinder

obstringō, obstringere, obstrinxī, obstrictum – bind; hamper

obtineō, obtinēre, obtinuī; obtentum – hold; obtain; acquire; possess

obviam (+ dat.) – in the way of; obviam venīre (+ dat.) – come to meet

occāsio, -ōnis (f.) – occasion; opportunity

occidō, occidere, occidī, occāsum – fall down; set (of sun)

occultē – in secret

occurrō, occurrere, occurrī, occursum (+ dat.) – meet

Oceanus, -ī (m.) – Ocean

oculus, -ī (m.) – eye

offendō, offendere, offendī, offensum – displease; offend

offensio, -ōnis (f.) – offense

officium, officiī (n.) – duty; function

omittō, omittere, omīsī, omissum – give up;
   neglect; reject

omnīnō – completely; altogether

omnis, -e – all

onerārius, -a, -um – carrying freight

onus, -eris (n.) – burden; trouble

opīnio, -ōnis (f.) – opinion; belief

oportet, oportuit (occurs only in 3rd person
   singular + infinitive) – one ought to; it is
   necessary to

Oppianicus, -ī (m.) – Oppianicus; step-father of
   Cluentius whom Cluentius was accused of
   poisoning

oppidum, -ī (n.) – town

opportūnissimus, -a, -um – most opportune

oppugnātio, -ōnis (f.) – attack

oppugnō, -āre – attack

optimus, -a, -um – best

optō, -āre – desire; choose

opus, -eris (n.) – work

opus est (+ abl.) – there is need of

ōra, -ae (f.) – border; margin; edge; shore

ōrātio, -ōnis (f.) – speech; language

ōrātor, -ōris (m.) – orator

ōrātōrius, -a, -um – relating to oratory

orbis, orbis (m.) – wheel

ordo, -inis (m.) – rank

orior, orīrī, ortus sum – rise; originate; begin

ornamentum, -ī (n.) – equipment; ornament

ostendō, ostendere, ostendī, ostensum – show;
   indicate

P. Lentulus, -i (m.) – Publius Lentulus, a fellow-
   conspirator with Catiline

P. Quinctius, -ii (m.) – Publius Quinctius,
   defended by Cicero

pābulātor, -ōris (m.) – forager

pābulō, -āre – forage (for food)

paene – almost; scarcely

paenitet – it repents (see Chapter 18)

palam – openly

Pān (gen. Pānos; acc. Pāna) (m.) – Pan

parātior, -ōris – more ready

parcō, parcere, pepercī, parsum (+ dat.) – spare

parens, -entis (m.) – parent

pāreō, pārēre, pāruī, pāritum (+ dat.) – obey

parō, -āre – prepare; (+ inf.) prepare (to)

pars, partis (f.) – part; division

particeps, -cipis (m.) – participant; partner

parvus, -a, -um – small

patefaciō, patefacere, patefēcī, patefactum – reveal

pateō, patēre, patuī – lay open

pater, -tris (m.) – father

patior, patī, passus sum – put up with; suffer;
   endure; undergo

patria, -ae (f.) – homeland

patrimōnium, patrimōniī (n.) – inheritance;
   patrimony

patrius, -a, -um – belonging to one's father;
   belonging to one's forefathers; ancestral

paulisper – for a little while

paulō – a little

pax, pācis (f.) – peace

peccō, -āre – commit an offense

pecūnia, -ae (f.) – money

peditēs, -um (m. pl.) – infantry

pellō, pellere, pepulī, pulsum – repel; drive
   back

per (+ acc.) – through

percipiō, percipere, percēpī, perceptum –
   understand

perditus, -a, -um – (participle from perdo)
   degenerate; ruined; broken

perdō, perdere, perdidī, perditum – destroy; ruin

perfundō, perfundere, perfūdī, perfūsum –
   moisten; bathe; fill

pergō, pergere, perrexī, perrectum – proceed

perīculum, -ī (n.) – danger; risk

permisceō, permiscēre, permiscuī, permixtum –
   mix

permoveō, permovēre, permōvi, permōtum –
   move deeply; influence

perniciēs, -ēī (f.) – disaster; destruction

perpetuus, -a, -um – enduring; lasting

persequor, persequī, persecūtus sum – pursue

perspiciō, perspicere, perspexī, perspectum – look
   at; examine; consider closely

perspicuē – clearly; manifestly

persuādeō, persuādēre, persuāsī, persuāsum (+ dat.) – persuade

perturbātus, -a, -um – troubled

perturbō, -āre – perturb; frighten; throw into confusion

perveniō, pervenīre, pervēnī, perventum (+ *ad* + acc.) – come to; arrive at

pestis, -is (m.) – plague

petō, petere, petīvī, petītum – seek; seek out; attack; (+ *ab* + abl.) ask of

pietās, -ātis (f.) – piety; loyalty; respect

piget – it troubles (see Chapter 18)

pīlum, -ī (n.) – javelin

piscīna, -ae (f.) – fish-pond

placeō, placēre, placuī, placitum – please

placō, -āre – calm; appease; placate

plānē – clearly; completely; entirely; certainly

plebs, plēbis (m.) – the people

plēnus, -a, -um – full

plūrimum – greatest; most; exceedingly

plūrimus, -a, -um – most; a great many

poena, -ae (f.) – punishment; penalty

poēta, -ae (m.) – poet

Polemarchus, -ī (m.) – Polemarchus (a man's name)

polliceor, pollicērī, pollicitus sum – promise

Pompeius, -ī (m.) – Pompey, a Roman general, opponent of Julius Caesar

pondus, -eris (n.) – weight

pons, pontis (m.) – bridge

pontifex, pontificis (m.) – high priest

populus, -ī (m.) – people

porta, -ae (f.) – gate

portō, -āre – carry

portus, -ūs (m.) – port

possideō, possidēre, possēdī, possessum – hold; possess

possum, posse, potuī – be able; have power; have influence

post (+ acc.) – after

posteāquam – after that; from that time

posteritās, -ātis (f.) – future generations; posterity

posterus, -a, -um – next; following; future

posthāc – in future

postquam – after

potior, potīrī, potītus sum (+ abl.) – take possession of

potissimum – especially

potius – rather

praecaveō, praecavēre, praecāvī, praecautum – to take care (in advance)

praecēdō, praecēdere, praecessī, praecessum – excel; surpass; precede

praeceptum, -ī (n.) – precept; rule

praeclārus, -a, -um – magnificent; opulent; valuable

praeda, -ae (f.) – booty

praedicātio, -ōnis (f.) – proclamation

praedor, praedāri, praedātus sum – plunder

praefectus, -ī (m.) – commander; prefect

praeferō, praeferre, praetulī, praelātum – carry in front; put on display

praemittō, praemittere, praemīsī, praemissum – send ahead; send in advance

praepōnō, praepōnere, praeposuī, praepositum – (+ dat.) put in charge (of)

praescriptio, -ōnis (f.) – precept; rule

praesidium, praesidiī (n.) – defense; protection; guard

praestans, -antis – outstanding

praestō, praestāre, praestitī, praestātum – be superior to; surpass; guarantee

prabtereā – besides

praetereō, praeterīre, praeterī(v)ī, praeteritum – pass over; omit

praetermittō, praetermittere, praetermīsī, praetermissum – pass over; leave out

praetor, -ōris (m.) – praetor (Roman official)

prāvus, -a, -um – crooked; vicious; depraved

pretium, pretiī (n.) – price

prīdiē – on the day before

prīmā nocte – at nightfall

prīmum – in the first place; first

prīmus, -a, -um – first; early

princeps, -cipis – first; most eminent

princeps, -cipis (m.) – prince; chief; leader

principātus, -ūs (m.) – commander-in-chief

prior, -ōris – former

pristīnus, -a, -um – former

prīvātus, -ī (m.) – private citizen

prō (+ abl.) – on behalf of; before

probābilior, -ōris – more likely

prōcurrō, prōcurrere, prōcurrī, prōcursum – run forward

prōdigium, prōdigiī (n.) – monster; prodigy

prōdō, prōdere, prōdidī, prōditum – betray

prōducō, prōducere, prōdūxī, prōductum – lead forward

proelior, proeliārī, proeliātus sum – battle

proelium, proeliī (n.) – battle

proelium (acc. n. sing.) committō, committere, commīsī, commissum – join battle

profectio, -ōnis (f.) – setting out

profectō – surely

prōferō, prōferre, prōtulī, prōlātum – bring forward

proficīscor, proficīscī, profectus sum – set out

profiteor, profitērī, professus sum – declare; confess; admit

profugus, -ī (m.) – fugitive; exile

prōhibeō, prōhibēre, prōhibuī, prōhibitum – keep out; prevent

propinquus, -a, -um – neighboring; nearby; (+ dat.) near (to); related (to)

propinquus, -i (m.) – relative

propius – nearer

prōpōnō, prōpōnere, prōposuī, prōpositum – set out; threaten

prōpraetor, -ōris (m.) – propraetor (a Roman magistrate)

propter (+ acc.) – on account of

propterea quod – because

prōvideō, prōvidēre, prōvīdī, prōvīsum – exercise foresight; look after; take thought for

provincia, -ae (f.) – province

proximus, -a, -um – next to; following

Ptolomaeus, -i (m.) (also Ptolemaeus) – ruler of Egypt; brother of Cleopatra

pūblicus, -a, -um – public

pudet – it shames (see Chapter 18)

pudīcitia, -ae (f.) – modesty; virtue

puella, -ae (f.) – girl

puer, puerī (m.) – boy

pugnō, -āre – fight; (+ *cum* + abl.) – fight with; fight against

pulcher, -chra, -chrum – beautiful; handsome

purgō, -āre – purge; cleanse

Q. Titinius, -iī (m.) – Quintus Titinius, a jurist and Fannius' brother (see above)

quaerō, quaerere, quaesīvī, quaesītum – ask; inquire; seek

quaestor, -ōris (m.) – quaestor (public official; magistrate)

quamdiū – for as long as

quantus, -a, -um – how great

quartus, -a, -um – fourth

quasi – as if; as it were

-que – and (added to the end of a word: *arma virumque canō* – I sing of arms **and** the man)

quī, quae, quod – who; which; that

quia – since; because

quīdam, quaedam, quoddam – a certain

quidem – indeed; certainly

quiēs, -ētis (f.) – quiet

quīnquāgintā (indeclinable) – twenty

Quintus, -ī (m.) – Quintus (abbreviated Q.)

quis?, quid? – who?; what?

quisquam, quaequam, quidquam (*or* quicquam) – anyone; anything (with negative) no one; nothing

quō – where

quō? – where (to)?

quod – because

quoque – also

rapidus, -a, -um – rapid; swift; swift-flowing

ratio, -ōnis (f.) – method; manner; reason; account; motive

ratiōcinor, ratiōcinārī, ratiōcinātus sum – reckon; argue

recens, -entis – new; fresh

recitō, -āre – recite; read out

rectissimus, -a, -um – most correct; most appropriate

reddō, reddere, reddidī, redditum – return; give back; give up; grant redintegrō, -āre – renew; start again

reditus, -ūs (m.) – return

redūcō, redūcere, redūxī, reductum – lead back

refellō, refellere, refellī – disprove; refute

referō, referre, retulī (*or* rettulī), relātum – report, refer (to)

refugus, -a, -um – fleeing back; receding

rēgius, -a, -um – royal; of the king

regnō, -āre – rule; reign

regnum, -ī (n.) – reign; rule; power; kingdom

regō, regere, rēxī, rēctum – rule

relinquō, relinquere, relīquī, relictum – leave (behind); abandon; give up

reliquus, -a, -um – remaining; (pl.) the rest; the others

remaneō, remanēre, remansī – remain; stay

Rēmī, -ōrum (m. pl.) – Remi (a people of Gaul)

remulcum, -ī (n.) – tow-rope

repentē – suddenly

repentīnus, -a, -um – sudden

reperiō, reperīre, reperrī, repertum – find; discover; perceive

repetō, repetere, repetī(v)ī, repetītum – ask back; return to; go back to

reprehendō, reprehendere, reprehendī, reprehensum – find fault with; blame

reputō, -āre – think; consider

rēs, reī (f.) – thing; matter; event

rēs gestae, rērum gestārum (f. pl.) – accomplishments

rēs novae, rērum novārum (f. pl.) – revolution; rebellion

rēs pūblica, reī pūblicae (f.) – state; republic (sometimes written as one word)

resistō, resistere, restitī (+ dat.) – resist

respondeō, respondēre, respondī, respōnsum – reply

restituō, restituere, restituī, restitūtum – restore

retineō, retinēre, retinuī, retentum – retain

reus, -ī (m.) – defendant (in court)

revertō, revertere, revertī, reversum – return

revertor, revertī, reversus sum – return

rex, rēgis (m.) – king

Rhēnus, -ī (m.) – the Rhine river

Rhodanus, -ī (m.) – the river Rhône

rīdiculus, -a, -um – ridiculous; amusing; laughable

rīpa, -ae (f.) – bank (of a river)

rīvus, -ī (m.) – stream

Rōma, -ae (f.) – Rome

Rōmānus, -a, -um – Roman

ruō, ruere, ruī, rutum – rush

Sabīnī, -ōrum (m. pl.) – Sabines (an Italian tribe)

sacramentum, -ī (n.) – oath

sagitta, -ae (f.) – arrow

saltem – at least

salūtō, -āre – greet

sanctus, -a, -um – holy; sacred

sānē – truly; by all means

sanguis, -inis (m.) – blood

sānus, -a, -um – sane

sapiens, sapientis – sensible; wise; as noun = wise man

sapientia, -ae (f.) – wisdom

Sardinia, -ae (f.) – Sardinia

satis – enough

saxum, -ī (n.) – rock

Scaevola, -ae (m.) – Quintus Mucius Scaevola, a renowned lawyer (during Cicero's lifetime)

scandō, scandere – climb

scapha, -ae (f.) – boat

Sceledrus, -ī (m.) – Sceledrus (slave name)

scelus, sceleris (n.) – crime

scrība, -ae (m.) – clerk

scrībō, scrībere, scrīpsī, scrīptum – write

Scythia, -ae (f.) – Scythia (an area in the north beyond the Black Sea)

sē – themselves (for declension, see Chapter 10)

sē recipiō, recipere, recēpī, receptum – retreat; withdraw; recover

sed – but

sed etiam – but also

sedeō, sedēre, sēdī, sessum – sit; remain seated

sēditiōsus, -a, -um – seditious; rebellious

sempiternus, -a, -um – eternal

senātus, -ūs (m.) – senate

senātūs consultum, -ī (n.) – decree of the senate

senex, senis (m.) – old man

sensus, -ūs (m.) – sense; feeling

sententia, -ae (f.) – opinion; feeling; purpose; idea; topic

sentiō, sentīre, sēnsī, sēnsum – sense; feel; perceive

Sēquanus, -a, -um – belonging to the Sequani, a Gallic tribe from the Seine area

sequor, sequī, secūtus sum – follow

sermo, -ōnis (m.) – conversation

serviō, servīre, servī(v)ī, servītum (+ dat.) – be devoted to; care for; serve

servitium, servitiī (n.) – slavery

servus, -ī (m.) – slave; servant

sēsē = sē

sevēritās, -ātis (f.) – severity; seriousness

sex (indeclinable) – six (see Appendix 3)

sī – if

sīc – thus

Sicilia, -ae (f.) – the island of Sicily

sīdus, -eris (n.) – star

signum, -ī (n.) – sign; seal; banner; military standard; statue

sileō, silēre, siluī – be silent

silva, -ae (f.) – forest; wood

similiter – in a like manner; similarly

sine (+ abl.) – without

singulāris, -e – singular; extraordinary; outstanding

sinō, sinere, sīvī, situm – allow

situs, -ūs (m.) – site; position

socer, -erī (m.) – father-in-law

socius, sociī (m.) – friend; ally

Sōcratēs, -is (m.) – Socrates (Greek philosopher, 5th century BC)

Sōcraticus, -a, -um – belonging to Socrates; Socratic

sōl, sōlis (m.) – sun

solum, -ī (n.) – ground; soil; region

sōlus, -a, -um – alone; only

soror, sorōris (f.) – sister

spatium, spatiī (n.) – distance; space; space (of time); opportunity

speciēs, -ēī (f.) – appearance

spērō, -āre (+ acc.) – hope (for)

spēs, -eī (f.) – hope

spīceus, -a, -um – made of ears of corn

spīritus, -ūs (m.) – air; breath

splendor, -ōris (m.) – splendor; brilliance

spoliō, -āre – despoil; rob

spolia, -ōrum (n. pl.) – spoils

stabiliō, stabilīre, stabilīvī, stabilītum – make firm; make stable

statim – immediately; at once

statua, -ae (f.) – statue

statuō, statuere, statuī, statūtum – establish; decide; consider

status, -ūs (m.) – state; condition

sterilis, -e – sterile; barren

stipula, -ae (f.) – stalk

studeō, studēre, studuī – be eager; apply onself to; study

stultus, -a, -um – stupid

stupeō, stupēre, stupuī – stop; stand still

stuprum, -ī (n.) – dishonor; disgrace

suādeō, suadēre, suāsi, suāsum (+ dat.) – advise (someone)

suāvis, -e – sweet; delightful

subeō, subīre, subi(v)ī, subitum – undergo

subitō – suddenly

subsidium, subsidiī (n.) – assistance

subsum, subesse – underlie

subveniō, sunvenīre, subvēnī, subventum – help

succurrō, succurrere, succurrī, succursum (+ dat.) – come to the help of; occur to; come to mind

Suēbī, -ōrum (m. pl.) – the Suebi (a people of northeastern Germany)

Suessiōnes, -um (m. pl.) – Suessiones (a people of Gaul)

Sulla, -ae (m.) – Lucius Cornelius Sulla, Roman dictator 81-79 BC

Sulpicius, Sulpiciī (m.) – Publius Sulpicius Rufus; an orator, tribune 88 BC; put to death by Sulla in 88

sum, esse, fuī – be; exist (note: *est* can mean "there is" and *sunt* can mean "there are")

summus, -a, -um – highest; greatest

sūmō, sūmere, sumpsī, sumptum – take

sumptus, -ūs (m.) – expense

superbus, -a, -um – proud

superī, -ōrum (*or* -um) – the gods above

superior, -ius – higher; (of time) past; previous

superō, -āre – overcome; be victorious; surpass

supplicātio, -ōnis (f.) – public prayer; public thanksgiving

supplicium, -iī (n.) – punishment

suspicor, suspicārī, suspicātus sum – suspect; believe; suppose

sustineō, sustinēre, sustinuī, sustentum – withstand

suus, -a, -um – his own; her own; their own

Syrācūsae, -ārum (f. pl.) – Syracuse, a city in Sicily

Syria, -ae (f.) – Syria, a country in Asia

T. Ampius, -iī (m.) – Titus Ampius, a Roman politician

tabernaculum, -ī (n.) – tent

tabula, -ae (f.) – written document; will; (pl.) records

taceō, tacēre, tacuī, tacitum – be silent

tālis, -e – such, of such a kind

tam . . . quam – so (much) . . . as; as . . . as

tamen – however; nevertheless

tandem – at last; (in questions) pray; now

Tantalus, -i (m.) – punished in the Underworld; he stands in water and fruit trees are just above his head; however, when he tries to drink the water flows away and the fruit remains just beyond his grasp

tantum – only

tantus, -a, -um – so great; so much

tardius – more slowly

Tarquinius, -ii (m.) – Tarquinius Superbus, the last king of Rome

taurus, -ī (m.) – bull

tectum, -ī (n.) – roof; house

tegō, tegere, tēxī, tēctum – cover; protect; conceal

tellūs, -ūris (f.) – earth; region; land

tēlum, -ī (n.) – javelin; spear; weapon

tempestās, tempestātis (f.) – time; season; weather

templum, -ī (n.) – temple

tempus, -oris (n.) – time; crisis; (pl.) circumstances; troubles

teneō, tenēre, tenuī, tentum – hold; have; maintain

tergum, -ī (n.) – back; in tergum – in the rear; behind

tertius, -a, -um – third (see Appendix 3)

testātus, -a, -um – manifest; attested

testificātio, -ōnis (f.) – testimony

testimōnium, testimōniī (n.) – testimony; evidence

testis, -is (m.) – witness

testūdō, testūdinis (f.) – tortoise; shelter (to protect besiegers)

Thēbae, -ārum (f. pl.) – Thebes

timeō, timēre, timuī – fear; be afraid of

timidus, -a, -um – fearful; frightened

titubō, -āre – totter; stagger; be in doubt; waver

tollō, tollere, sustulī, sublātum – lift up; raise; take away; remove

tormentum, -ī. (n.) – catapult

tot (indeclinable) – so many

tōtus, -a, -um – the whole of; all

trādō, trādere, trādidī, trāditum – hand over

trādūcō, trādūcere, trādūxī, trāductum – lead across

tranquillitās, -ātis (f.) – tranquillity

trans (+ acc.) – across

transeō, transīre, transī(v)ī, transitum – cross over

transfīgō, transfīgere, transfīxī, transfīxum – transfix

tres, tria – three (see Appendix 3)

tribūnus, -ī (m.) – tribune

tristis, -e – sad

Troia, -ae (f.) – Troy

tū, tuī – you (sing.)

tumulus, -ī (m.) – hill; mound

turbulentus, -a, -um – turbulent; stormy; restless; troublesome

turgeō, turgēre, tursī – swell

turpis, -e – foul; disgraceful; shameful

turpitūdō, -inis (f.) – disgrace; shamefulness

turris, turris (f.) – tower; siege-tower

tūtus, -a, -um – safe

tuus, -a, -um – your (sing.)

ubi – when; where

ubi? – where?

ullus, -a, -um – any

ultio, -ōnis (f.) – act of revenge

ultra (+ acc.) – beyond

ūnā – together

unda, -ae (f.) – wave; water (in poetry)

unde – whence; from where

ūniversus, -a, -um – whole; entire

ūnus, -a, -um – one; alone (see Appendix 3)

urbs, urbis (f.) – city

urna, -ae (f.) – urn

urus, -ī (m.) – wild ox; ure-ox

usque – continuously

usque (+ *ad* + acc.) – up to

ūsus, -ūs (m.) – use; experience

ut (+ indicative) – when; as

ut (+ subjunctive) – that; so that, etc.

uter, utra, utrum – which (of two)

ūtilis, -e – useful; beneficial

ūtor, ūtī, ūsus sum (+ abl.) – use; exercise

vacō, -āre (+ dat.) – be at leisure for; rest from

vadimōnium vadimōniī (n.) – appearance in court; hearing

vagus, -a, -um – scattered; wandering

vallēs, -is (f.) – valley

vallum, -ī (n.) – rampart

vastitās, -ātis (f.) – waste; desert; devastation

vehementer – vehemently

vendō, vendere, vendidī, venditum – sell

venēnum, -ī (n.) – poison

veneō, venīre, veni(v)ī, venītum – be sold

venia, -ae (f.) – favor; forgiveness; veniam dō = grant forgiveness

veniō, venīre, vēnī, ventum – come

ventus, -ī (m.) – wind

vēr, vēris (n.) – spring

verbum, -ī (n.) – word

Vercingetorix, -igis (m.) – Vercingetorix (commander of the Gauls)

vērē – truly

vereor, verērī, veritus sum – fear

vergō, vergere – lie; be situated

vērō – assuredly; however; but; in truth

versor, versārī, versātus sum – spend one's time; engage (in); dwell; remain; concern oneself with

vertō, vertere, vertī, versum – turn

vērus, -a, -um – true

vester, -tra, -trum – your (pl.)

vestis, vestis (f.) – clothes

vetō, vetāre, vetuī, vetitum – forbid

vetus, -eris – old; former

vetustās, -ātis (f.) – long duration; great age

via Aurēlia, viae Aurēliae (f.) – the Aurelian Way

victor, -ōris (m.) – victor

vīcus, -ī (m.) – village

vidēlicet – evidently; clearly (literally = "it is plain to see")

videō, vidēre, vīdī, vīsum – see

vigeō, vigēre, viguī – flourish

vigilia, -ae (f.) – watch (time of keeping watch at night – four watches per night)

vigilō, -āre – watch; be watchful; be vigilant

vīgintī (indeclinable) – twenty

vincō, vincere, vīcī, victum – defeat

vindicō, -āre – punish

vinea, -ae (f.) – siege-shelter

violō, -āre – violate

vir, -ī (m.) – man

vireō, virēre, viruī – be green; flourish

viridis, -e – green

virtūs, -tūtis (f.) – virtue; courage

vīs, vis (f.) – power; force; violence

vīta, -ae (f.) – life

vitium, vitiī (n.) – vice; fault

vītō, -are – avoid; escape

vīvō, vīvere, vīxī, vīctum – live

vocō, -āre – call

volō, velle, voluī – want; wish

volucer, volucris (m. and f.) – bird

voluntās, -ātis (f.) – wish; desire

voluptās, -ātis (f.) – pleasure

vōs, vestrī (vestrum) – you (pl.); yourselves

vulnerō (*or* volnerō), -āre – wound

vulnus, -eris (n.) – wound

vultus, -ūs (m.) – face; expression

Abbreviations: *a.* adjective, *adv.* adverb, *comp. a.* comparative adjective, *conj.* conjunction, *interj.* interjection, *n.* noun, *pl.* plural, *pr.* preposition, *pro.* pronoun, *sg.* singular, *vi.* verb (intransitive), *vt.* verb (transitive)

abandon *vt.* – *see* leave *vt.*

able, be *vi.* – possum, posse, potuī

about (= concerning) *pr.* – *see* concerning

about (= roughly) *adv.* – circiter

above *adv.* – suprā

absent, be (be away from) *vi.* – absum, abesse, āfuī

accomplish *vt.* – gerō, gerere, gessī, gestum; agō, -ere, ēgī, actum

acquainted with, be (know) *vt.* – *use* nōvī (perf. of noscō)

across *pr.* – trans (+ acc.)

administer *vt.* – administrō, -āre, -āvī, -ātum

advance *vi.* – prōgredior, prōgredī, prōgressus sum

adviser *n.* – auctor, -ōris (m.)

Aedui *n. pl.* (Gallic tribe) – Aeduī, -ōrum (m. pl.)

afraid (frightened) *a.* – timidus, -a, -um; be afraid – *see* fear

Africa *n.* – Āfrica, -ae (f.)

against *pr.* – in (+ acc.)

agree *vi.* – consentiō, -īre, consēnsī, consēnsum

all *a.* – omnis, -is; all their goods – *use* all their things (*n. pl.*)

also (even) *adv.* – etiam; et

although *conj.* – cum (+ subjunctive); quamquam (+ indicative)

ambassador (legate) *n.* – legātus, -ī (m.)

among *pr.* – in (+ abl.); inter (+ acc.)

ancestors *n. pl.* – māiōrēs, -um (m. pl.)

and *conj.* – et; atque; -que

and so *adv.* – itaque

angry *a.* – īrātus, -a, -um (angry with – īrātus + dat.)

another *a.* – alius, alia, aliud; (of two) alter, alterius

any *a.* – ullus, -a, -um

anything *pro.* – quicquam

approach *vt.* – accēdō, -ere, accessī, accessum

Apronius (a tax-collector, associate of Verres) – Aprōnius, -iī (m.)

Arar (river) *n.* – Arar, -āris (m.)

argument *n.* – argūmentum, -ī (n.)

Ariovistus *n.* – Ariōvistus, -i (m.)

arise *vi.* – coorior, coorīrī, coortus sum

arms (weapons) *n. pl.* – arma, -ōrum (n. pl.)

army *n.* – exercitus, -ūs (m.)

arouse *vt.* – adferrō, -ferre, attūlī, allātum

arrange *vt.* – agō, -ere, ēgī, actum

arrival *n.* – adventus, -ūs (m.)

art *n.* – ars, artis (f.)

as *adv.* – ut

as soon as *adv.* – ut primum

ashamed (to be) *vi.* – pudet, -ēre, puduit (impersonal)

ask *vt.* – quaerō, -ere, quaesīvī (*and* -iī), quaesītum; petō, petere, petīvī (*and* -iī), petītum; ask for – rogō, -āre, -āvī, -ātum; ask back – repetō, repetere, repetīvī (*and* -iī), repetītum

assembly *n.* – cōntio, -ōnis (f.)

assistance *n.* – auxilium, -iī (n.)

at all *adv.* – omnīnō

at last *adv.* – tandem

at this point *adv.* – hīc

attack *vt.* – oppugnō, -āre, -āvī, -ātum; aggredior, aggredī, aggressus sum; impetum faciō, -ere, fēcī, factum

Atuatuci (Gallic tribe) *n. pl.* – Atuatucī, -ōrum (m. pl.)

authority *n.* – dignitās, -ātis (f.); auctoritās, -ātis (f.)

avoid *vt.* – vītō, -āre, -āvī, -ātum

Wiley's Real Latin: Learning Latin from the Source, First Edition.
Robert Maltby and Kenneth Belcher.
© 2014 John Wiley & Sons, Inc. Published 2014 by John Wiley & Sons, Inc.

await *vt.* – exspectō, -āre, -āvī, -ātum

away (be) *vi.* – absum, abesse, āfuī

baggage *n.* – impedimenta, -ōrum (n. pl.); sarcinae, -ārum (f. pl.)

barber's shop *n.* – tonstrīna, -ae (f.)

baseness *n.* – nequitia, -ae (f.)

battle *n.* – proelium, -iī (n.); pugna, -ae (f.)

be *vi.* – sum, esse, fuī

be accustomed *vt.* – soleō, -ēre, solitus sum (usually + infinitive)

because *conj.* – quod

before *adv.* – antea; ante; *conj.* antequam; priusquam; *a.* = preceding – superior, -ōris

begin *vt.* – incipio, -ere, incēpi, inceptum; began – coepī (perfect)

beginning *n.* – initium, -iī (n.)

behind (their backs) *adv.* – post tergum

believe (in) *vt.* – crēdō, -ere, crēdidī, crēditum (+ dat.)

belittle *vt.* – contemnō, -ere, contempsī, contemptum

beneficial *a.* – ūtilis, -e

betray *vt.* – prōdō, -ere, prōdidī, prōditum

between *pr.* – inter (+ acc.)

blood *n.* – sanguis, -guinis (m.)

boat *n.* – scapha, -ae (f.)

boldly *adv.* – fortiter; audācter

born *a.* – nātus, -a, -um

boy *n.* – puer, -ī (m.)

bravely *adv.* – fortiter

break (camp) *vt.* – moveo, -ēre, mōvī, mōtum

break (down) *vt.* – frangō, -ere, frēgī, fractum

brevity *n.* – brevitās, -ātis (f.)

bridge *n.* – pons, pontis (m.)

bring *vt.* – ferō, ferre, tūlī, lātum

bring (back) *vt.* – adportō, -āre, -āvī, -ātum

bring (forward) *vt.* – prōferō, -ferre, prōtūlī, prōlātum

brother *n.* – frāter, frātris (m.)

build *vt.* – *use* faciō, -ere, fēcī, factum

but *conj.* – sed

but also *adv.* – sed etiam

by (*agent*) *pr.* – ā/ab (+ abl.); by all means *adv.* – sāne

Caesar *n.* – Caesar, -aris (m.)

camp *n.* – castra, -ōrum (n. pl.)

can (am able) *vi.* – possum, posse, potuī

captive *n.* – captīvus, -ī (m.)

capture *vt.* – capiō, -ere, cēpī, captum

carefully *adv.* – diligenter

cart *n.* – plaustrum, -ī (n.)

case *n.* (*legal*) – causa, -ae (f.)

cash *n.* – nummī, -ōrum (m. pl.)

catch sight of *vt.* – conspicio, -ere, conspexī, conspectum; conspicor, conspicārī, conspicātus sum

Catiline *n.* – Catilīna, -ae (m.)

Catullus *n.* – Catullus, -ī (m.)

cavalry *n.* – equitātus, -ūs (m.); cavalry man; horseman – eques, equitis (m.)

certainly *adv.* – certe; quidem

changing *a.* – *use* incertus, -a, -um

charge (accusation) *n.* – crīmen, -inis (n.); offensio, -ōnis (f.)

cheat *n.* – fraudātor, -ōris (m.)

children *n.* – līberī, -ōrum (m. pl.)

choose *vt.* – dēligō, -ere, -lēgī, -lectum

citizen *n.* – cīvis, cīvis (m.); Roman citizens – Quirites, -um (m. pl.)

city *n.* – urbs, urbis (f.); (= state) cīvitās, -ātis (f.)

clear *a.* – clārus, -a, -um; make clear – *see* make clear

close *vt.* – claudio, -ere, clausi, clausum

clothes *n.* – vestis, -is (f. sg.)

cohort *n.* – cohors, cohortis (f.)

come *vi.* – venio, -īre vēnī, ventum

commander *n.* – imperātor, -ōris (m.)

complete *vt.* – conficio, -ere, confēci, confectum

concerning *pr.* – dē (+ abl.)

condemn *vt.* – damnō, -āre, -āvī, -ātum

conference *n.* – colloquium, -iī (n.)

confess *vt.* – confiteor, -ērī, confessus sum

confirm *vt.* – confirmō, -āre, -āvī, -ātum

Conscript Fathers (= senators) *n. pl.* – Patres Conscripti

consider *vt.* – perspiciō, -ere, perspexī, perspectum

consider the interests of *vt.* – consulō, -ere, consuluī, consultum (+ dat.)

consul *n.* – consul, -is (m.)

contend with *vt.* – conflīgō, -ere, conflīxī, conflīctum

corn *n.* – frūmentum, -ī (n.)

corrupt *vt.* – corrumpō, -ere, corrūpī, corruptum

countless *a.* – innumerabilis, -is

country *a.* – rusticus, -a, -um

courage *n.* – virtūs, virtūtis (f.)

course *n.* – cursus, -ūs (m.)

crime *n.* – facinus, -ōris (n.); crimen, -inis (n.); scelus, sceleris (n.)

crisis *n.* – discrīmen, -inis (n.); *or use* tempus, -oris (n.)

crops *n.* – frumenta, -ōrum (n.)

cross *vt.* – transeo, -īre, transīvī (*or* -iī), transitum

crowd *n.* – multitūdō, -inis (f.)

cruelty *n.* – crūdēlitās, -ātis (f.)

Curio *n.* – Cūrio, -ōnis (m.)

daily *adv.* – cottīdiē

dare *vi.* – audeō, -ēre, ausus sum

daring *a.* – audāx, -ācis

daughter *n.* – fīlia, -ae (f.)

dawn (at) – prīmā lūce

day *n.* – diēs, diēī (m.)

day by day *adv.* – in dies singulos

death *n.* – mors, mortis (f.)

decide *vt.* – statuō, -ere, statuī, statūtum

deed *n.* – facinus, -oris (n.)

defaulter *n.* – infitiātor, -ōris (m.)

defeat *vt.* – vincō, -ere, vīcī, victum

defend *vt.* – dēfendō, -ere, dēfensī, dēfensum

defense *n.* – dēfēnsio, -ōnis (f.)

defenseless – *see* leave defenseless

defy *vt.* – contemnō, -ere, contempsī, contemptum

demand *vt.* – postulō, -āre, -āvī, -ātum

demonstrate *vt.* – dēmōnstrō, -āre, -āvī, -ātum

deny *vt.* – negō, -āre, -āvī, -ātum

depart *vi.* – discēdō, -ere, discessī, discessum

departure *n.* – dīgressus, -ūs (m.)

depravity *n.* – turpitūdō, -inis (f.)

desert *vt.* – dēserō, -ere, dēseruī, dēsertum

despise *vt.* – dēspiciō, -ere, dēspexī, dēspectum

deter *vt.* – dēterreō, -ēre, dēterruī, dēterritum

die *vi.* – morior, morī, mortuus sum

difficult *a.* – difficilis, -e

diligence *n.* – dīligentia, -ae (f.)

direct *vt.* – mandō, -āre, -āvī, -ātum

directions (in all) *adv.* – passim

disregard *vt.* – neglegō, -ere, neglexī, neglectum

dissolute *a.* – dissolūtus, -a, -um

ditch *n.* – fossa, -ae (f.)

division *n.* – pars, partis (f.)

do *vt.* – agō, agere, ēgī, actum; faciō, facere, fēcī, factum; gerō, -ere, gessī, gestum

Domitius *n.* – Domitius, -iī (m.)

do not – *use* nōlī, nōlīte (+ inf.)

door *n.* – forēs, forum (f., usually in plural)

double *a.* – duplex, -icis

doubt *vt.* – dubitō, -āre, -āvī, -ātum

down from *pr.* – dē (+ abl.)

drive out *vt.* – ēiciō, -ere, ēiēcī, ēiectum

eager, to be *vi.* – cupiō, -ere, cupīvī (*or* -iī), cupītum

eagerly *adv.* – ācriter

eagerness *n.* – alacritās, -ātis (f.)

easily *adv.* – facile

easy *a.* – facilis, -e

East (the) *n.* – Oriens, -entis (m.)

encourage *vt.* – cōnfirmō, -āre, -āvī, -ātum

end *n.* – fīnis, -is (m.); exitus, -ūs (m.)

end *vt.* – *use passive of* facio, -ere, fēcī, factum

endeavor *n.* – cōnātus, -ūs (m.)

enemy *n.* – hostis, -is (m.)

engaged (be engaged in) *vi.* – versor, -ārī, versātus sum

enjoy *vt.* – fruor, fruī, frūctus sum (+ abl.)

enthusiasm *n.* – studium, -iī (n.)

entire *a.* – tōtus, -a, -um

envoy *n.* – *use* ambassador; legate

escape *vt.* – effugiō, -ere, effūgī

establish *vt.* – constituō, -ere, constituī,
  constitūtum

even *adv.* – etiam

event *n.* – *use* rēs, reī (f.) *or* cāsus, -ūs (m.)

everything *n.* – *use n. pl. of* all

evidence *n.* – argumentum, -ī (n.)

example *n.* – exemplum, -ī (n.)

excellent *a.* – *use* optimus, -a, -um

exercise forethought *vi.* – prōvideō, -ēre, prōvīsī,
  prōvīsum; exercise (moderation) – *use*
  moderation

exile *n.* – exsilium, -iī (*n.*)

expert *a.* – expertus, -a, -um

explain *vt.* – expōnō, -ere, exposuī, expositum;
  explicō, -āre, -āvī, -ātum; exprōmō, -ere,
  exprompsī, expromptum

extravagance *n.* – luxuriēs, -ēī (f.)

eye *n.* – oculus, -ī (m.)

fail *vt.* – dēficio, -ere, dēfēcī, dēfectum

fall *vi.* – concidō, -ere, concidī

false *a.* – falsus, -a, -um

family *n.* – famīlia, -ae (f.)

far *adv.* – longe

fear *n.* – timor, -ōris (m.)

fear *vt.* – timeō, -ēre, timuī; pertimēscō, -ēscere,
  pertimuī; vereor, -ērī, veritus sum

fearless *a.* – impavidus, -a, -um

feel *vt.* – sentiō, -īre, sēnsī, sēnsum

feeling *n.* – sensus, -ūs (m.); feelings – *use* animus,
  -ī (m.)

few *a.* – paucī, -ae, -a (pl.)

field *n.* – ager, agrī (m.)

fiercely *adv.* – ācriter

fight *vt.* – pugnō, -āre, -āvī, -ātum

find *vt.* – inveniō, -īre, invēni, inventum

find fault with *vt.* – accūsō, -āre, -āvī, -ātum

first *a.* – prīmus, -a, -um

flank (of an army) *n.* – cornū, -ūs (n.)

flee *vi.* – fugiō, -ere, fūgī, fugitum; profugiō, -ere,
  profūgī

fleet *n.* – classis, -is (f.); *or use* nāvēs, -ium (f. pl.)
  (*ships*)

flight *n.* – fuga, -ae (f.)

follow *vt.* – (con)sequor, -sequī (con)secūtus sum

for *conj.* – nam

for (on behalf of) *pr.* – pro (+ abl.)

for a long time *adv.* – iam dūdum

force *n.* – vīs (*acc.* vim, *abl.* vī; *pl.* vīrēs,
  vīrium) (f.)

forces *n. pl.* – cōpiae, -arum (f. pl.)

forever *adv.* – in perpetuum

forget *vt.* – oblīvīscor, oblīvīscī, oblītus sum

forgive *vt.* – ignōscō, -ere, ignōvī, ignōtum
  (+ dat.)

former *a.* – prīstinus, -a, -um; prior, -ōris

fortify *vt.* – mūniō, -īre, mūnīvī (*or* -iī), mūnītum

forum *n.* – forum, -ī *n.*

four *num.* – quattuor

fourth *a.* – quartus, -a, -um

free *a.* – līber, -era, -erum

free from *a.* – expers, expertis

friend *n.* – amīcus, -ī (m.); amīca, -ae (f.); (=
  relative) necessārius, -iī (m.)

frighten off *vt.* – dēterreo, -ēre, dēterruī,
  dēterritum

from *pr.* – ab (a); ex (e) (+ abl.)

frugality *n.* – frūgālitās, -ātis (f.)

full *a.* – plēnus, -a, -um (+ gen. "full of")

function *n.* – officium, -iī (n.)

future (for the) *adv.* – in posterum

gate *n.* – porta, -ae (f.)

Gaul *n.* – Gallus, -ī (m.)

general *n.* – imperātor, -ōris (m.); belonging to a
  general *a.* – imperātōrius, -a, -um

German *n.* – Germānus, -ī (m.)

get up *vi.* – consurgō, -ere, consurrēxī,
  consurrēctum

girl *n.* – puella, -ae (f.)

give *vt.* – dō, dare, dedī, datum

give up *vt.* – reddō, -ere, reddidī, redditum

go *vi.* – eo, īre, īvī (*or* iī), itum

go on board *vi.* – conscendō, -ere, conscendī,
  conscensum (+ *in* + acc.)

god *n.* – deus, -ī (m.); by the gods – per deōs

gold *n.* – aurum, -ī (n.)

good *a.* – bonus, -a, -um

grateful (be) *vi.* – gratiam habeō, -ēre, habuī, habitum

great *a.* – magnus, -a, -um; so (such) great – tantus, -a, -um; how great; what great – quantus, -a, -um; greatest – maximus, -a, -um, summus, -a, -um; a great many – plurimus, -a, -um; greater – māior, -ōris

great number – *use* multitūdō, -inis (f.)

greed *n.* – cupiditās, -ātis (f.)

grounds *n. pl.* – locus, -ī (m. sg.)

guard *n.* – praesidium, -iī (n.)

halt *vi.* – constō, -āre, constitī, constātum

hand over (surrender) *vt.* – dēdō, -ere, dēdidī, dēditum

happen *vi.* – accidō, -ere, accidī; fīō, fierī, factus sum

harass *vt.* – vexō, -āre, -āvī, -ātum

hard *a.* – labōriōsus, -a, -um

harsh *a.* – acerbus, -a, -um

have *vt.* – habeō, -ēre, habuī, habitum

have built, have made, etc. – *use* cūrō, -āre, -āvī, -ātum + gerundive

he, she, it *pro.* – is, ea, id

hear *vt.* – *see* listen

heart *n.* – cor, cordis (n.); = mind – animus, -ī (m.)

help *n.* – auxilium, -iī (n.)

help *vt.* – iuvō, -āre, iūvī, iūtum; adiuvō, -āre, adiūvī, adiūtum

Helvetii (Gallic tribe) *n.* – Helvetiī, -ōrum (m. pl.)

Hercules (by) *interj.* – mehercule

hesitate *vi.* – dubitō, -āre, -āvī, -ātum

higher *comp. a.* – superior, -ōris

himself (herself, itself) *pro.* – ipse, ipsa, ipsum; *reflexive pro.* se

hold *vt.* – teneō, -ēre, -uī; hold (the senate) *vt.* – *use* habeō, *see* have

homeland (fatherland) *n.* – patria, -ae (f.)

honesty *n.* – fidēs, -ēī (f.)

honor *n.* – dignitās, -ātis (f.)

honorable (eminent) *a.* – amplus, -a, -um

hope *n.* – spēs, speī (f.)

hope (for) *vt.* – spērō, -āre, -āvī, -ātum

horse *n.* – equus, -ī (m.)

horseman – *see* cavalry man

house *n.* – domus, -ūs *and* -ī (f.)

how I wish – *use* utinam *adv.*

however *adv.* – tamen

humanity *n.* – hūmānitās, -ātis (f.)

hurl *vt.* – *see* throw

hurry *vi.* – contendō, -ere, contendī, contentum

I (me) *pro.* – ego, meī

idleness *n.* – inertia, -ae *f.*

if *conj.* – sī; if not *conj.* – nīsī

immortal *a.* – immortālis, -a, -um

impudence *n.* – impudentia, -ae (f.)

impunity (with) *adv.* – impūne

in (inside) *pr.* – in (+ abl.)

in fear – *use* afraid

in general, mostly, usually *adv.* – plērumque

in secret *adv.* – occultē

in the presence of *pr.* – apud (+ acc.)

indicate *vt.* – ostendō, -ere, ostendī, ostentum

induce *vt.* – addūcō, -ere, addūxī, adductum

infantry (foot soldier) *n.* – pedes, peditis (m.)

influence (have) (be influential) *vi.* – *use* possum, posse, potuī

injustice *n.* – iniūria, -ae (f.)

innocent *a.* – innocens, -entis

insolence *n.* – insolentia, -ae (f.)

instill *vt.* – inicio, -ere, iniēcī, iniectum

into *pr.* – in (+ acc.)

invent *vt.* – inveniō, -īre, invēnī, inventum

investigate *vt.* – investigō, -āre, -āvī, -ātum

involve *vt.* – complector, complectī, complexus sum

Italy *n.* – Ītalia, -ae (f.)

javelin *n.* – tēlum, -ī (n.); pīlum, -ī (n.)

join (battle) *vt.* – (proelium) committō, -ere, commīsī, comissum

journey *n.* – iter, itineris (n.); cursus, -ūs (m.)

judge *n.* – iūdex, -icis (m.)

judgment (form a) *vt.* – existimō, -āre, -āvī, -ātum

keep silent – *see* silent

kill *vt.* – interficio, -ere, interfēcī, interfectum

know *vt.* – sciō, -īre, scīvī, scītum

knowledge of (have no) – *see* unaware of (be)

lack *n.* – inopia, -ae (f.)

land *n.* – ager, agrī (m.)

large *a.* – magnus, -a, -um

large number *n.* – multitūdō, -inis (f.)

last (previous) *a.* – proximus, -a, -um

lasting *a.* – perpetuus, -a, -um

law *n.* – lēx lēgis (f.)

lead *vt.* – dūcō, -ere, dūxī, ductum

lead across *vt.* – trādūcō, -ere, trādūxī, trāductum

lead back *vt.* – redūcō, -ere, redūxī, reductum

leader *n.* – dux, ducis (m.)

learn *vt.* – discō, -ere, didicī

learn (of) *vt.* – cognōscō, -ere, cognōvī, cognitum

learned *a.* – doctus, -a, -um

least (of all) *adv.* – minimē

leave *vi.* – discēdō, -ere, discessī, discessum;
    excēdō, -ere, excessī, excessum

leave *vt.* – relinquō, -ere, relīquī, relictum

leave defenseless *vt.* – nūdō, -āre, -āvī, -ātum

leave out (omit) *vt.* – praetermitto, -ere,
    praetermīsī, praetermissum

legate – *see* ambassador

legion *n.* – legio, -ōnis (f.)

letter *n.* – epistula, -ae (f.); litterae, -ārum (f. pl.)

letter (of alphabet) *n.* – littera, -ae (f.)

lie about; lie broken *vi.* – iaceō, -ēre, iacuī,
    iacitum

lie hidden *vi.* – lateō, -ēre, latuī

lieutenant-general *n.* – *use* ambassador, legate

life *n.* – vīta, -ae (f.)

life breath (spirit) *n.* – spīritus, -ūs (m.)

listen (hear) *vt.* – audiō, -īre, audīvī (*or* -iī),
    audītum; accipiō, -ere, accēpī, acceptum

little (a) *adv.* – paulum

live *vi.* – vīvō, -ere, vīxī, vīctum

long-lasting *a.* – diūturnus, -a, -um

look after *vt.* – prōvideō, -ēre, prōvīdī, prōvīsum

lose *vt.* – āmittō, -ere, āmīsī, āmissum

lust *n.* – libīdō, -inis (f.)

luxury *n.* – luxuria, -ae (f.)

make clear (open up) *vt.* – aperiō, -īre, aperuī,
    apertum

make light of (despise) *vt.* – contemnō, -ere,
    contempsī, contemptum

man *n.* – vir, virī (m.); homō, -inis (m.)

many *a. pl.* – multī, -ae, -a; complūres, -ium

marriage *n.* – mātrimōnium, -iī (n.)

matter – *use* thing

matters – *see* old

Menapii (people of Belgic Gaul) *n.* – Menapiī,
    -ōrum (m. pl.)

mention *n.* – mentio, -ōnis (f.)

mercy *n.* – mānsuētūdō, -inis (f.)

middle *a.* – medius, -a, -um

mile *n.* – *use* a thousand paces – mīlle passūs (sg.);
    mīlia passum (pl.)

military *a.* – mīlitāris, -e

military standards *n. pl.* – signa, -ōrum (n. pl.)

mind *n.* – mens, mentis (f.)

misery *n.* – miseria, -ae (f.)

Mitylene *n.* – Mitylēnae, -arum (f. pl.)

moderation *n.* – moderātio, -ōnis (f.)

moon *n.* – lūna, -ae (f.)

more *comp. a.* – plūs, plūris

more and more *adv.* – magis magisque

most *adv.* – māxime

mound *n.* – tūmulus, -ī (m.)

move *vt.* – moveō, -ēre, mōvī, mōtum

much (= greatly) *adv.* – multum; (=
    by much) – multo

much (*pl.* many) *a.* – multus, -a, -um

my *a.* – meus, -a, -um

nature *n.* – nātūra, -ae (f.); = type, character –
    genus, -eris (n.)

near *adv.* – prope; *comp.* nearer – propius

nearby *a.* – fīnitimus, -a, -um

negligence *n.* – neglegentia, -ae (f.)

neighboring *a.* – propinquus, -a, -um

never *adv.* – numquam

nevertheless *adv.* – tamen

next *a.* – posterus, -a, -um, proximus, -a, -um

new *a.* – novus, -a, -um

night *n.* – nox, noctis (f.)

no *a.* – nullus, -a, -um

no one *pro.* – nēmō, -inis (m. and f.)

nod (will) *n.* – nūtus, -ūs (m.)

not *ad.* – nōn; haud

not know (be ignorant of) *vt.* – nesciō, -īre, nescīvī
(*or* -iī), nescītum

not only *adv.* – non solum

nothing *n.* – nihil

notice *vt.* – animadvertō, -ere, animadvertī,
animadversum

now *adv.* – nunc; iam

now at last *adv.* – *use* at last

number *n.* – numerus, -ī (m.)

oath *n.* – sacramentum, -ī (n.)

obscurity *n.* – obscūritās, -ātis (f.)

obtain *vt.* – capiō, -ere, cēpī, captum

occupy (fill) *vt.* – compleō, -ēre, complēvī,
complētum

offend *vt.* – peccō, -āre, -āvī, -ātum; (= offend
against) – offendō, -ere, offendī, offensum

oh *interj.* – ō

old *a.* – vetus, veteris (old matters – use n. pl. of
"old")

omit *vt.* – *see* leave out

on *pr.* – in (+ abl.)

on account of *pr.* – propter (+ acc.)

one (*numeral*) – ūnus, -a, -um

one (of two) *a.* – alter, -ius

opinion *n.* – opīnio, -ōnis (f.)

opportune *a.* – opportūnus, -a, -um

opportunity *adv.* – spatium, -iī (n.)

oratorical (of oratory) *a.* – ōrātōrius, -a, -um

order *n.* – mandātum, -ī (n.)

order *vt.* – iubeō, -ēre, iussī, iussum; mandō, -āre,
-āvī, -ātum (+ dat.)

Orgetorix *n.* – Oregetorix, -icis (m.)

ornament *n.* – ōrnamentum, -i (n.)

other (of two) *a.* – alter -ius

ought *vi.* – dēbeō, -ēre, dēbuī, dēbitum

our *a.* – noster, nostra, nostrum

outcome *n.* – eventum, -ī (n.)

outside *pr.* – extrā (+ acc.)

outstanding *a* – eximius, -a, -um

own (his own, her own, its own, their own) *a.*
– suus, -a, -um

painful (difficult) *a.* – gravis, -e

painting *n.* – tabula picta, tabulae pictae (f.)

pardon *vt.* – parcō, -ere, pepercī, parsum
(+ dat.)

part *n.* – pars, partis (f.)

pass over *vt.* – praetereo, praeterīre, praeterīvī (*or*
-iī), praeteritum

past (previous) *a.* – superior, -ōris

peace *n.* – pax, pācis (f.); concordia, -ae (f.)

penalty *n.* – poena, -ae (f.)

people *n.* – populus, -ī (m.); *or use* men *pl.*

perhaps *adv.* – forsitan

perjury, commit *vi.* – pēierō, -āre, -āvī, -ātum

persuade *vt.* – persuādeo, -ēre, persuāsī,
persuāsum (+ dat.)

piety *n.* – pietās, -ātis (f.)

place *n.* – locus, -ī (m.)

place *vt.* – pōnō, -ere, posuī, positum

plan *n.* – cōnsilium, -iī (n.)

poison *n.* – venēnum, -ī (n.)

Pompey *n.* – Pompeius, -ī (m.)

position *n.* – *see* place *n.*

possession *n.* – *for* with all their possessions *use*
with all their things

praise *n.* – laus, laudis (f.); laudationes,
-um (f. pl.)

prefect *n.* – praefectus, -ī (m.)

presence *n.* – praesentia, -ae (f.)

present *a.* – praesēns, -entis

present, be *vi.* – adsum, adesse, adfuī

pretend *vt.* – dissimulō, -āre, -āvī, -ātum

prevent (= restrain) *vt.* – retineō, -ēre, retinuī,
retentum; be prevented – *use* impedior, -īrī,
impeditus sum

promise *vt.* – prōmittō, -ere, prōmīsī, prōmissum;
polliceor, -ērī, pollicitus sum

protection *n.* – praesidium, -iī (n.)

provided that *adv.* – dum modō

province *n.* – prōvincia, -ae (f.)

punish *vt.* – vindicō, -āre, -āvi, -ātum; pūniō, -īre, pūnīvī (*or* -iī), pūnītum; (*with a penalty*) adficiō, -ere, adfēcī, adfectum

punishment *n.* – supplicium, -iī (n.)

purpose *n.* – cōnsilium, -iī (n.)

purse *n.* – sacculus, -ī (m.)

pursue *vt.* – consequor, -sequī, consecūtus sum

rampart *n.* – vallum, -ī (n.)

rank *n.* – ōrdō, -inis (m.)

rather *adv.* – potius

ready *a.* – parātus, -a, -um

realize *vt.* – intellegō, -ere, intellēgī, intellectum

reason *n.* – ratio, ratiōnis (f.); causa, -ae (f.)

recently *adv.* – nūper

reckless *a.* – audāx, -ācis

recklessness *n.* – audācia, -ae (f.)

recover *vt.* – se recipiō, -ere, recēpi, receptum

refute *vt.* – refellō, -ere, refellī

regret (longing) *n.* – dēsīderium, -iī (n.)

reject *vt.* – omittō, -ere, omīsī, omissum

remain *vi.* – remaneō, -ēre, remansī

remain seated – *see* sit

remaining *a.* – reliquus, -a, -um

remind *vt.* – commoneō, -ēre, commonuī, commonitum

remove *vt.* – tollō, -ere, sustulī, sublātum

repair *vt.* – reficiō, -ere, refēcī, refectum

repeat *vt.* – repetō, -ere, repetīvī (-iī), repetītum

reply *vt.* – respondeō, -ēre, respondī, respōnsum

report *vt.* – nuntiō, -āre, -āvī, -ātum

report back *vt.* – referō, -ferre, rettūlī, relātum

reproach *vt.* – exprobrō, -āre, -āvī, -ātum

republic *n.* – rēs pūblica, reī pūblicae (f.)

resist *vi.* – resistō, -ere, restitī (+ dat.)

rest *vt.* (a case) – repōnō, -ere, reposuī, repositum

retreat *vi.* – se recipiō, -ere, recēpī, receptum

return *n.* – reditus, -ūs (m.)

return *vi.* – revertō, -ere, revertī

reverence *n.* – rēligio, -ōnis (f.)

reward *n.* – frūctus, -ūs (m.)

Rhine *n.* – Rhēnus, -ī (m.)

ride towards *vi.* – adequitō, -āre, -āvī, -ātum

right *n.* – iūs, iūris (n.)

right (direction) *a.* – dexter, dextra, dextrum

ripe *a.* – matūrus, -a, -um

river *n.* – flūmen, fluminis (n.); fluvius, -iī (m.)

rock *n.* – saxum, -ī (n.)

Roman *a.* – Rōmānus, -a, -um

Rome *n.* – Rōma, -ae (f.)

route *n.* – iter, itineris (n.)

rule *n.* – praeceptum, -ī (n.)

run forward *vi.* – prōcurrō, -ere, prōcucurrī (*or* prōcurrī), prōcursum

rush out *vi.* – se ēiciō, -ere, ēiēcī, ēiectum

safety *n.* – salūs, salūtis (f.)

sake, for the sake of – causā (+ gen.); grātiā (+ gen.)

same *a.* (*pro*) – īdem, eadem, idem (same thing – use n. sg. of "same")

Sardinia *n.* – Sardinia, -ae (f.)

satisfied (be) (= atone for) *vt.* – luō, -ere, luī

say *vt.* – *see* speak

say . . . not – *use* deny

see *vt.* – videō, -ēre, vīdī, vīsum; cernō, -ere, crēvī, crētum

see (to it) that – *use* facio ut (+ subjunctive)

seek *vt.* – peto, -ere, petīvī (*or* -iī), petītum; quaerō, -ere, quaesīvī (*or* -iī), quaesītum

seem *vi.* – *use passive* of videō (*under* see)

sell *vt.* – vendō, -ere, vendidī, venditum (*pass.* vēneō)

senate *n.* – senātus, -ūs (m.)

send *vt.* – mittō, -ere, mīsī, missum

send forward *vt.* – praemitto, -ere, praemīsī, praemissum

sentence (court sentence) *n.* – iudicium, -iī (n.)

set out *vi.* – proficīscor, proficīscī, profectus sum

severely *adv.* – ācriter

shamefulness *n.* – turpitūdō, -dinis (f.)

shameless *a.* – immoderātus, -a, -um

shamelessness *a.* – impudentia, -ae (f.)

sheep *n.* – ovis, -is (f.)

ship *n.* – nāvis, -is (f.)

shore *n.* – lītus, -oris (n.)

short *a.* – brevis, -e

shout *n.* – clāmor, -ōris (m.)

show (= prove, demonstrate) *vt.* – convincō, -ere, convīcī, convictum

sight *n.* – cōnspectus, -ūs (m.); aspectus, -ūs (m.)

signal *n.* – signum, -ī (n.)

silent (be, keep) *vi.* – taceō, -ēre, tacuī, tacitum

silver (money) *n.* – argentum, -ī (n.)

since *conj.* – cum (+ subjunctive)

singular *a.* – singulāris, -e

sister *n.* – soror, -ōris (f.)

sit, remain seated *vi.* – sedeō, -ēre, sēdī, sessum

six *num.* – sex

slave *n.* – servus, -ī (m.); *in plural "slaves"* – mancipia, -ium (n. pl.)

so (in such a way) *adv.* – sīc

so (to such an extent) *adv.* – ita; tam

someone/something *pro.* – aliquis/aliquid

sorrow *n.* – dolor, -ōris (m.)

source of gain – *use* esse quaestuī (dat.)

speak (say) *vt.* – dīco, -ere, dixī, dictum

speak (talk) *vi.* – loquor, -ī, locūtus sum

spear *n.* – tēlum, -ī (n.)

speech *n.* – orātio, -ōnis (f.)

spider's web, cobweb *n.* – arānea, -ae (f.)

spirit (mind) *n.* – animus, -ī (m.)

soldier *n.* – mīles, mīlitis (m.)

some degree of – *use* aliquid (+ gen.)

soon *adv.* – mox; iam

starting from – dē (+ abl.)

state *n.* – cīvitās, -ātis (f.); (= Roman Republic) – rēs pūblica

statue *n.* – signum, -i (n.); statua, -ae (f.)

stone *n.* – lapis, lapidis (m.)

storm *n.* – tempestās, -ātis (f.)

stream *n.* – rīvus, -ī (m.)

strong *a.* – firmus, -a, -um

study *n.* – stūdium, -iī (n.)

subject-matter *n.* – māteria, -ae (f.)

such *a.* (= of such a kind) – talis, -is; (= so great) – tantus, -a, -um; in such a way *adv.* – ita

sudden *a.* – repentīnus, -a, -um

suddenly *adv.* – repente; subitō

suited *a.* – aptus, -a, -um (suited to = aptus ad + acc.)

summon *vt.* – vocō, -āre, -āvī, -ātum

summon together *vt.* – convocō, -āre, -āvī, -ātum

suppose (think) – arbitror, -ārī, arbitrātus sum; putō, -āre, -āvī, -ātum

surely *adv.* – profectō; certē

surrender *n.* – dēditio, -ōnis (f.)

surrender *vt.* – *see* hand over

surround *vt.* – circumsistō, -ere, circumstetī; circumveniō, -īre, circumvēnī, circumventum

suspicion *n.* – suspīcio, -ōnis (f.)

swamp *n.* – palūs, -ūdis (f.)

swiftly *adv.* – celeriter

sword *n.* – gladius, -iī (m.)

take (up) *vt.* – capiō, -ere, cēpi, captum

take care *vt.* – caveō, -ēre, cāvī, cautum

take place *vi.* – *use the passive of* gerō, gerere, gessi, gestum

tear apart *vt.* – revellō, -ere, revellī, revulsum

that *a.* (*pro.*) – is, ea, id; ille, illa, illud

then *adv.* – tum

there *adv.* – ibī

therefore *adv.* – igitur; (= and so) *adv.* – itaque

thing *n.* – rēs, reī (f.)

think *vt.* – arbitror, -ārī, arbitrātus sum; existimō, -āre, -āvī, -ātum

this *a.* (*pro.*) – hīc, haec, hōc; (defendant in court) – iste, -a, -ud

threaten *vt.* – immineō, -ēre, -uī

threatening *a.* – mināx, minācis (f.)

throw (hurl) *vt.* – cōnicio, -ere, cōniēcī, cōniectum

throw away *vt.* – abicio, -ere, abiēcī, abiectum

throw back *vt.* – reicio, -ere, reiēcī, reiectum

thus *adv.* – sīc

time *n.* – tempus, -oris (n.); for all time *adv.* – in omne tempus; at that time – *use* then

tithe *n.* – decuma, -ae (f.)

to, towards *pr.* – ad (+ acc.)

topic *n.* – sententia, -ae (f.)

torture *n.* – crūciātus, -ūs (m.)

touch *vt.* – attingō, -ere, attigī, attāctum

transact *vt.* – gerō, -ere, gessī, gestum

transfix *vt.* – transfīgō, -ere, transfīxī, transfīxum

tribune *n.* – tribūnus, -ī (m.)

troubled *a. (past. part.)* – perturbātus, -a, -um

troubling (troublesome) *a.* – molestus, -a, -um

true *a.* – vērus, -a, -um

try *vt.* – cōnor, -ārī, cōnātus sum

turn (away) *vt.* – āvertō, -ere, āvertī, āversum

two *num.* – duo

unaware of (be), have no knowledge of *vt.* –
   ignōrō, -āre, -āvī, -ātum

uncle *n.* – avunculus, -ī (m.)

understand *vt.* – intellegō, -ere, intellexī,
   intellectum; animo percipiō, -ere, percēpī,
   perceptum

unhappy *a.* – miser, -era, -erum

unless *conj.* – nīsī

unparalleled. *a.* – singularis, -e

us – *pro.; see* – we

use *vt.* – ūtor, ūtī, ūsus sum (+ abl.)

utmost *a.* – summus, -a, -um

valley *n.* – vallēs, vallis (f.)

Vercingetorix *n.* – Vercingetorix, -icis (m.)

Verres *n.* – Verrēs, -is (m.)

very (= very same) *a.* – *use* ipse, ipsa, ipsum

voice *n.* – vox, vōcis (f.)

voting tablet *n.* – tabella, -ae (f.)

wage (war) *vt.* – gerō, -ere, gessī, gestum

wall *n.* – mūrus, -ī (m.)

want (wish for) *vt.* – volō, velle, voluī

war *n.* – bellum, -ī (n.)

watch *n.* – vigilia, -ae (f.)

watchful (be) *vi.* – vigilō, -āre, -āvī, -ātum

wave *n.* – unda, -ae (f.); flūctus, -ūs (m.)

way, in this *adv.* – ita

we *pro.* – nos, nostrum

weapons *n. pl.* – arma, -ōrum (n. pl.)

when *conj.* – ubi; ut; cum

where? *adv.* – ubī?; (= whither?, where to?) –
   quō?

where *adv.* – ubī

whether . . . or *conj.* – utrum . . . an

who? what? *pro.* – quis, quis, quid?

whole *a.* – tōtus, -a, -um; omnis, -is

why? *adv.* – cūr?, quid?

wicked deed *n.* – maleficium, -iī (n.)

will – *see* nod

wing (of an army) *n.* – cornū, -ūs (n.)

wise *a.* – sapiēns, -entis

wish *vt.* – volō, velle, voluī; not wish – nōlō, nōlle,
   nōluī

with *pr.* – cum (+ abl.)

withdraw – *use* retreat

withstand *vt.* – sustineo, -ēre, sustinuī, sustentum

witness *n.* – testis, -is (m.)

wolf *n.* – lūpus, -ī (m.)

woman *n.* – mulier, mulieris (f.)

wondrous, wonderful *a.* – mīrābilis, -e

word *n.* – verbum, -ī (n.)

workman *n.* – faber, fabrī (m.)

worn out *a.* – cōnfectus, -a, -um

wound *n.* – vulnus, vulneris (n.)

wound *vt.* – vulnerō, -āre, -āvī, -ātum

wretched *a.* – miser, -era, -erum

write *vt.* – scrībō, -ere, scrīpsī, scrīptum

year *n.* – annus, -ī (m.)

you *pro. sg.* – tu, tui

you *pro. pl.* – vōs, vestri (vestrum)

young man *n.* – adulēscēns, -entis

your *a. sg.* – tuus, -a, -um

your *a. pl.* – vester, -tra, -trum

INDEX

Wiley's Real Latin: Learning Latin from the Source, First Edition.
Robert Maltby and Kenneth Belcher.
© 2014 John Wiley & Sons, Inc. Published 2014 by John Wiley & Sons, Inc.